ANNE SEXTON

UNDER DISCUSSION

Donald Hall, General Editor

Elizabeth Bishop and Her Art
  edited by Lloyd Schwartz and Sybil P. Estess

Richard Wilbur's Creation
  edited and with an Introduction by Wendy Salinger

Reading Adrienne Rich
  edited by Jane Roberta Cooper

On the Poetry of Allen Ginsberg
  edited by Lewis Hyde

Robert Bly: When Sleepers Awake
  edited by Joyce Peseroff

Robert Creeley's Life and Work
  edited by John Wilson

On the Poetry of Galway Kinnell
  edited by Howard Nelson

On Louis Simpson
  edited by Hank Lazer

Anne Sexton
  edited by Steven E. Colburn

Anne Sexton

Telling the Tale

Edited by Steven E. Colburn

Ann Arbor
THE UNIVERSITY OF MICHIGAN PRESS

1991   1990   1989   1988   4   3   2   1

Library of Congress Cataloging-in-Publication Data

Anne Sexton : telling the tale / edited by Steven E. Colburn.
   p.   cm. — (Under discussion)
  Bibliography: p.
  ISBN 0-472-09379-7 (alk. paper) ISBN 0-472-06379-0
(pbk. : alk. paper)
  1. Sexton, Anne—Criticism and interpretation.   I. Colburn,
Steven E., 1953– .   II. Series.
PS3537.E915Z55 1988
811'.54—dc19   88-14373
                                                        CIP

As the African says:
This is my tale which I have told,
if it be sweet, if it be not sweet,
take somewhere else and let some return to me.
—Anne Sexton, "Rowing"

Preface

After more than a quarter-century's attention to Anne Sexton's work, there is still no substantial consensus on her importance as a poet, her place in our literary history, or her relationship to other poets of her generation. The present collection of essays and reviews is an attempt to provide an overview of the issues that recur in reviews and criticism of her work.

Because Sexton's poetry is personal, even autobiographical, the volume begins with a chronology of Sexton's life and career. This is followed by the biography, memoirs, and reminiscences of part one, which span the entire course of Sexton's career, in chronological order, from Diane Wood Middlebrook's view of the poet's apprenticeship in "Becoming Anne Sexton," to contrasting views of the final phase of her career in Maxine Kumin's "A Friendship Remembered" and Denise Levertov's "Light Up the Cave."

Within the multiplicity of responses to Sexton's work lie some clear turning points in her career that serve as cruxes for dissension among her critics and reviewers. I have arranged the material in part two in three sections that correspond to these critical points of reference.

The first section covers the period from *To Bedlam and Part Way Back* and *All My Pretty Ones*, with their traditional verse forms, to *Live or Die*, her first sustained poem-sequence, for which she was awarded the Pulitzer Prize. Included in this section are classic statements on Sexton's work, which establish the questions and points of disagreement that remain unresolved for many later critics and reviewers.

The second section begins with the period of experimentation that followed Sexton's success with *Live or Die*. During this period, Sexton not only continued her use of the poem-sequence (in *Love Poems*), but also attempted to extend the limits of the medium itself, mingling poetry with music for Anne Sexton and

Her Kind, the group with which she performed in the Boston area during 1968 and 1969. Sexton's only foray into drama, *Mercy Street*, was produced in October of 1969. The middle period concludes with another experiment, *Transformations*, Sexton's most extended reworking of a traditional literary source.

The third section opens with Ben Howard's omnibus review of *The Book of Folly*, *The Death Notebooks*, and *The Awful Rowing Toward God*, which connects these volumes and identifies the outlines of Sexton's later work. In this period Sexton returned to her experiments with form, continuing the use of traditional sources, first explored in *Transformations*, with "The Jesus Papers" (*The Book of Folly*) and "O Ye Tongues" (*The Death Notebooks*). Yet a number of elements that separate these later volumes from the earlier work are equally prominent: her increasing concern with religious belief, her elaboration of a personal cosmology, and her use of eschatological content, language, and tone. The section concludes with a pair of opposing reviews of *The Complete Poems*, which demonstrate the continuing lack of consensus about Sexton's work.

A bibliography of material by and about Anne Sexton follows part two.

Acknowledgments

For their assistance in providing bibliographic information and research materials, I would like to thank: Kay Ellen Capo for her invaluable bibliographic research on Sexton's work; Emma Marras and Maria Carmela Coco Davani for their assistance with Sexton scholarship in Italian; Barbara von Bechtolsheim for her assistance with Sexton scholarship in German; the Boston Public Library, the Teachers and Writers Collaborative, and the *Christian Science Monitor* for their assistance in locating Sexton's uncollected work; Heather Cam for sharing her research on Sexton's early uncollected poetry; Viola C. Ayer and Catherine T. Jones of the Amelia Gayle Gorgas Library, University of Alabama; LeAnn Fields and Allison Rolls of the University of Michigan Press; Vicki Scheurer; Chua Keng Siew; the *Indian Journal of American Studies*; the *Baltimore Sun*; and the *Boston Globe*.

For their various forms of editorial assistance, I would like to thank: Doris J. Scott for her tireless work in researching and revising the chronology; Diane Wood Middlebrook for her expert assistance with details of Sexton's biography; Lawrence Jay Dessner, Gary Blankenburg, Katherine F. McSpadden, and Ruth Quebe for their cooperation and assistance in preparing their manuscripts for publication; Lucy Martinico Sullivan for her assistance with translation from Italian; E. R. Colburn and the Modern Language Association of America for technical assistance and support; Ralph J. Mills, Jr., Karen Alkalay-Gut, and all the other Sexton scholars who generously offered their support to the project.

My special thanks go to: Donald Hall for providing me once again with the opportunity to publish the results of my research on Sexton; Juanita Colburn for serving as unpaid secretary and personal assistant; Diana Hume George for her encouragement, expert counsel, and assistance during the latter stages of this project; and Linda Howe, as always, for her sound advice, which saved me from many embarrassing errors.

Grateful acknowledgment is also made to Linda Gray Sexton, Executor of the Estate of Anne Sexton, and to the Harry Ransom Humanities Research Center, University of Texas at Austin, for permission to quote from unpublished materials in the Anne Sexton Archive.

Contents

Anne Sexton: A Chronology
DORIS J. SCOTT   I

Part One   Biography, Memoirs, and Reminiscences

Becoming Anne Sexton
DIANE WOOD MIDDLEBROOK   7

Reminiscence Delivered at Memorial Service for
Anne Sexton in Marsh Chapel, Boston University
MAXINE KUMIN   22

Anne Sexton
ROBERT LOWELL   24

Poets and Friends
KATHLEEN SPIVACK   25

A Reminiscence
BARBARA SWAN   39

A Friendship Remembered
MAXINE KUMIN   46

Anne Sexton: Light Up the Cave
DENISE LEVERTOV   54

Part Two   Essays and Reviews

Review of *To Bedlam and Part Way Back*
JAMES DICKEY   63

Anne Sexton and Confessional Poetry
M. L. ROSENTHAL   65

From "The Poetry of Anne Sexton"
BEVERLY FIELDS   73

Redeeming Words
KAY ELLEN CAPO   88

Anne Sexton: The Voice of Illness
GARY BLANKENBURG   103

Review of *All My Pretty Ones*
  JAMES DICKEY   106

Review of *All My Pretty Ones*
  CECIL HEMLEY   107

Anne Sexton
  RALPH J. MILLS, JR.   110

The Witch's Life: Confession and Control in the Early
Poetry of Anne Sexton
  JEANNE H. KAMMER   125

Anne Sexton's "The Abortion" and Confessional Poetry
  LAWRENCE JAY DESSNER   135

Review of *Live or Die*
  CHARLES GULLANS   148

Strong Stuff
  PHILIP LEGLER   150

Live or Die: The Achievement of Anne Sexton
  ROBERT BOYERS   155

Plath and Sexton
  JON ROSENBLATT   167

The Achievement of Anne Sexton
  GREG JOHNSON   170

From "Anne Sexton's Suicide Poems"
  DIANA HUME GEORGE   188

Anne Sexton, Her Kind Mix Poetry with Music
  EUGENE POOL   202

The Poet on Stage
  CHARLES MARYAN   204

A Woman upon the Altar
  WALTER KERR   211

Review of *Love Poems*
  WILLIAM DICKEY   213

The Sacrament of Confession
  PAUL LACEY   216

Walt Whitman and Anne Sexton: A Note on the Uses of
Tradition
  MYRA STARK   242

Anne Sexton's *Love Poems*: The Genre and the
Differences
  WILLIAM H. SHURR   245

Review of *Transformations*
VERNON YOUNG 255

The Expanded Use of Simile in Anne Sexton's
Transformations
BRIAN GALLAGHER 257

That Story: The Changes of Anne Sexton
ALICIA OSTRIKER 263

The Poet in the Poem: A Phenomenological Analysis of
Anne Sexton's "Briar Rose (Sleeping Beauty)"
CYNTHIA A. MILLER [CYNTHIA M. ANTONELLI] 288

Shattered Glass
BEN HOWARD 303

"The Awful Babble of That Calling"
JOAN NUCIFORA 311

The Questing Self
RUTH EVELYN QUEBE 320

Anne Sexton
KARL MALKOFF 322

"The Excitable Gift": The Poetry of Anne Sexton
SUZANNE JUHASZ 333

From "The Nursing Mother and Feminine Metaphysics"
STEPHANIE DEMETRAKOPOULOS 357

Anne Sexton's Rowing Toward God
STEVEN GOULD AXELROD 359

Sexton's *The Awful Rowing Toward God*
MAXINE KUMIN 363

Anne Sexton: Demystifier or Mystic?
CAROLE FERRIER 365

Inventory of Loss
KATE GREEN 376

The Hungry Beast Rowing Toward God: Anne Sexton's
Later Religious Poetry
KATHLEEN L. NICHOLS 381

The Woman of Private (but Published) Hungers
ROSEMARY JOHNSON 387

The Self in the Poetry of Anne Sexton: The Religious
Quest
KATHERINE F. MCSPADDEN 403

How We Danced: Anne Sexton on Fathers and
Daughters
  DIANA HUME GEORGE   411

Malevolent Flippancy
  HELEN VENDLER   437

Poet of Weird Abundance
  DIANE WOOD MIDDLEBROOK   447

Bibliography   471

DORIS J. SCOTT

Anne Sexton

A Chronology

1928   November 9, Anne Gray Harvey born (in Weston, Massachusetts), to Mary Gray Staples Harvey and Ralph Churchill Harvey, youngest of three sisters, Jane (1923) and Blanche (1925). Namesake of Anna Ladd Dingley ("Nana") spinster great-aunt and confidante.

1934–45   Educated in Wellesley, Massachusetts, public schools. Summers spent at Squirrel Island, Boothbay Harbor, Maine.

1945–47   Attended Rogers Hall (preparatory school for girls) Lowell, Massachusetts, where she began writing poetry, which was published in *Splinters* (school yearbook). Accused of plagiarism by her mother, she stopped writing.

1947–48   Attended the Garland School, Boston (finishing school for women).

1948   August 16, eloped with Alfred Muller Sexton II ("Kayo"). Moved to Hamilton, New York, where Kayo attended Colgate University. November, moved back to Massachusetts, living alternately with both sets of parents. Kayo worked as sample boy in a woolen firm.

1949   Moved to apartment, Cochituate, Massachusetts, (near Newton). Completed modeling course (Hart Agency).

1950   Summer, Korean War began; Kayo joined the Naval Reserve. November, Kayo sent to Baltimore for navigation training; Anne accompanied him.

1951   May, Kayo shipped out on aircraft carrier *Boxer*; Anne returned to Massachusetts to live with in-laws. Modeled for Hart Agency, Boston.

1952   *Boxer* (damaged in combat) returned to San Francisco. Anne joined Kayo in a small walk-up apartment at Hunter's Point (naval housing), south of San Francisco.

Published by permission of the author.

1953   Kayo shipped out, Anne returned to her parents' home. July 21, Linda Gray Sexton born. Kayo discharged from service. August, Anne and Kayo purchased home at 40 Clearwater Road, Newton Lower Falls, Massachusetts.

1954   Began seeking counseling for recurring depression. July 15, 1954, great-aunt Anna Ladd Dingley died.

1955   August 4, Joyce Ladd Sexton ("Joy") born.

1956   First psychiatric hospitalization. Linda sent to Grandmother Harvey, Joy to Grandmother Sexton. November 8, first suicide attempt. December, encouraged by her psychiatrist ("Dr. Martin"), resumed writing poetry.

1957   January, enrolled in John Holmes's poetry workshop, Center for Adult Education, Boston, where she met Maxine Kumin. May, second suicide attempt.

1958   August, received scholarship to Antioch Writers' Conference, where she met W. D. Snodgrass. September, attended Robert Lowell's graduate writing seminar, Boston University, with Sylvia Plath and George Starbuck. Continued to attend Holmes's workshop with Kumin, Starbuck, and Sam Albert until Holmes's death in 1962.

1959   Awarded *Audience* Poetry Prize for 1958–59. February, John Holmes advised Anne not to seek publication for *To Bedlam and Part Way Back*. March 10, mother, Mary Gray Staples Harvey, died. April, signed contract with Houghton Mifflin, Boston, for publication of *To Bedlam and Part Way Back*. June 3, father, Ralph Churchill Harvey, died. July, received a Robert Frost Fellowship to attend the Breadloaf Writers' Conference. October, hospitalized for pneumonia, appendectomy, and ovarectomy. December 10, delivered the Morris Gray Poetry Lecture at Harvard.

1960   April 22, *To Bedlam and Part Way Back* published.

1961   Spring, Anne Sexton and Maxine Kumin appointed the first scholars in poetry at the Radcliffe Institute for Independent Study.

1962   *All My Pretty Ones* published. Prompted by John Holmes's death, wrote "Somewhere in Africa." June, hospitalized. Fall, first television appearance (with Peter Davison; interviewed by P. Albert Duhamel, critic for the *Boston Herald*). November, awarded Levinson Prize (*Poetry* magazine).

1963   *Eggs of Things* published. First of four children's books written in collaboration with Maxine Kumin. May, received first traveling fellowship from American Academy of Arts and Letters (for three months' travel in Europe). Summer, notified she had been awarded a Ford Foundation grant to work on her play *Tell Me Your Answer True* (begun in 1961). August 22 to October 27, toured France, Belgium, Holland, Switzerland, Italy, and Germany with "Sandy" Robart (friend and next-door neighbor). October 27, returned a month early due to emotional disturbance.

1964   *More Eggs of Things* (Sexton and Kumin) published. *Selected Poems* published in London. June, toured Europe with Kayo. July, when "Dr. Martin" moved his practice to Philadelphia, Anne began seeing a new psychiatrist, "Dr. Samuel Deitz." August, hospitalized. Began treatment with new antipsychotic drug, Thorazine. September, with a Ford Foundation grant, in residence at the Charles Playhouse, Boston, Anne began rewriting her play, *Tell Me Your Answer True*. December, moved to 14 Black Oak Road, Weston.

1965   Elected a Fellow of the Royal Society of Literature, London. Received a travel grant from the International Congress for Cultural Freedom. Summer, met Lois Ames.

1966   *Live or Die* published. August, African safari with Kayo. November, underwent surgery for broken hip.

1967   April, received the Shelley Award from the Poetry Society of America. May, awarded the Pulitzer Prize for *Live or Die*. July, read at the International Poetry Festival in London. September, taught English literature at Wayland (Massachusetts) High School.

1968   Taught poetry at McLean's Hospital (private mental institution), Belmont, Massachusetts. June, awarded honorary Phi Beta Kappa from Harvard (first woman ever to join the 187-year-old chapter). July, rock group Anne Sexton and Her Kind formed.

1969   *Love Poems* published. April, awarded Guggenheim Fellowship. April to August, worked on play *Mercy Street* (revision of *Tell Me Your Answer True*) for American Place Theatre. October 8, *Mercy Street* opened (off Broadway). While in New York, met Brian Sweeney, Australian businessman who admired her work. May, sister-in-law, Joan, killed in automobile accident. August, began seeing new psychiatrist, "Dr. Constance Chase." Fall, began teaching poetry seminar at Boston University. Began work on *Transformations*.

1970   Appointed Lecturer in English, Boston University.

1971   *Transformations* published. *Joey and the Birthday Present* (Sexton and Kumin) published. Began working on *The Book of Folly*.

1972   *The Book of Folly* published. Made full professor, Boston University. Held Crashaw Chair in Literature at Colgate University.

1973   *O Ye Tongues* published in London. February, hospitalized. March, filed for divorce. May 5, premiere of Conrad Susa's operatic adaptation of *Transformations* (Minnesota Opera Company, Cedar Village Theater, Minneapolis). August, hospitalized. November 5, divorce granted. Winter, hospitalized.

1974   *The Death Notebooks* published. Completed final editing of *The Awful Rowing Toward God*. Made tentative arrangement of poems in *45 Mercy Street*. June 1, made recording for *Anne Sexton Reads Her Poetry* (Caedmon Records). October 3, last reading (Goucher College, Maryland). October 4, committed suicide (carbon monoxide poisoning in the garage of her home, 3:30 PM).

1975   *The Awful Rowing Toward God* published. *The Wizard's Tears* (Sexton and Kumin) published.

1976   *45 Mercy Street*, edited by Linda Gray Sexton, published.

1977   *Anne Sexton: A Self-Portrait in Letters*, edited by Linda Gray Sexton and Lois Ames, published.

1978   *Words for Dr. Y.,* edited by Linda Gray Sexton, published.

1981   *The Complete Poems* published.

PART ONE   *Biography, Memoirs, and Reminiscences*

DIANE WOOD MIDDLEBROOK

Becoming Anne Sexton

Anne Gray Harvey became Mrs. Alfred Muller Sexton II on
August 16, 1948, after eloping from the family home in Weston,
Massachusetts, to be married before a justice of the peace in
North Carolina. She was nineteen years old. According to her,
an action equally precipitous and defiant changed her identity
nine years later into Anne Sexton, poet. On her twenty-eighth
birthday in 1956 she attempted suicide. A month later she began
writing poetry; two and a half years later her first book was
published with the title, *To Bedlam and Part Way Back* (1960). "It
was," she said, "a kind of rebirth at twenty-nine."[1]

A large collection of manuscripts and correspondence makes
it possible to reconstruct the years 1956–60 in enough detail to
conclude that while Anne Sexton's professional development
was both rapid and improbable, her success, like that of most
writers, resulted from a combination of talent, hard work and
well-timed good luck. But Sexton always claimed that her ca-
reer as a poet had the shape of a story; and that it opened not
with the event of writing her first poem, but with the suicide
attempt that separated her from a former life. In the following
pages I want to explore the ways in which her emphasis on
suicide expresses an ambivalence Sexton learned from her
mother, a writer's daughter, regarding the roles of mother,
daughter, and writer.

Sexton began telling, in print, the story of how she became a
writer after she was well on the way to being famous, in "craft
interviews" published mainly in literary journals between 1965

Denver Quarterly 18, no. 4 (1984). Reprinted by permission of the author. Quota-
tions from unpublished materials in the Anne Sexton Archive by permission of
Linda Gray Sexton, Executor of the Estate of Anne Sexton, and the Harry
Ransom Humanities Research Center, the University of Texas at Austin. Diane
Wood Middlebrook is currently at work on the authorized biography of Sex-
ton.—ED.

and 1976.[2] In each, Sexton found an occasion to remind the questioner that poetic truth is not "just factual." A preference for poetic truth seems to have determined the selection of details she provides about her beginnings as a poet. Particularly artful is the lengthy interview that appeared in the *Paris Review* shortly after Sexton received the Pulitzer Prize for Poetry in 1967. In four paragraphs she discloses much of what she ever had to say about the origins of her vocation.

Until I was twenty-eight I had a kind of buried self who didn't know she could do anything but make white sauce and diaper babies. I didn't know I had any creative depths. I was a victim of the American Dream, the bourgeois, middle-class dream. All I wanted was a little piece of life, to be married, to have children. I thought the nightmares, the visions, the demons would go away if there was enough love to put them down. I was trying my damnedest to lead a conventional life, for that was how I was brought up, and it was what my husband wanted of me. But one can't build little white picket fences to keep nightmares out. The surface cracked when I was about twenty-eight. I had a psychotic break and tried to kill myself.

She began writing as a form of therapy, Sexton told the interviewers:

I said to my doctor at the beginning, "I'm no good; I can't do anything; I'm dumb." He suggested I try educating myself by listening to Boston's educational TV station. He said I had a perfectly good mind. . . . One night I saw I. A. Richards on educational television reading a sonnet and explaining its form. I thought to myself, "I could do that, maybe; I could try." So I sat down and wrote a sonnet. The next day I wrote another one, and so forth. My doctor encouraged me to write more. "Don't kill yourself," he said. "Your poems might mean something to someone else someday." That gave me a feeling of purpose, a little cause, something to *do* with my life, no matter how rotten I was. . . .

After I'd been writing about three months, I dared to go into the poetry class at the Boston Center for Adult Education taught by John Holmes. I started in the middle of the term, very shy, writing very bad poems, solemnly handing them in for eighteen others in the class to hear. The most important aspect of that class was that I felt I belonged somewhere. When I first got sick and became a displaced person, I thought I was quite alone, but when I went into the mental hospital, I found I wasn't, that there were other people like me. It made me feel better—more real, sane. I felt, "These are my people." Well, at the John Holmes class that I attended for two years, I found I belonged to the poets, that I was *real* there, and I had another, "These are my people."

Asked whether she had never tried her hand at poetry before age twenty-eight, Sexton acknowledged writing little beside light verse for family occasions.

I wrote some serious stuff in high school; however, I hadn't been exposed to any of the major poets, not even the minor ones. . . . I read nothing but Sara Teasdale. I might have read other poets but my mother said as I graduated from high school that I had plagiarized Sara Teasdale. I had been writing a poem a day for three months, but when she said that, I stopped.[3]

From a factual point of view, this account of her development is incomplete and inexact: Sexton condenses the time periods and exaggerates the severity of the mental breakdown. But the narrative or storytelling truth is substantial. Suddenly, in 1956, through a cracked surface a buried self emerged and began looking for something to do. Like many of the housewives Betty Friedan was interviewing for her book *The Feminine Mystique*,[4] Sexton experienced the home as a sphere of confinement and stultification. Her usage three times in two paragraphs indicates that for her the verb *do* meant action in a social realm other than the family. Among both mental patients and poets she found she felt "more real, sane"; and it was within the realm of psychotherapy that she discovered and began to develop her talents. In the hospital she learned with infinite relief that as a mad housewife she was not merely the selfish monster she knew herself to be at home. She discovered that she belonged to a social category with its own language, its own system of symbol-making. Melville said of Ishmael in *Moby-Dick* that a whaling ship was his Harvard College and his Yale. So too for Anne Sexton were Westwood Lodge and the Boston Center for Adult Education. In these institutions she began to grasp both madness and metaphor as symbol systems, and to cultivate an understanding of them as ways of exploring and expressing her existence.

Sexton amplifies this arresting association between mental hospital and poetry class in both a letter and an early poem, "For John, Who Begs Me Not to Enquire Further." Addressed to her teacher at the Boston Center, the poem tells him that an asylum was the site of her first real education.

> in that narrow diary of my mind,
> in the commonplaces of the asylum
> . . . the cracked mirror
> or my own selfish death
> outstared me.
> . . . .
>
> And if you turn away
> because there is no lesson here
> I will hold my awkward bowl
> with all its cracked stars shining
> like a complicated lie.
> . . . .
>
> This is something I would never find
> in a lovelier place, my dear,
> although your fear is anyone's fear,
> like an invisible veil between us all . . .
> and sometimes in private,
> my kitchen, your kitchen,
> my face, your face.[5]

In the poem "For John," the reference to a cracking surface she uses in the interview appears as a metaphor for a kind of writing and a kind of speech. Her mind itself is a diary; the commonplaces of the asylum, a field of meanings she has learned to interpret in therapy and in the study of poetry. The poem is about the discovery of signs. Two years before her suicide attempt in 1956, Sexton had begun consulting a doctor in order to deal with recurring depression. Among other forms of treatment she undertook psychotherapy—sometimes called the "talking cure": the process of verbalizing or free association in which the psyche is coaxed to disclose its private symbolisms. The "buried self" thus uncovered is a linguistic self whose associations and metaphors are, in theory, keys to the origins of the illness.

Listening to the primitive speech of the buried self in herself and other mental patients, Sexton discovered what she later called "language," the convention-exploding imposition of new meanings on clusters of words produced by urgent personal associations. "It is hard to define," she wrote a friend.

> When I was first sick I was thrilled . . . to get into the Nut House. At first, of course, I was just scared and crying and very quiet (who me!) but then I found this girl (very crazy of course) (like me I guess) who talked language. What a relief! I mean, well . . . someone! And then later, a while later, and quite a while I found out that [her psychiatrist] talked language . . . I don't know who else does. I don't use it with everyone. No one of my whole street, suburb neighbors.[6]

In the interview, Sexton positions the proto-poet beneath what can be observed on the surface: "I didn't know I had any creative depths." The surface was a mirror reflecting back to parents and husband "the American Dream" girl. Not appropriate for exposure were other dreams: nightmares, visions, demons; when the mirror "cracked," these were released for speculation in therapy and poetry. Sexton referred to the releasing event as a "psychotic break." She was of course aware that "psychotic" had a specific meaning in psychiatry that did not apply to her case. By 1968 a variety of diagnostic labels had been attached to Sexton's ongoing mental illness—"hysteric," "psychoneurotic," "borderline," and "alcoholic"—but "psychotic" was not among them.[7] For the purposes of the interview, however, the term implied a significant poetic lineage. It connected her not only to such luminous contemporaries as Robert Lowell, Theodore Roethke, John Berryman, Delmore Schwartz, and Sylvia Plath, but Eliot and Pound, and, before the age of mental hospitals, Rimbaud, Baudelaire, Coleridge and others whose careers in poetry had included, in Rimbaud's widely translated words, "a lengthy, immense and systematic derangement of the senses." As she said to the interviewer, "These are my people."

Sexton's term "break," then, has a range of references in the story of her transformation from housewife into poet. Most obviously, it denotes her break into language and into the fellowship of poets, much assisted by the lucky breaks of having at her disposal the resources of literary Boston, and an affluent, cooperative family to take over the responsibilities of childcare and housekeeping. I want to pause, though, over what is concealed in Sexton's emphasis on discontinuity and transformation. For to become a poet did not mean for Anne Sexton breaking away from family ties, or breaking up a marriage. Rather than breaking out of the conventions of what she called "the bourgeois, middle-class dream," Sexton found ways to break into the meanings repressed there, and bring them over into brilliant metaphors. By 1968 when she granted the *Paris Review* interview, Anne Sexton was established as the poet of female bedlam. But in person Sexton presented to the world the carefully maintained image of an ordinary middle-class woman on whom unexpected fame has fallen. She kept a wardrobe of long dresses for important readings, and made entrances in them like an actress. Except during her severest illnesses, Sexton visited her hairdresser weekly and tinted her hair to cover the gray. Photographs invariably show large diamonds on both manicured hands. Despite her protestations that she was a "victim of the bourgeois, middle-class dream," Sexton maintained its insignia to furnish context for her art. Garbed in her finery, cigarette in hand, Anne Sexton mounted the stage and took the podium to speak lines uniting the buried self with her social stereotype, the suburban housewife.

Earlier I suggested that Sexton's account of her origins was incomplete as well as inexact. Now I want to turn to the question of what she left out or glossed over: the relevance of literary forebears, and most pertinently, the role her mother played in shaping Sexton's literary vocation.

In the fairy-tale version of her life reported to the interviewer, Sexton's suicide attempt precipitates the turn of the plot. Like the Briar Rose and the Snow White of her poems based on Grimm, Sexton wakened from the numb, deathlike state of a drug overdose into a new life. The doctor's confidence in her intelligence conflicted with the family drama in which Sexton had been assigned the role of the dumb daughter. The sense of being rotten, purposeless, dumb was of course an issue in Sexton's therapy, where it was treated as a symptom. But in the story she told of her transformation from housewife into poet, it was linked directly to a struggle with her mother over being a writer.

Anne's mother, always called Mary Gray, was the "adored" only child born late in life to Jane Dingley and Arthur Gray Staples in the small town of Lewiston, Maine. Mary Gray's father was editor of the *Lewiston Evening Journal*. A genteel man of letters, he collected his weekly editorials in several books of essays; on his retirement a eulogistic book of memoirs was published in his honor. One of his books survives in Anne Sexton's library with an inscription by Mary Gray: "to the author's youngest grandchild . . . from the author's daughter."[8]

Mary Gray was not a published author herself, but in a family which assigned older members younger namesakes and appointed family members different roles, Mary Gray and Arthur Gray formed the literary cohort. Several years after her mother's death from cancer in 1959, Sexton discussed the alliance of mother and grandfather with her psychiatrist. Your father always spoke of your mother as a writer, the doctor reminded her. And your grandfather published some books. Were they any good? "The opposite way my poetry is good—folksy—human—He wasn't original—he was homespun—. . . My mother must have had a tremendous Oedipus complex—she imitated him—grandfather drank a lot." The doctor pursued the question of mother's writing. Grandfather ran a newspaper; did mother work on it? "She never worked at anything—she wrote letters, charming letters. I can't spell." Sexton goes on to comment that Mother had beautiful handwriting and wrote the girls "elegant" excuses for school absences—but "she never really wrote real letters—she just composed letters."[9]

He wasn't original; she just composed. The question, Who are the writers in the family? evokes from Sexton distinctions similar to those that appear in the interview: those people (the family), my people (the poets); the conventional, the real. A feeling of rivalry with her mother had grown especially intense in the period following Sexton's recovery from the suicide attempt of 1956. Diary entries suggest that Sexton, who had only a high school education, thought of enrolling in college courses and broached the subject with Mary Gray. "Mother says she won't help pay for any college," Sexton noted. "Also said she got highest marks ever recorded on I.Q. test at Wellesley College. In other words there is nothing I could do to equal her genius."[10] But the conflict between mother and daughter that counted most in Sexton's discovery of her own genius had occurred much earlier, at the time of Anne's graduation from Rogers Hall. Anne had been writing poems; two were published in the school yearbook. Anne's sister Blanche validated Anne's memory that Mary Gray at that time accused Anne of plagiarism. Another girl had been expelled from Rogers Hall for submitting her father's work as her own; the scandal may have elicited Mary Gray's suspicions about Anne. She sent a sheaf of Anne's writing to "someone she knew in New York," for an expert opinion.[11] He assured Mary Gray that the work was original, but from Anne's point of view, the damage was irreversible. Her account of this episode to the *Paris Review* indicates she believed Mary Gray's intervention ended a phase of development and effected a moratorium that lasted ten years. No one else's encouragement would have mattered to her, Sexton insisted. "My mother was top billing in our house."[12]

Mary Gray expressed her sense of being an author's daughter by composing inscriptions, notes and verses to accompany gifts and celebrate special occasions. Given that Sexton was from a young age a scrapbook keeper and hoarder of letters, it is interesting that very few of Mary Gray's manuscripts in these genres survived among Anne Sexton's papers. But three of them which Sexton did save—a letter and two short poems—suggest ways in which Mary Gray served as both censor and precursor during the evolution of Sexton's identity as a poet. All are undated, but from internal evidence all seem to be responses to Sexton's second suicide attempt, which took place in May, 1957, after she had begun writing poetry.

Mary Gray's letter, shattered by long dashes, sounds far from "composed." It poses the predictable question of a parent to a suicidal offspring: where have I failed you?

We have always been a two-way radio, with perhaps one exception—Do *you* suppose subconsciously you feel—that *if* you don't please ME you are losing an anchor? I would not know—but I have a feeling that your love for me and my "sympatica" for you—could be licking you— . . .

You—Anne—my sweet daughter find life unattractive— Sometimes I do, *too*—and cry and cry—all full of self-pity and utter misery—So I can understand how you feel—Yet— you have something to give—*a* word—The word—a beautiful appreciation of what life—nature—and human relationship does . . . Every time you look at Joy—or Kayo—or me—or Linda with love in your heart *You* are happy—when you think of yourself and all of your failings you are *un*-happy—It happens to me—today—tomorrow—End of sermon—*Bless you darling*—Your very *im*perfect mother.[13]

In the forward drive of feeling, she addresses Anne as both a daughter and a mother and, identifying with both positions, expresses the point of view that the mother's responsibility requires the sacrifice of the daughter's point of view. Daughter finds life unattractive; but mother's duty is "to give—a word— The word—a beautiful appreciation." Closing from the "motherly" position, Mary Gray's letter seems to justify Sexton's claim that the way she was brought up required the suppression of demons, "if there was enough love to put them down." Mary Gray's poems, however, speak from the other, the demonic position. One ends in unambiguous identification with the daughter's despair: "with you I am a frail / Expression of the will to fail." The other, titled "Misery," contains a vivid portrait of Anne returning to consciousness from a drug overdose:

> She lay there very still and much too cool
> And though she hoped disaster yet could fool
> A mortal. But often her red tongue
> Kept flicking at her lips. How very young
> She seemed to me and when those long white toes
> Exposed among the bedclothes rose
> They told me she was on this plane
> So I could love her desperately again.[14]

The daughter's deathwish places the mother in a double bind, damned whether the daughter dies, or lives to be loved "desperately again." Yet it is disaster that inspires poetry, and the "author's daughter" in the mother who writes it.

Sexton viewed Mary Gray's poems not as messages of compassion, but as outrageous appropriations of the position of writer in the family, according to a letter she wrote poet James Wright about a year after Mary Gray's death. "When my mother wrote me these poems it was to show me that she too could write. But she was a little too late, thank God—I already knew I could do better than this. I remember, now, the scorn with which I read these." Proving she could, indeed, do better, Sexton "improved" the poem "Misery" a bit in process of retyping it for her mentor to read, undermining her rival and improving her own standing as an author's daughter at the same time.[15]

Sexton's unending rivalry with Mary Gray illuminates yet another meaning in the metaphor of "breaking" by which Sexton characterized the liberation of her talent. Accusing Anne of plagiarism at an early age, then "proving" Anne's originality by consulting a specialist, Mary Gray effectively halted her development as "the author's granddaughter," writer of "elegant excuses" and verse in the manner of Sara Teasdale. What survived to be uncovered as the "real" poet required breaking with the conventions that identify poetry with "beautiful appreciation"; yet she had her convention-imposing mother to thank. Breaking with convention meant, among other things examined here, breaking mother's code. For Mary Gray's communications suggest an identification of Daughter with unacceptable subjectivity, with self-centered authority—with poetry of the sort written by both Sexton and Mary Gray; and Mother with its repression.

The struggle to comprehend the contradiction between the roles of mother and daughter as she had learned them from Mary Gray provided Sexton the subject of what is arguably her most important early poem, "The Double Image" (*CP*, 35–42), written in 1958. Addressed to her younger daughter, Joy, the poem is an explanation of why Sexton "chose two times / to kill myself" rather than live within the family as Joy's mother. "Why did I let you grow in another place" than the family home? The answer is a long autobiographical poem incorporating many factual details about the period between July 1956, when Joy was sent to live with her paternal grandmother, and November 1958, when "you stay for good . . . You learn my name . . . You call me *mother*." The poem has a roughly chronological structure, and recounts that Sexton had been hospitalized, attempted suicide, convalesced in her parents' home; that her mother had been diagnosed and treated for breast cancer, blaming Sexton for the illness; that Sexton had attempted suicide a second time. Sexton condenses and interprets these events in the course of developing the rich metaphor of the poem's title. The double image is in fact a pair of portraits, of Mary Gray and Anne, painted during convalescence. In implication it is the situation of the mother in relation to the daughter she was and has; and the situation of the daughter, who must both separate from and approximate the mother.

Sexton speaks in the poem *as* a daughter *to* a daughter, *against* the dominance of mothers. Motherhood in this poem is depicted in images of invasion of personal boundaries, and in the imposition of conventions—as in these lines characterizing Anne's return to the family home, infantilized by illness.

> Part way back from Bedlam
> I came to my mother's house in Gloucester,
> Massachusetts. And this is how I came
> to catch at her; and this is how I lost her.
> I cannot forgive your suicide, my mother said.
> And she never could. She had my portrait
> done instead.
>
> I lived like an angry guest,
> like a partly mended thing, an outgrown child.
> I remember my mother did her best.
> She took me to Boston and had my hair restyled.
> Your smile is like your mother's, the artist said.

> (*CP*, 37)

The mother's effort to remake the daughter in her own image and dissolve the boundaries between their identities has a tragic outcome when the daughter's unforgiven deathwish shows up in the mother's aging body. "As if death were catching," Mary Gray developed cancer; following hospitalization for a mastectomy, she had her own portrait painted in a pose like that of Anne's portrait: "matching smile, matching contour." When, toward the end of the poem, Sexton returns to the question of "why I would rather / die than love," she offers Joy as an answer these symbolic portraits.

> In north light, my smile is held in place,
> the shadow marks my bone.
> What could I have been dreaming as I sat there,
> all of me waiting in the eyes, the zone
> of the smile, the young face,
> the foxes' snare.
>
> In south light, her smile is held in place,
> her cheeks wilting like a dry
> orchid; my mocking mirror, my overthrown
> love, my first image. She eyes me from that face,
> that stony head of death
> I had outgrown.
> . . . .
>
> And this was the cave of the mirror,
> that double woman who stares
> at herself, as if she were petrified.

(*CP,* 40–41)

Across a passageway in the parental home the generations eye each other, reproductions, surfaces concealing the nightmares of the recent past in both their lives. In this complex of images—of the cave of the mirror, the zone of the smile, the implication of receiving and passing on womanhood as a fatal legacy—is condensed material that fills book after book of poetry by Anne Sexton. And the last lines of "The Double Image" beautifully extend the implications of the metaphor, as Sexton ruefully acknowledges that she has stepped into the mother's position.

> we named you Joyce
> so we could call you Joy.
> . . . .
>
> I needed you. I didn't want a boy,
> . . . .

I, who was never quite sure
about being a girl, needed another
life, another image to remind me.
And this was my worst guilt; you could not cure
nor soothe it. I made you to find me.

(*CP*, 41–42)

Doubleness now denotes not only proliferation, but du-
plicity. Naming a daughter for a desirable state of mind, like
having her portrait painted, appropriates the daughter's identity,
turns her into a mirror; implies that the struggle to separate will
have to be violent: cracked mirror, psychotic break. In this
poem, Sexton apparently concurs with the assumption that her
suicide attempt has been a pathological rather than a creative
form of separation. But the "guilt" she accepts at the end of the
poem does not refer to her suicide attempt. It refers to the guilt
of mothers who wish to reproduce themselves in daughters. For
all its tenderness, the poem's point of view is catastrophic: the
birth of a child turns the daughter into a mother; if the daughter,
a buried self, emerges it must be to kill herself or the mother. Or
the mother's image.

In the psychiatric interrogation of her deathwish that began in
1956, Sexton was to grasp that inability to separate from her
mother was a central issue in her pathology. In the symbolic
structures of her art, however, the hunger for mothering and the
boundariless connection to the restless daughter in the repressed
mother was fertile ground for exploring the interconnectedness
of suffering and love, particularly across the generations of
women in a family. Sexton acknowledged this complex debt, in
which her pathology and her gift were interdependent, in the
enclosure that accompanied her Christmas gift to Mary Gray in
1957:

"Dear Mother, Here are some forty-odd pages of the first
year of Anne Sexton, Poet. You may remember my first
sonnet written just after Christmas one year ago. I do not
think all of these are good. However, I am not ashamed of
them. . . . I love you. I don't write for you, but know that
one of the reasons I do write is that you are my mother." (*L*,
31, 33)

"The Double Image," which Sexton claimed as the first poem in which she had truly found her voice as a writer,[16] was not to be written for another two years, after zealous work in the mastery of poetics. But by the end of 1956 Sexton had begun the process of separation and rebirth as the unique talent who for eighteen more years survived her own impulse to self-destruction: Anne Sexton, Poet.

NOTES

1. "Interview with Anne Sexton (1965)," by Patricia Marx, in *Anne Sexton: The Artist and Her Critics,* edited by J. D. McClatchy (Bloomington: Indiana University Press, 1978), 30.

2. *Anne Sexton: The Artist and Her Critics* contains a complete list of such interviews, 292–93.

3. "The Art of Poetry: Anne Sexton (1968)," interview with Barbara Kevles, in *Anne Sexton: The Artist and Her Critics,* 3–7.

4. In the introduction to the tenth anniversary edition of *The Feminine Mystique,* Friedan describes the origins of this groundbreaking study: "In 1957, getting strangely bored with writing articles about breast feeding and the like for *Ladies' Home Journal,* I put an unconscionable amount of time into a questionnaire for my fellow Smith graduates of the class of 1942, thinking I was going to disprove the current notion that education had fitted us ill for our roles as women. But the questionnaire raised more questions than it answered. . . . The suspicion arose as to whether it was the education or the role that was wrong" (New York: W. W. Norton, 1974), 2.

5. "For John, Who Begs Me Not to Enquire Further," *The Complete Poems,* edited by Linda Gray Sexton, with a foreword by Maxine Kumin (Boston: Houghton Mifflin, 1981), 34–35. Further quotations from this edition will be annotated *CP.*

6. *Anne Sexton: A Self-Portrait in Letters,* edited by Linda Gray Sexton and Lois Ames (Boston: Houghton Mifflin, 1977), 244–45. Further quotations from this edition will be annotated *L.*

7. These diagnostic labels appear in Sexton's hospital records, and in transcripts of tape-recorded therapy sessions she kept from January, 1961, to May, 1964. The latter are deposited as restricted materials in the Anne Sexton Archive, Humanities Research Center, The University of Texas, Austin, and quoted with the permission of Linda Sexton.

8. Inside cover of Arthur G. Staples, *Just Talks on Common Themes* (Lewiston, Me.: J. Scudney, 1920). Copy in the collection of Linda Sexton.

9. Entry in Anne Sexton's therapy transcript June 12, 1962. Quoted from restricted material in the Anne Sexton Archive, Humanities Research Center, The University of Texas, Austin, with the permission of Linda Sexton.

10. Holograph notes on loose calendar pages dated February 14–19, 1957; filed among letters to her psychiatrist deposited as restricted materials in the Anne Sexton Archive, Humanities Research Center, The University of Texas, Austin, and quoted with the permission of Linda Sexton.

11. Interview with Blanche Harvey Taylor, Scituate, Massachusetts, April 27, 1983.

12. "Art of Poetry: Anne Sexton," 5.

13. Sexton, Anne, Miscellaneous file, Humanities Research Center, The University of Texas, Austin.

14. Sexton, Anne, Recipient: from Harvey, Mary Gray Staples, Humanities Research Center, The University of Texas, Austin. I have reproduced Mary Gray's first two lines as written; the uses of "to" and "And" seem to be errors.

15. Wright, an established poet slightly older than Sexton, had become her lover and mentor; both relationships were conducted chiefly in an enormous correspondence, much of which has been lost. However, Sexton kept a carbon of this undated letter in a file reserved for notes written in the course of therapy with the psychiatrist who had proposed writing poetry. Quoted from restricted materials, Humanities Research Center, The University of Texas, Austin, with permission from Linda Sexton.

16. Letter to W. D. Snodgrass, November 26, 1958, L, 43.

MAXINE KUMIN

Reminiscence Delivered at Memorial Service for Anne Sexton in Marsh Chapel, Boston University

October 15, 1974

Yesterday at my desk, trying to sort out a few things to say here, I spent hours going through folders of old letters, work sheets, scraps of poems. For one thing, I was trying to pinpoint what year it was—1956? 1957?—that Anne and I met, two shy housewives, a pair of closet poets, in John Holmes's class at the Boston Center for Adult Education. For another, I was trying to sort out people's names, who and where we were, how Sam Albert was in that class, and Ruth Soter, the friend to whom "With Mercy for the Greedy" is dedicated, and how we first met George Starbuck when he read at the New England Poetry Club in 1958.

Most of this I gleaned from Holmes's letters, traveling from Medford to Newton, from 1957 to a month before his death in 1962, letters written between our workshop meetings, or because of them, or even in spite of them. George's name comes up frequently, and Sam Albert's name, and specific poems we are working on get mentioned. The group came down hard on Anne's poem, "Housewife," and she revised it well. Anne read the poem "For Eleanor Boylan Talking with God" at a workshop and it was enthusiastically received, except for some pruning needed at the end. There was no more determined reviser than Anne. She worried and snipped and pounded the ending into its final, poignant form.

Remembering this, the whole complex rich interplay of workshop comes back, of Holmes and Starbuck and Albert and Sexton and Kumin during the three years we held forth on our

From *To Make a Prairie* (Ann Arbor: University of Michigan Press, 1979). Reprinted by permission of the author and the publisher.

own over coffee and whiskey and carbon copies of our poems, and before that, around the long oak table at 5 Commonwealth Avenue in a second-story room that smelled of chalk and wet overshoes. There, Anne and I, in a funny mixture of timidity and bravado, prayed that our poems would rise to the top of the pile under Professor Holmes's fingers as he alternately fussed with his pipe and shuffled pages, and one of us would thus be divinely elected for scrutiny.

Later, for one semester, there were Ted and Renee Weiss, Ted a visiting professor at MIT. Anne had just written "Woman with Girdle." The poem's mischief roused Ted to such heights of ribaldry that night and we were all so raucous that the couple overhead—this was at Weiss's borrowed apartment somewhere in Cambridge—thumped on the floor and threatened us with the police and we were, to our shame, even noisier. That same winter John Crowe Ransom came to Tufts at Holmes's invitation and Anne and I drove to Medford in a blizzard to hear him. Somehow we drove back again too, at three o'clock in the morning, straddling the yellow line that divided a deserted and snow-clogged highway. We were sleepy and exalted and a little drunk on bourbon and fish chowder and the marvelous voice of the poet saying his own best lines.

I found an old poem of John's about another, earlier workshop that lasted through three winters in the forties, a workshop consisting of Ciardi, Wilbur, Eberhart, May Sarton, and John Holmes. It says what we were, too, and why, and now I'd like to close with these few lines from it:

> Good God bless all such big long bickering nights
> Among the cheeses and bottles, coffee and carbon copies,
> In Medford or Cambridge—or Nashville or Chicago!
> The fact is that everything we read is in our books,
> Our best poems. If those confrontations were painful,
> Rowdy, sometimes the bloom of fire and absolute,
> We couldn't hear a clank of armor some of us wore,
> Or see which came naked and afraid, but it was so.
>
> Look at us now, in the long story's foreseeable ending,
> Such a yardage of books on shelves . . .
> We remind one another, when we meet now, of those nights,
> How we had what we remember, the warmth of the poems.

ROBERT LOWELL

Anne Sexton

I met Anne Sexton in 1957,* and at a moment to be impressed, because I was writing my first autobiographical poems and was carried away by Snodgrass's marvelous *Heart's Needle* sequence. Anne was lean-faced, white-armed, thirty, and a poet for only a few months. She had met Snodgrass that summer and become a "confessional" poet overnight. How many laborious, often useless, steps of apprenticeship she had bypassed. Unlike Snodgrass and Sylvia Plath, she was an amateur. I am not sure I know what I mean by this. In my writing class, which she attended for a year or so, her comments and questions were more to the point than the more studious. In the beginning, her lines were overpoetic; she gave promise of becoming a fifties Edna Millay. Yet on her own, she developed a more sensitive, realistic idiom. Her gift was to grip, to give words to the drama of her personality. She did what few did, cut a figure. What went wrong? For a book or two, she grew more powerful. Then writing was too easy or too hard for her. She became meager and exaggerated. Many of her most embarrassing poems would have been fascinating if someone had put them in quotes, as the presentation of some character, not the author.

At a time when poetry readings were expected to be boring, no one ever fell asleep at Anne's. I see her as having the large, transparent, breakable, and increasingly ragged wings of a dragonfly—her poor, shy, driven life, the blind terror behind her bravado, her deadly increasing pace . . . her bravery while she lasted.

From *Anne Sexton: The Artist and Her Critics*, edited by J. D. McClatchy (Bloomington: Indiana University Press, 1978).

*Lowell met Sexton in the fall of 1958, not 1957.—ED.

KATHLEEN SPIVACK

Poets and Friends

Who can measure how precious we are to each other? Anne Sexton and I were friends and colleagues for fifteen years, sharing poetry and lives. Her death confirms the importance of staying alive, not to cut off one's options and development prematurely, but to continue to grow. Poets, and perhaps especially women, belong to each other. We exist side by side, writing for our friends as well as for ourselves. We are each other's listeners, the sharers of the heart. Society provides too few roles for creative people, especially women. We must no longer allow our gifts to categorize us: "paying the price," stopping our work and lives, depriving ourselves of growth, maturity, wisdom, and old age.

I met Anne Sexton during the beginning of her poetic career, in Robert Lowell's class at Boston University in the spring of 1959,* and remained close to her until her death on October 4, 1974. Sylvia Plath and George Starbuck, among others, were also in that class. I was nineteen, attending the class as a special student from Oberlin College. Anne, ten years older than I, had been writing for several years. Anne was warm, generous, humorous. For fifteen years we continued to work together, laugh, talk, swim in her pool, write, read poems, gossip, commiserate, and share. For five years during that period, from 1964 to 1969, I worked at Brandeis University, near Anne's house, and saw her several times a week. My job at Brandeis was that of a psychological counselor. But though I knew of Anne's unhappiness and attraction toward death, the focus of our friendship was on joy, the discipline of our work, shared experiences, and that most complex preoccupation, poetry.

Anne had an exceptional ability to inspire empathy. One

Boston Globe Magazine, August 9, 1981. © Kathleen Spivack. Reprinted by permission of the author.

*Sexton began attending Lowell's class in the fall of 1958.—ED.

cringes at the thought of the hundreds of Sexton imitators, perhaps even gifted, who will now emerge, working themselves up and killing themselves in order (they hope) to become poets. The poet as mad, the poet as suicide, the vulnerable deranged woman: Anne herself was a believer in, as well as a victim of, that myth. The myth, with its attendant diminution of the person of talent, makes the artist more "bearable" to those around her. How difficult it is to deal with the ideas of strength in creativity: the poet as see-er, namer; the poet as Poet, an intact human being, experiencing and recording life in all its dimensions.

Anne was a dedicated and hard-working poet, and her best material included not only her own suffering, but a more universal outreach. Anne started writing as a result of her psychotherapy. Though she wrote a great deal out of her own personal history, her finest poems went beyond it: the "Fury" poems, for instance; "Some Foreign Letters"; "Man and Wife"; "The Angel" sonnets; and others.

Anne came to Lowell's seminar with a desperate ambition and tremulous nerve. She was not yet thirty, but it was considered that she had started writing "late in life"; late, that is, when compared with the undergraduates who dominated the class. Her fine poem "The Double Image" had appeared in the *Hudson Review,* and a few others had been published here and there. *To Bedlam and Part Way Back* was still in manuscript. Lowell advised her on the organization of that first collection.

"Who is your favorite poet?" Robert Lowell opened his class with that question. Anne's favorite, that first day, was William Carlos Williams, a strange choice when considered against the kind of personal poetry she was to share with the class. Sylvia Plath chose Wallace Stevens. I felt skeptical of Sylvia, certain that she was putting on airs. It was hard to imagine Wallace Stevens as a "favorite" poet: dispassionate, intellectual. The category "favorite" demanded a more passionate partisanship. But Sylvia was at that time writing very formal intellectual poems, unable to break out into the passionate feeling of *Ariel* and subsequent books. Those earlier poems, later to be included in *The Colossus,* were intelligent and admirable. Lowell praised them, but with a certain disinterest, for the poems were technically perfect and there was not much to say. (Sylvia, I was told, was paid $50 by her publisher as an advance for *The Colossus.* Such is the cult of suicide that, following Sylvia's death, several publishers advanced prospective biographers more than $20,000 each. Suicide definitely increased Sylvia's worth, much as she could have used the money during her lifetime.)

Sylvia had had an excellent education and had read everything. She could be a devastating critic. "Reminds me of Empson," she might drawl as a student's poem was handed around the table. Or she might cite a more obscure poet, out of another century. Lowell would be impressed. The student author would be doubly embarrassed: first, because the suspicion of plagiarism had been raised; and second, because most of us had never heard of, let alone read, the poets she referred to. Many of Sylvia's critical comments had the effect of making the rest of us feel judged as cheats or ignoramuses in the face of her scholarship and unusual poetic recall.

Sylvia sat on one side of the long table, composed, neat, held in, in a tightly buttoned print blouse and neat cardigan. She spoke quietly, with utmost control. She was married to the poet Ted Hughes, who seemed her opposite in every way. Anne, on the other hand, was often late, and wore splashy, flowing dresses and flashy jewelry. Her hoarse voice breathed extravagant enthusiasm and life. Her hands shook when she read her poems aloud. She smoked endlessly. Anne's poems were ragged; they flew off the page. She was an instinctual poet rather than, as Sylvia, a trained one. Anne wrote out her private pain without censoring. She was not always successful in her attempts to transform her feelings into poetry, and she wrote as much bad poetry as good. At the same time she was humble and wanted to learn. Closely connected with her own psychotherapy, Anne's poems seemed to be validating her neuroses. What is not generally known is how hard she worked to go beyond the outpourings of her "fifty-minute hour," to become a serious artist. She worked to prune and shape a poem.

Her striking gifts as a poet were those of an image-maker, somewhat related to the open, imagist state of psychosis. Anne's best poems were strong, startling, and courageous; they exploded with original imagery. It was her ability to walk that fine line between sanity and madness that makes so many of her poems astonishing. Her flaws as a poet were the reverse of this:

private unrelated images, an indulgence in the personal and the morbid, and insufficient editing. Since poetry was a way of dealing with her mental distress, it was sometimes hard for her to throw a bad poem away or leave it out of a collection.

In Lowell's class, Anne rewrote and revised diligently. "Some Foreign Letters," "The Bells," "The Double Image," as well as "You, Doctor Martin" were first seen in class.

The poet W. D. Snodgrass had just published his volume *Heart's Needle,* a book of poems dealing mainly with divorce and bereft fatherhood. This was a striking departure from the restrained academic poetry, dominated by the New Critics, which was being written at that time. Though formal in structure, *Heart's Needle* dealt directly with pain. Lowell as well as his students thought the collection remarkable. Anne's poem "The Double Image" is based on the Snodgrass sequence in its attempt to deal with real experience, but with a certain formality and structure. Her poem deals with a breakdown and relation to motherhood:

> I, who was never quite sure
> about being a girl, needed another
> life, another image to remind me.
> And this was my worst guilt; you could not cure
> nor soothe it. I made you to find me.

While Anne was working on poems that were to be included in *To Bedlam and Part Way Back,* Robert Lowell was finishing *Life Studies.* He shared many of the poems in manuscript and draft form with the class. Though Anne's work has been called confessional, the urge to write directly from personal experience was being explored by Snodgrass and Lowell as well.

Both Sylvia and Anne were sensitive to the subjects of madness, breakdowns, and suicides. There were times during Lowell's classes when the two women exchanged knowing glances and withdrew into themselves. Lowell himself suffered mental breakdowns during this period. During one class, in which he seemed agitated, we had the distinct fear that he was going to throw himself out of the window. The class sat completely hushed. Anne fixed me firmly with her green eyes, as if to communicate something. Lowell hospitalized himself directly after this class meeting. Anne's poem "Elegy in the Classroom" documents this moment.

Sylvia, Anne, and George Starbuck had a special relationship born out of the class. They were approximately the same age but came from different circumstances. George seemed the most stable; in class he was kind, urbane, and encouraging. It was only after the publication of *Ariel* that those of us who had not gotten drunk with George and Anne and Sylvia at the Ritz realized the extent of Sylvia Plath's desperation. She had seemed reserved and totally controlled as well as unapproachable to the younger writers. Anne herself felt a barrier to the friendship with Sylvia; it was not until Sylvia had left the country that openness grew between the two women, then only in correspondence. Anne was always open, even without liquor—perhaps too much; vulnerable and frightened. But her honesty gave her a rare sort of poise.

After Sylvia's suicide, Anne felt a mixture of emotions, from anger and betrayal and abandonment to jealousy that Sylvia had actually managed to kill herself, that act that both women had discussed endlessly. Anne was obsessed with death—one has only to read *Live or Die* to see to what extent. Anne felt Sylvia had achieved immortality by her suicide.

The desire to be immortal was a strong motive for Anne's writing, she said. Death, while allowing her immortality, was to be a lover, a mother, a comfort, as well as assuring that Anne would be remembered: She wrote about it constantly, in many guises. As in, for instance, her poem "The Addict":

> Don't they know
> that I promised to die!
> I'm keeping in practice.
> I'm merely staying in shape.
> The pills are a mother, but better,
> every color and as good as sour balls.
> I'm on a diet from death.

Death was the easiest solution, to be turned to when unhappy, upset, confused, or just plain tired—as was perhaps the case in her final successful attempt. Anne wanted her husband

and daughters to fill the comfort functions, but her need was greater than anyone's ability to fill it. For a time, Anne's writing helped keep her alive. It gave her a reason to work, a preoccupation beyond her own problems, a focus for her imagination and intensity. It was, at least for a time, her solace, her secret, and her one real love. Ultimately, death took precedence in her imagination. Anne had, her friends felt, almost a what-the-hell attitude toward death: Her wish to destroy herself was a deep compulsion and, at the same time, a whim that might be postponed if something nicer came along to distract her.

Whatever their troubles in their womanhood, both Anne and Sylvia had suffered emotional deprivation as young children. Their childhoods had a lasting and terrible effect on them. However, this does not explain why they became poets, or why other poets, equally deprived, and gifted, have managed to stay alive. Sylvia documents her violent emotion in a final outcry, *Ariel,* unleashing all the pent-up anger, the passion, and the sense of irreparable loss that had been so repressed in her earlier work. And there is some relation, I think, in both Anne's and Sylvia's work, between the view of themselves as object or victim and a fear of the largeness of their anger toward key figures in their lives.

Writing a poem about a disturbing aspect of her life did not seem to relieve the emotion for Anne. Rather, it opened the door to more and more brooding upon it. This is the reverse of the usual sequence of emotions for a poet; in most cases, a poem is a crystallization of feelings, which are somewhat solved writing of them. But for Anne, writing the poem was just the beginning, as if poetry were free association. Then she would go on to obsess about the subject in her daily life. Her obsessions were her relation to her mother and her attempts to salvage it through seeking union in madness, love, fantasies of death, and finally, in her last year and a half, God. "The Death Baby" sequence in *The Death Notebooks* speaks of the childhood relationship directly and the extent to which Anne could not accept herself (and felt her mother could not accept her). "Those Times" in *Live or Die* is also an especially literal poem, as are many of the first group in *The Book of Folly*. Anne craved sustenance: maternal love, a breast, and acceptance of her own being and body.

She was also beginning to explore her sense of separation from her father and her fear that she was illegitimate. (See "The Death of the Fathers" sequence in *The Book of Folly*.) She also wrote about her marriage, and it is evident, in its recording throughout her work, that during the later years the relationship disintegrated, as in the poem "The Wifebeater." *The Book of Folly* is almost a direct record of Anne's psychotherapy and of her preoccupations at the time of its writing, which were to continue through the last years of her life.

To Bedlam and Part Way Back, Anne's first book, is about a breakdown and a woman's relation to her family. Carefully constructed and arranged, the book is intense and poignant. *All My Pretty Ones,* one of Anne's best collections, continues to shape and form the poems, and the work moves from Anne's inner self to focus on the outside world a bit more. *Live or Die* is a journey into illness and despair, though there is some hope of redemption in the end. *Love Poems,* which Anne had originally wanted to call *For My Beloved,* has beauty, feeling, and grace, and there are some stirring poems in the volume. *Transformations* was a deliberate attempt on Anne's part to write about something other than herself, and she had a lot of fun doing the book. The outcome is a fascinating collection of Grimm's tales retold, with all of Anne's imagery, human empathy, and humor. *The Book of Folly* is a varied collection, with a focus on psychotherapy, with the exception of the "Angel" poems. There, as in *The Death Notebooks,* Anne achieved an almost Rilke-like clairvoyance, a transcendent energy and ecstasy that make this work luminescent.

Psychotherapy played a large part in Anne's life and work. She had started writing poetry at the suggestion of one of her earlier psychiatrists, after a breakdown. She tape-recorded most of her psychiatric sessions and played them over to herself. Since her poems were, many of them, records of her psychological struggles, we speculated on what they would have been like had Anne been involved in a form of therapy other than Freudian.

But both Anne and Sylvia were, in fact, obsessed with a Freudian framework. Had they not been members of an East Coast orientation, with all its focus on the past, perhaps their work would have been different. For Anne, especially, what was going on in her present was quite positive. The constant focus on "self" in both poets' work perhaps accounts for the airless, sometimes self-indulgent quality one senses. There is also a tremendous focus on their anger, which in their imagination transforms the poets into demons, witches, madwomen, and man-eaters. The poem "Her Kind" was especially important to Anne. She always started her poetry readings with these lines from it:

> I have gone out, a possessed witch,
> haunting the black air, braver at night;
> dreaming evil, I have done my hitch . . .
> A woman like that is not a woman, quite.
> I have been her kind.

Sylvia Plath wrote, in "Lady Lazarus":

> Dying
> Is an art, like everything else.
> I do it exceptionally well.
>
> I do it so it feels like hell.
> I do it so it feels real.
> I guess you could say I've a call.
> . . . .
> Herr God, Herr Lucifer
> Beware
> Beware.
>
> Out of the ash
> I rise with my red hair
> And I eat men like air.

Anne, especially, made the great gap between poetry and psychiatry dangerously close. Later, she turned more and more to religion. Her gifts as a poet allowed her to pull it off. This has not been true for her imitators.

Vibrant and beautiful, Anne was very attractive to men in an appealing and vulnerable way. One of her many psychiatrists used the therapeutic situation to make love to her, according to Anne (documented in *Love Poems*). Anne talked this over extensively with her friends, who advised her to break it off. The therapist's colleagues also felt the situation was potentially disastrous. Anne was unable to break free of this relationship. When finally the psychiatrist terminated the therapy, and the affair, Anne was devastated. This rejection had far-reaching effects.

Anne's psychiatric expenses during the last year of her life, she told me, were enormous (over $60,000). For this reason, though she disliked poetry readings, which made her feel unusually vulnerable and exposed, she took a number of engagements to meet her bills.

She was, in fact, seriously mentally ill. By this I refer not only to the multiple suicide attempts, triggered apparently by a range of emotions, from rage and anguish to boredom, but to the fact that she often hallucinated, heard voices, and so forth, when in distress. Her illness increased, her friends felt, during the last two years of her life, and it was harder for us to be of help to her. Her marriage suffered, undergoing unbearable strain.

She was given a variety of drugs, but none worked. Thorazine, which for a time seemed helpful, had a number of side effects, including an allergy to the sun. Anne loved the sun and sunbathing and was forced, for a number of years, to give that up because of the Thorazine. It was impossible to be with her when she was severely distressed without resonating to her state. Listening again to the recordings of Anne reading her poems, I am struck by the near-madness of some of them; they hover on the edge of psychosis, though at the same time they are brilliant.

During the last two years of her life, Anne said that she thought she would have been a healthier woman had the women's liberation movement come along sooner. In many ways I feel this is true. Both Anne and Sylvia had a strong drive toward conventionality and perfection, a view of "life as it should be" that left no room for their wild emotions and imagination. Sylvia's anger and hatred, when finally unleashed, were insatiable (see *The Bell Jar* as well as *Ariel*).

In her twenties, Anne tried to live the conventional life of a married young mother in the suburbs, and she went mad. She was isolated, secluded, and surrounded, she said, by people who did not understand her. She had not had a college education, and it was not until she got a teaching job at Boston University that she was able to overcome her feelings of inferiority about her lack of formal education. Anne drank, worried about her appearance, and took mood-controlling pills. The first time she left her young children (and she stayed in, she said, for the first five years of their lives), it was to see a psychiatrist. For a while she sold cosmetics door to door to pay for her psychiatric appointments.

Despite her difficulties, Anne was strong. Warm and outgoing with her friends, she was a hard worker, dedicated and ambitious. She was the leading businesswoman in the poetry world, and she loved the wheeler-dealer aspects of publishing her work. She commanded, and got, the largest fees ever given to a poet for publishing and for readings, with the possible exceptions of Allen Ginsberg and James Dickey. They have done more to help other poets get paid for their work than the entire polite generation of academic poets who preceded them. Anne negotiated a good job for herself and got paid decently. She loved to give advice, had a huge correspondence, and encouraged poets, would-be poets, and scores of mental patients who wrote to her. She enjoyed a good joke, sunning, swimming, and being with friends.

Anne had a great gift for friendship, and she kept her friends for years. Her closest friends were the writers Maxine Kumin and Lois Ames. Lois was later designated by Anne as "my official biographer." Both women were immensely loyal, and it was Lois who accompanied Anne on many reading tours, providing the support, security, and companionship that is so important when one is among strangers. Maxine gave strength and nurturance to Anne during the many difficult periods in her marriage. Both Maxine and Lois are unusually gifted professional women in their own right. Both were managing nearly full-time jobs as well as writing and caring for their families; yet, with all that, they retained qualities of depth and wisdom, as well as humor. It is a credit to the friendship of the three women that each maintained her own integrity and identity while supporting the life and work of her friends. These were total friendships, with great generosity and love.

I remember accompanying them to a restaurant on Anne's fortieth birthday. I had just passed my thirtieth. They assured me that the forties were wonderful, without the mortality-brooding that accompanied the early thirties. Because I was expecting my first child, and their children were more or less grown, there was some rueful laughter around the subject of child care. Everyone drank a bit more, and Anne and Lois had a poetry competition. Lois had given Anne a necklace, engraved "Don't let the bastards win." Anne had then given Lois one, which read "Don't let the bastards get you." Which was a better line of poetry? I chose Lois's, on account of the rhythm and heavy accent on "win." Anne's mood changed, and she referred to this with dismay for years. How could I have been so disloyal?

It was commonly thought that Anne Sexton had rushed into print, experiencing no difficulty in getting published once her first brilliant poems had been created. This was untrue. In fact, Anne had tried to publish consistently for several years before the acceptance of her first manuscript. She had an entire file drawer full of magazine letters. Some were printed rejection forms; others, nasty letters. It was comforting to be shown them by Anne, to know that the struggle to publish was a common one and that everyone got rejected. Anne enjoyed the process of sending out material. She had envelopes addressed to the magazines she favored, and when her poems came back in the mail, she immediately transferred them to new envelopes and sent them right out again.

She worked continually, in her good periods writing three and four poems a day. She worked on several manuscripts at once, and poems went into various looseleaf notebooks, to be scrawled on and edited. She planned ahead and was working on at least three more books, including *The Life Notebooks,* when she died.

At the time we all met in Robert Lowell's writing workshop, there was a great prejudice against "women writers." This particularly referred to women who tried to combine female and poetic roles. Exempt were those few poets of stature: Elizabeth Bishop and Marianne Moore, who had neither married nor had children. "She writes like a man" was still the highest male praise given a clear-minded woman. Both Muriel Rukeyser and Denise Levertov had disqualified themselves, according to

Lowell, by writing about, in fact celebrating, the vagina, thereby managing to offend both Boston propriety and male prerogative in a few quick scribbles.

One must be pure for one's art, it was argued: A woman who opted for both art and family life was expected to pay for that compromise, either by inferior art or by emotional casualties. Men were not expected to compensate for having families by producing second-rate art. But in the case of women poets, this was a given, the price. Some of these attitudes toward women writers are changing now. But in 1959 the men poets still had to be exceptionally macho and the women monkishly dedicated, or suffer the punishment of men's negative judgment on their poems when they put their children first.

Sylvia Plath and, at Radcliffe, Adrienne Rich had partially managed to become exempt, at least for a time. In Sylvia's case, we know the later hardship she struggled against in order to write and care for her children—a hardship that overcame her finally, so that she wanted only to sleep and sleep. Adrienne, too, struggled to maintain her work. But in a system that rewarded young women chiefly for being worshipful and self-effacing, both women had managed to win prizes, recognition, and approval from the male establishment.

Sylvia had won every possible prize at Smith, published in national magazines while still an undergraduate, and had won a fellowship abroad. Adrienne, while still a junior at Radcliffe College, had won the Yale Younger Poets prize, which included publication of her first book. The poems in that volume demonstrated a crystalline translucent intellectual quality that is still so much a part of her poetry today. Nevertheless, she was not admitted to the upper-level English courses at Harvard on the grounds that no women had ever been admitted to them—and no exceptions were to be made. Women achievers were designated "castrating," and male poets were the most damning of their female contemporaries. I was told, in my own search for a publisher, to take my name off my poems and substitute a male pseudonym. Only then would my work be given a reading by an editor. The subsequent women's movement freed women as well as men to admit openly to deep human loyalties and responsibilities in addition to their commitment to their art.

Anne, by virtue of her lack of formal education and by her

"excessive" emotionality and obvious vulnerability, was attacked most bitterly. She inspired controversy, and though I have questioned many of her male contemporaries, I have yet to discover why. Perhaps because of her own insecurity, always so close to the surface, she threatened the precarious security, so easily destroyed, in more defended male writers. Nevertheless, this did not stop with her success.

In the spring of 1974, Anne gave a poetry reading at Harvard that was in some way the climax of her career. The place was jammed; the audience sat hushed and then leapt to its feet. Anne said of the reading that she had been very nervous beforehand, and that suddenly, onstage during her introduction, a calm had descended on her, and she was able to communicate entirely with her audience. It was a brilliant and moving reading. The next day the *Boston Globe* carried a devastating attack on Anne for her reading, accusing her of self-exploitation, commercialism, and debased poetry. The accusations were aimed at her as a woman. What was most regrettable about the attack was that it was the first review the *Globe* had carried about any poetry reading in the Boston area. It is impossible to conceive of such a personal attack being called forth upon a male poet happening to read at Harvard; the ambivalence of the male reviewer spilled over into vitriol. Recent history has somewhat changed the climate of understanding of women writing.

However, the East Coast academy, the last stronghold, still much prefers its writers male, preferably dead. For instance, when Muriel Rukeyser read at Harvard at the invitation of the *Harvard Advocate* less than a year before her death, severely crippled by a stroke and using a walker, her electric energy poured forth. It was an incredibly moving reading, and not one member of the Harvard faculty was present. That same year, when the British poet Stephen Spender read, the Anglophiliac academics came out in droves.

When I started this article, I wanted to examine why women poets of my acquaintance chose to glorify madness and end by suicide, as if these were the only options open for women of their generation. The closer one looks, the more complex the question of suicide becomes. And yet, amid all the complexity is the sense that Anne felt herself, at the time of her death, to be exhausted and depleted; that she, like Sylvia, was merely desperate to sleep. And that is a simple yet frightening aspect. I hoped there would be, somewhere, the possibility, for all of us, of integrating our lives and our work. Anne's struggle was complicated by her illness. I wanted to talk of Anne's strengths as well as her unique problems, her commitment to her craft, her continued hard work, her friendships, as well as a troubled personal history.

Anne had used her fellowship from the Radcliffe Institute of Independent Study (given at least partially on the basis of need) to build herself an outdoor swimming pool. This fact did not please the worthy ladies of Radcliffe. Nevertheless, that swimming pool gave her, as well as friends, a great deal of pleasure. I remember swimming nude in the pool, looking at trees and drinking Anne's newest drink discovery, "Champale," giggling over vague poetic jokes. Or sitting in the sun, reading each other's poems. Maxine Kumin and her children would arrive. Maxine dove into the pool, cool, competent, and graceful. Anne, on Thorazine, would move a bit into the shade. The phone rang and was dragged outside.

Anne's children came home from school. The Dalmatian dragged its puppies outside. Figures were commented on. I had a baby. Lois got her divorce. Maxine's daughter entered Radcliffe. Anne's children grew up. We wrote and wrote and read and revised and wrote. Poems were shared and magazines passed around. We read aloud to each other. We talked and laughed. Steam rose from the pool; the light grew thin; the leaves fell. And we swam until late October.

BARBARA SWAN

A Reminiscence

Anne Sexton and I met as recipients of grants from the Radcliffe Institute during its first year of existence in 1961. The application form had clearly stated that a candidate must have a Ph.D. or the equivalent. Both Anne and I shared a certain awe at those with a Ph.D. and were uncertain about what an equivalent might be. The creative mind deals with a world of the imagination. The artist and the poet carry this world around in their heads. They inhabit it. The scholar with a Ph.D. can study this world, analyze it, criticize it, even try to recreate it in biography, but the scholar can never really know the crazy, intuitive nonsense that whirls around in the mind of an artist.

During our years of friendship Anne moved into my world and I had the lovely privilege of moving into hers. We shared on an intuitive level knowing instinctively the kind of thing that would spark a creative idea. I could open up my book on Edvard Munch, show her the lithograph titled *The Scream,* and know it would fascinate her. It did. Later in the poem "Briar Rose" from *Transformations* she was to use this line:

> The court fell silent.
> The king looked like Munch's *Scream.*

Early in our friendship Anne acquired my lithograph called *The Musicians.* It was framed and hung in her study. My lithograph has a flute player, a figure playing a recorder, and a great deal of murk that could be anything. Frankly, I was experimenting with the newly discovered possibilities of texture in lithography and wanted an aura of mystery, but beyond that I had nothing specific in mind.

From *Anne Sexton: The Artist and Her Critics,* edited by J. D. McClatchy (Bloomington: Indiana University Press, 1978). Reprinted by permission of the author.

One day there was a phone call and an excited Anne said, "Barbara, I've written a poem about your lithograph!" She sent me a copy and at that stage it had the title "The Musicians." Later the title was changed to "To Lose the Earth." How could I be prepared for what she saw in my lithograph? I was astonished!

> He plays his flute in a cave
> that a pharaoh built by the sea.
> He is blowing on light,
> each time for the first time.
> His fingers cover the mouths of all the sopranos,
> each a princess in an exact position.

And on it went, images building on images. My harmless fellow playing the recorder became:

> At the far right,
> rising from an underground sea,
> his toes curled on a black wave,
> stands the dwarf;
> his instrument is an extension of his tongue.

Anne had moved into my world like a tornado. She shook it up, rattled it, possessed it like a demon. Naturally, I adored the poem. I had had no idea at all what lurked beneath my murky textures.

Some years later Anne again used a work of mine as inspiration for a poem. It was a large drawing called *Man Carrying a Man,* inspired by a fifteenth-century German sculpture of Christ being carried on the back of a man. We were then in the throes of the Vietnam War and I wanted the drawing to express universal compassion for man's fate, the way we all share in it. Anne's poem "Jesus Walking" expresses exactly what I wanted my drawing to say and in the last line she used my title.

> To pray, Jesus knew,
> is to be a man carrying a man.

One other poem deals with me and not my work. In "Hurry Up Please It's Time" she describes a day spent in Rockport when we drank vodka and ginger beer and I drew a line drawing, and she says, "Of such moments is happiness made."

It *was* a happy day. I did two line drawings and one appeared on the back of the cover for *The Book of Folly*. Line drawings go very quickly and I drew while we talked. Later we all had drinks with my friends, Professor Edwin Miller and Roz Miller. Then there was seafood at a rather primitive lobster place with an open porch and a Munch-like view of the setting sun across the water. Anne loved it—the mess of the seafood (steamers and lobster), the dramatic sky over Folly Cove. We all said that we must do it again, but of course nothing is ever the same and we never did.

Anne and I collaborated in three areas concerning her work— a broadside, book covers, and the drawings for *Transformations*. At the Impressions Workshop where I was learning lithography the owner, George Lockwood, decided to launch a series of broadsides with various artists doing prints in collaboration with contemporary poets. It was obvious that I should work with Anne. She chose the poem "For the Year of the Insane." Because it was so autobiographical I felt I should use her face, and this resulted in a number of working drawings from life. I think it was around this time that I did a portrait drawing for my own pleasure. As an artist, I loved to draw her. Anne was a beauty and the challenge was to go beyond that beautiful face to what lay beneath. Also, when I draw someone I like to explore who the person really is, and these sittings further deepened our friendship. In the broadside I tried to show the outer Anne Sexton, fingering rosary beads, and in the background the darker side, the side that perhaps no one ever really understood.

As for book covers, Anne and I suffered together when dealing with the production department of her publisher. The book itself is designed by one person but the cover is controlled by a different department and our views and the views of the person in charge of book covers did not always converge. It was with *Live or Die* that Anne called me in despair to say, "They've sent me a terrible book cover with pink and blue flowers and green frogs. It looks like a children's book. Have you anything I can use?" I found a drawing called *Gothic Heads,* and since Anne did have some control over her book covers it was offered and accepted. It was a delicate drawing and the heads were supposed to be diagonal but the book cover designer made them vertical and then plastered thick black letters across the top of the drawing. Later, after the book came out the person in charge of book covers said that even she was offended by the lettering. I still shudder when I look at it.

When Anne asked me to do a drawing for *The Book of Folly* cover I decided to control the lettering by incorporating my images within the letters as in medieval manuscripts. Anne had sent me the entire manuscript of her book, so my letters became inhabited by the girl with the chair, the girl with long hair, Lazarus, an angel. Folly became half skeleton, half a masked costume figure. Jesus nailed to the cross fitted within the confines of a Y. It was not easy to draw in this way and I suffered more with those letters than if I had done a simple drawing. For this cover it was I who said the border should be red, a bloody red. As I read the poems I was struck by such lines as "Tonight all the red dogs lie down in fear" or "Once there was blood as in a murder" or "and the vibrating red muscle of my mouth." I could go on. The color red seemed to me pervasive.

Anne and I corresponded about the cover for *The Death Notebooks*. On July 26, 1973, I received this letter from Anne in Pigeon Cove, where I spend the summer:

Dear, dear Barbara

I am interested in what you say about the "underbelly" of our lives.

The color blue sounds right to me. At least I trust you more than I trust myself. As a matter of fact, those poems were always kept in a blue notebook. All of your ideas and your miniature drawing appeal, but that is not surprising, for you are very sensitive to the poet's word—at least *your* two poets.

I am interested in what you said about the nine psalms at the end. I worry about them. I'm afraid they are excessive or maybe just plain bad writing. Of course, they involve life's stages as well as praising many of life's or God's objects.

Do write again when you get back from Maine. I would love to hear from you.

Love,
A.

My idea for a cover drawing was to create the look of a crack opening across the cover revealing what I referred to as the "underbelly" of our lives. The eye peering out at the bottom is, of course, Anne's. Again I was struck by a dominant color . . . "expecting a large white angel, with a blue crotch" . . . "The shocking blue sky" . . . "Take the blue eyes of my mother" . . . "The autumn sky, Mary blue."

I also pointed out to Anne that she seemed to like the word "belly" and I would love to draw a fat belly and also a rounded rear end. I said that any book calling itself *The Death Notebooks* had to have at least two nudes on the cover to boost sales. Besides, the poems had a great deal to do with life. Because my drawing zoomed across the cover, the lettering was forced to behave itself.

Our collaboration with *Transformations,* based on *Grimms' Fairy Tales,* was the most sustained and the most rewarding for me. It all began when Anne asked me if I knew a woodcut artist who could illustrate these poems. She had in mind a kind of Gothic, slightly expressionist style. We went together to the print department of the Boston Public Library, but what we saw seemed suitable only for children's books. Then, over lunch at Joseph's, a favorite restaurant of Anne's, she said, "Barbara, would you consider it?" I had never done a book but my reply was, "Send me a poem." In the mail came "Snow White" and I loved it. Immediately I was on the phone. "Anne, I don't know about you but I identify with the poor old queen." "So do I," said Anne. I made a drawing that portrays the universal problem of the aging beauty, needing every beauty prop available, and the young girl, smug and indifferent, temporarily secure in her glorious youth. In the last lines of the poem Snow White begins to look in her mirror and you know that twenty years later, she, too, will face a middle-age crisis.

After that, poem after poem came to me in the mail. Anne and I agreed that I should absorb each poem individually, do a drawing, and then await the next poem. Between the poem and the drawing there would be a phone call and I would tell Anne my visual reaction to the poem, what I felt I could express. Always my reactions intrigued her. When it came to the poem "Iron Hans" what I wanted to draw surprised her because it was not her vision. She had imagined a drawing with Iron Hans battling around in a cage as a wild man. My drawing showed the young prince being carried into the woods on the shoulders of Iron Hans because the prince saw through his wildness and trusted him. "The poem has to do with compassion," I said. Anne had identified with the wild man in a cage, like a madwoman trapped in an asylum. But for me in Anne's poems there is a cry of compassion. As for my drawing, Anne said, "You're right."

Two of my drawings are in the style of Edvard Munch because it seemed appropriate. In the poem "Briar Rose" Anne even refers to Munch's *The Scream,* and the tormented incestuous relationship seemed best served by stark curves of black and white. In "The Wonderful Musician" I was influenced by the way Munch's lines seem to give out the sound of a scream, and so I curved and twisted the lines from the violin to give the sound and the shape of a death dance. Even skulls emerge.

Cinderella and her prince are a dull pair and I had to do a dull drawing.

> Regular Bobbsey Twins.
> That story.

"Rapunzel" was a pleasure for me because of the relationship of Mother Gothel to the beautiful Rapunzel.

> A woman
> who loves a woman
> is forever young.

I don't think anyone had ever before thought of the lesbian aspect in Mother Gothel's isolation of Rapunzel in a tower. I tried to show the possessive love of Mother Gothel and I turned Rapunzel into a Victorian beauty perhaps like the heroine of John Fowles's novel *The French Lieutenant's Woman.*

What a good time we had with "The Twelve Dancing Princesses." In Anne's poem there is no doubt they are freaked out. In my drawing I came up with a combination of Busby Berkeley and Isadora Duncan. Anne and I laughed over that, the chorus line and the free spirit.

In "Red Riding Hood" Anne enjoyed my idea that the hunter

should be listening for the fetal heartbeat in the wolf who had just eaten Red Riding Hood and the grandmother. As Anne wrote, "He appeared to be in his ninth month."

As for "Hansel and Gretel," I felt it would be an ironic touch to put BLESS THIS HOME over the kitchen stove as the witch is about to be baked.

> Gretel,
> seeing her moment in history,
> shut fast the oven,
> locked fast the door,
> fast as Houdini,
> and turned the oven on to bake.

I would also like to say that any little girl who bakes an old lady is not a dear little girl. She is a rather nasty little girl.

My drawing for "The Frog Prince" has a great deal that is phallic going on behind the plate of liver and bacon that the frog is sitting on. I was not certain that the publisher would be comfortable with it so I pointed it out. The editor smiled and said, "We've grown up quite a bit here at Houghton Mifflin."

When *Transformations* was published Anne inscribed a book to me, writing "with love and with awe at your genius." It was typical of her generous spirit that she could write exactly what might please my ego. Who ever knows what genius is? I prefer to turn the compliment her way. She and I tilted at windmills together. It was exhilarating.

A Friendship Remembered

As the world knows, we were intimate friends and professional allies. Early on in our friendship, indeed almost as soon as we began to share poems, we began to share them on the telephone. Since we lived initially in the same Boston suburb and later in contiguous ones (Ma Bell's unlimited contiguous service be praised!), there were no message units to reckon with, which surely would have inhibited me, though probably not Annie, whose long-distance phone bills were monumental down the years. It was her habit when alone at night (and alone at night meant depressed always, sometimes anxious to the point of pain as well) to call on old friends. But that's a digression. What I wanted to say was I don't know what year, but fairly early on, we both installed second phone lines in our houses so that the rest of each of our families—the two husbands, the five children—could have equal access to a phone and we could talk privately for as long as we wanted. I confess we sometimes connected with a phone call and kept that line linked for hours at a stretch, interrupting poem-talk to stir the spaghetti sauce, switch laundry, or try out a new image on the typewriter; we whistled into the receiver for each other when we were ready to resume. It worked wonders. And to think that it only cost seven or eight bucks a month!

How different from January and February of 1973, when I went to Centre College in Danville, Kentucky, as a writer-in-residence. We agreed ahead of time to divide the phone bill we would incur. Anne called me every afternoon at five; she was then writing *The Awful Rowing Toward God* at white heat—two, three, even four poems a day. I tried hard to retard the process for I felt it was all happening too fast and it scared me. It was too

From *Anne Sexton: The Artist and Her Critics,* edited by J. D. McClatchy (Bloomington: Indiana University Press, 1978). Reprinted by permission of the author.

much like Plath spewing out those last poems. Nevertheless, I listened, commented, helped, tried to provide some sort of organizational focus. We averaged one hour a day on the phone, only because I was too cheap to talk longer. My share of the bill came to about $300, which was pretty liberated for me. I am descended from a lineage that panics as soon as the three-minute mark is passed.

Writing poems and bouncing them off each other by phone does develop the ear. You learn to hear line-breaks, to pick up and be critical of unintended internal rhyme, or intended slant rhyme or whatever. We did this so comfortably and over such an extended period of time that indeed when we met—usually over lunch at my house, for Anne almost always stopped off to lunch with me after seeing whichever of her infamously inept psychiatrists—we were somewhat shy of each other's poem there on the page. I can remember so often saying, "Oh, so *that's* what it looks like" of a poem I had heard and visualized through half a dozen revisions.

Over the years, her lines shortened and the line-breaks grew, I think, more unexpected. In the early days we were both working quite strictly in form. We measured and cut and pasted and reworked arduously, with an intense sense of purpose, both of us believing in the rigors of form as a forcing agent, that the hardest truths would come right if they were hammered to fit (see the title poem, "All My Pretty Ones"). I confess we both had rhyming dictionaries and we both used them. Typically, we had totally different kinds. Anne's grouped rhyme-words according to their common endings—all the one-syllable words, for example, followed by the two-syllable ones, and so on— whereas mine worked by orthography, which made it quirkier because it went not by sound but by spelling. It was Anne's aim to use rhyme unexpectedly, brilliantly but aptly; even the most unusual rhyme, she felt, must never obtrude on the sense of the line, nor must the normal word order, the easy tone of natural vernacular usage, be wrenched to save a rhyme. She would willingly push a poem through twenty or more drafts; she had an unparalleled tenacity and abandoned a "failed" poem only with regret if not downright anger after dozens of sessions.

Nevertheless, I would say that Anne's poems were frequently "given" ones. "Riding the Elevator into the Sky" (in *The Awful*

Rowing Toward God) is an example. The newspaper article mentioned in its first stanza gave rise to the poem and the poem itself came quite easily and cleanly, as if written out beforehand in the clean air and then transcribed onto the page with very few alterations. "Letter Written on a Ferry While Crossing Long Island Sound" (in *All My Pretty Ones*) was a "given" poem, too; given by the fortuitous sight of the nuns. As I remember it, the poem was written much as it now appears on the printed page, except for the minor skirmishes required to effect that marvelous closure in each stanza where the fourth from the last and the last lines rhyme (save for the first stanza, and "cup" and "up" in the middle of the last stanza). Also, it was originally called "Letter Written on the Long Island Ferry" and was made more specific on the advice of Howard Moss. "Young" and "I Remember" (both also in *All My Pretty Ones*) required very little revision, as my memory serves, whereas "The Truth the Dead Know" went through innumerable workings to arrive at its final form. In this poem, the poet is locked into an *a b a b* rhyme-scheme with little room for pyrotechnics. The language is purified to an amazing degree, I think, reflecting Anne's wish to open *All My Pretty Ones* with a spare, terse, tough elegy for her parents, one without biographical detail, the very detail she would get into later, in the title poem or in "The House." That title poem was one which underwent many revisions to force it into the exigency of an *a b a b, c d c d, e e* stanza. We both admired the multi-syllabic rhymes of "slumber"/"disencumber" and "navigator"/"later," to say nothing of the *tour de force* final couplet.

The initial impetus for her poems usually came as a direct visitation to the cave of her desk. She invoked the muse by reading other poets and playing her favorite records over and over. The background of music acted in some way to free her to create, which always astonished me, for whom it is an intrusion. Often with the volume turned up loud, loud enough to drown out all other sounds, she could pull an intricate rhyme-scheme out of the air. Is it worth noting that massed orchestral strings, full volume, served too as a device for her to cover and block out the bad voices? (The time before the time she killed herself, it was with music at crescendo: a scream, I thought when I got there. I don't know if the radio was playing that last time; I think so.) As for her subject matter, we all know it came for the most part directly out of her own life and times, with little if any psychological distance on the trauma or pleasure that gave rise to the poem. Still, she transmuted the events. She was able to take the rawest facts—her mother's agonizingly slow death from cancer, her father's stroke, her entire wretched childhood experience as what was undoubtedly an undiagnosed hyperkinetic youngster, kept behind a gate in her room—and to make of them a whole.

Someone once said that we have art in order not to die of the truth. Not only did Sexton's confessional poems most vividly and truly keep her alive, but they sustained and spoke to a vast audience. I would say that she drew great sustenance and comfort from the knowledge that her work reached out to and beyond the normal sensitive reader of poetry (though, for god's sake, what is "normal" or "sensitive"?) and touched the minds of many deeply troubled people. For a while it seemed that psychiatrists all over the country were referring their patients to Anne's work, as if it were the balm in Gilead. At the same time that it comforted and fed her to know that she mattered as a poet beyond the usual sphere of self-congratulating, self-adulating bards, she had considerable ambivalence about her work. Accused of exhibitionism, she was determined only to be more flamboyant; nevertheless, the large Puritan hiding inside suffered and grieved over the label "confessional" poet. For instance, when she wrote "Cripples and Other Stories" (in *Live or Die*), a poem that almost totally "occurred" on the page, she crumpled it up, as if in embarrassment, and tossed it into the wastebasket. We fished it out and saved it; I thought it then and think it now a remarkable document.

The "saving" of that poem was to make the tone consistent and to smoothe out some of the cruder rhythmical spots. This was the sort of mechanical task Anne could fling herself into gladly. The results were often doubly effective. In "The Operation" (a key poem in *All My Pretty Ones*), for example, the experience—awesome and painful—is hammered into art by way of form and rhyme. Both squeeze the raw event until the juice runs in the reader, I think. I do not mean to downplay the force of metaphor in the poem—the "historic thief," the "humpty-dumpty," etc.—but it is the impact of rhyme and the shape of the poem's three parts (its form) that bring it off.

For instance, the retardation of the rhyming sounds at the end of the first section—"leaf"/"straw"/"lawn"/"car"/"thief"/ "house"/"upon"—in those short, fairly sharply end-stopped lines, build to the impact. Or, to take yet another poem, I remember "Faustus and I" (in *The Death Notebooks*) was headed for the discard pile; it was then a free-verse poem and as such had, for me, an evilly flippant tone. I seem to remember that I often helplessly suggested, "Why don't you pound it into form?" and often it worked. In the case of "Faustus and I" the suggestion worked because the rhyme scheme gave the poem a dignity and nobility it deserved. It worked because the pounding elicited a level of language, a level of metaphor she hadn't quite reached in the early versions.

Anne also had an almost mystical faith in the "found" word or image, as well as in metaphor by mistake, by typo or misapprehension. She would fight hard to keep an image, a line, a word usage, but if you were just as dogged in your conviction that the line didn't work, was sentimental or mawkish, that the word usage was ill-suited or trite, she would capitulate—unless she was totally convinced of her own rightness. Then there was no shaking her. We learned somehow, from each other and from trusting each other's critical sense, not to go past the unshakable core, not to trespass on style or voice. Perhaps we learned this in the early years of our student workshops, first at the Boston Center in classes with John Holmes, and later in our own house-by-house workshops with John Holmes and George Starbuck and Sam Albert. These were often real encounters, real square-offs, but we all respected and admired one another—an idea that seems terribly old-fashioned somehow today, that poets could be competitive and full of ego but genuinely care for one another's well-being. That was a good group, now that I think back on it; we all wrote at white heat and many of the best poems any of us ever wrote were tested in that crucible. Anne, in fact, as a result of this experience, came to believe in the value of workshops. She loved growing this way herself, and she urged the technique on her students. Her whole *Bedlam* book grew during her workshop years and virtually every one of those poems was scrutinized across the table. We were still at it when *All My Pretty Ones* was in process. It was awesome the way Anne could come to the workshop biweekly with three, four, five new and complicated poems. She was never meek about it, but she did listen and she did care. She gave generous help and she required, demanded, insisted on generous response.

We might talk for a moment about *Transformations*. Anne was fascinated by fairy tales. They were for her what the Greek myths had been, perhaps, for others. Since she had not had—and she was grim about this—the advantage of a higher education (by which she meant *Beowulf,* the Norse Eddas, Homer, Milton, etc.—all denied her), she lapsed back to what must have been a halcyon time in her life, the time when her great-aunt, the colossal mother figure of her past, had read German fairy tales to her. Now she reread them all and scoured the libraries for more, even asking my daughter Judy to translate and retranslate some tales from the German so that she could be sure she had gotten every final variant on the story. The wonderful self-mocking, society-mocking wit of *Transformations* is entirely her own; she was a very funny person, quick to satirize a given situation. The book more or less evolved; she had no thought of a collection at first, and I must immodestly state that I urged and bullied her to go on after the first few poems to think in terms of a whole book of them. I also take outright credit for the title. We had been talking about the way many contemporary poets translated from languages they did not themselves read, but used trots or had the poems filtered through an interpreter, and that these poems were *adaptations*. It struck me then that Anne's poems about the fairy tales went one step further and were *transformations*. And for the record let me state that in that same conversation Annie was urging me to collect the "pastoral" poems I'd written, and I said, "But what will I call it?" and she said, "*Up Country,* of course."

The Book of Folly gives further evidence of Anne's interest in myth-making. Whether or not they succeed, she has written three myths of her own and she labored strenuously in the vineyard of prose, finding it foreign and harsh work. But it is true that the storyteller inside the poet sometimes yearns desperately to be let out. Anne's storyteller burst out in these tales and in the Daisy play she wrote early in her career on a Ford grant. (*Tell Me Your Answer True* was its original title, though it ended up as *Mercy Street*—an image that turned up in a dream, the dream a plea for mercy from somewhere, anywhere, from Life.) It wasn't the first verbalization of her Christ fascination, nor was it destined to be the last. Christ as Prime Sufferer and God (any kind of god who'd be there) became her final obsessions, perhaps because as her life deteriorated, people were less dependable. But Jesus figured prominently from the very beginning. But what I chiefly remember is how much fun Anne had working on the play, how richly she enjoyed working in dialogue, for which she had a considerable talent. Her ear was quick and true; I always trusted implicitly her criticism of the dialogue in my fiction, and could point to dozens of lines—responses, usually—in my own work which came pure out of Sexton's mouth. She also loved the excitement of being in the theater and being in New York and staying at the Algonquin. She adored her leading actress Marian Seldes (as who would not!), and loved most of all the late late nights after a rehearsal when she would sit up till dawn reworking a speech here, a phrase there, loving the tinkering even more than the glamour of actually having her play produced.

Anne's way of working, whether with a poem or the play or an attempted story, was to try out the draft on as many listeners as she could amass. I felt sometimes that she was putting the matter to a vote, and indeed in her classes at Boston University she fell into the always amusing pattern of inviting the students to vote for or against an image, a line-break, an ending. But she invited and needed the interchange of ideas and attitudes, something that is anathema to most writers who cannot brook outside interference or involvement in an unfinished piece. Anne took strength from outside reactions, as much strength from the negative as from the positive remarks (I am not now speaking of reviewers!), and she genuinely felt that there was always something to be gained in this sharing process. It was her conviction that the least-experienced student could bring something to bear on a worksheet; she weighed and evaluated opinions, keeping some, discarding others, but using them all as a kind of emotional ballast for going on with her work. And she was equally willing to bring her own energy to bear on the meanest poem. She was generous, yes; but it transcends generosity, really. It was evangelical, it was for Poetry, the Higher Good. She lived her poetry, poetry was her life. It had saved her life in a real sense when, in the mid-1950s, she began to write poems as a therapeutic act urged on her by her current psychiatrist. The clear thread that runs through all the books of poems is how tenuous that life was. She was on loan to poetry, as it were. We always knew it would end. We just didn't know when or exactly how.

DENISE LEVERTOV

Anne Sexton

Light Up the Cave

The news of Anne Sexton's death saddened a great many people, and startled those who had assumed that, despite all the troubles of which her poetry told, she had come to the long stretch of middle age with some reserves of strength; though—I am told— the friends who knew her best were confirmed in their fear that her determination towards suicide had not really been deflected. My own sadness at the death of a fellow poet is compounded by the sense of how likely it is that Anne Sexton's tragedy will not be without influence in the tragedies of other lives.

She herself was, obviously, too intensely troubled to be fully aware of her influence or to take on its responsibility. Therefore it seems to me that we who are alive must make clear, as she could not, the distinction between creativity and self-destruction. The tendency to confuse the two has claimed too many victims. Anne Sexton herself seems to have suffered deeply from this confusion, and I surmise that her friendship with Sylvia Plath had in it an element of identification which added powerfully to her malaise. Across the country, at different colleges, I have heard many stories of attempted—and sometimes successful—suicides by young students who loved the poetry of Plath and who supposed that somehow, in order to become poets themselves, they had to act out in their own lives the events of hers. I don't want to see a new epidemic of the same syndrome occurring as a response to Anne Sexton's death.

The problem is not, however, related only to suicide per se. When Robert Lowell was at the height of his fame among student readers (his audience nowadays is largely an older one) many of them seemed to think a nervous breakdown was, if not imperative, at least an invaluable shortcut to artistry. When W. D. Snodgrass's *Heart's Needle* won the Pulitzer Prize, young couples married and divorced, it seemed, especially in order to have the correct material to write about.

I am not being flippant. Innumerable young poets have drunk themselves into stupidity and cirrhosis because they admired John Berryman or Dylan Thomas and came to think they must drink like them to write like them. At the very least it is assumed that creativity and hang-ups are inevitably inseparable. One student (male) said to me recently, "I was amazed when the first poet I met seemed to be a cheerful person and not any more fucked up than anyone else. When I was in high school I got the idea you *had* to be fucked up to be a real artist!" And a young English teacher in a community college told me she had given up writing poetry because she believed there were unavoidable links between depression and anxiety and the making of art. "Don't you feel terrible when you write poems?"

What exactly is the nature of the confusion, and how has it come about? The mistake itself lies in taking what may possibly be an occupational hazard as a prescriptive stimulus to artistic activity. Whether artists as a class are in fact more vulnerable than other people, or whether their problems merely have more visibility, a serious and intelligent statistical study might perhaps tell us. It makes no difference: the point is that while the creative impulse and the self-destructive impulse can, and often do, co-exist, their relationship is distinctly acausal; self-destructiveness is a handicap to the life of art, not the reverse.

Yet it is the handicaps themselves that so often allure the young and untried. The long lives of so many of the greatest artists, sometimes apparently uneventful, sometimes full of passion and suffering, but full too of endurance, and always dominated by love of their work, seem not to attract as models. Picasso, Matisse, Monet, Cezanne, Pissarro, Corot, Rembrandt, Titian, J. S. Bach, Stravinsky, Goethe, William Carlos Williams, Stevens, Pound, Neruda, Machado, Yeats, Shakespeare, Whitman, Tolstoi, Melville. . . . There is romance in their tenacity, their devotion, but it is overlooked. Why is this? There are topical reasons, but their roots are in the past, their nature historical and political.

In summary, Western culture began, during the Renaissance—only recently, that is to say, in the calendar of human history—to emphasize individuality to a degree merely foreshadowed in Greece and Rome or in the theological dramas of the Old Testament. Geographical and scientific discoveries spurred the sense of what humanity on its own could do. The "Elizabethan world picture" had wholeness and consistency; but it held the seeds of an expanded view of things. And as feudal social systems underwent economic changes with the rise of the merchant class and the growth of banking procedures, so, too, the social and economic circumstances in which art was produced underwent changes that heightened the new sense of individuality.

The relationship of the artist to other people rapidly altered. The people began to become "the public," "the audience," and the poet, set aside from that "public," began to become more private, more introspective. When his work (or hers—but it was a long time before there were women poets in any numbers) was printed it was increasingly a revelation to the public of the highly personal, rather than being to a large degree the voice of the people itself which it had been the bard's task, in earlier times, to sound forth. The value put on individual expression, the concept of "originality," and ultimately even upon individualism as a creed, had been pushed further by the time we reach the period of Romanticism, which developed alongside the Industrial Revolution and was in part reactive to the prospect of facelessness presented to the prophetic eye by that phenomenon.

Twentieth-century alienation is another phase of the reaction. What began as a realization of human potential, a growth of *individuated* consciousness (to use Jung's useful term) out of the unconscious collective, became first a glorification of willful, essentially optimistic individualism, echoing the ambitious, optimistic individualism of its capitalist context, and then, as that turned sour and revealed more and more of greed in its operations, led to the setting of a high esthetic and moral value upon alienation itself.

But alienation is of ethical value, is life-affirmative and conducive to creativity only when it is accompanied by a political consciousness that imagines and affirms (and works toward) an alternative to the society from which it turns away in disgust. Lacking this, the alienated person, if he or she is gifted, becomes especially a prey to the exploitation that characterizes capitalism and is its underlying principle. The manifestations—in words, music, paint, or what have you—of private anguish are exploited by a greedy public, a public greedy for emotion at second hand because starved of the experience of community. Concurrently, for the same reasons, a creative person—whether a pop star or a Sylvia Plath, a John Berryman, an Anne Sexton—internalizes the exploitive, unwittingly becoming *self*-exploitive.

And if the public is greedy, the critics, at their worst, are positively ghoulish, or at the least, irresponsible. I feel, for instance, that it is irresponsible for one local columnist, in a memorial eulogy, to have written of Anne Sexton, "The manner of her death is at once frightening and fascinating to those who responded to her poetry, sharing as they do many of the same fears and insecurities she articulated so well. Her death awakens those fears and insecurities, the way some of her poems did, it raises them up from where they hide, buried by ordinary, everyday things." It is irresponsible because it is a statement made without qualification or development in a context of praise, and without, therefore, helping readers to see (as I suppose the writer herself does not see) that to raise our fears and insecurities into consciousness in order to confront them, to deal with them, is good; but that if the pain is confused with art itself, then people at the receiving end of a poem describing a pain and insecurity they share are not really brought to confront and deal with their problems, but are instead led into a false acceptance of them as signs or precursors of art, marks of kinship with the admired artist, symptoms of what used to be called "the artistic temperament."

Again, when I read the blurbs on the back of the late John Berryman's prizewinning *Delusions, etc.,* and see what A. Alvarez wrote of Berryman's work and death, I feel that a poisonous misapprehension of the nature of poetry is being furthered. "For years," Alvarez says, "I have been extolling the virtues of what I call extremist poetry, in which the artists deliberately push their perceptions to the very edge of the tolerable. Both Berryman and Plath were masters of the style. But knowing now how they both died I no longer believe that any art—even that as fine as they produced at their best—is worth the terrible cost."

At first glance this statement might be taken as being in accord with my own viewpoint; but its effect (since it is obvious that Alvarez believes their art to have been of the highest possible quality, perhaps the best poetry of their time) is still to extol the pursuit of the almost intolerable, the deliberate driving of the self to extremes which are not the unavoidable, universal extremes imposed by the human condition, but—insofar as they are deliberately sought—are luxuries, or which, if part and parcel of individual mental illness, should rather be *resisted* than encouraged in the name of art. In assuming that the disasters of those writers' lives were a form of payment for the virtues of their art, Alvarez, even while he says he has come to feel it is not worth the cost, perpetuates the myth that confounds a love-affair with death with a love-affair with art.

Thus it is that long lives devoted to the practice of art seem lacking in allure, and young would-be artists, encouraged by people older than themselves but equally confused, equally apt to mistake handicap for power, model their lives on the lives of those who, however gifted, were vanquished by their sorrows. It is not understood that the greatest heroes and heroines are truly those who hold out the longest, or, if they do die young, do so unwillingly, resisting to the last.

An instance would be the young guerrilla poets of Latin America, so many of whom have been killed so young. (At least one of them, Javier Heraud, of Peru, would surely have been a major poet. He was shot down at the age of twenty-three.) They were not flirting with death, any more than Victor Jara, the extraordinary and beloved Chilean musician and poet who was murdered in the Stadium in Santiago just over a year ago. They died politically conscious deaths, struggling for a better life, not just for themselves but for their people, for The People. Their tragedy is very different from the tragedy of suicide; they were conscious actors in dramas of revolutionary effort, not helpless victims.

Anne Sexton's struggle has its political dimensions too—but hers is the story of a victim, not a conscious participant. Anne

Sexton the well-to-do suburban housewife, Anne Sexton in Bedlam, Anne Sexton "halfway back," Anne Sexton the glamorous performer, Anne Sexton: timid and insecure, Anne Sexton saying she had always hoped to publish a posthumous volume, Anne Sexton in her garage breathing in the deadly fumes, was—whatever the clinical description of her depression—"caught in history's crossfire." Not because she was a woman—the problem is not essentially related to gender or to sexual stance. Not because she didn't have radical politics—god knows they are not a recipe for great art or for long life (though I can't help feeling that a little more comprehension of the relation of politics to her own life might have helped her). But because she herself was unable to separate her depression and her obsession with death from poetry itself, and because precisely her most enthusiastic readers and critics encouraged that inability.

The artist, the poet (like Hokusai, who called himself "the old man mad about painting" and felt that at seventy he had begun to learn, at ninety would have some command of his powers, and at one hundred would begin to do justice to what he saw in Nature) needs the stamina of an astronaut and the energy derived only from being passionately in love with life and with art. "This is this world, the kingdom I was looking for!" wrote John Holmes. And "You must love the crust of the earth on which you dwell. You must be able to extract nutriment out of sand heap. Else you will have lived in vain," wrote Thoreau.

Such purity, integrity, love, and energy—rarely fully attained but surely to be striven for—are undermined by our exploitive society, which romanticizes its victims when they are of a certain kind (thus distracting us from the unromanticizable lives of the suffering multitude). It romanticizes gifted individuals who have been distorted into an alienated individualism, a self-preoccupation, that is *not* individuation, *not* maturation.

Anne Sexton wrote in "Wanting to Die":

> Suicides have already betrayed the body.
> Still-born, they don't always die,
> but dazzled, they can't forget a drug so sweet . . .
> To thrust all that life under your tongue!—
> that, all by itself, becomes a passion.

Too many readers, with a perversity that, yes, really does seem to me to be bound up with white middle-class privilege and all its moral disadvantages, would sooner remember, and identify with, lines like those than with these, which (in *The Death Notebooks*) she also wrote:

> Depression is boring, I think
> and I would do better to make
> some soup and light up the cave.

To recognize that for a few years of her life Anne Sexton was an artist *even though* she had so hard a struggle against her desire of death is to fittingly honor her memory. To identify her love of death with her love of poetry is to insult that struggle.

PART TWO   *Essays and Reviews*

JAMES DICKEY

Review of *To Bedlam and Part Way Back*

Anne Sexton's poems so obviously come out of deep, painful sections of the author's life that one's literary opinions scarcely seem to matter; one feels tempted to drop them furtively into the nearest ashcan, rather than be caught with them in the presence of so much naked suffering. The experiences she recounts are among the most harrowing that human beings can undergo: those of madness and near-madness, of the pathetic, well-meaning, necessarily tentative and perilous attempts at cure, and of the patient's slow coming back into the human associations and responsibilities which the old, previous self still demands. In addition to being an extremely painful subject, this is perhaps a major one for poetry, with a sickeningly frightening appropriateness to our time. But I am afraid that in my opinion the poems fail to do their subject the kind of justice which I should like to see done. Perhaps no poems could. Yet I am sure that Mrs. Sexton herself could come closer than she does here, did she not make entirely unnecessary concessions to the conventions of her literary generation and the one just before it. One can gather much of her tone and procedure from quotations like "You, Doctor Martin, walk / from breakfast to madness," and "All day we watched the gulls / striking the top of the sky / and riding the blown roller coaster." "Riding the blown roller coaster" is a kind of writing I dislike to such an extent that I feel, perhaps irrationally, that everyone else including Mrs. Sexton ought to dislike it, too, for its easy, A-student, superficially exact "differentness" and its straining to make contrivance and artificiality appear natural. One would hope that a writer of Mrs. Sexton's seriousness, and with her terrible story to tell,

From "Five First Books," *Poetry* 97 (1961). Copyright © 1961 by The Modern Poetry Association. Reprinted by permission of the author and the Editor of *Poetry*.

would avoid this kind of thing at any price. Yet a large part of her book is composed of such figures. In the end, one comes to the conclusion that if there were some way to relieve these poems of the obvious effort of trying to be poems, something very good would emerge. I think they would make far better short stories, and probably in Mrs. Sexton's hands, too, than they do poems. As they are, they lack concentration, and above all the profound, individual linguistic suggestibility and accuracy that poems must have to be good. As D. H. Lawrence once remarked in another connection, they don't "say the real say." But Mrs. Sexton's candor, her courage, and her story are worth anyone's three dollars.

M. L. ROSENTHAL

Anne Sexton and Confessional Poetry

Confessional poetry is a poetry of suffering. The suffering is generally "unbearable" because the poetry so often projects breakdown and paranoia. Indeed, the psychological condition of most of the confessional poets has long been the subject of common literary discussion—one cannot say gossip exactly, for their problems and confinements in hospitals are quite often the specific subjects of their poems. It is not enough, however, to relegate the matter to the province of the mentally disturbed. A heightened sensitivity to the human predicament in general, for reasons developed in the first chapter, has led to a sharper sense, as a by-product perhaps, of the pain of existence under even "normal" conditions. Sentimentality, self-dramatization, and the assumption that universal feelings are the private property of the poet himself as a uniquely seismographic instrument are among the manifest dangers of this situation. It is probably inevitable that many of the best practitioners in this age should at times fall into these traps, and that many of them pay for their gifts of sympathy and perception by mental illness. We must, in any case, finally read them as artists. The slogans of the confessional movement are well summed up in the quotations that Anne Sexton uses as epigraphs to her books *To Bedlam and Part Way Back* (1960) and *All My Pretty Ones* (1962). The first is from a letter of Schopenhauer's to Goethe; the second from a letter of Kafka's to Oskar Pollak:

It is the courage to make a clean breast of it in face of every question that makes the philosopher. He must be like Sophocles' Oedipus, who, seeking enlightenment concerning his

From "Other Confessional Poets," in *The New Poets* (New York: Oxford University Press, 1967). © M. L. Rosenthal, 1967. Reprinted by permission of the author.

terrible fate, pursues his indefatigable enquiry, even when he divines that appalling horror awaits him in the answer. But most of us carry in our heart the Jocasta who begs Oedipus for God's sake not to inquire further. . . .

and:

> . . . the books we need are the kind that act upon us like a misfortune, that make us suffer like the death of someone we love more than ourselves, that make us feel as though we were on the verge of suicide, or lost in a forest remote from all human habitation—a book should serve as the ax for the frozen sea within us.

"To make a clean breast of it in face of . . . appalling horror" and to write a book that is "the ax for the frozen sea within us" is not just a matter of intention but one of art. Force of character, clarity of line, a hard yet sensitive simplicity at the center and in the total outline, however complex the surface detail and the chains of implication may grow, would seem essential.

The poet in this school who comes closest to Lowell and Sylvia Plath at her best in the second and third of these essential qualities is Anne Sexton. A good many of the poems in her first book—as the title, *To Bedlam and Part Way Back,* implies—are explicitly about her experience in mental asylums. They are distinguished by an unambiguous presentation in each of the basic situations, and at the same time by the discovery of an appropriate music for each. At her most successful, as in "Ringing the Bells," the harmony of situation and formal embodiment is perfect:

> And this is the way they ring
> the bells in Bedlam
> and this is the bell-lady
> who comes each Tuesday morning
> to give us a music lesson
> and because the attendants make you go
> and because we mind by instinct,
> like bees caught in the wrong hive,
> we are the circle of the crazy ladies

The nursery rhythm is both true to the condition to which the "crazy ladies" have been for the time being reduced and to the irony, which is directed at once against herself and against the institutional situation. It enables the poet to present cleanly and economically the pathos of the situation without breaking the rhythm or dissipating the concreteness:

> and this is the small hunched squirrel girl
> on the other side of me
> who picks at the hairs over her lip,
> who picks at the hairs over her lip all day

Another poem, "Music Swims Back to Me," has already been mentioned as one of the pieces discussed by the critics on the BBC. As I noted at the beginning of this chapter, it illustrates the fact that Anne Sexton's poetry seldom explicitly includes the cultural criticism of Lowell's or Sylvia Plath's. But it is not entirely without it, either. The "they" of "Ringing the Bells" refers to the hospital administration, of course, and to what might be called the impersonal tradition of managing the mentally ill. Behind these literal meanings there is at least a faint suggestion of the way the strong and unconsciously brutal folk of the world, and all the institutional structures including the governments, handle the innocents, each lost in his own needs, sufferings, and self. "Music Swims Back to Me" illustrates this faint but not quite expendable implication a shade more emphatically:

> Wait Mister. Which way is home?
> They turned the light out
> and the dark is moving in the corner.
> There are no sign posts in this room,
> four ladies, over eighty,
> in diapers, every one of them.
> La la la, Oh music swims back to me
> and I can feel the tune they played
> the night they left me
> in this private institution on a hill.

"The poetry is in the Pity," as Wilfred Owen says—the ultimate referent is the private suffering, whose public dimensions were more self-evident in his poetry of war than in Mrs. Sexton's poems of madness. I do not wish to push this point any further—*poetry* is the issue. Anne Sexton's art is particularly notable for the way it picks up the rhythms of the kind of sensibility with which she is concerned. The examples I have so far given catch the note of the self reduced to almost infantile regression (what hostile critics have called "baby-talk"), but the mature intelligence of the speaker is ultimately that of one no longer in the literal predicament presented by the poems. The climactic section of "Music Swims Back to Me," in which the poet describes how it felt the first night in the institution and how the music that was played became the focus of that feeling, is the discovery of the paralysis of the adult self by way of a brilliant image of its incomplete transference to nature. The image at first resembles the famous one in the second and third lines of Eliot's "Prufrock," but the rhapsodic development, the sense of an ecstasy of pain, is peculiarly Anne Sexton's:

> It was the strangled cold of November;
> even the stars were strapped in the sky
> and that moon too bright
> forking through the bars to stick me
> with a singing in the head.
> I have forgotten all the rest.

The relationships, in the poems of *To Bedlam and Part Way Back,* between the tones of mockery and of childlike vulnerability, with appropriate rhythms, and those of rhapsodic realization bring Anne Sexton close to the spirit of Sylvia Plath. These two young women may well have affected one another's styles, for they were certainly aware not only of each other's work but also of their common indebtedness to Lowell. Some of Anne Sexton's images and effects could easily have influenced "Lady Lazarus" and other poems of *Ariel*. Thus, in "Lullaby" she forms the kind of ironic and tentative bridge, for just an instant, between a plain fact (associated, needless to say, with her maladies) and a self-contained symbolic image that becomes its own world. Not only the process, but the image of the woman as "linen," recalls Sylvia Plath:

> My sleeping pill is white.

It is a splendid pearl;
it floats me out of myself,
my stung skin as alien
as a loose bolt of cloth.
I will ignore the bed.
I am linen on a shelf.

The beginning of "The Double Image" is still more striking
in this respect. The mother is addressing the child from whom
she has been separated by commitment to an asylum. The age of
the speaker, the attempted suicides, the witch-imagery, even the
"Lazarus" effect are almost the same as in Sylvia Plath:

I am thirty this November.
You are still small, in your fourth year.
We stand watching the yellow leaves go queer,
flapping in the winter rain,
falling flat and washed. And I remember
mostly the three autumns you did not live here.
· ·

I, who chose two times
to kill myself, had said your nickname
the mewling months when you first came;
until a fever rattled
in your throat and I moved like a pantomime
above your head. Ugly angels spoke to me. The blame,
I heard them say, was mine. . . .

Death was simpler than I'd thought.
The day life made you well and whole
I let the witches take away my guilty soul.
I pretended I was dead
until the white men pumped the poison out,
putting me armless and washed through the rigamarole
of talking boxes and the electric bed.

Nevertheless, these poems exist on a narrower scale than Syl-
via Plath's. Their high points are not the magnificent fusion of
private and universal motifs, but piercing, isolated strains of
music and finely compassionate impressions of pitiful life. The

former, and greater, kind of success is a purification of the expression of private pain, as in the climax of "Music Swims Back to Me" or the beginning of "You, Doctor Martin":

> You, Doctor Martin, walk
> from breakfast to madness. Late August,
> I speed through the antiseptic tunnel
> where the moving dead still talk
> of pushing their bones against the thrust
> of cure. And I am queen of this summer hotel
> or the laughing bee on a stalk
>
> of death. . . .

The second kind of success can be seen, in Anne Sexton's first book, in a poem like "The Waiting Head," about her mother in a rest home, sitting always at the upper front window and "watching for anyone from her wooden seat," and always writing in "her leather books" that "no one came"—apparently whether it was true or not. It can be seen in her second book as well, in "The Hangman," in which the speaker is the father of an extremely retarded child; and in the title poem, "All My Pretty Ones," about her parents, who died within three months of one another in 1959. But again, the highest poetic points are those of private expression, especially the brief, perfect "The Starry Night."

> The town does not exist
> except where one black-haired tree slips
> up like a drowned woman into the hot sky.
> The town is silent. The night boils with eleven stars.
> O starry starry night! This is how
> I want to die.
>
> It moves. They are all alive.
> Even the moon bulges in its orange irons
> to push children, like a god, from its eye.
> The old unseen serpent swallows up the stars.
> O starry starry night! This is how
> I want to die:

> into that rushing beast of the night,
> sucked up by that great dragon, to split
> from my life with no flag,
> no belly,
> no cry.

All My Pretty Ones has its recognizably confessional poems. Some continue pretty much in the spirit of "The Double Image," in the first book. "The House," for instance, is a portrait of the poet as an adolescent girl, again with various remarkable resemblances, in its vehement and satirical objectivity of detail and its unforgetting resentments, to Sylvia Plath's work. "The Flight" is an original, bitterly humorous account of an attempt, hysterical and disorganized at best, to flee to a lover. It was frustrated by the grounding of planes at the airport. Yet there is a growth of new, hardier skin on these pieces, comparable with that in Lowell's *For the Union Dead*. For the most part, the poems are not as vulnerable as before in their self-exposure. "The Fortress," though like "The Double Image" it is an address to a child and a confession of a kind of helplessness, is not autobiographical as much as contemplative. "Housewife" changes what might have been pure whining into a compelling symbolism of the house as an extension of the body of a woman, underlining the identity that develops between herself and her mother. "Letter Written on a Ferry While Crossing Long Island Sound" begins as a wrily melancholy account of the end of a love-affair and becomes a magnificently humorous prayer that the four solemn nuns on the ferry with the speaker may become visibly miraculous:

> Oh God,
> although I am very sad,
> could you please
> let these four nuns
> loosen from their leather boots
> and their wooden chairs
> to rise out
> over this greasy deck,
> out over this iron rail,
> nodding their pink heads to one side,

flying four abreast
in the old-fashioned side stroke;
each mouth open and round,
breathing together
as fish do,
singing without sound.

BEVERLY FIELDS

From "The Poetry of Anne Sexton"

*Author's note: Anne Sexton was born November 9, 1928, in Newton, Massachusetts, and grew up in Wellesley, where she attended local schools. She has been married for fifteen years and has two daughters— Linda, nine, and Joyce, seven. She began writing five years ago. Her poetry has appeared in numerous periodicals and anthologies. Houghton Mifflin Company has published two volumes of her work—*To Bedlam and Part Way Back *and* All My Pretty Ones. *In 1958–59 she won the* Audience *poetry prize and in 1959 she held the Robert Frost Fellowship at Breadloaf, Vermont. She was awarded a grant as assistant scholar to the Radcliffe Institute for Independent Study during 1961–62, and she won the* Poetry *prize in 1962. This year she was awarded the first traveling literary fellowship of the American Academy of Arts and Letters for a year's residence at the American Academy in Rome. When* Poetry *sent her a biographical form to fill out, she wrote under the heading of education "none" and under the heading of occupation she wrote "homebody."*

The poetry of Anne Sexton expresses a number of symbolic themes which have been read as literal autobiography. Because her work is difficult, the biographical approach to the poems has been a temptation; but while there are elements of autobiography in it, the poetry cannot always be interpreted in this way. It seems more profitable to credit her with a degree of esthetic distance and to consider some of the recurrent themes that create relationships among the individual poems. What follows is intended to direct readers to the poems as poems rather than as memoirs.

There are no new seasons in hell, but the old ones from time to time toughen up new visitors who are able to describe in verse the climate of descent. Anne Sexton's hell is more like Dante's

---

Tri Quarterly, o.s., 6, no. 1 (1963). © 1963 Beverly Fields. Reprinted by permission of the author.

than like Milton's; her images clarify rather than veil the ineffable. "The Moss of His Skin," for example, is ostensibly a dramatic monologue, its voice started by a quotation from an article in a psychoanalytic journal. The quotation appears as epigraph to the poem:

> Young girls in old Arabia were often buried alive next to their dead fathers, apparently as sacrifice to the goddesses of the tribes.

But the form of the poem—the dramatic monologue—is a metaphor that reveals naked a personal fantasy:

It was only important
to smile and hold still,
to lie down beside him
and to rest awhile,
to be folded up together
as if we were silk,
to sink from the eyes of mother
and not to talk.
The black room took us
like a cave or a mouth
or an indoor belly.
I held my breath
and daddy was there,
his thumbs, his fat skull,
his teeth, his hair growing
like a field or a shawl.
I lay by the moss
of his skin until
it grew strange. My sisters
will never know that I fall
out of myself and pretend
that Allah will not see
how I hold my daddy
like an old stone tree.

The *liebestod* experience here is given more straightforwardly than even Antigone's; none of its elements is in doubt—the sense of sin, or tabu, that requires the grave as the most secret bed and also as punishment is directly produced in the four grave figures that establish sin (black), privacy (cave), annihilation (mouth), and the complex female need not only to share the father with the mother but also to share the mother with the father (an indoor belly).

Like all her poems, this one doubles its strength and clarity through sound. There is almost no rhyme except at the end, where *see* and *tree* reach a climax intensified by the intervening *daddy,* with its extra syllable that contributes to the syncopation of the last two lines. The poem proceeds to this final syncopation from its beginning jump-rope rhythms, expressive of childhood, and through a meter that is struck almost exclusively with two beats to a line, expressive of this secret and disastrous coupling. Where three beats occur in a line the mother is to be found, an extra yet necessary presence: "to sink from the eyes of mother"; her presence is implied strongly also in the trimeter lines that recognize the need to hide from the sisters and from Allah, since all these censors refer psychologically to the mother, against whom the sin is after all committed:

> . . . My sisters
> will never know that I fall
> out of myself and pretend
> that Allah will not see

It may be no more than coincidence that "The Moss of His Skin" occurs almost at dead center of Anne Sexton's first published volume, *To Bedlam and Part Way Back;* but it is possible to look before and after it to radiant elements in the large discourse of this book. The metaphorical use of the dramatic monologue makes four more poems, of which one, "Where I Live in This Honorable House of the Laurel Tree," speaks in a *double-entendre* of lament both for the cold pastoral, the death–in–life of poetry, and for the erotic paralysis that results from refusing courtship that is divine or otherwise tabu:

> . . . The air
> rings for you, for that astonishing rite
> of my breathing tent undone within your light.

I only know how this untimely lust has tossed
flesh at the wind forever and moved my fears
toward the intimate Rome of the myth we crossed.
. . . .

You gave me honor too soon, Apollo.
There is no one left who understands
how I wait
here in my wooden legs and O
my green green hands.

The tree of the father literally imprisons her here, in an ancient and durable symbol; and in another sense she is imprisoned in poetry, the shibboleth that promises to open the gates of the dead.

But a dead voice chants in another monologue, "Portrait of an Old Woman on the College Tavern Wall," with the narcotic repetitiveness of a ballad, its refrain the voices of the living, about poets and about the locks on the gates of the dead that prevent the poets from really reaching the deep truth:

> I only said
> how I want to be there and I
> would sing my songs with the liars
> and my lies with all the singers.
> And I would, and I would but
> it's my hair in the hair wreath,
> my cup pinned to the tavern wall,
> my dusty face they sing beneath.
> Poets are sitting in my kitchen.

As in Donne, the dead voice asks a question whose answer is made impossible by another question:

> Why do these poets lie?
> Why do children get children and
> *Did you hear what it said?*

> I only said
> how I want to be there,
> Oh, down at the tavern

> where the prophets are singing
> around their round table
> until they are still.

Poetry is a lying art undertaken perhaps in a witch's "kitchen," not only because of the nature of the poet, who is always aware of the lie behind the truth, but also because the city of the dead, the buried life, is closed, and because even the dead would lie if they could.

To lie or not, to publish or withhold, is the concern of the fourth dramatic monologue in this volume. The "Unknown Girl in the Maternity Ward" speaks to her illegitimate infant, six days old. From the dramatic surface of the poem, however, a lyrical note thrusts up as the girl tells the infant that

> . . . Your lips are animals; you are fed
> with love. At first hunger is not wrong.

This is surely out of character; it knows too much; and it is a direction toward the undramatic pulse that beats *sotto voce* beneath the monologue where it is not difficult to detect the poet pinned sprawling to the wall:

> The doctors are enamel. They want to know
> the facts. They guess about the man who left me,
> some pendulum soul, going the way men go
> and leave you full of child. But our case history
> stays blank. All I did was let you grow.
> Now we are here for all the ward to see.
> . . . .
> . . . I am a shelter of lies.
> Should I learn to speak again, or hopeless in
> such sanity will I touch some face I recognize?

The decision is made at last, as involuntary and natural an act as when

> . . . I burst empty
> of you, letting you learn how the air is so.
> . . . .

> . . . the doctors return to scold
> me. I speak. It is you my silence harms.
> I should have known; I should have told
> them something to write down. My voice alarms
> my throat. "Name of father—none." I hold
> you and name you bastard in my arms.
>
> And now that's that. There is nothing more
> that I can say or lose.
> Others have traded life before
> and could not speak. I tighten to refuse
> your owling eyes, my fragile visitor.
> I touch your cheeks, like flowers. You bruise
> against me. We unlearn. I am a shore
> rocking you off. You break from me. I choose
> your only way, my small inheritor
> and hand you off, trembling the selves we lose.
> Go child, who is my sin and nothing more.

This is the poem that has led some to speculate whether or not Anne Sexton has had an illegitimate child—an interpretation that amuses her. Such error is not merely simple-minded, however; it is a response to the poet's trick of investing the experience of *the other* with her own emotional realities. What is primary in the poem is of course the experience of childbirth with its essential pain of separation; but here again, as in many of her poems, there is a *double-entendre*. The undramatic *sotto voce* appears to refer associatively to the long poem, "The Double Image," and to "For John, Who Begs Me Not to Enquire Further"; and it expresses precisely the problem that is called attention to in the epigraph to *To Bedlam and Part Way Back*. The epigraph is a quotation from a letter of Schopenhauer to Goethe:

> It is the courage to make a clean breast of it in face of every question that makes the philosopher. He must be like Sophocles' Oedipus, who, seeking enlightenment concerning his terrible fate, pursues his indefatigable enquiry, even when he divines that appalling horror awaits him in the answer. But most of us carry in our heart the Jocasta who begs Oedipus for God's sake not to inquire further.

This is an afterthought, of course, in the context of the volume; but it puts neatly the tension that motivates all the poems. A small composition history may be illuminating. After Anne Sexton had written the long poem "The Double Image" she showed it to her teacher John Holmes, who was angry and dismayed to find her revealing so much of herself in her verse and attempted to prevent her publishing it. Her answer to him was "For John, Who Begs Me Not to Enquire Further"; but even here, in her rebuttal, his censorship appears to be the voice of her own inner Jocasta. The poem begins in explanation, justification; and the attempted liberation of her Oedipus from her Jocasta is reinforced by means of free verse:

> Not that it was beautiful,
> but that, in the end, there was
> a certain sense of order there;
> something worth learning
> in that narrow diary of my mind,
> in the commonplaces of the asylum
> where the cracked mirror
> or my own selfish death
> outstared me.
> And if I tried
> to give you something else,
> something outside of myself,
> you would not know
> that the worst of anyone
> can be, finally,
> an accident of hope.

The movement away from solipsism, the only possibility for a poet who works from the specific to the general, who does not stop at the moment of lyrical narcissism, begins the middle of the poem:

> I tapped my own head;
> it was glass, an inverted bowl.
> It is a small thing
> to rage in your own bowl.
> At first it was private.

> Then it was more than myself;
> it was you, or your house
> or your kitchen.

The witch's kitchen again. But the poem ends with a return to the lyrical moment, enlarged, however, by the experience of reaching out, so that the final declarative sentence is twice qualified:

> There ought to be something special
> for someone
> in this kind of hope.
> This is something I would never find
> in a lovelier place, my dear,
> although your fear is anyone's fear,
> like an invisible veil between us all . . .
> and sometimes in private,
> my kitchen, your kitchen,
> my face, your face.

"My face, your face," Jocasta's face; it is the awareness of "my own selfish death" that sees more than one face in "the cracked mirror"—cracked to reflect both sides of the overwhelming question whether or not to inquire, whether or not to express the results of inquiry.

Like the "Unknown Girl in the Maternity Ward," Anne Sexton makes her decision, but it is a difficult one. The *double-entendre* in "Unknown Girl," made in alternate rhyme to express its internal debate, and in "Where I Live in This Honorable House of the Laurel Tree," is her manner of clarifying the difficulty by means of the metaphors of childbirth and mythology. Equivalence between childbirth and poem-making is by no means new, and neither is the fear of annihilation in poetry that is expressed in the metaphor of the tree. Keats and Tennyson both felt such fear, and so did Frost and Eliot; Plato was impelled to exclude poets from his ideal republic, himself a poet; and it was Vergil, after all, who invented the metaphor of the golden bough.

Just how personally Anne Sexton pursues her fearful inquiry, however, is a matter of more conjecture than most of her readers are likely to understand. Where the lyric leaves off and the dramatic monologue takes up is frequently not clear. "For Johnny Pole on the Forgotten Beach," for example, looks like a lyric: its refrain, "Johnny, your dream moves summers / inside my mind," separates two sections of the poem that are concerned respectively with Johnny on the beach of a resort summer and with Johnny on a "beach of assault" in war, and the voice says that "He was my brother, my small Johnny brother, almost ten." But whose voice tells the truth? The poem's? Or Anne Sexton's, telling an interviewer "something to write down"—that she did not have a brother who was killed during the war?

The answer is irrelevant. The infernal journey requires what can probably be called vision, a state of heightened or intensified perception that can apprehend the nature of both the self and the other, separately as well as together, the kind of ego mobility that can slide freely between inner and outer reality.

One major literary device for attaining and expressing vision, in this sense, is synesthesia, as old as Saint John of Asia and as new as Rimbaud or as Anne Sexton. Her synesthetic figures radiate most frequently from the sense of hearing. In "Music Swims Back to Me," where the synesthesia is at its simplest, she presents the Proustian notion that "the song . . . remembers more than I." The sense of vertigo and of loss is heavy:

> Wait Mister. Which way is home?
> They turned the light out
> and the dark is moving in the corner.
> There are no sign posts in this room,
> four ladies, over eighty,
> in diapers every one of them.
> La la la, Oh music swims back to me
> and I can feel the tune they played
> the night they left me
> in this private institution on a hill.

It is loss of the self that you feel here; and in an attempt to find it, the persona is impelled toward pathetic fallacy:

> Imagine it. A radio playing
> and everyone here was crazy.

> I liked it and danced in a circle.
> Music pours over the sense
> and in a funny way
> music sees more than I.
> I mean it remembers better;
>
> remembers the first night here.
> It was the strangled cold of November;
> even the stars were strapped in the sky.

"Stars . . . strapped in the sky" conveys of course the sense of restraint—literal, physical restraint—"in this private institution"; vision here operates to merge the self consolingly with elements of the external world. The result, however, is not consoling, but suggests that the persona and the stars are fellow inmates in a prison-house, so that the poem moves, by implication, from the immediate, lyrical moment toward a larger statement about the nature of the universe.

Like the stars, the persona is strapped in, but paradoxically, since she remarks the lack of sign posts as if she were able to move like "the dark" itself:

> They lock me in this chair at eight a.m.
> and there are no signs to tell the way,
> just the radio beating to itself
> and the song that remembers
> more than I. Oh, la la la,
> this music swims back to me.
> The night I came I danced in a circle
> and was not afraid.
> Mister?

Paradise is lost here too, even though there is irony in the lost circle of dancing confidence where she may have felt preserved like the Old Testament prophets in a circle of flames or like anyone in any magic circle anywhere.

Another ironic paradise lost is evoked in "The Bells," where again sound stirs the memory and where the circle in "Music Swims Back to Me" becomes "three rings of danger":

> Today the circus poster

is scabbing off the concrete wall
and the children have forgotten
if they knew at all.
Father, do you remember?
Only the sound remains,
the distant thump of the good elephants,
the voice of the ancient lions
and how the bells
trembled for the flying man.
I, laughing,
lifted to your high shoulder
or small at the rough legs of strangers,
was not afraid.
You held my hand
and were instant to explain
the three rings of danger.

There is no narcissism here, only the knowledge of the serpent in paradise, whose wounding nature is made evident by means of the circus poster that is "scabbing off"—still scabbing off the hurt place which is referred to ironically as a "concrete wall." Here, as in "Music Swims Back to Me," the persona "was not afraid"—a phrase that is terrifying in context, since it is perfectly clear that there is in both situations a great deal to fear: in "Music Swims" the fear is of vertigo, restraint, and loss of self; in "The Bells" the fear is of the father's courtship, which is tabu, and which also produces restraint, as the metaphorical paralysis of "Where I Live in This Honorable House of the Laurel Tree" makes plain.

The courtship, and the response to it, is one of the most vivid infernal events in the volume:

Oh see the naughty clown
and the wild parade
while love love
love grew rings around me.
This was the sound where it began;
our breath pounding up to see
the flying man breast out
across the boarded sky
and climb the air.

> I remember the color of music
> and how forever
> all the trembling bells of you
> were mine.

The word choice is designed to understate the elements of the *liebestod* experience that were seen so plain in "The Moss of His Skin," which, by the way, has a kind of tactile association with "the rough legs of strangers"; the reason behind the understatement is the awareness that for children experience has to be toned down in order to be acceptable to the adult world. Thus sin becomes only "naughty" in this poem, and is furthermore projected onto the other, the clown; and the "three rings of danger" which clearly refer to "love love / love" which "grew rings around me" can be simply the literal circus rings. The divine lover, identified in "Where I Live" as Apollo, is here reduced to the childlike "flying man"—another instance of substituting one image for another: here it is a matter of displacing the divine, or tabu, attribute of the father onto the trapeze artist—and even the need for the mother is timidly expressed in a verb as the flying man is seen to "breast out across the boarded sky" so that the undifferentiated, or hermaphroditic, love object, left over from childhood, is only vaguely indicated, as it is in dreams.

The excitement and suspense (and fear) shared with the father take on an erotic color at the point where the two have only one breath: "our breath pounding up to see"; and it is preparatory to this moment of climax that the perception becomes synesthetic, as music becomes a place—"This was the sound where it began"—and then afterward becomes visual—"I remember the color of music." The equation of the flying man, or divine lover, with the father is firmly established at the conclusion, which reverts to the image of "the bells" that "trembled for the flying man" and which makes the bells the father in liquid consonants and murmuring alliteration that evoke the sense of touch: "all the trembling bells of you / were mine."

The bells recur in "Said the Poet to the Analyst":

> My business is words. Words are like labels,
> or coins, or better, like swarming bees.

I confess I am only broken by the sources of things;
as if words were counted like dead bees in the attic,
unbuckled from their yellow eyes and their dry wings.
I must always forget how one word is able to pick
out another, to manner another, until I have got
something I might have said . . .
but did not.

Your business is watching my words. But I
admit nothing. I work with my best, for instance,
when I can write my praise for a nickel machine,
that one night in Nevada: telling how the magic jackpot
came clacking three bells out, over the lucky screen.
But if you should say this is something it is not,
then I grow weak, remembering how my hands felt funny
and ridiculous and crowded with all
the believing money.

Two major preoccupations—truth and the father—come to-
gether here when the persona, after saying flatly that "I /
admit nothing," does make an admission in her memory of "how my
hands felt funny / and ridiculous and crowded with all / the
believing money." The admission appears to be that the money
is the father's love, since it is the result of hitting the jackpot
with "three bells." The technique of substitution is at work
again here, in the displacement of the attitude of "believing," in
the sense of "credulous," from the persona to the money itself, a
displacement that operates to strengthen the association of the
money with the father's love by suggesting that this literal pater-
nal love believed itself innocent. The displacement also permits
the persona to draw back from her own credulousness, to dis-
avow it, as if to say that she had known all along what the
analyst had said about her narrative, "that this is something it is
not."

The first stanza of the poem prepares the way for the second,
in the admission that "Words are like labels, / or coins," and in
the afterthought that a better simile is "bees" which have been
"unbuckled" from everything that gave them life in general and
from their seeing eyes in particular. There is life behind words
too, or separate from them, which the words cannot always see;

and in the second stanza there is the knowledge that there is life behind or separate from things and events, life that words, things, events, can only "pick out" or "manner." The limitations of poetry here are almost as strong as they are in "Portrait of an Old Woman on the College Tavern Wall."

The image of the bees recalls the first poem in this volume, "You, Doctor Martin," where a mental hospital is referred to as a "summer hotel":

> You, Doctor Martin, walk
> from breakfast to madness. Late August,
> I speed through the antiseptic tunnel
> where the moving dead still talk
> of pushing their bones against the thrust
> of cure. And I am queen of this summer hotel
> or the laughing bee on a stalk
>
> of death. We stand in broken
> lines and wait while they unlock
> the door and count us at the frozen gates
> of dinner. The shibboleth is spoken
> and we move to gravy in our smock
> of smiles. We chew in rows, our plates
> scratch and whine like chalk
>
> in school. There are no knives
> for cutting your throat. . . .

Again the bee is an alternate image, a second thought, chosen perhaps because it can sting like words or like a fatal woman; and it leads to the first of a series of chilling anticlimaxes in the poem. Following the Dantean image of the dead who do not know they are in hell, an image expressed in sexual terms, the "laughing bee on a stalk" suggests pollination, but this expectation is sharply defeated in the next stanza by the qualifying words, "of death," until you recognize that what is given here is another form of the *liebestod*. If there is any doubt that this "summer hotel" is really hell itself, it is dispelled "while they unlock / the door and count us at the frozen gates"; but again an anticlimax is presented, this time to insist on the ordinariness of hell: the "frozen gates" open only to "dinner." Juxtaposed with the childhood reference to "school," the statement that "There are no knives" is not surprising until you get to the coda: "for cutting your throat."

Various images from childhood pattern through this poem: besides "chalk" and "school" there is "our smock," and in a subsequent stanza the persona remarks, "What large children we are / here," in the same way that she later observes in "Music Swims Back to Me" that there are in the room with her "four ladies, over eighty, / in diapers every one of them." The mood of infantile regression among the patients is conveyed not only through such explicit images, however; the rhyme scheme is designed to resemble the repetition of the abc's.

KAY ELLEN CAPO

Redeeming Words

From one perspective, *To Bedlam and Part Way Back* is Anne Sexton's attempt to dramatize her mental illness. In certain poems the reader meets personae who are living in an illusory world of madness or near-madness ("You, Doctor Martin," "Music Swims Back to Me," "Noon Walk on the Asylum Lawn," "Ringing the Bells"). However, many poems in this book endeavor to justify the analytic process which can be a way back to normalcy. For example, in "Said the Poet to the Analyst," "The Lost Ingredient," "A Story for Rose on the Midnight Flight to Boston," "The Double Image," "The Division of Parts," and "For John, Who Begs Me Not to Enquire Further," Sexton's personae are confronting the exposure of their own illusions.

Any illusion is a psychic safety device. What is painful is the shattering process of unmasking one's illusions. For beneath that guarded network is the vulnerable identity who has erected a symbol system to serve as a self-defense. When that symbolic world is exposed as an elaborate lie, the naked self must stand, bereft of all protection, and face the burden of its failures. Such painful exposure is a prerequisite for building healthy communication with oneself or others. Thus, the "inward look that society scorns"[1] may be the only way to recover secular grace—that ability to be candid which forms the basis of human trust.

In *Bedlam,* Sexton is aware of the tension between the human desire for secure illusions and the call to reduce her life to its authentic identity. Any identity-quest can bring painful revelations, as Oedipus the King found out. Yet in the prefatory note

From "Redeeming Words: A Study of Confessional Rhetoric in the Poetry of Anne Sexton" (Ph.D. diss., Northwestern University, 1978). Copyright © 1978 by Kay Ellen Merriman Capo. Edited version reprinted by permission of the author.

which opens *Bedlam,* Sexton invokes the courage of Oedipus as she cites from a letter of Schopenhauer to Goethe: "It is the courage to make a clean breast of it in face of every question that makes the philosopher. He must be like Sophocles' Oedipus, who, seeking enlightenment concerning his terrible fate, pursues his indefatigable enquiry, even when he divines that appalling horror awaits him in the answer. But most of us carry in our heart the Jocasta who begs Oedipus for God's sake not to inquire further. . . ."

In one of the last poems of *Bedlam,* "For John, Who Begs Me Not to Enquire Further," Sexton explores her own version of the Oedipus-Jocasta controversy. This poem is framed as an apologia to John Holmes, the poet and teacher with whom she first studied her craft. It defends the publication of her confessional self-scrutiny against his objections.[2] In a larger sense, the poem serves as Sexton's justification to her readers for the intimate personal examination of which *Bedlam* is made. Pieces that John or the reader might consider dangerously inward or downright self-indulgent are defended as offering Sexton an escape from the confines of her own mind. Thus the personal consequences of her poetic self-confrontation, "a certain sense of order," and "something worth learning," have been salutary. However, there are negative consequences of her self-inquiry which must be faced by the redeemed persona: estrangement from John and perhaps from the reader.

Despite the heroic overtones of Oedipal probing and the almost Grecian illusion of necessity which tinges this speaker, her moralistic tone is not carried to an extreme, lest it destroy the chance to make peace with John. Haughtiness or superiority would not be the way to create appeal or to overcome disapproval in her auditor. Because the poem is structured to bridge a gap between the speaker and John, its overall tone is low-key and conciliatory.

Nevertheless, Sexton felt stung by the disapproval of her mentor, John Holmes. This is apparent in her complaint that Holmes saw her as a dangerous person whom Maxine Kumin should avoid: "He told me I shouldn't write such personal poems about the madhouse. He said, 'That isn't a fit subject for poetry.'"[3] In a contrite aside, Sexton claims that she had intended to reform her ways: "I tried to mind them. I tried to write the way the others, especially Maxine, wrote, but it didn't work. I always ended up sounding like myself."[4] Her defiant inner truths kept surfacing. In this poem, Sexton neutralizes the student-mentor controversy to some extent by picturing both parties in a posture of mutual supplication; he begs her to withdraw from introspection, and she implores him to understand her need for it. Thus they are identified at the level of communicative style.

From the outset, Sexton's speaker uses a tone which suggests that she is humbly repentant about her acts of self-inquiry. There is irony and rhetorical necessity in this tone, since the confessional opening of one's life could be construed as a form of narcissism, exhibitionism, or impiety. Confession demands that one's auditor be faced with the naked truth, but such unveiling could be regarded as impudent. However, in Sexton's poem the potentially immodest act of revealing inner weakness is counterbalanced by the modesty of her opening remark: "Not that it was beautiful."

It should be pointed out that the persona's contrite attitude does not constitute a simple admission of guilt; rather, it bows to the need for decorum for courting an offended party—John. True, there is some indication that the poet is embarrassed about her failings; yet she never throws herself at John's mercy, as an admitted sinner might do. While her humility reflects the desire for sympathy and understanding, she also seeks justification. The poem uses contrition as a strategy to encompass her sorrow at losing John's confidence, and rhetoric of apologia to encompass Sexton's conviction that her actions really were salvific and honorable. Although there are no stanzaic divisions in the poem, it is comprised of six different stages, each of which constitutes a discrete moment in Sexton's attempt to conciliate John. Each section is marked by a shift in attitude, and most are comprised of a single sentence.

In the exposition of section one (lines 1–9), the poet introduces her problematic conduct: madness, suicide, and self-analysis. From the outset, she emphasizes the good consequences of poeticizing her difficulties in a written diary; versification has brought order and truth to her experience. In the second phase of the poem (lines 10–16), Sexton differentiates the sordid subject matter of her verse ("the worst of anyone") from the salvific—even edifying—effect such a painful record may have on others ("an accident of hope"). What emerges is an elaboration of the aesthetic argument between John and herself, for she represents her poetic self-discovery as a gift he shouldn't refuse. Lines 17–24, section three, condense the persona's history of self-discovery into a narrative of four short sentences, naming poetry as the vehicle which admitted other people to her solitary universe.[5] Succeeding this mini-history is a gentle admonition to John (section 4, lines 25–32), where the poet warns her mentor not to prefer ornamental verse over the plain, naked truth. What follows in lines 33–37 (section 5), is a recapitulation and compression of the arguments made in sections 1 and 2. Finally, the concluding lines (38–44) raise the problem of estrangement between student and teacher to a universal, transcendent level: "although your fear is anyone's fear, / like an invisible veil between us all. . . ."

In the first part of the poem, a series of verbal sidesteps creates a humble posture for the persona, enveloping in mystery the act to which she alludes. Yet this section also establishes terms for the contrary aesthetic position she upholds throughout the poem: Conventional forms of beauty and moral balance are not the only wellspring of poetic truth; there is hope and order in the awful truths uncovered by her true confessions.

> Not that it was beautiful,
> but that, in the end, there was
> a certain sense of order there;
> something worth learning
> in that narrow diary of my mind,
> in the commonplaces of the asylum
> where the cracked mirror
> or my own selfish death
> outstared me.

Self-humbling and contrition are apparent as the speaker describes her debased condition in the asylum. She asserts that her poetic probes into madness, though not beautiful, did uncover a valuable sense of personal order. Yet deep humility characterizes her claim; it is meek, deferential, and even somewhat stammering. One could diagram the hesitant self-assertion thus:

$$\begin{matrix} \text{not that} & \rightarrow & \text{there was} \\ \text{but that} & & \end{matrix}$$

There is a clear rhetorical function served by the speaker's irresolute, even negative attitude toward herself. This doubtfulness does not so much reflect her own inner qualms as it appeals to and anticipates the doubt she senses in John. Her posture thus becomes a rhetorical means to identify with the skepticism or disapproval of her auditor. Also, by taking on an attitude of self-recrimination, she mitigates John's tendency to blame her. Why should he (or the reader) doubt the motives of one who has subjected herself to such merciless scrutiny? Through ad hominem arguments she blames herself more cruelly than a sympathetic confessor ever would, relentlessly cataloging her sins: She is narrow, cracked, selfish, not beautiful. Such obvious contrition reduces the listener's inclination to criticize. Moreover, although John fears that she is on a dangerous psychological and aesthetic path, the persona proves herself capable of objectivity, logical argument, and even the detachment of skepticism.

It has been mentioned that the speaker uses circumlocution to avoid any direct naming of her supposed sin; even the site of the act is problematic. For example, she modifies the "sense of order" which was "something worth learning" by two locative phrases. Her place of confinement was both the "narrow diary" of her own mind, and the "commonplaces of the asylum." One infers that by finding the keys to her mind, she will be able to unbolt the doors of Bedlam. Sexton's association of "narrow diary" with "mind," "cracked," "commonplaces," "mirror," "outstared," and "asylum" creates dual referencing. For example, one's mind can be a refuge for peaceful contemplation. (Being crazy is to be "out of one's mind.") However, in the insane asylum the institutionalized person is faced with other people who mirror his own psychic division. For this speaker, neither her disturbed psyche nor the insane asylum offers any retreat; they are places of bedlam where one is locked into the necessity of painful self-realization.

In the opening passage, Sexton's feeling of entrapment is em-

bodied through language that is self-reflexive and ultimately sol-
ipsistic. Every noun and pronoun refers to the landscape of her
own soul. Thus her intense program of self-scrutiny surfaces in a
series of subjective images that circle back to the ego like some
maddening hall of mirrors. "It," "something," "narrow diary
of my mind," "commonplaces of the asylum," "cracked mir-
ror," and "selfish death" all refer to her attempts at verbalizing
and visualizing a self-image. From a rhetorical point of view, the
reduction of her sphere of identity to a tiny microcosm reduces
the arena of the persona's ethical responsibility.

By adopting a contrite tone toward her madness and suicide,
Sexton admits that these were negative actions; she is guilty.
Thus, she bolsters negative attitudes which her audience would
probably have toward such taboo experiences, and aligns herself
with conventional morality. In this respect, her rhetoric is refor-
mative. A more radical, transformative strategy occurs when
she undermines John's implied criticism by differentiating poetic
beauty from order and truth ("learning"). All three are positive,
readily acceptable qualities, and each is normally associated with
poetry. Yet Sexton's controversial aesthetic position is revealed
by her forced separation of beauty from order and truth. What
remains is a poetic norm that will admit grotesque or ugly sub-
ject matter if it yields truth and order. This is exactly the case
that must be made if she is to defend her poetry against John's
objections. Thus, without ever taking on an argumentative
tone, she makes her point. Her explanative form of discourse
(bolstering plus differentiation) assumes that if he could appreci-
ate the noble results of her confessional writing he would exon-
erate her verse. By establishing her own aesthetic terms for
judging confessional poetry, Sexton undercuts John's objection
to her unbecoming, ignoble revelations.

In the second phase of the poem, the persona still appears
meek and deferent. Yet there is an underlying message here that
overturns John's professorial authority; the teacher-student rela-
tionship is cleverly reversed. While insisting on the moral value
of her experience, Sexton reminds her mentor of the lesson she
taught him:

> And if I tried
> to give you something else,
> something outside of myself,

you would not know
that the worst of anyone
can be, finally,
an accident of hope.

What saves Sexton from appearing impudent is the delicate tone of her delivery. She pursues her point indirectly, warding off any offense to John by a fragile web of negative logic. The somewhat defiant implications of this sentence are muted by negative logic which inverts an open declaration (if $p \rightarrow$ then q) into the statement if $p \rightarrow$ then *not q*.

As in the earlier section discussed, Sexton does not name her disapproved action directly. Though she clearly claims to have given something personal to John, the gift itself is somewhat shrouded. It was *not* "something else," nor "something outside of myself." While in the asylum, she delved into "the worst" truths of her own existence and now offers John, in poetic form, the "accident of hope" wrought by her acceptance of those truths. This use of indirect referents creates several effects. First, the poet suggests intimacy between John and herself. Estranged they may be, but their fund of mutually shared experience establishes a pool of common referents which allows them to communicate through inference and ellipsis. Second, Sexton assumes that the reader who has been following her journey back from Bedlam also possesses the background to decipher this rather oblique apologia. Indeed, her employment of general terms helps universalize the lesson for John and the reader. Using strategies of differentiation and transcendence, she argues that knowing even the worst things about one human life can help other lives. Such edifying rhetoric assumes that confessions of exemplary guilt can, like exemplary virtue, offer anecdotes for living. This reaffirms Sexton's aesthetic position on confessional poetry: The subjective life, however gruesome, is a proper subject for verse. One need not offer "something outside of" oneself.

The final rhetorical effect of this section's indirect referents is that they create an aura of taboo. Freud has described taboo as a syndrome based on fear which causes primitive or neurotic persons to avoid using the name of a repellent object or person.[6] It would be logical to see euphemism (tact) as a species of taboo that is working in this poem. For example, the words "suicide" and "madness" are replaced by elusive phrases ("my own selfish death" and "the worst of anyone"). Perhaps as a courtesy to John or perhaps in deference to her fears about recurring problems, Sexton never names her sins directly.

It is in the third section of "For John . . ." that the process of self-discovery which has been defended is shown directly. Her breakdown and renewal are represented in a condensed narrative:

> I tapped my own head;
> it was glass, an inverted bowl.
> It is a small thing
> to rage in your own bowl.
> At first it was private.
> Then it was more than myself;
> it was you, or your house
> or your kitchen.

In this self-dramatization the speaker has reduced the narrow diary of her mind to an even tinier microcosm. This condensation of a lengthy history of self-analysis into several brief phrases indicates a recovery of her capacity to select and order experience. Not only did she survive the maelstrom; she has transcended it sufficiently to gain the perspective required for social intercourse—the ability to see oneself as others do.

There is another effect created by these lines. By reducing the site of her downfall to a tiny, self-enclosed sphere, the persona manages to reduce the guilt and fearsome taboo of her madness: "It is a small thing / to rage in your own bowl."[7] Also, the choice of inert materials to describe her mind ("glass," "inverted bowl") emphasizes her helplessness. Glass, already present in the mirror image of section 1, connotes fragility, implying that the speaker is a victim who can be easily hurt and must be handled with care. This display of weakness pleads mercy and consideration, suggesting that Sexton could crack again if she is subjected to harsh criticism.

One way to defend a deplored action is to claim helplessness or lack of control, and this speaker seems bereft of free will. Trapped in a solipsistic prison, she is ultimately depersonalized. Her head is like a material vacuum which, when "tapped," belies a loss of subjective awareness. Like any vacuous space, her psyche does not resonate. While an upright glass will ring when tapped, because it has resonance, not so "an inverted bowl." Because she lacks the echoes of self-awareness provided by internal speech, this speaker aligns herself with inert beings.

In the earliest section of this poem Sexton had described how the cracked mirror of her selfish death provided some self-definition.[8] Since the echo is an acoustic analogue of the mirror, one might expect self-awareness to issue from the reverberance of private rage. Yet her mind lacked this reverberating capacity. What saved her from isolation was communication with other people like John. His kitchen, representative of the informal family gathering place, refers to the poetry workshop where Sexton met other people like herself. The socialization provided by shared poetic expression was her cure.

Not only does the speaker gain ethos by describing her escape from solipsism. In this passage John is being flattered as the agent of deliverance. No longer is her mind a narcissistic mirror, because his workshop has provided a window to the outside world. By casting John as the rescuing knight of her story, Sexton makes it difficult for him to reject her arguments. He is transformed from a displeased teacher into a redeemer.

Having humbly pleaded the pathos of her situation, and having praised John as the hero of her self-transcendence, Sexton tries yet another method to sway her disapproving mentor. His admonition had been the pretext for this poem (cf. title), but now she offers an admonitory anecdote of her own:

> And if you turn away
> because there is no lesson here
> I will hold my awkward bowl,
> with all its cracked stars shining
> like a complicated lie,
> and fasten a new skin around it
> as if I were dressing an orange
> or a strange sun.

In this fourth section, Sexton somewhat reverses the student–teacher relationship. Earlier postures of self-abasement, confessional honesty, and flattery are forsaken for a gentle threat: "And if you → I will." She does not threaten to regress into her previous introversion, but promises to continue the exhibition of herself ("I will hold my awkward bowl") until she convinces John of her point. If necessary, she will forsake the naked truth for more ornamental verse ("dressing"), hoping to fire his imagination with her sunny new garments.

In this section the aesthetic quarrel between student and teacher emerges again. While Sexton prefers the honesty of subjective truth, however grotesque, John would opt for decorous poetic masks and subjects. And while she had praised him as her rescuer in section 3, now she implicates him in her possible downfall, insinuating that: either John must understand her need for self-disclosure or take responsibility for her relapse into solitude. This leaves the reader wondering: would the chivalric teacher who saved Sexton from the cave of herself toss her into solitary confinement again?

Another rhetorical feature of this passage is Sexton's imagery of dressing and undressing, which takes advantage of stereotypic male-female interaction. A lady should be, above all, modest. Yet this speaker confesses nakedness; she has disrobed herself as one would unpeel an orange. Such a vulnerable state calls for chivalrous conduct in her auditor. Unless he accepts this lady's proffered gift of herself, she will have to put on some clothes ("dressing") to maintain her decency.

What softens Sexton's contention of John's responsibility is that she does not resort to nasty threats. For example, the grotesque creature she could become is more comic than menacing. Rather than mutilate or victimize herself, she will employ a variant of the silent treatment. By donning the mask of a grotesque, she can show, rather than tell, John her meaning. Also, the image of cracked stars shining in the bowl of her head recalls a familiar comic strip convention. "Seeing stars" is the caricatured behavior of people who are dazed by losing consciousness or being in love.

Having exhausted the possibilities of her quasi-aggressive stance toward John, Sexton softens her tone even more in the fifth section and recapitulates the argument with which she began:

> Not that it was beautiful,
> but that I found some order there.
> There ought to be something special
> for someone
> in this kind of hope.

Although the speaker resumes her earlier posture of contrition and humility, there is evidence of growing hope in this passage. What had been introduced initially as "a certain sense of order" is now "some order" and the "accident of hope" is seen more definitely as "*this kind* of hope." One feature that betrays Sexton's growing confidence is her use of verbs. Before, she had urged that there "can be" hope in the revelation of sordid experience. Now she utters what sounds like a moral proclamation: there "*ought* to be" hope in her communiqués from Bedlam. This is justificative rhetoric. Not only does the speaker want approval and understanding, she sees her painful experience as a way to edify others; the mere fact of her survival should be heartening. For this reason she does not merely seek atonement, but lays claim to an exemplary status.

It is because the persona has acquired order and hope from her experience that she grows stable enough to counsel her literary mentor. In the final section, a soothing, almost superior apostrophe to John addresses him as "my dear." Throughout the poem Sexton has gradually strengthened her position relative to John until transcendent rhetoric finally draws him and all persons into her purview:

> This is something I would never find
> in a lovelier place, my dear,
> although your fear is anyone's fear,
> like an invisible veil between us all . . .
> and sometimes in private,
> my kitchen, your kitchen,
> my face, your face.

Mildness and defiance coexist in this passage. Although Sexton is tender toward John, she insists that she could never accept an alternative route. Her path to poetic truth is fated and irrevocable.

Moreover, her aesthetic position has universal value and is reiterated in a poem of *All My Pretty Ones*. This second apologia for confessional verse, "With Mercy for the Greedy," defines all poems as part of the tongue's continuing wrangle for justification.

In this final section of her apologia the persona mixes forgiveness with accusation. On the one hand, John's frailty in facing the unknown is excused, since anyone might fear as he does. This is a form of bolstering that diagnoses his reservations about self-disclosure as a universal malaise. Yet in this seemingly gracious pardon are the seeds of accusation: John's flawed character makes him seem rather commonplace, and not an ideal source of moral or aesthetic advice. His ethos is reduced.

Juxtaposed against John's fear of openness, Sexton's brazen disclosure is transformed into an act of courage. Discovering the worst of anyone may offer the accident of hope, while fear is the invisible veil that blocks out the light of truth or the hope of reform. Surely there is irony in this reversal of pardoner-petitioner roles. Even as Sexton forgives her mentor, she classifies his reservations about her writing as a brand of cowardice. What makes her impudence rhetorically workable is the indefinite pronoun "anyone's," which implies that Sexton also shares John's frailty. This pronoun transcends division, absorbing all parties into a generic condition of mutual weakness. In a way, she has sought the ultimate acquittal (or the ultimate cop-out), by classifying her differences with John as part of a fateful condition analogous to classical (Greek) necessity.

The persona's graphic image of fear establishes an impersonal, material force, and a sense of foreboding. For although she has evolved from her former isolation, meeting John's objections with reasonableness and calm, the veil of fear could close them off at any moment. Defensive capacities are a resource that prevent one from suffering unwarranted rejection. But such protective devices can also create isolation. Although the relationship between John and the persona seems reconciled for the moment, it is still vulnerable to the inevitable breakdowns which separate human beings. At any time, without warning, the curtain of estrangement may drop, eclipsing the open light that fosters honest fellowship.[9] One is left wondering if, given

Sexton's aesthetic position as a confessional writer, she considers the poetic mask to be just another unnecessary veil between people.

A poem which began gingerly, as an attempt to attune a damaged human relationship, ends with a transcendent strategy that draws all humanity into the curse of threatened isolation. Sexton's problem, and thus her solution, is enlarged to include much more than a teacher-student controversy. This is an open, contrite piece, which initially seeks to win favor for poetry of personal revelation but ends on a note of universal edification.

"For John . . ." solves a difficult rhetorical task. The persona must do penance for the derogatory charge of an authority figure, while maintaining enough integrity to defend her work against his charges. To appease John's hostility, Sexton avoids stridency and uses the humble rhetoric of contrition. Yet the terms of her opposing aesthetic position are established right away: Poetry must first bring order and truth; conventional beauty is a secondary attribute. To prove this point, rhetoric of apologia comes into play.

The speaker's contrition is apparent in her various attempts to win mercy, forgiveness, and renewed fellowship. For example, images of shattered glass communicate Sexton's sense of vulnerability and act as a buffer against further criticism. But the self-defense of this poem is persistent, as well as polite. In the end it is clear that moral exhortation, however humbly veiled, is a strong rhetorical feature of Sexton's plea. Far from seeking mere absolution or vindication, she wants her action to be universally justified. Moving away from the particulars of John's accusation, she shows his objections in a context of general reproof. They are based on the fear of self-exposure. From this vantage, her controversial poetic revelations are implicitly transformed into edifying, heroic acts.

NOTES

1. This is a quotation from "Kind Sir: These Woods" *(Bedlam)*, where Sexton describes her psychological probe as an endeavor that meets with general disapproval.

2. For information about the autobiographical context of this poem,

see Beverly Fields's article "The Poetry of Anne Sexton," in *Poets in Progress,* edited by Edward Hungerford (Evanston: Northwestern University Press, 1967), 258. Fields comments: "After Anne Sexton had written the long poem 'The Double Image,' she showed it to her teacher John Holmes, who was angry and dismayed to find her revealing so much of herself in her verse and attempted to prevent her publishing it." Fields explains that Sexton's answer to him was "For John, Who Begs Me Not to Enquire Further."

3. Barbara Kevles, "The Art of Poetry XV: Anne Sexton," *Paris Review,* no. 52 (Summer 1971):166.

4. Kevles, 166.

5. In her interview with Kevles, Sexton explains the positive influence that Holmes's poetry class had on her life: "After I'd been writing about three months, I dared to go into the poetry class at the Boston Center for Adult Education taught by John Holmes. . . . The most important aspect of that class was that I felt I belonged somewhere. When I first got sick and became a displaced person, I thought I was quite alone, but when I went into the mental hospital, I found I wasn't, that there were other people like me. It made me feel better—more real, sane. I felt, 'These are my people.' Well, at the John Holmes class that I attended for two years, I found I belonged to the poets, that I was *real* there, and I had another, 'These are my people'" (164).

6. "Taboo and Emotional Ambivalence," in *Totem and Taboo (1913 [1912–13]), The Complete Psychological Works of Sigmund Freud,* vol. 13 (London: Hogarth Press, 1955), 56.

7. Sexton's image of her mind as an inverted glass dome has much in common with the central image of Sylvia Plath's novel *The Bell Jar* (London: Faber and Faber, 1966). The heroine of this story explains to the reader (196) that she is beset by mental isolation: ". . . wherever I sat . . . I would be sitting under the same glass bell jar, stewing in my own sour air." It was the stifling distortion of the bell jar which drove Esther to attempt suicide, and toward the end of her story (250) Esther says: "To the person in the bell jar, blank and stopped as a dead baby, the world itself is the bad dream."

8. Anthony Wilden, translator of *The Language of the Self: The Function of Language in Psychoanalysis* (Baltimore: Johns Hopkins University Press, 1968), by Jacques Lacan, describes Lacan's theory of the "stade du miroir." (See Wilden's commentary on p. 144 of the text.) This theory refers to the child's startling realization that his mirrored image is something other than and outside of himself. Such a sense of the self as something to be observed objectively helps form personal ideals and the awareness that other people are outside one's immediate consciousness and control. In the poem being discussed, Sexton's capacity

to see herself objectively in the "cracked mirror" is a prelude to mental health.

9. In this poem Sexton personifies fear as a material determinant of human separation. This determinacy is featured in another poem called "Imitations of Drowning" *(Live or Die):*

> There is no news in fear
> but in the end it's fear
> that drowns you.

GARY BLANKENBURG

Anne Sexton
The Voice of Illness

It would be an overstatement to say that Anne Sexton writes only of mental, physical, and spiritual illness; however, it would not be much of an overstatement. The title of her earliest book, *To Bedlam and Part Way Back,* supports a notion that is very prevalent in confessional poetry: once one has "cracked," once he has been "to bedlam," he can never fully recover regardless of the number or the sincerity of his attempts; he can only get "part way" back home, but never can he reach that home from which he departed. It seems that madness begins with the loss of innocence through exposure to a contaminated world, that madness is intensified by a self-defeating intellectual curiosity that leads, in turn, to the burden of insight, and that the final straw is the resulting self-examination and introspection that fail to bring health or the recovery of home, a former state of well-being.

NOON WALK ON THE ASYLUM LAWN

The summer sun ray
shifts through a suspicious tree.
though I walk through the valley of the shadow
It sucks the air
and looks around for me.

The grass speaks.
I hear green chanting all day.
I will fear no evil, fear no evil

From "A Rhetorical Approach to Confessional Poetry: Plath, Sexton, Lowell, Berryman, and Snodgrass" (Ph.D. diss., Carnegie-Mellon University, 1983). Edited version reprinted by permission of the author.

The blades extend
and reach my way.

The sky breaks.
It sags and breathes upon my face.
in the presence of mine enemies, mine enemies.
The world is full of enemies.
There is no safe place.

"Noon Walk on the Asylum Lawn" (in *To Bedlam and Part Way Back*) finds the "cracked" and "broken" persona confined to a mental hospital; rhetorically, the "split" in the persona is evidenced by the presence of two voices at work: the main voice describing how it feels to walk on the asylum lawn and an interior voice repeating scattered lines from Psalm 23. The main voice in "Noon Walk" is a paranoid one; even though it is a sunny, summer day, the "sun ray / shifts through a suspicious tree." The sun doesn't shine; it "shifts," suggesting that there is something "shifty" about even the sun, something that the persona can't trust. This inconstancy is expected from the moon because that is her way, but that the constant and reliable sun should "shift" seems like an ultimate betrayal. The "sun ray" not only "looks around for" the persona, but it also "sucks the air." Sadly, the persona blames the sun, the source of life, for her lack of breath and breathing space—she is like Plath's Esther Greenwood suffocating under "the bell jar." The subjective mind of the persona knows that her feelings are very real and must project the threat to her upon something tangible—the sun, a false enemy—rather than upon her very mind, her world vision, that is her own worst enemy. There is, moreover, a strong sense of ego here in that the sun, according to the persona, "looks around for me," not for any of the other inmates. The grass is also a threat. The persona hears "green chanting all day," the grass chanting ominously as a Greek chorus, a foreboding prefiguration of the doom and tragedy to come. She then notices that "the blades extend / and reach [her] way," the implication being that they are capable of cutting her, in fact may want to cut her.

The Sexton persona also regards the sky fearfully, for "it sags and breathes upon [her] face." In the midst of all this negative personification of nature—a shifty sun that vampirelike sucks what is necessary for life, "a suspicious tree," "chanting" grass with "blades," and a sky that "sags and breathes"—the only conclusion to come to is that "the world is full of enemies. / There is no safe place."

Psalm 23, often considered the most comforting of the psalms, does not soothe the persona. As she walks under the tree, her inner voice repeats, *"though I walk through the valley of the shadow."* It is "the shadow of death" that haunts her. The "green chanting" that she hears makes her think, *"I will fear no evil, fear no evil,"* but she does not conclude the line with "for thou art with me." No one is with the persona, she says in stanza 3, *"in the presence of mine enemies, mine enemies."* "Thou preparest a table before me" is the missing introduction to the words that she remembers; for, of course, the persona can find no table prepared for her. Though both poems are pastoral, Sexton's poem is totally antithetical to the meaning of the psalm: the "green pastures" of the psalm act as a foil to the "asylum lawn," and "the house of the Lord," an eternally safe asylum, is juxtaposed with the asylum itself, "no safe place." In her paranoia, the persona has taken only those lines from the psalm that support her present world view, which is inseparable from the omnipresence of death, illness, evil, and enemies. Like the voice heard in Eliot's "The Hollow Men," attempting to remember the words to "The Lord's Prayer," this Sexton persona has likewise forgotten, or has elected to forget, the most crucial and saving words of Psalm 23.

JAMES DICKEY

Review of *All My Pretty Ones*

In Anne Sexton's work the main sense is that of indignity—of being outraged by the world and its henchmen, like surgeons and alcoholic lovers and dying parents. It would be hard to find a writer who dwells more insistently on the pathetic and disgusting aspects of bodily experience, as though this made the writing more real, and it would also be difficult to find a more hopelessly mechanical approach to reporting these matters than the one she employs.

Her attitude, widely cited as "compassionate," is actually a curious compound of self-deprecatory cynicism and sentimentality-congratulating-itself-on-not-being-caught, as when Mrs. Sexton sees her stomach, after surgery, as being "laced up like a football / for the game" (as though footballs were laced up for games) or when she says to "K. Owyne": "I washed lobster and stale gin / off your shirt. We lived in sin / in too many rooms." Most of Mrs. Sexton's book is like this; her recourse to the studiedly off-hand diction favored by Randall Jarrell and Elizabeth Bishop and her habitual gravitation to the domestic and the "anti-poetic" seem to me as contrived and mannered as any romantic poet's harking after galleons and sunsets and forbidden pleasures.

The confessional quality in much recent verse, of which the works of Robert Lowell and W. D. Snodgrass are also cases in point, is giving rise to a new kind of orthodoxy as tedious as the garden-and-picture-gallery school of the forties and fifties. Though it is eminently orthodox in this respect, Mrs. Sexton's work seems to be very little more than a kind of terribly serious and determinedly outspoken soap-opera, and as such will undoubtedly have an appeal in some quarters.

From "Dialogues with Themselves," *New York Times Book Review*, April 28, 1963. Copyright © 1963 by The New York Times Company. Reprinted by permission.

CECIL HEMLEY

Review of *All My Pretty Ones*

The most memorable poems in Anne Sexton's new book in-
volve death and the response to death. The title of the volume is
taken from the scene in *Macbeth* in which MacDuff, learning of
the entire extinction of his family, cries out "All my pretty
ones?" in a poignant exclamation of disbelief. How this relates
to Mrs. Sexton is made explicit in the dedication to the very first
poem, "The Truth the Dead Know": "For my mother, born
March 1902, died March 1959, and my father, born February
1900, died June 1959." It is easy to understand how so much
catastrophe coming so quickly can create crisis. Mrs. Sexton's
book is a record of her crisis.

> Gone, I say and walk from church,
> refusing the stiff procession to the grave,
> letting the dead ride alone in the hearse.
> It is June. I am tired of being brave.

The sure attack, the fine use of sound, make it clear from the
start that Mrs. Sexton is a lyricist of power. If one does not read
carefully and accepts the hypnotic music of the lines, one can
even think one is reading a conventional elegy. But of course the
poem is no such thing. Earlier epochs would have found it im-
mensely shocking. Not only does the mourner refuse to accom-
pany the body to the grave, but she drives off to the Cape to
"cultivate myself where the sun gutters from the sky." We are in
a post-Christian world where ceremonial has ceased to be
important and death is something one seeks to dismiss from
one's mind.

There is no doubt that the poet wants us to associate herself
with the "I" of the poem; it is Anne Sexton who has not driven

Reprinted by permission from "A Return to Reality," *The Hudson Review,* Vol.
XV, No. 4 (Winter 1962–63). Copyright © 1963 by The Hudson Review, Inc.

to the cemetery. This identification with the writer has the advantage of intensifying our feelings, but the disadvantage of embarrassing us slightly. There were good reasons why past eras were reticent on such matters. However, the poem rises above the confession and achieves great beauty. For one thing the serious tone of the verses shows that the refusal to mourn is not successful. The mourner does not escape her grief. She is haunted.

Mrs. Sexton has a fine gift for metaphor and in this poem she is at her best. "In another country people die," she tells us. It is not only forcefully said, but true. The death of the psyche, if indeed it does occur, is never witnessed. She goes on to ask:

> And what of the dead? They lie without shoes
> in their stone boats. They are more like stone
> than the sea would be if it stopped.

These lines I think are an example of Mrs. Sexton's power of creating images that are amazingly suggestive. She is on the Cape looking out at the sea. The dead are in stone boats, and actually they are enclosed. Presumably then they are sailing. But not on the sea that she is watching. They are surely sailing away from her in time. And this in a sense is what she wants. But she remains haunted by their stillness and their unknowability. The sea that she is watching could become dead also but its calm would not be as frozen as the stone faces she has looked upon.

Anyone who has experienced the shock of bereavement will realize that Anne Sexton has captured the feelings of the recent mourner marvellously. The landscape becomes infected with death; death enters the brain. But yet the fact of death remains incomprehensible. The corpse that one viewed is not one's loved one. So Anne Sexton writes of ghosts, of the search for religious consolation which she rejects because "need is not quite belief." No wonder she suffers nervous collapse. She is the mourner who cannot stop mourning. The very first word in the book is "gone," and the last poem, viewing the catastrophe from a year later, finds the dead still present.

> Dearest,
> It is snowing, grotesquely snowing,

upon the small faces of the dead.
Those dear loudmouths, gone for over a year,
buried side by side
like little wrens.
But why should I complain?
The dead turn over casually,
thinking . . .

There is a terrifying quality to these lines, for the dead are not accepted as dead, but are viewed as incarcerated in the earth. They have an underground existence which is not that of spirits. The snow is falling on them. Perhaps this is the way secular man is doomed to view death. He cannot give up the reality of those he has held dear, but can find no container in which the past is held. Mrs. Sexton is a ruthlessly honest poet of great ability. Her book is both shocking and poignant.

RALPH J. MILLS, JR.

Anne Sexton

Anne Sexton is, by any standards, a bold and impressive poet.
At first glance, the unsuspecting reader may be jolted by the self-
revelation that so plainly serves as the basic raw material of her
art. To be sure, we have already discussed personal disclosure as
it is variously employed in the writing of Robert Lowell,
Brother Antoninus, Denise Levertov, and James Wright; but
few poets—perhaps Lowell and Antoninus are the chief excep-
tions—have attempted to convey the feeling of the continuity of
a single life, the poet's own, in something approximating its full
complexity. Undisguised revelation and examination—of her
parents, her lovers, her friends; of the unbelievable torment of
both mental and physical illness as she has had to endure them;
of her struggles with a religious belief that eludes her but doesn't
leave her; of the face of death as she has frequently seen it—
comprise Mrs. Sexton's poetic cosmos. The eye the poet brings
to bear on these contents of her life is mercilessly lucid; yet she
can be compassionate toward others and is without self-pity.
Her life, as must be clear by now, has been graced only slightly
with what we ordinarily conceive as happiness; its occasional
joys and moments of tenderness are wrung from the general
pain of experience. Yet these pleasures and affections are the
more precious because of the cost involved in obtaining them,
and also because of the poet's strong love which brings them
about in spite of the odds. Mrs. Sexton has further discovered an
ability to introduce order into existence, to allow valued things
to survive through the imaginative act that in the making of a
poem can create its own patterns of justice, meaning, and love.

From *Contemporary American Poetry* (New York: Random House, 1965). Re-
printed by permission of the author.

Lacking a firm religious faith, she seeks in the performance of her work a redeeming task:

> My friend, my friend, I was born
> doing reference work in sin, and born
> confessing it. This is what poems are:
> with mercy
> for the greedy,
> they are the tongue's wrangle,
> the world's pottage, the rat's star.
>
> ("With Mercy for the Greedy")

In her first book, *To Bedlam and Part Way Back* (1960), Anne Sexton concentrates her sharp and fertile imagination a number of times on the period of her mental illness and hospitalization, as well as on the effects of this illness in her relationships with others (her daughter and mother, for instance, in "The Double Image"). One of the best poems directly treating the subject, "Ringing the Bells," should help to demonstrate, through its frighteningly realistic picture of therapy at a hospital, the kind of marvelous artistic proficiency combined with an uncompromising vision of human actuality that we can usually expect of Mrs. Sexton. The mixture of simplicity and sophistication in rhythm and diction, building up through one long sentence, terrible in its understatement, and concluding in another, three-word sentence that compresses all the agony and helplessness and resignation of her dilemma, exhibits this poet's brilliant technical mastery, in addition to her toughness of mind, to real advantage:

> And this is the way they ring
> the bells in Bedlam
> and this is the bell-lady
> who comes each Tuesday morning
> to give us a music lesson
> and because the attendants make you go
> and because we mind by instinct,
> like bees caught in the wrong hive,
> we are the circle of the crazy ladies
> who sit in the lounge of the mental house

and smile at the smiling woman
who passes us each a bell,
who points at my hand
that holds my bell, E flat,
and this is the grey dress next to me
who grumbles as if it were special
to be old, to be old,
and this is the small hunched squirrel girl
on the other side of me
who picks at the hairs over her lip,
who picks at the hairs over her lip all day,
and this is how the bells really sound,
as untroubled and clean
as a workable kitchen,
and this is always my bell responding
to my hand that responds to the lady
who points at me, E flat;
and although we are no better for it,
they tell you to go. And you do.

A few poems, such as "You, Doctor Martin" and "Said the Poet to the Analyst," present different, and less harrowing, accounts of her days of hospitalization and psychiatric treatment. Still other poems like "Music Swims Back to Me" and "Her Kind" undertake to render the author's disturbed psychic and spiritual states; certain less directly focused poems like "The Double Image" and "Lullaby" occasionally touch this theme. This spell of confinement and the poems dealing with it provide merely one part of the life Mrs. Sexton suggests to us. She sometimes includes poems that do not depend upon her biography but are efforts to step into more objective dramatic or lyrical roles; but these pieces are, in my opinion, generally weaker because so much of this poet's power lies in her talent for dramatizing *her own* existence in the wide range of its moods, memories, relationships, aspirations, desires, and for doing this without evading the necessary consequence of having to face herself squarely in the mirror of her art.

Mrs. Sexton also devotes poems in this first book to her parents and other close relatives, a practice that carries over into her next collection. She traces with the utmost scrupulousness her own attitudes in these family relations. What we get, in a phrase borrowed from the title of a poem about the poet, her daughter, and her mother, is a type of "double image," in which the subject of the particular poem and, simultaneously, the poet's ties with and approach to that subject are sketched. Through this indirect but revelatory method we learn even more about the poet herself.

The predominant mood of the family poems is elegiac. Mrs. Sexton's parents are both dead—her mother died of cancer, her father died a few months after her mother; her brother was killed on a beachhead during the war;* the great aunt she loved so fiercely in her childhood succumbed to deafness and to a resulting mental breakdown. Thus the poetry founded on such figures is one of bittersweet memory and loss. The elegy for her brother, "For Johnny Pole on the Forgotten Beach," admirably exhibits these qualities. The poem starts out with a fairly long stanza of pleasant recollections of summers on the beach as children. There they rode the breakers in, sunned themselves, and dreamed their futures. The boy's last name even becomes evocative of youth, stalwartness, and masculine potentiality as the poet describes him:

> In his tenth July some instinct
> taught him to arm the waiting wave,
> a giant where its mouth hung open.
> He rode on the lip that buoyed him there
> and buckled him under. The beach was strung
> with children paddling their ages in,
> under the glare of noon chipping
> its light out. He stood up, anonymous
> and straight among them, between
> their sand pails and nursery crafts.
> The breakers cartwheeled in and over
> to puddle their toes and test their perfect
> skin. He was my brother, my small
> Johnny brother, almost ten. We flopped
> down upon a towel to grind the sand
> under us and watched the Atlantic sea

---

*Sexton had no brother.—ED.

> move fire, like night sparklers;
> and lost our weight in the festival
> season. He dreamed, he said, to be
> a man designed like a balanced wave . . .
> how someday he would wait, giant
> and straight.
>
> Johnny, your dream moves summers
> inside my mind.

Following the brief transition in the last lines above, the poem leaps across another decade in the poet's memory. The scene of the second long stanza is again a beach, but this one Mrs. Sexton has had to imagine for herself in all its horror and waste. At its edge is sprawled the dead body of her brother, aged twenty. With an overwhelming yet deft irony she introduces words and images recalling the happy innocence and human possibility of the earlier stanza into the depiction of its tragic outcome. The beach, the youthful bodies with their connotation of life's copious physical vitality, the waves, the bright, warm sunlight of another ocean, and the posture of the brother are warped out of recognition—or perhaps we should say that they are still recognizable enough to thrust their terrible implication upon us:

> He was tall and twenty that July,
> but there was no balance to help;
> only the shells came straight and even.
> This was the first beach of assault;
> the odor of death hung in the air
> like rotting potatoes; the junkyard
> of landing craft waited open and rusting.
> The bodies were strung out as if they were
> still reaching for each other, where they lay
> to blacken, to burst through their perfect
> skin. And Johnny Pole was one of them.
> He gave in like a small wave, a sudden
> hole in his belly and the years all gone
> where the Pacific ocean chipped its light out.
> Like a bean bag, outflung, head loose
> and anonymous, he lay. Did the sea move fire
> for its battle season? Does he lie there

forever, where his rifle waits, giant
and straight? . . . I think you die again
and live again,

Johnny, each summer that moves inside
my mind.

In poem after poem Mrs. Sexton discloses to us her mind
populated and haunted, as it is in this elegy for her brother, by
persons and events of the past, reviving them in the act of writ-
ing and so bringing to them through her imagination the mutual
effort of love and understanding. That is true of the pair of
poems about her mother with which her initial book finishes,
and likewise fits several pieces in *All My Pretty Ones* (1962) about
her father and her family life when she was a girl. Another early
poem, "Some Foreign Letters," develops a very moving de-
scription of the poet's great aunt from a group of letters she left
behind. In Paul Engle's and Joseph Langland's anthology *Poet's
Choice,* Mrs. Sexton has made some observations about this
poem:

> "Some Foreign Letters" is a mixture of truth and lies. I
> don't feel like confessing which is which. When I wrote it I
> attempted to make all of it "true." It remains true *for me* to
> this day. But I will say that it was written to my great aunt
> who came to live with us when I was about nine and very
> lonely. She stayed with us until she had a nervous break-
> down. This was triggered by her sudden deafness. I was sev-
> enteen at the time she was taken away. She was, during the
> years she lived with us, my best friend, my teacher, my confi-
> dante and my comforter. I never thought of her as being
> young. She was an extension of myself and was my world. I
> hadn't considered that she might have had a world of her own
> once. Many years later, after her death, I found a bound
> volume of her letters from Europe. (My family were the type
> that bound letters in leather.) The letters are gay and intimate
> and tragic.

As the poem begins Mrs. Sexton sits perusing the dead aunt's
letters and, at the same time, remembering the aunt as she knew
her in old age. The world this aunt so freely traveled and the

experiences she recorded in her correspondence come to the poet out of a "graceful innocent age," one the latter "loved," as she notes in *Poet's Choice,* "but never knew." The opening stanza then goes on to offer a summary picture based on the letters that captures beautifully and succinctly the flavor of life for this New England woman journeying through Europe at the end of the nineteenth century. We need also to see how Mrs. Sexton keeps us conscious both of her presence as a reader of the letters and as the person who recalls a later phase of the aunt's life and so can contrast it with the earlier.

> You posted them first in London, wearing furs
> and a new dress in the winter of eighteen-ninety.
> I read how London is dull on Lord Mayor's Day,
> where you guided past groups of robbers, the sad holes
> of Whitechapel, clutching your pocketbook, on the way
> to Jack the Ripper dissecting his famous bones.
> This Wednesday in Berlin, you say, you will
> go to a bazaar at Bismarck's house. And I
> see you as a young girl in a good world still,
> writing three generations before mine. I try
> to reach into your page and breathe it back . . .
> but life is a trick, life is a kitten in a sack.

The final line of this stanza predicts the fate awaiting the young lady traveler, first in disappointments, ultimately in her sudden attack of deafness and nervous collapse. Indications of Johnny Pole's destiny are not so obvious in the first half of the poem about him. The trick of fate is nearly a commonplace in Mrs. Sexton's work, as apparently it has been in her experience. The "kitten in a sack," one of this poet's most unbalancing metaphors, points to human helplessness in the grip of forces that unexpectedly twist individual lives from their normal course, threaten them, or lead them to conclusion without warning. We are all, the implication runs, included in the image of that kitten imprisoned in a sack and will be drowned at last. However, any translation of the line's significance pales next to the line itself; Mrs. Sexton uses her metaphor to great effect. As she muses on her aunt's letters the past and future (though both of these are now periods of the past from the writer's location in time) fall together, with a death in between: the beloved aunt has escaped "the sack of time" and left the poet to bind the pieces of her life for her.

The poem continues, and further excerpts from the aunt's European travels turn up, occasionally interrupted by the poet's memories of the dissolution of what that lady had known and been:

> This is Italy. You learn its mother tongue.
> I read how you walked on the Palatine among
> the ruins of the palaces of the Caesars;
> alone in the Roman autumn, alone since July.
> When you were mine they wrapped you out of here
> with your best hat over your face. I cried
> because I was seventeen. I am older now.

In the last years of her life she had come to stay with Mrs. Sexton's parents, as the remarks from *Poet's Choice* explain. The aunt's world, the world of the 1880s, as the poet sees, had long since crumbled into an unfamiliar and disastrous age. This old lady's expectations, the most important ones, have gone unfulfilled. Her romance with a German count was fruitless. She finishes as a spinster great-aunt loved by a young girl who, much later, will discover her letters and start to comprehend her life. In the closing stanza Mrs. Sexton summons with dexterity and deeply felt emotion the pathos of a person's existence whose hopes have dispersed and whose conclusion is near. In spite of the inevitable human failure, the poet's love and sympathy reinforce the aunt's persistent endeavor to speak her own truth, and lend this last stanza a sense of redemption:

> Tonight I will learn to love you twice;
> learn your first days, your mid-Victorian face.
> Tonight I will speak up and interrupt
> your letters, warning you that wars are coming,
> that the Count will die, that you will accept
> your America back to live like a prim thing
> on the farm in Maine. I tell you, you will come
> here, to the suburbs of Boston, to see the blue-nose
> world go drunk each night, to see the handsome

children jitterbug, to feel your left ear close
one Friday at Symphony. And I tell you,
you will tip your boot feet out of that hall,
rocking from its sour sound, out onto
the crowded street, letting your spectacles fall
and your hair net tangle as you stop passers-by
to mumble your guilty love while your ears die.

Redemption, as was previously suggested, arrives by the poem, so far as Mrs. Sexton is concerned. In her poetry character, motive, and experience receive evaluation and judgment; in this respect she is one of those poets who seems to be winning back property that fiction writers had almost completely annexed. And, of course, Mrs. Sexton is presenting a segment of her own life when she portrays her aunt or some other person, for that life is the true origin of her poetry.

Anne Sexton's new poems, gathered in *All My Pretty Ones* (the title of which, taken from *Macbeth,* suggests a preoccupation with death and ruin), though they sacrifice none of their harsh devotion to the facts of experience, do enter some different areas of her life as well as resuming prior explorations. Several notable poems are given over to her family relationships when she was a girl; her father is portrayed, as her mother was in the preceding book. In "The Truth the Dead Know," an elegy for both parents, she leaves the place of their death and burial in an attempt to regain, by geographical change and the play of the senses, her awareness of being alive:

We drive to the Cape. I cultivate
myself where the sun gutters from the sky,
where the sea swings in like an iron gate
and we touch. In another country people die.

Nature seems barely to agree with human wishes in these lines: the guttering sun, the mechanical motion of the sea are, at best, indifferent; at worst, sinister. Human contact does, however, provide momentary relief before the final stanza puts us back where we began with the disquieting question, "And what of the dead?" That stanza ends with the poet's realization of her small comforts of the flesh that her mother and father, by dying, have relinquished: "They refuse / to be blessed, throat, eye and knucklebone."

The truth the dead know in the poem of that title contributes an integral part of the knowledge with which Mrs. Sexton tries to meet her experience. Such recognition of mortality colors the whole of her vision, even though she is still quite capable of salvaging images of beauty from the prospect of general destruction. The life of the body and the temporary warmth of love it can feel are always endangered by the exacting costs of time or by disorder and loss. Again, in the somewhat longer poem "The Operation," the poet takes as a point of departure the grim coincidence that she too is suspected of having cancer just a short while after her mother's death from the disease. Once she submits to the indignities of the doctor's examination, the precariousness of existence has become a fundamental theme:

> After the sweet promise,
> the summer's mild retreat
> from mother's cancer, the winter months of her death,
> I come to this white office, its sterile sheet,
> its hard tablet, its stirrups, to hold my breath
> while I, who must, allow the glove its oily rape,
> to hear the almost mighty doctor over me equate
> my ills with hers
> and decide to operate.

The next stanzas look retrospectively over her mother's illness and the last months of her life. At the opening of the second section we are confronted with the poet prepared for surgery, her body deprived of its identity: she hangs suspended, a floating consciousness in a flesh gone alien, between memories of past pleasure and a future in which she has no certainty of existing. Waiting fills her mind with nightmares of tense expectancy:

> Clean of the body's hair,
> I lie smooth from breast to leg.
> All that was special, all that was rare
> is common here. Fact: death too is in the egg.

Fact: the body is dumb, the body is meat.
And tomorrow the O.R. Only the summer was sweet.

The rooms down the hall are calling
all night long, while the night outside
sucks at the trees. I hear limbs falling
and see yellow eyes flick in the rain. Wide eyed
and still whole I turn in my bin like a shorn lamb.
A nurse's flashlight blinds me to see who I am.

In these stanzas Mrs. Sexton apprehends within the human individual the seeds of his own decay and death. Like Dylan Thomas, who saw the conclusion of life contained in the instant of its conception, she thinks of herself in sacrificial terms, as "a shorn lamb." (A comparison of this sacrificial theme of surgery might profitably be made with W. D. Snodgrass's poem "The Operation.") And the operation realizes her premonitions as she passes into a bizarre universe where the spirit, lacking any control, must live out the victimized body's fate. The course pursued by her mind or spirit in an anaesthetic dream draws near to death, but then returns; the poet's self, cut and patched, is reborn to a world almost lost:

The great green people stand
over me; I roll on the table
under a terrible sun, following their command
to curl, head touching knee if I am able.
Next, I am hung up like a saddle and they begin.
Pale as an angel I float out over my own skin.

I soar in hostile air
over the pure women in labor,
over the crowning heads of babies being born.
I plunge down the backstair
calling *mother* at the dying door,
to rush back to my own skin, tied where it was torn.
Its nerves pull like wires
snapping from the leg to the rib.
Strangers, their faces rolling like hoops, require
my arm. I am lifted into my aluminum crib.

The poem closes with its author, her "stomach laced up like a football / for the game," getting ready to take up ordinary living again. But that resumption does not put an end to Mrs. Sexton's thought, nor does it resolve the problems to which she is heir. Given her acute sensitivity to human frailty, to the agonies built in men's bones which she knows so well and has stated so plentifully in her verse, we could guess that she must finally grapple with questions of supernatural belief. Indeed, in *To Bedlam and Part Way Back* the last poem, "The Division of Parts," entertains a comparison between the poet's sorting of goods her mother has willed her and the dividing of Christ's possessions after His crucifixion. The religious parallel is called up naturally because Mrs. Sexton notices that the day on which she is performing her difficult family duty is Good Friday. Her meditations prompt her to consider both her religious upbringing and her present state of skepticism:

> The clutter of worship
> that you taught me, Mary Gray,
> is old. I imitate
> a memory of belief
> that I do not own. I trip
> on your death and Jesus, *my stranger*
> floats up over
> my Christian home, wearing his straight
> thorn tree. I have cast my lot
> and am one third thief
> of you. Time, that rearranger
> of estates, equips
> me with your garments, but not with grief.

Mrs. Sexton's concern with faith extends to *All My Pretty Ones,* specifically to a series of poems grouped in one section of that book and prefaced by the following statement of the Catholic theologian Romano Guardini: "I want no pallid humanitarianism—If Christ be not God, I want none of him; I will hack my way through existence alone. . . ."

We cannot take it for granted that these words, written by a man of profound religious faith, automatically assert Mrs. Sexton's belief, when they would appear in fact to signify her selection of the alternative: stoicism, loneliness, and self-reliance. But if this is her choice, it has not been lightly made, as the poems of this group indicate. Three that strike at the very heart of Mrs. Sexton's interests involve the figure of Christ: "With Mercy for the Greedy," "For God While Sleeping," and "In the Deep Museum." Since she is a poet without mystical inclinations, but rather is earthbound, committed to a vision that shocks by its unvarnished realism, it is hardly surprising that she should approach religious belief through the person of Christ, who is, for her, the man claiming to be God and subjecting Himself to the extremes of bodily and spiritual torture as proof of His appointed task. He is the one who reminds her again of the destiny to which all flesh is ordered—death. The Christ she envisages so vividly recalls the beaten, ravaged images of the Crucifixion painted by Gruenewald and, in our own time, by Graham Sutherland. The poem "For God While Sleeping" displays the durable human emotion she feels for Christ. It first mentions the poet's own sickness, but shifts in revery to Jesus' sufferings. The brutal details should not be permitted to obscure Mrs. Sexton's compassion and the desire she has to resolve her troubled relationship with this crucified figure who inhabits her dreams:

> Sleeping in fever, I am unfit
> to know just who you are:
> hung up like a pig on exhibit,
> the delicate wrists,
> the beard drooling blood and vinegar;
> hooked to your own weight,
> jolting toward death under your nameplate.
>
> Everyone in this crowd needs a bath.
> I am dressed in rags.
> The mother wears blue. You grind your teeth
> and with each new breath
> your jaws gape and your diaper sags.
> I am not to blame
> for all this. I do not know your name.
>
> Skinny man, you are somebody's fault.
> You ride on dark poles—
> a wooden bird that a trader built

for some fool who felt
that he could make the flight. Now you roll
in your sleep, seasick
on your own breathing, poor old convict.

There is a development from the first hallucinatory images growing out of the poet's fitful sleep in the beginning stanza to a participation in the milling crowd witnessing the Crucifixion; then, after further comment on Christ which seems adverse but is really tender, the dream subsides. "Poor old convict" is not very clear and may suggest several meanings, the most likely of which is, I think, an identification of the poet's fate with that of Christ—that is, the conclusion of all human effort in failure and death. This identification is, of course, based on the premise that Christ's execution is an example of defeat for an idealist ("some fool who felt / that he could make the flight"), and so Mrs. Sexton's own skepticism remains unchanged. But these last lines are perhaps too confused, too much like a dream, for us to be certain of identities. In any case, the suffering caused by the poet's illness, her feverish condition, allows the vision to form and links her in feeling to the dying Christ. The next poem, "In the Deep Museum," retains the device of fantasy and nightmare speculation in order to articulate the thoughts of Jesus, who, having been crucified, awakens in the sepulchre only to die a more horrible and degrading death, a death that succeeds (if that is the poet's aim) in turning the idea of a Resurrection into a hideous mockery.

Mrs. Sexton's poetry, then, is built upon an attitude of stoic pessimism that occasionally lapses into morbidity; yet we cannot doubt the biting honesty of her intelligence or the truth *to her* of the intuitions around which her art is modeled. There is also a more delightful side to some of her work; this is particularly evident in the exuberant lyricism of "Letter Written on a Ferry While Crossing Long Island Sound." In this poem she imagines that four nuns who are fellow-passengers on the ferry without warning "rise out / over this greasy deck" and ascend into the sky above the open waters. Here are two stanzas that give the general atmosphere:

Dearest,
see how my dark girls sally forth,

over the passing lighthouse of Plum Gut,
its shell as rusty
as a camp dish,
as fragile as a pagoda
on a stone;
out over the little lighthouse
that warns me of drowning winds
that rub over its blind bottom
and its blue cover;
winds that will take the toes
and the ears of the rider
or the lover.

There go my dark girls,
their dresses puff
in the leeward air.
Oh, they are lighter than flying dogs
or the breath of dolphins;
each mouth opens gratefully,
wider than a milk cup.
My dark girls sing for this.
They are going up.

The poems Anne Sexton has published so far read like the pages of an autobiography in verse which expose her without defense, though this is true only if we accept for a moment that poetry *is* her mode of defense and self-comprehension. It is precisely this fact which saves her work from the weaknesses of exhibitionism or of vain subjectivity. The private experience that Mrs. Sexton holds up so courageously to frank, imaginative scrutiny falls outside her possession once the poem has been written: that experience is transformed into a public one, that is to say, one capable of illuminating the lives of each of us.

JEANNE H. KAMMER

The Witch's Life

*Confession and Control
in the Early Poetry of Anne Sexton*

With her death in 1974, Anne Sexton confirmed for many read-
ers her place among the group of confessional, suicidal poets
(Berryman, Plath, and Lowell, for example) who inhabit and
invest with their prophetic presence the troubled decades of the
middle century. Approaches to her poetry are often correspon-
dingly handicapped by the voyeuristic interest which followed
her last volumes toward their inevitable outcome. There is more
interest in the substance of her writing, it seems, than in its
craft—and the limbo area where art touches life appears more
ill-defined than ever. In order to see more clearly what she be-
came as a poet, it is helpful to return to the place where she
began—to the first collections, whose strongest poetry has set-
tled securely into the American tradition, and by which she was
first known to the current generation of students and scholars.

The most striking aspect of her first book, *To Bedlam and Part
Way Back,* is the regularity of form which characterizes most of
the poems in it. In a sequence marked by recurrent themes of
grief and loss, explicit in its depiction of physical and emotional
distress, the horror of the institutional experience, Sexton's use
of reiterated stanza patterns and complex rhyme schemes comes
as a surprise to the reader expecting a "free" confessional nar-
rative. Some of this may indeed be therapeutic; "The ingenuity
of shape," says Richard Howard, "has something of the basket-
weaver's patience about it, it is the work of a *patient*."[1] But it is
also true that, like her literary predecessors and with her strong-
est contemporaries, Sexton perceived the general dilemma of the
woman artist as characterized by the culture ("A woman who

Language and Style 13, no. 4 (1980). Reprinted by permission of the author.

writes feels too much . . ."), along with her personal vulnerability as a poet inclined to the confessional mode. She responded to both conditions, in the early years of apprenticeship and reputation-building, by imposing upon the stuff of her experience the boundary and counterpoint of intense poetic control.

"You, Doctor Martin," the opening poem of the collection and one of the strongest, is a good example of her technique and can stand close scrutiny. The voice of the "queen of this summer hotel" is full of the gleeful, murderous, placating tones of the inmate/patient, held in check by an orderly visual pattern. Sexton's habit is to allow an initial stanza to take its own shape, then to repeat that form in the ones which follow. Here, the visual enclosure is tidy and symmetrical:

> You, Doctor Martin, walk
> from breakfast to madness. Late August,
> I speed through the antiseptic tunnel
> where the moving dead still talk
> of pushing their bones against the thrust
> of cure. And I am queen of this summer hotel
> or the laughing bee on a stalk
> of death.

The apparent symmetry of the stanza is opposed, however, by the run-on lines and the failure of the whole to be, in the end, self-contained. The form is both an ironic extension and a contradiction of the content: It swings, like Doctor Martin and his patients, "from breakfast to madness," a ritual pacing, a pushing of the "bones against the thrust of cure." At the same time there is a denial of motion; the "moving dead" only *talk* of resistance, and the final pun on "stalk" (contrasting with Dr. Martin's free "walk" in the first line) conveys the speaker's double sense of herself as aggressor and victim, "queen" and prisoner.

Walk/stalk/talk—rhyme is an important element in Sexton's early poetry, because it is a game played against visual uniformity even as the appearance of regularity is maintained: the patient's riddle and the witch's web. While the shape of the stanzas may remain consistent throughout a poem as an element of visual control, the rhyme scheme shifts, doubles back, deceives the eye. In the later stanzas of "You, Doctor Martin," for example, the dominant walk/talk of the first is moved to a secondary position, then buried in syntax and masked by spelling variations and half-rhyme. It persists, nevertheless, as a reminder of the poem's main axis: the attempt of the individual to move, to speak, to escape, opposed by the immobility, silence, inexorable sameness, and containment of the institutional group.

By the end of the poem the same rhyme is acting (like Denise Levertov's "horizon note") as a constant in the background which centers theme and tone. "Doctor," after all, has sounded the initial note, which becomes "god of our block" in stanza 4, to be echoed again in "foxes"/"boxes" and the "foxy children." Near the end of the poem, the block/smock sound softens to frost/lost, but we find "talking," "forgotten," and "moccasins" reflecting and repeating earlier terms. It is a painful sound, repeated over and over, sometimes sharp and sometimes muffled, cut off even as it begins—an appropriate vehicle for the speech and the feeling of Bedlam.

Other patterns of internal rhyme support the poem's core of control and feeling: the sequence, for example, of "moving"/"pushing"/"laughing"/"cutting"/"breaking"/"talking" emphasizes the contradictory doubleness of the human-but-confined; the repetition of "moving"/"move"/"moves," is poignantly linked to "love" in the fourth stanza; there is a humorously punning opposition of "I" and "eye" (patient to doctor) stretched to a painful edge in the echoes of "lines"/"smiles"/ "whine" / "knives" / "lives" / "sky" / "lights"/"cry"/*"life"*; the casual "breakfast"/"thrust" of the first stanza reappears sarcastically, desperately in the last ones as "most"/"best"/"nest"/ "twist"/"frost"/*lost.*" The total effect, says Richard Howard, is of rhyme slightly off-balance, "roughed-up, abandoned when inconvenient, psychologically convincing" (445).

It is the last phase which is important to an understanding of Sexton's poetic choices, where matters of form and style are involved. Control, for Sexton, is not simply an antidote to autobiography, but also a vehicle for communicating the individual experience. It is a means of making strong poems—sturdy baskets—while telling the truth. Nearly all the pieces in this first collection exhibit a similar use of set, visually repetitive stanza forms with varying sorts of contrapuntal, expressive sound activity. They range from the self-generated shape and patterns of "You, Doctor Martin" to a thick, sixteen-line unit with heavy end-rhyme in "Some Foreign Letters" to the childlike litany of "Ringing the Bells." "Elizabeth Gone" is composed of two sonnets, and "Her Kind" employs a rhythmic, incantatory stanza and refrain. The poet's technical concern, in all of these, deflects the imagination from the pain of direct confrontation and denies the temptation to self-pity, even as the experience is relived and named. In her later work, even as she moves beyond the visual security of the reiterated stanza form and loosens her grip on meter and syntax, Sexton preserves this early discipline of internal control.

The *Bedlam* poems, after all, do not simply represent the therapy of intricate weaving, the "counting . . . of moccasins," although that element is certainly present. Rather, the riddle—the game of order in disorder, structure in chaos—is an important aspect of their peculiar stance: dramatically unstable, but determined to have an authority which form and style alone do not create. One source of that authority is found in another aspect of control in Sexton's work which is more difficult to dismiss as therapeutic in origin or mechanical in nature. By the time of her second volume, *All My Pretty Ones,* her instinctive sense of the striking opening phrase is matched by her knack for a closure which is powerful and precise. In both cases, the principles of understatement and economy are uppermost, and rooted in the placement of sharp images within tight, often minimal sentences.

Here is the first stanza of "The Operation":

> After the sweet promise,
> the summer's mild retreat
> from mother's cancer, the winter months of her death,
> I come to this white office, its sterile sheet,
> its hard tablet, its stirrups, to hold my breath
> while I, who must, allow the glove its oily rape,
> to hear the almost mighty doctor over me equate
> my ills with hers
> and decide to operate.

"Recall if you can," says Peter Davison, "The opening of any recent poem to match that for economy, fullness, and power in setting a scene."[2] We may notice once again the strong presence of rhyme: the most painful or shocking words are saved for the ends of lines and joined firmly, faced up to. At the same time, they comment ironically on one another: "Sweet . . . sheet," "rape . . . equate . . . operate." The play of the long line against the short, the enclosure of present details within a hazier past and future, intensify the emotional stress. From the deceptively "sweet promise, the summer's mild retreat," we come quickly to a catalogue of horrors: "this white office, its sterile sheet, its hard tablet, its stirrups. . . ." "To hold my breath," in the center, is a temporary death, imaging the mother's even as it is an ironic acting out, in a hostile setting, of the "little death" of sexual fulfillment ("the glove's oily rape"). "My ills," in line 8, is more than a literal, physical term—encompassing as it does a span of seasons, generations of fear and grief. The effect of the stanza's shape and movement is to focus all our attention on the last word: "operate" is both abstraction and image, familiar and ominous, flat and charged with emotion. The patient is exposed in her vulnerability even as the artist remains supreme in her control.

Other poems demonstrate the same capacity in Sexton to summon to opening lines the emotional core of an experience while economically setting forth its key images and issues. In "The Truth the Dead Know," she provides a headnote with the dates of her parents, who died within months of each other, then begins with these blunt lines:

> Gone, I say and walk from church,
> refusing the stiff procession to the grave,
> letting the dead ride alone in the hearse.
> It is June. I am tired of being brave.

"Letter Written on a Ferry While Crossing Long Island Sound" opens with the sarcastic, understated strength of this declaration:

> I am surprised to see
> that the ocean is still going on.

"The Starry Night" in swift strokes recalls to mind the painting which occasions the poem and at the same time recasts it in the speaker's private images and emotional landscape:

> The town does not exist
> except where one black-haired tree slips
> up like a drowned woman into the hot sky.

Sexton's impulse to crisp, direct statement is a way of not appearing over-emotional, where the subject is highly personal and intensely felt. It is also a tactic that invites the reader's recognition and curiosity, and demands a close attention. So, too, in her endings. The effectiveness of poetic closure is often a means of distinguishing between the gifted and the merely competent writers, the interesting poetry and the great. In the *Bedlam* volume, the endings of Sexton's poems are for the most part unmemorable, except for the few that set up a complex resonance and mark the best pieces:

> A woman like that is not ashamed to die.
> I have been her kind.
>
> ("Her Kind")

> Go child, who is my sin and nothing more.
> ("Unknown Girl in the Maternity Ward")

> Allah will not see
> how I hold my daddy
> like an old stone tree.
> ("The Moss of His Skin")

By the time of *All My Pretty Ones,* however, she is hitting the mark more consistently; many poems end with phrases that strike us as singularly appropriate, collecting the poem's force in a few well-placed final words. There is humor in "Woman With Girdle":

> straightway from God you have come
> into your redeeming skin.

tenderness in "I Remember":

> and what
> I remember best is that

> the door to your room was
> the door to mine.

Death and pain are met with characteristic understatement and irony:

> The supper dishes are over and the sun
> unaccustomed to anything else
> goes all the way down.
>
> ("Lament")

> and run along, Anne, and run along now,
> my stomach laced up like a football
> for the game.
>
> ("The Operation")

Rhyme remains a strong element in Sexton's closure, even if camouflaged or postponed; the last phrases are kept deliberately minimal, isolated carefully—apparently artless, but powerful in their simplicity. Again, the structure of lines and sentences causes us to focus on the final image each time, which provides the testimony of the senses for what has been said.

It should be apparent by now that the structural means by which Sexton maintains a firm command over material which is nakedly personal are consistently supported, in these volumes, by a texture of language which is often as lean and cryptic as that of an Emily Dickinson. Yet James Dickey, in reviewing the *Bedlam* poems, comments that "they lack concentration, and above all the profound, individual linguistic suggestibility and accuracy that poems must have to be good";[3] and Barbara Howes, from the opposite corner, complains that Sexton "has a habit, which may be mere carelessness, of using verbs ungrammatically or of wrenching them away from their usual meaning, and sometimes she twists words cruelly. . . ."[4] Some of this critical scoring may be explained in its context: Sexton suffered in the early 1960s from competition (almost book for book) with Denise Levertov, a more widely recognized and experienced poet, and with such "delicate" poets as Katherine Hoskins, noted for her coolness and restraint.[5]

Nevertheless, carelessness and lack of concentration are hardly terms which can apply to Sexton in these volumes, particularly where language is concerned. She employs a diction that is characteristically simple, strong, and colloquial, in what Richard Howard accurately terms a "lucid obstruction to sentimentality" (447); a good example is found in "The Operation":

> There was snow everywhere.
> Each day I grueled through
> its sloppy peak, its blue-struck days, my boots
> slapping into hospital halls, past the retinue
> of nurses at the desk, to murmur in cahoots
> with hers outside her door, to enter with the outside
> air stuck on my skin, to enter smelling her pride,
> her upkeep, and to lie
> as all who love have lied.

The "ungrammatical" use of "grueled," the coinage of "blue-struck," the unusual sense of "upkeep" are all part of the effort to portray accurately the distorted hospital world, to preserve the delicate balance of feeling and saying required of patients, staff, and visitors.

Language in general for Sexton appears bound up with the act of *seeing,* of accurate observation and naming—truth sought out and confronted, reflected in the solidity of the printed word, the appropriate image. "Perception," says the poet Marvin Bell in a recent essay on the art, "has two meanings: sight and insight. I believe that both sight and insight derive from fierce consciousness, whether it begins in looking at a small object or in paying attention to all of the implications and resonances of an idea or image."[6] For Sexton a "fierce consciousness" of the real world as well as of the individual word was inextricably linked with self-consciousness as we find it in her literary ancestors: Dickinson, H.D., Marianne Moore.

"*See* how she sits on her knees all day," she says in "Housewife"; "let us consider the *view,*" in "From the Garden"; "*see* them rise on black wings" in "Letter Written on a Ferry. . . ." And the loon (crazy, ridiculous among birds) landing awkwardly in "Water" goes under "calling, I have *seen,* I have *seen.*" The contemporary need, of which Bell speaks, to *get closer to* rather than to accumulate more of poetic detail (38) is strong in Sexton and in the peculiar sort of confessional tradition associated with poets like Dickinson: the self revealed in the craft of the poem even more than in its content. It is also an effort to escape both self and outer world by getting *through* the image in the word—the same attempt described in Gerard Manley Hopkins's process of "inscape" and celebrated by Denise Levertov in the poetry of H.D.—to a still place of clarity and peace.

In these early books, however, the habit of seeing and of finding the precise words to articulate insight is primarily another means of control in a world which otherwise appears subjective, inchoate. In her later books, sight intensifies to vision, and is coupled with an increasingly oracular *persona* and images which take on archetypal, mythic dimensions. With *Live or Die,* unity of volume becomes the most apparent controlling factor in Sexton's poetry; the individual poem begins to be subsumed in the larger movement of which it is a part. And with *Transformation,* Suzanne Juhasz argues, Sexton is able to abandon her tight control of meter, rhyme, and syntax because she is in command of the poem at a different level.[7]

Without denying the effect of these developments in Sexton's poetry (longer, more prosaic poems and the use of poem sequences, for example) we may still pay attention to the means of its technical success—and find that the early discipline hangs on in the continuing love of the challenge of set forms (the sonnet sequence "Angels of the Love Affair," in *The Book of Folly*); the subtle internal control of rhyme ("Doctors," in *The Awful Rowing Toward God,* may be profitably compared with "You, Doctor Martin"); and the urgent effort to approach and enter the image/word which, at its best, allows us to see as she sees.

The outspoken, confessional poet of "The Abortion," "Menstruation at Forty," and "The Fury of Cocks" remains throughout her career a determined and beguiling shaper of words in the best tradition of the art. To see that her work, in Philip Legler's words, is in fact "crazily sane and beautifully controlled,"[8] is to understand that the witch's life has more solidity to it than fetishes and spells, and that the exploration of the self does not preclude the mastery of speech. It is an important lesson for those who read and teach Anne Sexton's poetry; it is even more important for those others who would practice that black art.

NOTES

1. "Some Tribal Female Who Is Known But Forbidden," in *Alone with America: Essays on the Art of Poetry in the U.S. Since 1950* (New York: Atheneum, 1969), 444.

2. "The New Poetry," *Atlantic,* November, 1962, 88.

3. "Five First Books," *Poetry* 97, no. 5 (February, 1961): 319

4. Review of *Bedlam* poetry in *New York Herald Tribune* Lively Arts Section, December 11, 1960, 37.

5. See, for example, Louis Simpson, "The New Books," *Harper's,* August, 1967, 91.

6. "Homage to the Runner," *American Poetry Review* 7, no. 1 (January–February, 1978): 38.

7. *Naked and Fiery Forms: Modern American Poetry By Women—A New Tradition* (New York: Harper and Row, 1976), 127.

8. "O Yellow Eye," *Poetry* 110, no. 2 (May, 1967): 127.

LAWRENCE JAY DESSNER

Anne Sexton's "The Abortion" and Confessional Poetry

Those students and readers for whom Anne Sexton is no more than a name in a textbook or at the foot of a mimeographed handout have an advantage over the rest of us for whom the tragic drama of Anne Sexton's suffering and premature death is literally and painfully unforgettable. The student reader, who has only the few Sexton poems in the textbook anthology, or only the one or two assigned, rarely thinks of the name on the printed page as belonging to a fellow human creature. At most the student assumes that the owner of the famous name led the celebrity's charmed life of universal homage and died peacefully in the fullness of years. Such readers, however, as we encounter them in our classrooms, may help us realize or regain to some extent a clearer sense of the nature and enduring value of Sexton's poetic achievement. We, who were more nearly her contemporaries, who, following her work as it appeared in the eight slender volumes could not help but follow as well the story of her life. And in the aftermath, shaken, we comforted ourselves with the one plump volume of poems[1] and the lovingly edited *Letters,*[2] both with their newly public revelations of the private life. It was not—it is not—easy to separate the facts from the fictions, the person from the poetry. Impinging too on our reading has been the debate in the papers and quarterlies about the propriety, the seemliness, the moral as well as the aesthetic decorum, of the putative confusion of fact with fiction, and the uses to which Sexton seemed to have put personal and private adversity.[3] That debate has increasingly seemed to us to be, and surely strikes us now as, pointless and absurd. Was it only a decade ago that "confessional" was so contentious a category

Published by permission of the author.

that Sexton felt compelled to disown it?[4] But what we learned about the personal and private, what we were given no choice but to learn about it, will not age for us or stiffen into similar irrelevance. And after such knowledge, what forgiveness, or at least what clearheadedness of critical judgment?

Standing between us and the untroubled and unmitigated appreciation of Sexton's high comic wit, of her best work's pungent health and exquisite technique, and perhaps most importantly, of the essentially dramatic nature of much of the best of that work fall the shadows of what we know of Sexton's life and of the questions her work raised about the nature and limits of poetry. Sexton herself contributed to the discussion of those troubling questions. She told an interviewer, "I mean it's a difficult label, 'confessional,' because I'll often confess to things that never happened. . . . If I did all the things I confess to, there would be no time to write a poem. . . . I'll assume the first person and it's someone else's story."[5] Do we not want, in this time of sophisticated, theoretical advances, to go further and argue that *all* of the confessions, like *all* of whatever may be written, "never happened," if for no other reasons than that the compression and selectivity of writing and the inherent slipperiness of language make fiction our only discourse? But such philosophical first principles of our moment are easier to utter than to remember in the heat of practice. Sexton herself let herself tell another interviewer that "Many of my poems are true, line by line, altering a few facts to get the story at its heart."[6] Difficult as it is to regain the innocent reader's ignorance of these matters, impossible as it is to sustain it, the poetry itself demands that we try.

"The Abortion," from *All My Pretty Ones* of 1962, is a moving dramatic fiction, touching in its pathos and insight, exhilarating in its linguistic precision, and because of its closing self-reflexive revelation of its own literary mode of being, particularly interesting for the light it throws on the vexed question of "confessional" poetry. An early reviewer, pairing this poem with "The Operation," wrote of both as part of Sexton's "journey into autobiography."[7] The unlikely claim, if true, I take to be irrelevant here.

> *Somebody who should have been born*
> *is gone.*

Just as the earth puckered its mouth,
each bud puffing out from its knot,
I changed my shoes, and then drove south.

Up past the Blue Mountains, where
Pennsylvania humps on endlessly,
wearing, like a crayoned cat, its green hair,

its road sunken in like a gray washboard;
where, in truth, the ground cracks evilly,
a dark socket from which the coal has poured,

Somebody who should have been born
is gone.

the grass as bristly and stout as chives,
and me wondering when the ground would break,
and me wondering how anything fragile survives;

up in Pennsylvania, I met a little man,
not Rumpelstiltskin, at all, at all . . .
he took the fullness that love began.

Returning north, even the sky grew thin
like a high window looking nowhere.
The road was as flat as a sheet of tin.

Somebody who should have been born
is gone.

Yes, woman, such logic will lead
to loss without death. Or say what you meant,
you coward . . . this baby that I bleed.

This poem is dramatic, multivocal, although all its voices
emanate from a single consciousness, the narrator's. The refrain
echoes in the mind of the narrator of what follows it while she
recalls the trip to the abortionist, well off the beaten track as such
places had to be in those years before legalization. The refrain
itself is stern, admonitory, guilt-provoking, ominous, but it is a
poet's line as well: both of the first two stressed syllables begin

with the same *s*, the vowels of the last two stressed syllables chime, and the progressive reduction of unstressed syllables between the increasingly thudding stresses accelerates the menace, as does the remarkable parade of *o*'s, the echoing middle two ("who should") separating the outer pairs. Stern and foreboding as the refrain is, its patterned sounds and cadences offer the pleasure of beauty even in lines whose apparent function is to deny the remorseful sufferer the relief of art.

In between the occurrences of the refrain, however, the recounting of the day's outing reaches toward lightness of tone and spirit. The lilting attack of "Just as the earth" (dah-di-di-dah), which is intensified by its immediate repetition, is of a piece with the suggestion that "just" means only, merely, without importance or consequence. The narrator's change of shoes is remembered breezily, as if it had been done joyfully and with little or no premeditation. "South" in this context means the civilized tropics where high fashion and gaiety reinforce each other. The burden of the story is of course quite otherwise. Try as she will to mitigate the facts that the refrain has announced, "just" does indeed express the bitter realization that at the very moment of Nature's spring rebirth, with seedlings pushing up to the surface of the earth and causing the shape of kissing lips to seem to have been imprinted on its surface, "just" when the buds, too, are, each one of them, blossoming in the act of reproducing their kind, "just" then did the narrator set out to end the new life stirring within her.

This conflict of opposed tones and implications can be seen in the stanza's ending: "and then drove south." On the one hand the delayed rhyme and the necessarily delayed revelation that lines 3 and 5 are rhythmically similar, each made up of two bursts of four syllables, provide the compelled pleasure of verbal music, what Tennyson wrote of, with troubled hesitation, as the "use [that "lies"] in measured language."[8] (What is at issue in *In Memoriam*, as in this and other Sexton poems, is the problematic relationship of history and poetry, pain and pleasure, truth and beauty.) On the other hand, this first of the poem's three-line stanzas ends with a shift from the tripping run of unstressed syllables with which it began to the three consecutive stressed, and therefore retarding, monosyllables and the gloomy "drove" with which it ends. The narrator's response to the chastening refrain is both to echo it and to deny it.

The next stanza continues this troubled doubleness of purpose. The verse has both its manic lilt and depressive falls. The sprightliness of its opening attack runs up against "humps"[9] and collapses into "endlessly." But the full, the eternal, stop which that word would seem to have announced, is short lived. The narrator bounces back with what would under other circumstances be a joyful and triumphant metaphor, the dreariness of Pennsylvania's never-ending mountains suddenly transcended by animating them into an immense and brightly colored cat. Lurking in the figure however is the child with the crayons and the delightful way of using them that suggests an animal's fur. With one component of her mind, the narrator dances away from her awareness of the "Somebody who . . . is gone," but the undertow of her own imaginative escape sucks her back to kindergarten and the lost child.

This working out of the tension between the escape of oblivion and the ordeal of remembrance continues in the ensuing stanzas, although with a perceptible darkening of tone and an increasing somberness of color and pace. The "gray washboard" of the third stanza, its color remembered with startling and touching accuracy, comes from a conventionally idealized domestic tableau from the past, but it is also "sunken" and virtually colorless. "Evilly" brings with it the literature of childhood and romance. It stirs nostalgia as well as expressing the narrator's horror at her vision of the earth splitting apart. "In truth," the narrator says, insisting that what seems a conventional and therefore distanced report, is not fictitious at all. And indeed the open or opening seam in the ground, however literary its sources in the apocalyptic earthquakes of Revelation, and however inflamed its resonance, marks as well an abandoned coal shaft. But that "dark socket" is even more strikingly the hidden uterus, site of the abortion that is being commemorated and of its menstrual flow, which is being remembered in the pouring of coal.[10]

After the second utterance of the refrain, the narrator's divided consciousness, her mood swings as it were, becomes more vehement and erratic, and the accumulating images increasingly play against each other and point forward to their recapitulation. The "grass" of line 14 names and recalls the green "crayoned" (line 8) hair worn by Pennsylvania's mountains. The reference to Rumpelstiltskin (line 18) picks up the movement toward fairy tale diction and vehicle. The natural world, which had been absorbed with the impending culmination of spring's fertility, now sympathetically imitates the aborted promise in the human world: The mountain's grass is "bristly and stout as chives," that is, dry, coarse, and while sweet to the taste, subtly coaxing tears from the eye. The ground which had cracked open (line 10) leads the narrator to wonder when the larger, general destruction will be announced by the revelation of the breaking of the "ground" (line 15) beneath her feet.

The fifth stanza stages a violent shift of tone after the direct expression of the narrator's despair over the impending cataclysm and the universal fragility of things. The children's fairy tale whose influence had been seen and felt is named. (What is not said, what the narrator knows but cannot bring herself to remind us of, is that Rumpelstiltskin's plot was foiled and the young Queen relieved of her obligation to give him her child.)[11] There is a pathetically forced return to the opening's lilting rhythm and sprightliness of demeanor in "Up in Pennsylvania, I met a little man." First the *p*'s are doubled, then the *t*'s tripled and the *m*'s repeated. The vowels of "in," "Penn*sy*lvania," and "little," link the line together, but the lyricism of the music and the play or pretense of high spirits collapses in the bald and rueful announcement that this is not a fairy tale, not a story told in celebration of the triumph of good over evil. Not "at all, at all." The mournful complaint expresses the narrator's sorrow, but because of its own elementary but persistent verbal play, the utterance also expresses and provides the distancing and aesthetic relief of art.

At this point the fact of the abortion itself is directly declared with minimal use of metaphor. "Love" (line 19), it might well be argued, is always metaphoric. The "fullness" is both a matter of emotional and anatomical circumstance. Then there is the bleak stanza recounting the narrator's bleak homeward journey. "North" answers the opening's "south." Nature's sympathetic imitation of the narrator's plight—flat stomach and depressed spirits—is insisted on: "*even* the sky grew thin" (line 20). The measureless emptiness of things, the *nada,* is figured by the empty horizon. The narrator's last words about the trip to Pennsylvania—"The road was as flat as a sheet of tin"—contrasts the mountainous terrain of the setting out with the flatness of the return. It is as if that setting out had been in fact, or was by comparison with the return, an occasion of, or even for, jaunty high spirits. The roads of course figure the narrator's outlook on the present condition and the prospects that loom ahead. The natural world no longer mocks or sympathizes with the narrator; it has vanished. There are no branches in the sky and the grassy mountains have been displaced by "a sheet of tin," man-made, conventionally thin, bland in color if not colorless, and cheap enough to be the material for throwaway cans. This line, however, which expresses so stark and barren a prospect, is not without its pleasing graces. It offers the comforts of its end rhyme and the consoling pattern—in the sense that all pattern is consoling—of balanced iambs enclosing a pair of anapests.

There is as well a larger pattern being brought to completion and closure here in this line. Since the next and last repetition of the refrain that follows it causes and marks a seemingly funda-mental shift in the narrator's approach to the retelling of her story, that narration in effect ends with that "sheet of tin," as does a remarkably sustained metaphor which was initiated with the "puckered" earth and "puffing" buds of the narrative's opening. In addition to expressing the motif of Nature's loving fertility, these are images of disruption of an otherwise smooth surface, images which might be said to be emotionally and morally neu-tral, a matter of physics or geometry. They are related to the final smooth flatness of the piece of tin through a series of intermediary images: "mountains," "humps," the ridges of a "washboard," the "crack[ed]" earth, the "break[ing]" "ground," and the "full-ness" of the distended belly. This sequence of images serves to hold the poem together by providing an underlying structure or framework. The images function as structural elements in much the same way as do the narrative's division into rhymed three-line stanzas and the lines' fundamental but not insistent loyalty to the patterned music of iambic tetrameter. Such patternings are arbi-trary, unrelated to the specific events recounted, unrelated to the emotional pressure behind their recounting. Nevertheless, the overall effect of our reading is that the poem moves us emo-tionally, but we know that it does so in part—how large or small a part is beyond knowing—through the agency of the arbitrary patterning of art. "The Abortion" expresses its narrator's most painful remorse and regret, yet we read the poem for and with that species of pleasure called aesthetic.

While the "confessional" poet may strive to "hold back nothing,"[12] to tell the most personal and intimate of painful and shocking truths, the manner of the telling of the home truths must put in question their truthfulness. The structures inherent in the shaped language we call a poem—and to the extent that grammar is equally a structure the principle holds for all language—those structures, while allowing the telling or summarizing of a series of events, do not permit the emotions with which the teller experienced or imagined those events to be conveyed in their fullness. One might say that language itself is a process of holding back. What is held back we call truth; what is made manifest through language we call beauty.

The admonitory refrain that echoes through "The Abortion" reminds the narrator of the rest of the poem of the "truth" that there has been an irremediable loss. But even the refrain itself is an instance of artful, patterned, and therefore pleasure-giving language. The triple verbatim repetition of the refrain and its pattern of recurrence, framing each group of three three-line stanzas, confirm its secret and subversive allegiance to the cause of beauty. And poor truth, the innocent idea of holding nothing back, remains an idle and impossible boast.

In Sexton's poem the protest against the nature of language, against its inherent conflict with truth-telling, is not made until the last three lines. And then it is a new voice, yet another aspect of the poem's narrator, which, by raising the issue almost directly, exposes the conflict that the poem has been tacitly engaged in from the beginning:

> Yes, woman, such logic will lead
> to loss without death. Or say what you meant,
> you coward . . . this baby that I bleed.

The "Yes" is bitterly ironic. The "logic" is everything that has been said up to this point about the abortion, or better, every *way* language has been used to refer or respond to it. "Logic" refers to the guilt-provoking menace of the refrain, the pathetic, recurring masked references to childhood and children, the swings into buoyant rhythms and their accompanying light-heartedness, and the darker tones and images. It encompasses as well all of the other aspects of linguistic form, including stanzaic design, metrical patterning, overall structure, and all of the varieties of rhyme and verbal music. It also refers to "logic" itself, rational discourse and the rationalizations it so readily discovers for us.

> Yes [this new voice says, tauntingly, to the earlier voices of the poem], the resources of language and reason you have been using, speech itself, is corrupt, false, and fatal. Rather than mourning the events, accepting your responsibility for them, bearing the pain of such guilt, the poem you have been uttering has been an exercise in evasion, self-deception, and hypocritical fraud. Only myself, that heretofore silent aspect of your complex consciousness, myself, who cannot or will not surrender anguish to "logic," whose cry is past syntax or paraphrase, is telling the truth. Your continuation of your cowardly practices must cease, or else!

The words which embody that threat, "Loss without death," and the "Or" that follows it are oddly but perhaps necessarily obscure, even irrational. The phrase would seem to mean eternal or never-ending regret at the loss, but this is inconsistent with the stanza's overall meaning, which is that the preceding stanzas, by their cowardly evasion of the brutal truth, their distancing language and prettifying imaginative play, have not said what was meant, have not accepted and borne the full weight of responsibility for what has occurred. The "Or" would seem to be offering an alternative to never-ending regret, but what it *is* offering is an alternative to the use of "such logic." That the elementary semantic functioning of this narrator's language should break down here in the midst of her angry outburst against precisely the results of the ordinary functioning of language is, despite itself, a rational phenomenon. It occurs again with the three dots of the last line. These do not designate an ellipsis but a pause, a speechless pause. The narrator's anger is beyond speech, beyond syntax and hence beyond reason. She does not write; she "bleeds." Her truth is beyond logic and language's logic. She will not trust it to those cowardly and falsifying arts of beauty.[13]

But of course the angry, distraught narrator of the poem's last stanza has no choice in the matter. To the extent that her utterance is more than a scream, a noise, it will obey the laws of its vehicle, language. And to the extent that this stanza, which rebels against the poem, is itself the culmination of the poem, it is guilty of precisely the crimes against truth that it has come into existence to arraign. The stanza's passionate rebellion is expressed in the same stanza form as its predecessors. The outburst is rich in complex alliteration: "*logic* wi*ll* *l*ead / to *l*oss." The fetus is sentimentally both elevated into a "baby" and diminished to a flow of blood. Its mother's bleeding is both literal and figurative. Her protest against poetry's art culminates in three regular iambic feet, and a word which completes both an alliterating triplet and the rhyme which links the stanza's beginning with its end. That rhymed word, "bleed," additionally, brings together the stanza's two multiply alliterating consonants.

What the poem's concluding protest "proves" is that language and therefore the mode of fiction is inescapable, that "confessional" writing is an impossibility, a contradiction in terms. The author of "The Abortion" cannot be identified with any one of the poem's voices nor with an inferred person from whom all the voices spring. (The act of writing turns persons into voices, truth into language.) The implied author of the poem exists apart from them, on a different metaphysical plane from them. The existence of the poem's voices imply a silent voice, a maker, but a maker of fictions.

The relationship between the anguish that Anne Sexton suffered and the poems she wrote, which we admire, appreciate, and enjoy, is then a complex and enigmatic one. Perhaps all we can feel sure of about Sexton's seemingly autobiographical poems is that what we have on the page represents, if not a deliberate fiction or falsification, at most a necessarily modulated or transfigured version of some original autobiographical impulse. "The Abortion" raises the theoretical question into plain sight. Whether the poem derives from events in Sexton's own life or in the life of someone personally known to her, we cannot know. Nor can we know how much, if anything, the poem owes to the political and ideological debates of its time. Those questions are not as much unanswerable as absurd. What we do know about the poem under discussion is that in it is dramatized the paradox of "confessional" poetry. "The Abortion" is about the absurdity of seeking expression outside of the constraints of language, about the impossibility of being a "confessional" poet. The only real historical event we *know* the poem describes is the aborting of what may have been an autobiographical impulse and intention.

Although "The Abortion" is a particularly extended and direct treatment of the problematic relationship of truth to beauty, of the question of "sincerity," other poems by Sexton refer to it. "Rowing," for example, from Sexton's *The Awful Rowing Toward God* of 1975, begins with the announcement that what is to follow is "A story, a story!" and ends with a coda about the "tale which I have told" and a concluding reference to "this story." That the events summarized—they are largely instances of deprivation, pain, and severe psychological distress—are announced as components of "a story" may have something to do with this poem's success when many of Sexton's later poems with similar content but without such self-conscious reference to their literary mode of existence are not successful. Writing to her friend William Snodgrass in 1959, Sexton referred to "her kind of poetry" as "sincere." She said she understood why some found her work "unseemly, too personal." It is because they "are afraid of something that is real."[14] Traditional poetry is, or was, by tradition, *not* "real," not the truth. Anne Sexton's poetry often purports to be autobiographical, but its presentation in her more successful poems is often marked by overt signs, often traditional signs, of the presence of art, which is artifice, something other than truth-telling. We do not believe that what the narrator says about herself in "Her Kind" (1960) is true of Anne Sexton because the poem's tightly rhymed and structured lines and stanzas mark the utterance to be a poem and hence *not* true, at least not literally true.

This same self-contradiction is apparent in "The Starry Night" (1962) which announces its narrator's passionate and almost overwhelming obsession with suicide with, among other elements of literary structure, a series of prominent voiced plosives: "black-haired," "boils," "bulges," "beast," and "belly." It is as if the "cry" with which the poem ends, the raw cry itself, before or beyond syntax, had been captured and frozen in that sensational series around which the poem's ordinary discourse is gathered. It is as if Sexton, in this early poem as well as in many that followed, were taking on as her mortal opponent the paradoxical limits of language and the gods who had ordained them to be what they are.

It is not easy to imagine Anne Sexton's true emotional history, whether it was more or less painful than her poems imply. But poems are, for better or for worse, transformations of experience, not experience itself. In many of her poems, the true history we learn about is one of pain defeated, or at least forestalled, by craft and all those forms of courage which make craft possible.

NOTES

1. *The Complete Poems* (Boston: Houghton Mifflin, 1981). I use this text for all quotations from the poetry.

2. *Anne Sexton: A Self-Portrait in Letters,* edited by Linda Gray Sexton and Lois Ames (Boston: Houghton Mifflin, 1977), hereafter, *Letters.*

3. A convenient sampling of that debate is in *Anne Sexton: The Artist and Her Critics,* edited by J. D. McClatchy (Bloomington: Indiana University Press, 1978), 115–89. Subsequent references cite this volume as McClatchy. Also useful in this regard is *Sylvia Plath and Anne Sexton: A Reference Guide,* edited by Cameron Northouse and Thomas P. Walsh (Boston: G. K. Hall, 1974).

4. William Heyen, ed., *American Poets in 1976* (Indianapolis: Bobbs-Merrill, 1976), 309: "Well, for a while, oh for a long while, perhaps even now, I was called a 'confessional poet.' And for quite a while I resented it." In a letter of 1960, Sexton wrote: "I have written a new longish poem called 'The Operation' which is (damn it as I really don't *want* to write any more of them) a personal narration about my experiences this fall" (*Letters,* 99).

5. Heyen, 309.

6. Barbara Kevles, "The Art of Poetry: Anne Sexton," in McClatchy, 22. This interview first appeared in the *Paris Review* 52 (1971): 159–91.

7. Thomas P. McDonnell's review in *America* 116 (May 13, 1967), is reprinted in McClatchy. His passing and unsupported judgment occurs there on p. 135. I know of no possible autobiographical basis for "The Abortion." The poem is not mentioned in *Letters.*

8. *In Memoriam,* section 5, line 6. Tennyson's long poem wrestles with the paradox that the expression of sorrow may, by easing it, attenuate the sorrow's cause, here, the narrator's love for his lost friend. Stanzas 48, 75, and 77, are especially interesting in this regard.

9. Several adventurous students of mine have become convinced that "humps" suggests that the narrator, in using the slang word for sexual intercourse, is remembering the union from which the pregnancy developed.

10. "Had poured" says the text, not "has poured," which would have suggested a single rather than a repeated event such as the flow of clotted blood and embryonic material.

11. *Grimms' Tales for Young and Old,* translated by Ralph Manheim (London: Victor Gollancz, 1978), 196–98. Sexton returned to the tale in *Transformations* (1971). Her "Rumpelstiltskin" there is a retelling of the story within a frame of psychoanalytic interpretation.

12. "For years I railed against being put in this category," Sexton told the readers of the *New York Times* in 1969. ". . . Then about a year ago, I decided I was the *only* confessional poet. Well . . . Allen Ginsberg too. He holds back nothing and I hold back nothing." Quoted by Robert Phillips in *The Confessional Poets* (Carbondale: Southern Illinois University Press, 1973), 76.

13. Richard Howard, "Anne Sexton: 'Some Tribal Female Who Is Known But Forbidden,'" (McClatchy, 200) makes this brief reference to "The Abortion": "What a relief when the design works against the poet's distemper, as in 'The Abortion' and 'The Operation,' instead of surrendering—condescending, really—to the awfulness of it all." Howard seems to have taken one of the poem's voices for all of it. He praises what the speaker of the poem's last stanza so vigorously condemns. Howard's essay originally appeared in his *Alone with America: Essays on the Art of Poetry in the United States Since 1950* (New York: Atheneum, 1971), 442–50. Jeanne H. Kammer in her "The Witch's Life: Confession and Control in the Early Poetry of Anne Sexton," *Language and Style* 13, no. 4 (Fall, 1980): 29–35, sees Sexton's use of the devices of formal control in the early poems as imitative, expressive, and rhetorical. She refers in passing to "The Abortion," calling it the work of "the outspoken confessional poet" (35). Suzanne Juhasz, in *Naked and Fiery Forms: Modern American Poetry by Women—A New Tradition* (New York: Harper and Row, 1976), 127, sees Sexton's later work developing different, more global, forms of poetic control.

14. *Letters,* 62.

CHARLES GULLANS

Review of *Live or Die*

The materials of Anne Sexton's third book are already familiar to us. Wanting to die, resisting suicide, checking into the mental hospital, talking to one's psychiatrist, insanity and the threat of it, and one's desperate resistance to that insanity—any of these might well be the materials of a serious poem; but these are not poems, unless we conceive of a poem as the simple delineation of anguish, or literal confession. These are not poems at all and I feel that I have, without right or desire, been made a third party to her conversations with her psychiatrist. It is painful, embarrassing, and irritating. The immediacy and terror of her problem are painful; the personal character of the confessional detail is embarrassing; and the tone of hysterical melodrama which pervades most of the writing is finally irritating. Either this is the poetry of a monstrous self-indulgence, in which case it is despicable; or it is documentation of a neurosis, in which case to pretend to speak of it as literature at all is simply silly. It is raw material for the understanding, like any other confusing experience. For the author, one might feel pity, if she could not control herself. This would be the pity one feels for the victim of psychosis; but to mistake such feeling for literary response implies a confusion among readers and critics of cause and effect. The Romantic stereotype says that the poet is sensitive and suffers; the neo-Romantic stereotype says that anyone who is sensitive and suffers is a poet. In the former view, poetry was the product of anguish; in the latter, the anguish has become the poetry. To suffer is to be creative; I feel, therefore, I am: the more strongly I feel, the greater my Being. To invite the reader to participate in violent feeling for its own sake is the final cause of the poem. This is the

From "Poetry and Subject Matter: From Hart Crane to Turner Cassity," *Southern Review* 7 (1970). Copyright by The Southern Review 1970. Reprinted by permission of the author.

sentimental view of literature and life, which argues that indulgence in feeling is a good in itself. The sentimental literature of the past invited us to participate in feeling of a rather idealized and genteel character; the sentimental literature of this century proposes violent feeling as a permanent mode of existence; one stumbles from disaster to disaster for the sake of the excitement which the disasters provoke. One might as reasonably propose Auschwitz as a model for communal living. But then, this is to take Miss Sexton's poems seriously; they are not poems, they are documents of modern psychiatry and their publication is a result of the confusion of critical standards in the general mind.

PHILIP LEGLER

Strong Stuff

In *Live or Die,* Anne Sexton continues to create a poetry all her own. Though in many ways similar to *To Bedlam and Part Way Back* and to *All My Pretty Ones,* this new book focuses more intensely on the poem as process and on that process as it discovers both the destructive and creative elements in us all.

For the most part these are poems in which Mrs. Sexton's craft is so perfect, so seemingly effortless and natural, that the reader cannot praise them enough. They do what the poet herself once said her poems should do—open up, go way out, and then close in. Many of the strict, formal patterns established in *To Bedlam* and in *All My Pretty Ones* are now thrown off; in *Live or Die* the formal control is still present, but the patterns are much freer, are more intrinsic to the emotional states the poems suggest. Technically, then, in the best pieces the line lengths, the rhythms, the occasional rhymes are never imposed upon the material but, as Frost has said of poetry, ride easy in harness.

Yet the reader who is fascinated with such a mastery of technical problems will, if he is careful and thoughtful, give attention to the voice; for while some critics have suggested echoes of W. D. Snodgrass and Robert Lowell, Mrs. Sexton's voice is always her own. Perhaps the only direct influence she might wish to acknowledge is found in her approach: she has learned from Snodgrass that poetry can be personal, that it can and must tell the truth.

And the truth is here!—shaped in a language that cries out, that sings of what man is, of what we are. In "Flee on Your Donkey" (a major work for the poet), the speaker returns to a mental institution to discover the futility of such a place, of such

Review of *Live or Die, New Mexico Quarterly* 37, no. 1 (1967). Reprinted by permission of the author.

a state of mind. But that very state, that knowing madness, asks some questions:

> Hornets have been sent.
> They cluster like floral arrangements on the screen.
> Hornets, dragging out their thin stingers,
> hover outside, all knowing,
> hissing: *the hornet knows.*
> I heard it as a child
> but what was it he meant?
> *The hornet knows!*
> What happened to Jack and Doc and Reggy?
> Who remembers what lurks in the heart of man?
> What did The Green Hornet mean, *he knows?*
> Or have I got it wrong?
> Is it The Shadow who had seen
> me from my bedside radio?

The poet knows!—an example of how she can take something very familiar, something unreal and stereotyped, and give to it a new meaning. All of us "heard it as a child" but have not wanted to admit such knowledge.

Many of the poems dramatize how we destroy ourselves and others. In "Man and Wife"—

> Now they are together
> like strangers in a two-seater outhouse,
> eating and squatting together.
> They have teeth and knees
> but they do not speak.
> A soldier is forced to stay with a soldier
> because they share the same dirt
> and the same blows.

Mrs. Sexton never lets up, the poems delivering such "blows," such brilliantly conceived images. In another piece, "Self in 1958," the narrator as "a plaster doll" confides that

> I live in a doll's house
> with four chairs,

> a counterfeit table, a flat roof
> and a big front door.
> Many have come to such a small crossroad.
> There is an iron bed,
> (Life enlarges, life takes aim)
> a cardboard floor,
> windows that flash open on someone's city,
> and little more.

The discovered reality is not the joy of life; it is not the joy of cooking, for

> Someone plays with me,
> plants me in the all-electric kitchen,
> Is this what Mrs. Rombauer said?

So the destructions go on and on—the killings, the mutilations—in the prisons and closets and memories of the self: "Cripples and Other Stories" is an ironically grotesque ballad in which a patient addresses her "father-doctor" (psychiatrist), saying

> *Each time I give lectures*
> *or gather in the grants*
> *you send me off to boarding school*
> *in training pants.*

And the child's world returns, a world crippled and maimed, twisted and horrifying.

But it is "The Addict"—one of the finest poems in the book—in which the poet finds her most striking metaphor for contemporary man, for his fascination with self-destruction, with death, with hell. We are all addicts, giving ourselves up to hate, love, deadly illusions, fears; we are all masochists trying to survive on "sweet pharmaceutical bottles"; we are living on some kind of drug:

> My supply
> of tablets

has got to last for years and years.
I like them more than I like me.
Stubborn as hell, they won't let go.
It's a kind of marriage.
It's a kind of war
where I plant bombs inside
of myself.

There are life-giving forces, too, the poem "Live" finding them in the gift of creation, in the sunlight world where

God! It's a dream,
lovers sprouting in the yard
like celery stalks
and better,
a husband straight as a redwood,
two daughters, two sea urchins,
picking roses off my hackles.

It's a world where—instead of being "an instant cripple" or "an addict," "a killer, / anointing myself daily / with my little poisons."—

I'm an empress.
I wear an apron.
My typewriter writes.
It didn't break the way it warned.

And the empress lives: in the poem "The Sun," where "Now I am utterly given. / I am your daughter, your sweet-meat,"; in "Somewhere in Africa," where a death is celebrated but "Let there be this God who is a woman who will place you / upon her shallow boat,"; in "Sylvia's Death" (for Sylvia Plath), where there is the perception that "what is your death / but an old belonging, / a mole that fell out / of one of your poems?", the dead friend seen as a "funny duchess?"; in "Your Face on the Dog's Neck," where a woman concludes that "I will crouch down / and put my cheek near you, / accepting this spayed and flatulent bitch you hold"; and in the moving "Little Girl, My

String Bean, My Lovely Woman," where a mother tells her daughter

> Oh, darling, let your body in,
> let it tie you in,
> in comfort.
> What I want to say, Linda,
> is that women are born twice.

And after conjuring the magical roots and sprouts of growth—

> *Oh, little girl,*
> *my stringbean,*
> *how do you grow?*
> *You grow this way.*
> *You are too many to eat.*

What poet wouldn't give years to have found those lines!
   Live or Die is a beautifully fashioned book. It is strong stuff.

ROBERT BOYERS

Live or Die

The Achievement of
Anne Sexton

Anne Sexton's *Live or Die* is the culmination, indeed the crowning achievement, of the confessional mode which has largely dominated American poetry in the last decade. No doubt, the very term "confessional poetry" may dismay many people, but it is a convenient catchall for the kind of work we have come to associate with the names of such poets as Robert Lowell, the late Sylvia Plath, W. D. Snodgrass, and Frederick Seidel, not to mention numerous other, if less distinguished, practitioners. Mr. Lowell's *Life Studies* is generally acknowledged as the driving force, perhaps even the inspiration for much of this poetry, and its influence on Miss Sexton's work has always been obvious. In her latest volume, though, Miss Sexton has brilliantly transcended, without wholly discarding, her allegiance to Lowell's verse, with its resolute dredging of a complex domestic past, its morbid self-disparagement, and its remorseless pursuit of an identity which is at once genuine and acceptable.

Miss Sexton's confessional, like Mr. Lowell's, is by no means wholly therapeutic in either purpose or effect. As A. Alvarez recently remarked of Sylvia Plath's later poetry, the Freudian notion that the artist is relieved of his fantasies simply by expressing them does not hold water: "the act of formal expression merely makes the dredged-up material more readily available." In the case of Miss Plath, the full destructive potential of the material was released by her violently excessive straining for authenticity, by her unquenchable desire to examine what was most unthinkable in herself and in history. Miss Sexton's propensities are similarly violent and suicidal, but she convinces

Salmagundi 2 (1967). Reprinted from *Salmagundi* by permission of the editors.

herself, and her reader, that she has something to live for. We are grateful to Miss Sexton as we can be to few poets, for she has distinctly enlarged and enhanced the possibilities of endurance in that air of lost connections which so many of us inhabit.

Miss Sexton's is a poetry of the nerves and heart. She is never abstract, never permits herself to be distracted from her one true subject—herself and her emotions. It is remarkable that she never flinches from the task at hand, never attempts to use her art as a device for warding off final perception. Unlike a poet like Frederick Seidel, she is willing to make her connections explicit. Her poems lack that hurtling momentum which keeps diverse elements in a sort of perpetual disrelation in the work of Seidel. Miss Sexton is painfully direct, and she refuses to keep her meaning at a tolerable distance. *Live or Die* projects an anguish which is profoundly disturbing precisely because its sources are effable, because the pressure of fantasy has not been permitted to distort or mediate Miss Sexton's vision.

One must admit that several poems in this volume are less than total successes. There are occasional crudities which should not be overlooked. Frequently, the debt to poets as far apart as Lowell, Roethke, and Emily Dickinson strikes one as almost obscenely unconcealed, nakedly thrusting itself before a gaping awareness. In the poem "Flee on Your Donkey," describing one of Miss Sexton's sojourns in a mental hospital, one is continually reminded of Mr. Lowell's poems on the same subject. One does not so much resent the echoing of details from Mr. Lowell as one resents the appropriation of his characteristic tone. And it is striking that whenever Miss Sexton mimics the man who was at one time her teacher, she comes off a very poor second. In the following passage, Miss Sexton sounds like a colorist, a collector of faintly absurd minutiae: "in another room someone tries to eat a shoe; / meanwhile an adolescent pads up and down / the hall in his white tennis socks." And later: "The permanent guests have done nothing new. / Their faces are still small / like babies with jaundice." One shudders to compare this with lines from Mr. Lowell's "Waking In the Blue": "and see the shaky future grow familiar / in the pinched, indigenous faces / of these thoroughbred mental cases, / twice my age and half my weight." At another point in her poem, Miss Sexton tries to establish a more detached vantage point. She vaguely wonders why she has returned to the institution that confines her, but concludes "what good are my questions / in this hierarchy of death," precisely as Mr. Lowell concluded after mentally making the rounds: "What use is my sense of humor?" Even the names of places and people echo from *Life Studies,* including such familiars as Marlborough Street and L. L. Bean, but they lack resonance in Miss Sexton's poem.

In a few of these poems, Miss Sexton demonstrates a grasp of poetic nuance which is hardly satisfactory. Her similes are often imprecise, or simply gratuitous. In "Flee on Your Donkey," she writes: "recommitted, / fastened to the wall like a bathroom plunger, / held like a prisoner / who was so poor / he fell in love with jail." One must be excessively charitable to grant validity to Miss Sexton's "bathroom plunger." It does not in any way make more distinctively manifest Miss Sexton's anxiety over recommitment to the asylum. The effect of the second simile is even less justifiable, for it strikes one as wholly unnecessary and irrelevant, as a sort of very feeble joke having no relation to the dominating seriousness of the poem. Even in a beautiful little piece like "Three Green Windows," one has questions to ask about some of Miss Sexton's similes.

On occasion, the poet grows rather too self-conscious about her role as a writer. She wants us to be sure and listen very carefully, now. In one poem, "The Legend of the One-Eyed Man," she dictates "Do not think of the intense sensation / I have as I tell you this / but think only. . . ." In "Flee on Your Donkey," she takes measures to ensure we are solemn enough for what she has to convey: ". . . for this is a mental hospital, / not a child's game." Neither is the poet's taste always security against excessive self-dramatization, even spilling into undertones of self-pity. In "Two Sons" she announces "I grow old on my bitterness," and proceeds to establish the disparity between the bustling past and her present loneliness, only Miss Sexton never quite succeeds in evoking the gilded past which comes alive in the work of Mr. Lowell. Her writing is strangely flat and unaffecting where one would expect her to invest a great deal of nostalgic enthusiasm, as though she did not quite believe the memories of a more baroque and securely enclosed heritage: "I sit in an old lady's room / where families used to feast / where the wind blows in like soot from north-northeast." One would care more about the soot if one had more of the sense of decline which Miss Sexton obviously wished to convey.

Notwithstanding such defects as these, Miss Sexton is an extraordinarily accomplished artist. It is a mark of her distinction that one never hesitates to grant her the privilege of being wholly self-centered in her poems. There is no real inclination to insist that she get beyond the relatively narrow range of problems that haunt her, for her evocation of these problems gives them a resonance which is unmistakably general, universally relevant. Miss Sexton's is a poetry of victimization, in which she is at once victim and tormentor. She has an inalienable sense of guilt and responsibility which is rendered pathetic by her recognition of contingency and ultimate chaos in the world. In "The Legend of the One-Eyed Man," she identifies with Judas Iscariot, and one has no doubt that she is convinced of her own guilt: "look into my face / and you will know that crimes dropped upon me / as from a high building." She wants desperately to be judged, for if her sins can be legitimately punished, so too might she be the recipient of a grace which is nowhere forthcoming. But she lacks proper faith. Her imagination is too bizarre to relax with singular explanations. It is always playing with alternatives, wryly amusing possibilities. In "Protestant Easter," she recaptures the naive meanderings of an eight-year-old, skeptical about conventional legends, who wonders whether the resurrected Jesus was able to accomplish his "miracle" by mere sleight of hand. She thinks of a tunnel she used to hide in as a child: "Maybe Jesus knew my tunnel / and crawled right through to the river / so he could wash all the blood off."

The naive archness, even cuteness of this poem is far from characteristic of Miss Sexton, whose tone is generally severe and intense. Her abasement is frequently so extreme that it threatens to become either mawkish or simply unbearable, but she succeeds nonetheless. An instance of her daring and skill is "For the Year of the Insane," in which she struggles valiantly to escape what she is, to transcend her condition, the arrogance of a mind which demands explanations where there are none. Her obsession with words is seen as ugly and corrupt, a sign of insufficient spirituality. She forces herself into a posture of utter abasement, but the exacerbation of will is everywhere apparent. Indeed, the frightful tension and pain implicit in the acquiescence indicates that Miss Sexton's salvational ordeal can be only temporarily relieved. She cannot truly be innocent again, as she wants to be. She is too aware of guilt and pain, too self-conscious ever to be open and free and humbly grateful. During communion, reverently silent and deliberately pious, "I am handed wine as a child is handed milk." But the mood is quickly broken. Miss Sexton's awareness of herself, imperfect and sinful, intrudes: "I have this fear of coughing." She sips the wine clumsily: "I see two thin streaks burn down my chin. / I see myself as one would see another. / I have been cut in two."

Miss Sexton's continuing, and largely unsuccessful struggle is to escape the image of herself which dominates and in a sense pollutes her projections of future possibility. Part of her self-disgust is not uncommon. She is dissatisfied with her performance as mother and wife, though the demands she customarily lays on herself are hardly conventional. The intimacy of married life seems absurdly ludicrous, with strangers inhabiting a common situation, powerless to affect the essential loneliness of the individual psyche. In "Man and Wife," Miss Sexton's image beautifully evokes the futility of the marital arrangement, and the peculiarly insufficient intimacy it often involves: "Now they are together / like strangers in a two-seater outhouse, / eating and squatting together."

Miss Sexton is terribly annoyed with herself. She hates to be a spectacle, a nuisance. Though her past is a nightmare of grisly proportions, she cannot evade its urgent appeals to her consciousness. In "Those Times. . . ," probably the best single poem in this volume, Miss Sexton recounts the humiliations of a childhood marked by early sexual distress, and dominated by the sense that she was an unwanted expediency used by her mother "to keep Father / from his divorce." She cannot really fight back, but withdraws instead. She delights in stillness, but fears everything. The young child is projected as "the me who stepped on the noses of dolls / she couldn't break . . . / They came from a mysterious country / without the pang of birth, / born quietly and well." What envy seethes in those lines, at once so fragile and violent! And what terrible transformations the poetic imagination at its best is capable of achieving. In "Those Times. . . ," the most conventionally beneficent phenomena are imbued with a quality of awesomeness that is both strange and disturbing. There is a sense of violent dislocation, as objects are ripped out of their familiar emotional contexts and charged with an electricity we had thought them incapable of transmitting. The rose in this poem becomes wholly different from what we expect, for its natural growth has been arrested. It is fixed in the endlessly repetitive, undeveloping pattern of wallpaper. The child thinks once, and then again, of "the same terrible rose repeating on the walls." What had been lovely and free to bloom and die in its own way is trapped, denied its autonomy.

The feeling is developed, made somewhat more explicit, in a further image, as the child hides from life in a closet, only to find that the inexorable voracity of her imagination inclines it to devour and transform everything, to invest the most mundane objects with an aura of menacing potency. An ordinary array of dresses is described as follows: "and then the dresses swinging above me, / always above me, empty and sensible / with sashes and puffs, / with collars and two-inch hems / and evil fortunes in their belts." The effect of these lines is to render everything intimidating, and to dwarf the huddling, frightened child by contrast. The experience which we have learned to live with, to tolerate as relatively benign and uncomplicated, appears suddenly to have acquired appalling dimensions. It is a revelation which brings us back to the root of things, to the nature of the freedom upon which we predicate our smugness, individually and collectively. The momentum of the poem marvelously prepares us to acquiesce in the development of Miss Sexton's vision, which grows more terrifying as it becomes more explicitly violent. The terrible rose becomes ". . . the wallpaper of the room / where tongues bloomed over and over, / bursting from lips like sea flowers—" and the window is described as ". . . an ugly eye / through which birds coughed, / chained to the heaving trees."

Everywhere in this volume the sense of entrapment is acute, and the spectre of violation is equally pervasive. The poetry is not correspondingly claustrophobic. The succession of images does not hammer one into painful submission before the spectacle of humanity furiously plundered and abandoned. Miss Sexton's ambience is severe, as suggested, but not torrential. At her best, the rhetoric is subdued. She employs irony as a counterpoint to intensity. In several poems, Miss Sexton expresses her sense of violation in terms of the sophisticated preoccupations "responsible" people are supposed to have, including a wide spectrum of items, from social problems and family affairs to literary fashions. She is always on the run from one thing or another, expressing in this the contours of an instinct for escape and purification which must obsess a great many of us. In "Walking in Paris," she announces "I have deserted my husband and my children, / the Negro issue, the late news and the hot baths," but her construction of a new possibility, a new reality, is flawed. The patchwork cannot hide its seams, for the tone of longing and faint regret, and the consciousness of what must be left behind, cling in the mind like foul odors which cannot be washed away. Miss Sexton is brave, and resolute, but her essential honesty prevents her from any easy accessions of peace and renewal. She identifies herself with Zola's Nana, and with Nana's Paris, "as if I might clean off / the made woman you became, / withered and constipated." What pain and desire ring in her assertion that "to be occupied or conquered is nothing— to remain is all!" One might almost be willing to tolerate such a sentiment, if only one could believe Miss Sexton capable of accepting it. Her longing is ultimately pathetic, however, and strangely beautiful in the very fact that it cannot be satisfied or assuaged. Miss Sexton must know, conjure as she will, that glorious invocations like "Come, my sister, / we are two virgins, / our lives once more perfected / and unused" cannot mitigate the pain she knows too well. There is a knowledge beyond words, which words must be forever powerless to affect.

The anonymity of Miss Sexton's oppressors makes her struggle all the more representative and relevant, for today we have all learned what it is like to perpetually stifle our complaints, not knowing to whom we can rightfully attribute a primary responsibility. Surrounded by middle-men, faceless bureaucrats and managers, we turn our anger inwards, growing bitter in the face of liberal platitudes about meaning well, respect for due process, and basic human frailty. Rarely, Miss Sexton erupts with a sputter of furious accusation, but she soon lapses into the tone of dogged, agonized reminiscence which we recognize. There is release, a kind of pyrrhic gratification, in a poem like "Cripples and Other Stories," with its "God damn it, father-doctor. / I'm really thirty-six. / I see dead rats in the toilet. / I'm one of the lunatics." But Miss Sexton knows that her father is only part of the story, a dubious source of her misery. She is confused about him, as about so many other things, earnestly groping for an image of consistency where there is always essential contradiction. She is mystified by tenderness, by apparently genuine displays of affection and whispers of love.

In search of an oppressor, of an object for the venomous resentment she carries in her like a knife, she seizes upon her mother in "Christmas Eve." The setting is evoked in words of bitter directness, memory stirred roughly as with a stick. Fiercely she stares at a portrait of her late mother, lighted by the multicolored bulbs of the Christmas tree: "Then they were a beehive, / blue, yellow, green, red; / each with its own juice, each hot and alive / stinging your face. But you did not move." And later: "Then I thought of your body / as one thinks of murder. . . ." One would suppose that passages of such ferocity would tend to alienate their witness, that the myopic eye of anguish, as one critic said of Sylvia Plath's work, would so obliterate the contours of the known and acceptable, that true participation on the part of readers would be rendered highly unlikely. It is not so. In this poetry, the passion to punish, to point an unswervingly accusatory finger, is everywhere balanced by a conviction of personal failure, by an altogether remarkable complexity in single lines, where one cannot be too hastily disposed to make absolute judgments. Even as the poet's mother is mercilessly dissected, with a simultaneously obsessive and self-conscious objectivity, there is a strange admixture of pervasive sorrow, a regret for an intimacy that might have flourished. The object of so much hatred and derision is a frail creature, pathetically human: "Then I watched how the sun hit / your red sweater, your withered neck, / your badly painted flesh-pink skin."

Where do such projections take us, and Miss Sexton? Presumably to guilt, impatience with our collective inability to fix blame and at least quell a bitterness that we more and more allow to turn inwards, and ultimately to the final despair of suicidal negation. Miss Sexton feels not only thwarted and impotent, but actively put upon, not only violated, but regularly manipulated. While her writing resists overt political commentary, she is very much aware of the unique character of our century, of the leveling of standards and the rampant destruction of individual identity at the roots of mass society. This awareness is reflected in "Self in 1958," where Miss Sexton sees herself as a plaster doll, "with eyes that cut open without landfall or nightfall / upon some shellacked and grinning person." The standard faces and counterfeit courtesy of our civilization, with its regular diet of homiletic banalities shoveled out with impeccable execution by statesmen and presidents, is remarkably conveyed in that image of "some shellacked and grinning person." How Miss Sexton loathes the way in which we have agreed to be dominated by the synthetic comforts we crave. Her house is a doll's house, with neat little, carefully measured cubicles thinly separated from one another, with "the all-electric kitchen," "a cardboard floor," "a counterfeit table," and, in a description suggesting total alienation from the world modern technology has wrought, "windows that flash open on someone's city, / and little more." The poet sees herself as a sort of free-floating element in a world at once confining and inhospitable, a world she can in no way embrace as belonging to her. She inhabits a universe which Robert Lowell has described as "our monotonous sublime," in which we must often wonder whom to properly acknowledge as the agents of our actions. "Someone plays with me," complains Miss Sexton. "Someone pretends with me—I am walled in solid by their noise." She knows what is expected of her, that she also must pretend to satisfy others, that she must show "no evidence of ruin or fears," no sign of the chaos within her and the senseless terror and destruction outside of her. She wants to flee from contingency, from her habits of acquiescence and patient self-hatred. She wants to be transcendently beautiful, unclassified, not a woman but something rare and detached, like the angelic creatures in "Consorting with Angels," "each one like a poem obeying itself, / performing God's functions, / a people apart."

Miss Sexton concludes her sequence with a poem called "Live," an affirmation of such "mundane" qualities as simple fortitude, self-reliance, and love of dogs and children. The poem is a triumph of determination and insight, a final resolution of irreconcilabilities that had threatened to remain perpetually suspended and apart. Miss Sexton's affirmation represents a rebirth of astounding proportions, a veritable reconstruction of her self-image in the face of a corrupt and corrupting universe. The poet strengthens herself by struggling to identify with her children, with the spontaneity of their responses to life. Miss Sexton's indomitable need to engage the reality of her own peculiar obsessions, jealousies, and cruelties does not spoil the poems in which she draws ever closer to her children, but instead imbues them with an air of desperation to which we cannot help responding. In the midst of "A Little Uncomplicated Hymn" for the daughter she names Joy, she fears that she is being dishonest, that she does not deserve to sing songs of pure peace and harmony. She yearns to participate in the innocent games and delightful fantasies of childhood, but she wonders, in another poem, watching her daughter's eyes open after retreating under closed lids: "Perhaps they will say nothing, / perhaps they will be dark and leaden, / having played their own game / somewhere else, / somewhere far off." As always, the poet is beset by uncertainties. She is still dependent, even with relation to her young daughter. She cannot take the initiative.

What Miss Sexton comes to see in the course of her book, covering three stormy years, is that to maintain innocence, an openness to life and a regular communion with diverse phenomena, the child must be oblivious to certain fundamental considerations. The innocence of the child is really nothing less than an ability to live blithely in the face of contingency, to live as though we held the key to our own fate. In "Your Face on the Dog's Neck," Miss Sexton recoils at her daughter's pastoral intimacy with "this spayed and flatulent bitch," "that infectious dog," but she sees that to truly enter the child's world, to partake of her simple vision, she must banish her inveterate hesitancy, and embrace life joyously in all its soiled and spotted variety. She must not be too mindful of the neighbor's symbolic lawnmower, as it ". . . bites and spits out / some new little rows of innocent grass."

Miss Sexton's salvation lies in her twin capacities for irony and love. At moments of intense depression, she retains an attitude of sardonic anger toward herself and toward a world which will not help her. This sardonic streak, obviously also a component of Miss Plath's later work, intermittently erupts as a peculiarly laughable and bitter form of self-mockery, as in "The Addict," where she describes herself as "the queen of this condition," "something of a chemical / mixture. / That's it!" and "a little buttercup in my yellow nightie." This poem is wonderfully effective in the way it undercuts the terrible worry and concern that originally occasioned the poem. Miss Sexton seems genuinely amused that her condition should have progressed as far as it has, that she is indeed a grotesque spectacle, as unbearable to herself as she must be to others. The irony, the mockery, has as its object, of course, a distancing, making tolerable that which is too painful to contemplate. The literary antecedents for such an aesthetic device are legion, though rarely has an artist been so deft and inventive as Miss Sexton in carrying it to great extremes. Aside from the aesthetic accomplishment, though, a poem like "The Addict" permits Miss Sexton to step back from herself, from the image of herself with which she is so constantly at odds. It permits her, that is, to accomplish, even if only for a moment, what she so desperately wanted—to escape the self-absorption which has kept her a prisoner of her own fantasies and delusions. The control implicit in the poet's manipulation of her self-image for aesthetic purposes becomes a demonstration of a capacity which had for too long lain unused and forgotten.

Miss Sexton's poems, then, come as close as we can expect anyone to come to that creation of a poetic universe which is at the same time a re-creation of the self, a restructuring of a general orientation to reality. As such, it is invigorating and significant in a way we had not thought great poetry could any longer be: it renews our capacity for delight and joy in the created world of the poem, and in the world of men which we inhabit. There is something awesome, even sublime in a woman who is not afraid to sound crude or shrill so long as she is honest, who in her best work sounds neither shrill nor crude precisely because she is honest. At the end of this long journey, this dark night of the soul, Miss Sexton emerges triumphant, deciding not to kill the eight inconvenient Dalmatian puppies everyone advises her to drown: "I promise to love more if they come, / because in spite of cruelty / and the stuffed railroad cars for the ovens, / I am not what I expected. Not an Eichmann. / The poison just didn't take. / So I won't hang around in my hospital shift, / repeating the Black Mass and all of it." Miss Sexton's decision to live, with her eyes open, and the responsibility for human values planted firmly on her competent shoulders, is a major statement of our poetry.

JON ROSENBLATT

Plath and Sexton

Even though many critics use the term *confessional* as a neutral label for a poetic movement, the word must indicate a narrowing of the range of literary possibility and achievement. Inevitably, confessionalism suggests that the writer has written so directly out of his personal experience and memory that he does not separate his autobiographical self from his projection in the poem. This sense of the term applies to many poets who rely on autobiography without any transforming or structuring principle in their poems. In much of Anne Sexton's poetry, for example, it is difficult to see how the impulse to self-revelation has been at all fashioned into a meaningful, self-sufficient aesthetic form. But this sort of confessionalism does not apply to Plath's work. Plath employs numerous personae; she establishes objective settings within which the speakers of her poems dramatize themselves; and she consistently employs imagery in a nonrealistic manner. Rather than using the personal image or autobiographical reference to reflect back upon herself, Plath uses personal allusions as the foundation for dramas of transformation and psychological process. . . .

Anne Sexton's work, on the other hand, defines how extraordinary a poet Plath really is. Working with similar material, particularly the subjects of suicide and madness, Sexton produces poems of sociological and biographical interest. The immediacy of Plath's work is absent in Sexton's because the tension between speaker and reader has collapsed. Sexton's poetry suggests no more than nonstop diary reading: the audience does not exist as a force inside or outside the poem. The poems suggest that they will enter into the complexities of the self, but they turn into loose-jointed, self-indulgent mono-

From *Sylvia Plath: The Poetry of Initiation* (Chapel Hill: University of North Carolina Press, 1979). Reprinted by permission of the author.

logues. Encountering nothing outside them[selves] of signifi-
cance, they tend to be wordy, repetitious, and self-inflated.
These faults could be exemplified at length from any of Sexton's
volumes, but a good contrast with Plath lies in the comparison
of "Daddy" with this passage from "Those Times . . . ," a
childhood reminiscence in Sexton's *Live or Die* (1966):

> I will speak of the little childhood cruelties,
> being a third child,
> the last given
> and the last taken—
> of the nightly humiliations when Mother undressed me,
> of the life of the daytime, locked in my room—
> being the unwanted, the mistake
> that Mother used to keep Father
> from his divorce.
> Divorce!
> The romantic's friend,
> romantics who fly into maps
> of other countries,
> hips and noses and mountains,
> into Asia or the Black Forest,
> or caught by 1928,
> the year of the *me,*
> by mistake,
> not for divorce
> but instead.

(Live or Die, p. 29)

The problem with Sexton's poem lies, first, in its failure to
objectify the memories of Father and Mother. While Plath leaves
no possibility for doubt about the nature of Daddy, dramatizing
each moment of awareness or memory of him, Sexton begins
portentously—"I will speak of the little childhood cruelties"—
and then provides only vague references to what happened to
her as a child. The "humiliations" when she undressed are un-
specified, for example, although it is not clear why she felt hu-
miliated in front of her mother. No clear image emerges of her
father or mother, whereas "Daddy" brilliantly enlarges the
memory of Plath's father to legendary proportions. Plath dra-

matizes the situation between daughter and father as if no time had passed since the father's death: the emotional situation is still burning in her consciousness. But Sexton's words suggest someone who is trying to call up a strong emotion that has lost much of its original power.

Second, Sexton's poem is marred by the triviality of its associations. It jumps from personal reference to personal reference, never elevating the material to anything more than personal nostalgia and grief. If 1928 is the "year of the *me,*" according to the poem, then the reader has the right to know why this *me* is of significance. The poet assumes a self-importance that she does not demonstrate, she becomes involved in her autobiography. But Plath is not interested in detailing the facts of her life—the year of her birth, the marital difficulties of her parents, the nature of the parents' argument over divorce—but in presenting the processes of consciousness. "Daddy" is brilliant precisely because of its wide-ranging associations to Nazism, to Freudian theories, and to ritual patterns. The wildness of the emotion is contained and channeled through these structures, whereas Sexton's work exemplifies the worst aspects of confessionalism: an impulse to confess without adequate means to transform the personal material.

GREG JOHNSON

The Achievement of Anne Sexton

When we must deal with problems, we instinctively resist trying the way that leads through obscurity and darkness. We wish to hear only of unequivocal results, and completely forget that these results can only be brought about when we have ventured into and emerged again from darkness. . . .
—*Carl Jung*, The Stages of Life

I

At the heart of Anne Sexton's poetry is a search for identity, and her well-known infatuation with death—the cause of her rather notorious fame, and the apparent reason her work is often dismissed as beneath serious consideration—has little to do with this search; in her best work, in fact, it is most often an annoying irrelevancy, however potent it seems in its occasional command of the poet's psyche. Quite simply, Sexton's poetry is a poetry of life, and if her work is "confessional" at times, or even most of the time, this does not mean that the poet's confessions (the word itself is misleading) necessarily describe experiences ridden with guilt or pain. This is where Sexton's poetry diverges so dramatically from that of Sylvia Plath, of whom she is frequently seen as a kind of epigonic follower. Plath mythologizes death with great power and succinctness, and places herself at the center of a myth whose message is "blackness—blackness and silence"; her vision is brutally nihilistic, and she embraces it willingly. Plath's struggle is that of the mythmaker—primarily artistic rather than personal, since the personal self is mercilessly pared away in her poetry (as are all other selves) in deference to the controlling myth. Anne Sexton, on the other hand, speaks longingly and

First appeared in *The Hollins Critic* 21, no. 2 (1984). Reprinted by permission of *The Hollins Critic*, holder of copyright.

lovingly of a world of health, of childlike wholeness—a world toward which she struggles valiantly and against insuperable odds. To understand her poetry as a record of this struggle, and as a testament to its value and importance, is to appreciate its special relevance to the contemporary world, a world of increasing disjunction between personal and social selves and one whose chaotic, literally "maddening" effect on the individual mind Anne Sexton manages to convey with that blend of craft and vulnerability that is her special magic.

Unlike Plath, and certainly unlike Robert Lowell—with whom her name is also frequently and pointlessly linked—Sexton is a Primitive, an extraordinarily intense artist who confronts her experience with unsettling directness, largely innocent of "tradition" and privately developing an idiom exactly suited to that experience. As Louis Simpson remarked after the publication of her first book, "This then is a phenomenon . . . to remind us, when we have forgotten in the weariness of literature, that poetry can happen." The reader's sense of the direct and seemingly spontaneous quality of Sexton's earliest volumes—*To Bedlam and Part Way Back* (1960), *All My Pretty Ones* (1962), and *Live or Die* (1966)—can partially be explained by noting that she first began writing poetry, at the age of twenty-eight, as a form of personal therapy, a way of formalizing past traumas and of coping with an increasing sense of disorientation in her conventional role of suburban wife and mother. Her emotional instability, including her suicidal impulses, contributed to the immediacy, rawness, and power of much of the poetry. This kind of therapy no doubt helped the poet in her personal life, but what is heroic in Sexton's case, and particularly relevant to her readers, is the earnestness and scrupulosity with which she mastered her craft, developed her highly original voice, and set about the task of communicating her experience to others. That Anne Sexton herself later succumbed to the "weariness of literature"—her later work, on the whole, is distinctly inferior to her early poetry, and verges at times on self-parody—and finally to her own destructive impulses, does not diminish the value and irresistible power of her finest achievements, which speak to us in a voice by turns inspired and beleaguered, joyful and aggrieved, lost in the confusions of self but found, ultimately, in her masterful articulation of her experience as a whole, a complex experience which serves as a painfully truthful mirror of the age.

II

Sexton's first two volumes have much in common, both in their multi-faceted handling of the identity theme and in their adherence to rather strict poetic forms. In both there is a constructive relationship between the deeply painful, inchoate materials—experiences in a mental institution, the loss of the poet's parents, and unceasing struggle to define her own selfhood—and the restraining, masterful form of the poems themselves. There is little sense that the poet is arbitrarily forcing her experiences into rigid, inappropriate shapes, primarily because she convinces us that she has pierced to the core of those experiences to discover shapes inherent in them; the formal, measured quality of the verse not only indicates the poet's necessary caution in dealing with her turbulent materials, but also establishes a crucial distance from which she may safely view her continuing struggle and present it to her readers in palatable form. Yet the controlled, meditative voice of these early poems is frequently mingled with an openly vulnerable, "confessional" voice, one which conveys genuine, childlike experiences of pain and terror. The poems are neither songs of innocence nor experience, but continually oscillate between conflicting states of mind, admitting continued disorientation while simultaneously creating an impressive poetic order.

An important difference between the first two books should be recognized, however. *To Bedlam and Part Way Back* comprises an ordering of a specific, urgent experience—the descent into madness and a partial return—while *All My Pretty Ones* broadens from this painful but rich experience to consider more general themes of loss (especially the loss of parents) and upon an explicit need to define the poet's self in terms of the world. Although Sexton's books describe an ongoing personal development and flow naturally one into the other, each of the early volumes has a distinct identity and merits separate discussion. As Geoffrey Hartman has noted, *To Bedlam and Part Way Back* is not merely a collection of poems but "truly a *book*," and there is ample evidence that Sexton organized the volume with meticulous care.

The shorter lyrics in part 1 deal with a cluster of obsessive themes, all related to the poet's search for identity, while the pair of long, meditative poems in part 2 achieve a tentative but emotionally satisfying resolution.

Anne Sexton expresses concern about her female identity in a way which links her, especially in her first book, to other American female poets. Many of these poets initiate the search for identity by complaining, in strikingly analogous language, of an original and mysterious feeling of loss. "A loss of something ever felt I," wrote Emily Dickinson in only one of her many expressions of this idea, and Sylvia Plath, in her long poem "Three Women," voices a similar lament: "What is it I miss? / Shall I ever find it, whatever it is?" Sexton's tone, however, is not wistful but strident, calmly determined "to question this diminishing" ("Funnel"); in "The Lost Ingredient" she laments the seeming futility of her search:

> Today is made of yesterday, each time I steal
> toward rites I do not know, waiting for the lost
> ingredient, as if salt or money or even lust
> would keep us calm and prove us whole at last.

"Am I still lost? Once I was beautiful," she says in a poem addressed to her psychiatrist ("You, Dr. Martin"). The revealing non sequitur—a familiar device in Sexton's work—raises another major concern in this first volume: her identity as a conventional woman (a "beautiful" wife, a devoted mother) has proved to be only a partial one; it is this recognition that has precipitated the speaker's crisis, but which may also lead to full self-realization, a recapturing of the "lost ingredient."

By far the majority of poems in *To Bedlam and Part Way Back* explore the poet's identity in terms of other women. There are poems about being buried alive ("The Moss of His Skin"), paralysis within a marriage and its "pantomime of love" ("The Farmer's Wife"), the literal paralysis of the goddess Diana, changed forever to a laurel tree and noting in despair that "blood moves still in my bark bound veins" ("Where I Live in This Honorable House of the Laurel Tree"). In one of the most moving of these poems, "Unknown Girl in the Maternity Ward," Sexton dramatizes the relationship between a mother and her daughter with a typical mingling of tenderness and a hopeless sense of estrangement. The mother can only consider her child a "fragile visitor," her "funny kin," and the reason is the mother's lack of her own selfhood, since she is, after all, "unknown":

> I touch your cheeks, like flowers. You bruise
> against me. We unlearn. I am a shore
> rocking you off. You break from me. I choose
> your only way, my small inheritor
> and hand you off, trembling the selves we lose.

The lost self, in this case, is one which fails to emerge even in the most basic relationship between a mother and child. Sylvia Plath, in a more direct and angry protest at this failure, says to her own child, "Off, off, eely tentacle! / There is nothing between us"—the child is envisioned as a mere hindrance to the achievement of the ruthlessly independent, mythologized self of *Ariel*. But Anne Sexton yearns back toward human connections, and her madness rises from her sharp awareness that these connections are lost, and that the loss is irrevocable.

In seeking to define her own identity through poetic fictions about other women, and about relationships between women, Sexton merely sees her own identity as inferior and finds that genuine relationship is unavailable. Later volumes will explore the causes behind her failure to "connect" meaningfully with others, but in *To Bedlam and Part Way Back,* her failure leads directly into madness. Although she pictured herself, wryly, as "a secret beatnik hiding in the suburbs in a square house on a dull street," any pride she might have taken in her role as poet seems cancelled by this image of herself as a misfit, someone who did not live in that "good world" she envied her great aunt and could not create for herself. One senses that Anne Sexton felt herself forced into poetry, that her inability to find satisfaction in a conventional role made the pose of a "secret beatnik," a rebel—in the sense that both poetry and madness are forms of rebellion—her only means of survival. Unlike Emily Dickinson, who felt that "Much Madness is divinest Sense" and whose extreme self-sufficiency (however "mad" it might have appeared to her Amherst contemporaries) was the sign of a fully realized identity, Sexton desperately needed the approval of others: "I want everyone to hold up large signs saying YOU'RE A GOOD GIRL." Her belief that she had failed to be "good," and that she had no way of finding a "good world," led to a madness that was not divinest sense but hellish chaos, a threatened disintegration of selfhood.

This linking of madness with evil, with the inability to be "good," recurs in Sexton's poems dealing with her experiences in mental institutions. She continues to lament her sense of loss and disorientation: "They lock me in this chair at eight a.m. / and there are no signs to tell the way" ("Music Swims Back to Me"). In the first stanza of this poem she pictures herself as an orphan seeking the way home:

> Wait Mister. Which way is home?
> They turned the light out
> and the dark is moving in the corner.
> There are no sign posts in this room,
> four ladies, over eighty,
> in diapers every one of them.
> La la la, Oh music swims back to me
> and I can feel the tune they played
> the night they left me
> in this private institution on a hill.

These lines, like Ophelia's mad speeches, blend irreality and the absence of sequential thought with a terrifying, sane intuition; immersed in a surreal, abandoned world, the speaker nonetheless understands her need to escape, to find "sign posts" back toward health.

Does Sexton imagine any way out of this impasse, any way to escape the debilitating terror of a consciousness plagued by a conviction of its own evil? One possibility is to replace self-loathing with an open acceptance of evil—even admitting the likelihood that she is "not a woman." What is remarkable, however, is not this admission itself but the lively, almost gleeful tone in which it is uttered:

> I have gone out, a possessed witch,
> haunting the black air, braver at night;
> dreaming of evil, I have done my hitch

over the plain houses, light by light:
lonely thing, twelve-fingered, out of mind.
A woman like that is not a woman, quite.
I have been her kind.

("Her Kind")

"A woman like that is misunderstood," Sexton adds wryly, but the poem is a serious attempt to understand such a woman—her sense of estrangement, her impulse toward death—by internalizing evil and giving it a voice: a chortling, self-satisfied, altogether amiable voice which suggests that "evil" is perhaps the wrong word after all. Sexton's witch, waving her "nude arms at villages going by," becomes something of value to the community, performing the function Kurt Vonnegut has called the "domestication of terror." Unlike Plath's madwoman in "Lady Lazarus"—a woman at the service of a private, unyielding anger, a red-haired demon whose revenge is to "eat men like air"—Sexton's witch is essentially harmless. Although she remains vulnerable—"A woman like that is not ashamed to die"—she rejects anger in favor of humor, flamboyance, self-mockery. She is a kind of perverse entertainer, and if she seems cast in the role of a martyr, embracing madness in order to domesticate it for the rest of the community—making it seem less threatening, perhaps even enjoyable—it is nevertheless a martyrdom which this aspect of Sexton accepts with a peculiar zest.

Poems like "Her Kind" and "Music Swims Back to Me" help create the famous, fatally glamorous mask of Anne Sexton—part lovable witch, part helpless madwoman—for which she became famous, and which is often discussed as if it were the only self present in Sexton's poetry. Denise Levertov, in her well-intentioned, somewhat patronizing remarks on Sexton's suicide, suggested that Sexton was "too intensely troubled to be fully aware of her influence or to take on its responsibility. Therefore it seems to me that we who are alive must make clear, as she could not, the distinction between creativity and self-destruction." But Sexton did take on a personal responsibility for the interest her work aroused—she sent cheerful, supportive letters, for instance, to the countless victims of mental illness who wrote to her—and much of her poetry, from the first volume onward, expresses anguish over her destructive impulses, with an awareness that they are threatening to her poetry as well as to her personal well-being.

Part 2 of *To Bedlam and Part Way Back* contains only three poems, but they are long, reflective works which attempt to take stock of the poet's progress, to state a rationale for her kind of poetry, and especially to acknowledge lifelong conflicts that have prevented a healthy development of self. These goals are directly addressed in the volume's longest and finest poem, "The Double Image." Here the poet gathers all her themes into a single autobiographical narration, seeking that "certain sense of order" through a careful, measured recounting of her seemingly chaotic and random experiences. Like many of Sexton's more somber, reflective poems, "The Double Image" is addressed to her daughter, establishing the crucial dynamic between the poet's desire for an affectionate, healthy relationship with the child, and her yearning toward the madness that threatens to separate them. The poem's tender, carefully modulated voice is firmly aligned on the side of health, but the poet remains aware of her continued vulnerability. She sees her madness as an unknown, demonic force, an "ugly angel" whose voice enchants the poet—much like the "disquieting muses" in Plath's analogous narrative. After giving way to madness and losing her child, Sexton has returned as a "partly mended thing," still unable to assume a healthy identity:

> . . . I had to learn
> why I would rather
> die than love, how your innocence
> would hurt and how I gather
> guilt like a young intern
> his symptoms, his certain evidence.

The poem's title refers to Sexton's mother and daughter, seen as potent forces pulling her simultaneously in two directions. Sexton's mother (certainly a cold, uncaring figure in this poem) represents "the stony head of death," while the final lines speak of the daughter's inestimable value for the poet's present self, not only as a symbol of the life-force but as a hopeful fore-shadowing of her own developing selfhood:

> . . . We named you Joy.
> I, who was never quite sure
> about being a girl, needed another
> life, another image to remind me.
> And this was my worst guilt; you could not cure
> nor soothe it. I made you to find me.

In the volume's concluding poem, "The Division of Parts," she admits that she cannot escape her dead mother, now a "god-in-her-moon," and she rehearses the religious guilt that will become an increasingly potent theme in her later work; but with the flowering of her poetic gift in a remarkable first volume, the birth of a daughter named Joy, and a general rise of self-esteem in her success as a woman of letters, Sexton makes a heroic effort to put Bedlam behind her, finding solace in the attempt to appreciate—and record—the complexities of her experience.

In Sexton's second volume, *All My Pretty Ones* (1962), she broadens her scope from consideration of the specific, urgent experience of madness to consider more universally comprehensible forms of loss. Sexton's parents died in 1959, and though she insisted at the time that she would not write poems about them, she later changed her mind. The first part of this volume contains "The Truth the Dead Know," "All My Pretty Ones" and "Lament," poems dealing with her parents' deaths and among the finest she ever wrote. Not surprisingly, the ostensible theme of bereavement is mingled with an examination of the poet's continuing struggle toward identity. In that strange, bitter elegy, "The Truth the Dead Know," Sexton seems to eschew the common rituals of mourning: "Gone, I say and walk from church, / refusing the stiff procession to the grave"; she prefers, instead, to "cultivate myself" and to avoid such a powerful intimation of mortality as the death of both parents within a few months. The poem ends, however, by emphasizing not her own refusals but those of the dead, and into her voice creeps something like envy:

> And what of the dead? They lie without shoes
> in their stone boats. They are more like stone

than the sea would be if it stopped. They refuse
to be blessed, throat, eye and knucklebone.

A far gentler, more nostalgic poem like "Young" recalls the
poet's innocence as a "lonely kid" whose relationship to her
mother was not yet perceived as a "funnel"; and in "Old Dwarf
Heart" she creates a separate, mythical self—again resembling
Plath's disquieting muses—who insists upon "the decay we're
made of": "When I lie down to love, old dwarf heart shakes her
head." Sexton can never escape this destructive self ("Where I
go, she goes"), which is perceived as having originated in a
vicious Oedipal "tangle," but the loss of her parents does give
her a kind of grim new beginning, and the rest of the volume
explores various avenues of escape.

In her attempt to counter the truth the dead know with a
gentler, more humanizing truth, Sexton seeks out two major
sources of comfort: religious belief and domestic love. Her early
cluster of religious poems, forming part 2 of *All My Pretty Ones,*
initiates a theme that will recur throughout her work—es-
pecially in her posthumous volume, *The Awful Rowing Toward
God* (1975)—but she seemed to find little solace in her religious
ponderings; at times, in fact, they only increase her sense of
guilt. In "With Mercy for the Greedy," addressed to a Catholic
friend who tried to convert the poet, Sexton says with childlike
sincerity: "I detest my sins and I try to believe / in The Cross. I
touch its tender hips, its dark jawed face, / its solid neck, its
brown sleep." Unlike Emily Dickinson, who saw herself locked
in a battle of wills with God the Father, a Puritan Nobodaddy
who threatened her own sense of self, Sexton was drawn toward
the image of a gentle, redemptive Christ, a God who was pal-
pably human. But she concludes, ruefully, "Need is not quite
belief," and explains, with typical Sexton wryness, "I was born
doing reference work in sin. . . ." In part 3, which consists of a
single poem, "The Fortress," Sexton insists that the love be-
tween herself and her daughter has greater redemptive power
than any religious belief. The poet has a sense of her own value,
however fleeting, in her protectiveness toward her daughter:
"What ark / can I fill for you when the world goes wild?"
Although she knows that "Life is not in my hands" and cannot
promise that her daughter will find happiness, the poem empha-
sizes their tender domestic alliance, the "fortress" their together-

ness forms against the "bombs" of experience.

In one of the volume's most impressive poems, "Letter Written on a Ferry While Crossing Long Island Sound," Sexton makes an ordinary boat ride into the occasion of an optimistic, even transcendent spiritual vision. Although the ocean seems "without miracles or rage / or unusual hope," she sees four nuns sitting together "like a bridge club," and in a long, striking passage, half prayer and half fantasy, she imagines them rising up from the poet's depressed vision of reality, her incalculable "sadness," to serve as messengers of hope. The poem mingles Sexton's gift for whimsical description and her ability to convey her own dire state of need. She sees "these four nuns / loosen from their leather boots / and their wooden chairs," and then:

> There go my dark girls,
> their dresses puff
> in the leeward air.
> Oh, they are lighter than flying dogs . . .
> They are going up.
> See them rise
> on black wings, drinking
> the sky, without smiles
> or hands
> or shoes.
> They call back to us
> from the gauzy edge of paradise,
> *good news, good news.*

Sexton yearns toward the gauzy edge of paradise, she hopes for good news, yet she remains surrounded by the "whitehearted water" of "The Truth the Dead Know," and that despairing truth affects even her most hopeful visions. Exercising her "black art" in a wide range of poetic styles and voices, giving definite form to hope as well as to despair, Sexton had yet to confront the most basic question of her poetic and personal lives.

III

With two accomplished volumes behind her, with a blossoming career and innumerable devoted readers, she summoned the courage to bluntly question the value of living—to decide whether, in fact, the pain of life does not outweigh its rewards. In "The Black Art" she insisted: "A woman who writes feels too much, / those trances and portents!" Her decision to explore fully those excessive feelings, to relate her mysterious "trances and portents" to her central concerns of identity, poetry and survival, helped her toward *Live or Die* (1966), winner of a Pulitzer Prize and the finest achievement of her career. The volume's title represents an ultimatum; the poems themselves, arranged in chronological order and reading, as Sexton herself noted, like a "fever chart," show the poet moving toward a stark confrontation with her suicidal impulses and with her "portent" that life as a whole—not only for her, but perhaps for everyone—is simply not worthwhile. And yet, as one astute reviewer, Thomas P. McDonnell, noted at the time *Live or Die* was first published, Sexton gives us more than "impulses": "(this) is not a poetry of spasmodic revelation or of occasional incident transformed from similitude to artifact: in its continuing wholeness one perceives the suggestion of a journey." It was a journey, as *Live or Die* makes clear, upon whose outcome rested her life itself, and one she approaches with great courage and her developed artistic powers.

Carl Jung, discussing the obstacles to personal growth, notes that venturing into "obscurity and darkness" is absolutely essential in the quest for a new stage of development, a higher individuation of self. For Anne Sexton, there were two kinds of "darkness"—her madness, which represented personal defeat; and that agonizing uncertainty about her life and her identity which could only be eased through poetry and whose resolution—even if temporary—could represent significant progress toward mental stability and a secure sense of self. In *Live or Die,* Sexton has greatly matured as woman and as poet: she does not glorify madness, setting herself apart from the rest of humanity, but rather perceives it as an ignoble escape and, most of all, as a colossal waste of time. The most fearsome "obscurity and darkness," Jung suggests, lies in a sane, ego-centered approach toward personal problems, not in a surrender to the chaotic promptings of the id. In her third volume Sexton recognizes this truth, and the recognition helps produce some of her finest poetry.

In her long, moving description of yet another confinement in a mental institution, "Flee on Your Donkey," the poet betrays little of her former fascination with madness; now the asylum is "the scene of the disordered senses," a place where she has wasted some of her best years:

> Six years of such small preoccupations!
> Six years of shuttling in and out of this place!
> O my hunger! My hunger!
> I could have gone around the world twice
> or had new children—all boys.
> It was a long trip with little days in it
> and no new places.

She now sees that her doctor represented a kind of crutch, someone who "promised me another world / to tell me who / I was." The poem concludes that madness is merely "the fool's disease," a way of "allowing myself the wasted life," and the poet finally exhorts herself: "Anne, Anne, / flee on your donkey, / flee this sad hotel. . . ."

Sexton, refusing the descent into madness, must now attempt to deal rationally with her nearly irresistible impulse toward suicide. Many poems in *Live or Die* deal explicitly with this subject: "To Lose the Earth," "Wanting to Die," "Suicide Note," and "Sylvia's Death," a poem about the suicide of Sylvia Plath. "The Addict" describes the part of Sexton that is a "death-monger": "I'm an expert on making the trip / and now they say I'm an addict." What has not been remarked about these poems, however, is that their imagery, tone, and often their explicit argument speak *against* suicide; Sexton is not flirting with death but attempting to exorcize personal demons, to understand her impulses and thereby transcend them. In "Wanting to Die" she addresses an unnamed "you"—perhaps the rational, questioning part of the poet's own psyche—and her voice seems rueful, melancholy. The poem's first stanza is one of the finest Sexton ever wrote:

> Since you ask, most days I cannot remember.
> I walk in my clothing, unmarked by that voyage.
> Then the almost unnameable lust returns.

Here the desire for suicide is a "lust," and therefore love—as the poem's final line claims—can only represent an "infection." Sexton emphasizes not only this perversity in the suicidal impulse but also its blatant irrationality: "suicides have a special language. / Like carpenters they want to know *which tools*. / They never ask *why build*." Summoning up her own former persona, the glamorous witch of her earlier volumes, Sexton realizes that she had "possessed the enemy," had "taken on his craft, his magic," but that this represented an erroneous course, a capitulation to destructive forces. In "Suicide Note" she admits that "I am only a coward / crying *me me me*" and in "Sylvia's Death," despite her acknowledged envy of Plath ("I know at the news of your death, / a terrible taste for it"), Sexton emphasizes Plath's defeat. She gained nothing through her suicide, Sexton implies, since death is nothing but an "old belonging," and she finally refers to Plath's diminishment, her new identity as a mere "blonde thing" who has relinquished her own "special language" and received nothing in return.

In "Wanting to Die," Sexton notes that her own body, her essential physical self, is only a "bad prison" that should be emptied of breath, of life. Through poetry she sought liberation from this cruel and unnecessary prison, a liberation that could come only through a compassionate acceptance of her own flawed but redeemable self. Thus her emphasis in *Live or Die* is not upon "confession," with its implication of guilt, but upon compassion for herself and for all those who have influenced her personal existence. Seeking out the origin of her illness in childhood traumas and inadequate relationships with her parents, she is not interested in assigning blame but in bringing to light the dismal facts themselves; there is a new, strong impulse to face past realities and to assess their impact on the present. If this produced only a partial liberation, at least it represented an *earned* freedom that could directly affect the poet's life—acting as a form of therapy—and intensify the honesty of her art as well.

"They put me in the Closet," Emily Dickinson wrote, "because they liked me 'still' "—but the poem focuses upon her elders' inability to imprison the poet's spirit (defined as inhering in her poetic faculties) even in childhood. Anne Sexton is far less confident than this; she lacks Dickinson's firm sense of mission, she frequently distrusts her own creative excitement, and she cannot conceive of her identity—even in its aspect of poetic creativity—as having sufficient strength to withstand external constraints. Her typical reaction to her own analogous experiences is one of fear. "Imitations of Drowning," for instance, includes this bleak reminiscence: "I was shut up in that closet, until, biting the door, / they dragged me out, dribbling urine on the gritty shore." The poem concludes: "in the end it's fear that drowns you." In her superb long poem, "Those Times . . . ," she elaborates upon the sufferings of her childhood:

> I was locked in my room all day behind a gate,
> a prison cell.
> I was the exile
> who sat all day in a knot.

Although this situation may recall that of Plath's "Daddy," in which the poet recalls living under her father's domination like a foot trapped inside a black shoe, "poor and white, / Barely daring to breathe or Achoo," Sexton's poem lacks vindictiveness or even anger; it simply tells what happened.

The poem's description brilliantly conveys her early terror and helplessness:

> The closet is where I rehearsed my life,
> all day among shoes,
> away from the glare of the bulb in the ceiling,
> away from the bed and the heavy table
> and the same terrible rose repeating on the walls.

Locked in her bedroom, the child retreats into an even smaller cell, her closet, but one whose conditions she could control. There she "rehearsed" her life, as if unconsciously attempting to ignore the distorting influences of her present experience. When her stern, punishing mother "came to force me to undress"— the phrase contains an unmistakable suggestion of rape—Sexton says that she "lay there silently, / hoarding my small dignity." Certain phrases recur throughout the poem, testifying to the child's ignorance: "I did not question it," "I did not ask," "I did not know." The poem is remarkable for its withholding of judgment: it creates sympathy for the mother as well as for the suffering child. As so often in Sexton's work, the true villain seems to be life itself, whose tragic process insists upon the movement away from innocence toward unending pain, and its resulting tragic awareness.

Live or Die is Sexton's first volume, after all, which simply arranges the poems in chronological order, as if surrendering to the flux of experience, its chequered pattern of elation and despair. Yet there are many elements which form a constant, hopeful strand in the fabric of Sexton's continued pain: humor and tenderness, the recognition of madness as a waste of time, a caustic, disapproving attitude toward suicide, and a remarkable development of the poet's artistic powers. The volume frequently celebrates personal relationships, and it exalts the artist's autonomy and necessary solitude. The poem "Live," which Sexton chose to conclude the volume, represents a new, mature attitude, a recognition of these positive elements as a possible starting point for a new stage of personal development. It ends with a positive, infectious excitement:

> The poison just didn't take.
> So I won't hang around in my hospital shift,
> repeating The Black Mass and all of it.
> I say *Live, Live* because of the sun,
> the dream, the excitable gift.

IV

After *Live or Die,* Sexton's personal evolution began to seem increasingly frenetic and directionless. In her later volumes she assumes various effective guises—the witty lover of *Love Poems* (1969), the ribald folklorist of *Transformations* (1971), the religious seeker of *The Awful Rowing Toward God* (1975)—but never again does she achieve the immediacy and fullness of *Live or Die,* a book that shows her largest, most personal issue examined with her utmost energy and clarity. In a sense, her later books are elaborate footnotes to that volume, developing ancillary themes and exploring areas of existence which become important once Sexton has made her crucial decision to live. And, as many critics have noted, she began to abandon the careful craftsmanship so evident in the early volumes, producing a larger number of poems but letting their quality suffer a noticeable decline. Increasingly uncertain about the direction of her career, Sexton began to rely on the familiar, melodramatic voice of her earlier work, frequently repeating herself and no longer seeming able, or willing, to hone that voice through a rigorous attention to form, or to deepen its implications through fresh or suprising insights. As an artist, in short, she seems to stop growing. As a result, the American literary myth that a writer is only as good as her last book has been extremely damaging to Sexton, as expressed in the form of harsh or dimissive reviews of her last volumes. The recently issued collected edition of her work, however, should force readers to take another look, and especially to rediscover the value of Sexton's important earlier work.

In a letter written a few weeks before her death, Sexton remarks upon the famous closing poem of *Live or Die:*

> I do not know how I feel about such an old poem as "Live" in *Live or Die.* The poems stand for the moment they are written and make no promises to the future events and consciousness and raising of the unconscious as happens as one goes forward and does not look backward for an answer in an old poem.

A typically breathless, headlong statement, one which contains—with the advantage of hindsight, we can see it easily—a veiled warning, as well as a surprisingly harsh contempt of "old poems" representing experiences that are past, dead, no longer available to the poet (and, it would seem, no longer interesting to her). On the surface, it also suggests an unwillingness to *learn* from experience, to assimilate past insights into the vulnerable present consciousness as talismanic reminders, if not as forms of positive moral instruction. But actually the statement is consistent with Sexton's poetry as a whole, and merely states once again the darker side of her belief: one cannot go backward, and the poet can "make no promises" that artistic resolutions can remain valid beyond the experience of a particular poem. "Experiment escorts us last," as Emily Dickinson wrote, and Sexton shared this frightening awareness of the uncertain, friable nature of personal evolution, of the pitfalls lying in wait at every turn of experience. What remains for us, after her death, is to admire her spirit in facing that experience, to rejoice in her momentary triumphs and to recognize, in the poems themselves, her ultimate survival.

DIANA HUME GEORGE

From "Anne Sexton's Suicide Poems"

> *Anne, I don't want to live. . . . Now listen, life is lovely, but* I Can't Live
> It. *I can't even explain. I know how silly it sounds . . . but if you knew how it*
> Felt. *To be alive, yes, alive, but not be able to live it. Ay that's the rub. I am*
> *like a stone that lives . . . locked outside of all that's real. . . . Anne, do you*
> *know of such things, can you hear???? I wish, or think I wish, that* I *were dying*
> *of something for then I could be brave, but to be not dying, and yet . . . and yet to*
> *[be] behind a wall, watching everyone fit in where I can't, to talk behind a gray*
> *foggy wall, to live but to not reach or to reach wrong . . . to do it all wrong . . .*
> *believe me, (can you?) . . . what's wrong. I want to belong. I'm like a jew who*
> *ends up in the wrong country. I'm not a part. I'm not a member. I'm frozen.*
> —*Anne Sexton, from a letter to Anne Clark, October 13, 1964*

In the interim between Anne Sexton's first suicide attempt and
her final and successful one, an interval of some seventeen years,
she wrote at least twenty poems primarily dedicated to explain-
ing what it feels like to want, or need, to die. These poems
translate into understandable idiom the language, so foreign to
most people, of the suicide. As poems, I find them various in
their degrees of successful achievement. I find them similarly
various—and more than incidentally, identically various—in
their degree of success in being persuasive, in rendering under-
standable the suicidal impulse. By "identically various," I mean
that those poems which are what I'd call excellent poetically are
also those which are polemically persuasive—if this can be called
a polemic, and I think it can. The least successful, ironically, is
the one she wrote for "Sylvia's Death" in her third collection,
Live or Die. Reading this poem, and this one only, I feel I am
overhearing a pathetic competition between suicides, one ac-
complished and one potential, full of petty jealousy and envy
masquerading as eulogy. (It is the masquerade I find unsuc-

Reprinted with permission from the *Journal of Popular Culture* 18, no. 2 (1984),
pp. 21–29.

cessful, even offensive, not the open admission of envy that Sylvia got "that ride home with *our* boy" before Sexton did.) But in the same collection is her finest single poem on the subject, "Wanting to Die" which I want to explicate with the attention to detail I think it, and the issue, deserve.[1]

> Since you ask, most days I cannot remember.
> I walk in my clothing, unmarked by that voyage.
> Then the almost unnameable lust returns.

The speaker answers a question asked outside the poem's frame. It's not possible to know exactly what that question was, but a reasonable inference is that the questioner has inquired about her feelings toward life. She has been asked, in other words, to explain herself. The reader should not lose sight of the implicit audience whose question is the occasion of the poem; that outsider *is* the reader, who comes to such a poem with predictable assumptions and resistances. The first two lines are distant, detached, calm, as well as open and frank. The speaker is answering the question as directly as she can. But the lines are end-stopped, clipped, flat, almost tired. Each day is a trip, a voyage, but one the speaker moves through rather than participates in. The third line shifts abruptly from the weary business of life to the desire for death. The diction suggests intense, passionate, almost sexual involvement, but even this line is still explanatory in tone. The speaker explains the sequence of emotional events:

> Even then I have nothing against life.
> I know well the grass blades you mention,
> the furniture you have placed under the sun.

This could be an institutional lawn where the speaker might be talking to her doctor. But the questioner could as well be any person who cares about the speaker: a husband, a friend, a lover. In any case, an attitude has been conveyed from outside the frame of reference in the poem, and that attitude says, "see how good life is." The simple diction points to forces of fertility and evokes the comfort of man-made things as well. The furniture under the sun recalls warmth, human company, even perhaps domesticity, things that ordinarily make life worthwhile. Again, the tone of her response is detached and assessive:

> But suicides have a special language.
> Like carpenters, they want to know *which tools.*
> They never ask *why build.*

The speaker has shifted here from acknowledging the argument for life, to asserting the desire for death. To effect this, she is forced to use a metaphorical language, an analogy with something ordinary that the hearer will understand. Now the speaker must begin the arduous task of translating from a foreign language. This job becomes the central work of the poem, the subtle and controlling metaphor on which the poem stands—or falls. The effectiveness and precision of the translation, the communication of nuance and idiom into words the hearer will understand through his or her own language, are measures of the poem's success. The "language" of the suicide, to make the matter conceptually and practically tougher, is essentially nonverbal, and has to do with act rather than word. The speaker is trapped doubly: not only must she translate into words the hearer can understand; she must deal with the problem that the only words at her disposal are in a language whose structure emphatically asserts life. The connotations of the words she must press to her service are all loaded against her: life is good, death is bad. The moral imperatives of this language censure her position from the outset, for its values are as foreign to her as are the values of her speechless language to the hearer. She will be forced literally to overturn the structure of the hearer's language.

The speaker begins with an elementary analogy, a concrete simile easy enough to understand. In order to explain this "lust" of hers to someone who does not feel it, she chooses a dry, uncharged, explicit image to convey a state of mind whose essence is passionate. The carpenter comparison implies an unmentioned third element, the architect or planner who *does* ask "why build," as contrasted with the carpenter whose job it is to arrive at the site and begin to work. Suicides are like this, says the speaker. There is no word for them that translates into "why;" there is only "how," because it is definitive of a carpenter that he find the way to build, and just as definitive of the suicide that she find a way to die. The irony is effective, and underscores the reversal of connotive value that the poem has begun: carpenters are creators and builders. Suicides, as normal perception sees them, are destroyers. The hearer, if he is to enter into the linguistic universe of the suicide, must begin to see that for the suicide, killing oneself is a kind of building, a kind of creating. A final advantage of this simile is that its detached, apparently logical construction will mark the suicidal speaker as reasonable, capable of explaining irrationality in a rational, credible manner.

> Twice I have so simply declared myself,
> have possessed the enemy, eaten the enemy,
> have taken on his craft, his magic.

The speaker characterizes her two previous suicide attempts as totally integrated declarations of self. But who is the "enemy?" Is it death, or the means to death, perhaps some kind of drug? If she is using language in an ordinary sense, the enemy is obviously death. But consider the speaker's linguistic dilemma; in the special language of·the suicide, everything has duplicitous and paradoxical meaning. The enemy may, then, be life itself. When she takes the drug she mentions later, she finally possesses life completely, eats it up, burns it out, ends it. The ambiguity of the grammatical and thematic referent is a problem only if the reader demands that the language of the poem be irreducible. That ambiguity represents the central problem of the poem, the attempt to balance between two paradoxical versions of linguistic and intellectual reality.

From this point on, the "double language" of the poem becomes increasingly important; words and images are always both double and connotively contradictory. With this stanza, Sexton introduces another mediator between the two languages. Ritual and magic are invoked, just at the moment when the reader is asked to make a leap that abandons logic. The suicide has already made that leap. The poem has gently led to this, carefully remaining within the realm of the rational until now; it is time to listen to the suicide talking as much in her own terms as in the listener's. We have been well prepared by the poem for this reversal of values.

> In this way, heavy and thoughtful,
> warmer than oil or water,
> I have rested, drooling at the mouth-hole.

The tone here is subtly but decidedly positive. The speaker might be talking about taking a good nap. But "warmer" and "thoughtful" are yoked to other words not easily understood in a positive way. She is "heavy," and she drools, not from the mouth, but from "the mouth-hole." That phrase manages to objectify the self and the body, making both a vacancy, an absence, a hole. On my first reading of this poem, I reacted negatively to this stanza. If the speaker was trying to convince me that dying isn't so bad, "drooling at the mouth-hole" was hardly the way to win my approval, or even my understanding. But after a close and careful reading during which I was persuaded to enter the linguistic world of the poem, my reaction was different. I understand now how such a repellent image could be appealing *for the suicide*. Even if the suicide's language is never to be my own, I have come to understand that uneasy, careful translation of images.

> I did not think of my body at needle point.
> Even the cornea and the leftover urine were gone.
> Suicides have already betrayed the body.

The speaker grows bolder and less apologetic, more trusting of the hearer's understanding. She remains direct and unwavering in the presentation of details, but now they are unmitigated by helpful analogy. Instead, the speaker shifts to a cryptic explanatory line with the statement that suicides have always already betrayed the body, even, by implication, before they try to leave it. This kind of assertion is considerably distant from the language and the tone of the first stanzas of the poem, a long way from the sun and grass and lawn furniture and reasonable explanations.

> Still-born, they don't always die,
> but dazzled, they can't forget a drug so sweet
> that even children would look on and smile.

The image of a child in happy contemplation of the sweetness of death is difficult to stomach; somehow, it is especially objectionable to think of children half in love with easeful death. Why does this poem insist on the complicity of children? Why would the poet risk arousing our passionate defense of innocence? According to the speaker, her particular kind of suicide is figuratively stillborn, always close to that thin line between life and death first differentiated in the womb. The implication is that such people should have been born dead, and since they were not, they naturally spend their lives trying to return to the security of the womb, nexus of the boundary between life and death. The use of "children" attempts to communicate the purity and innocence of that feeling, from the suicide's perspective.

As the speaker moves further into the experience and language of the suicide, she maintains minimal but vital contact with the listener:

> To thrust all that life under your tongue!—
> that, all by itself, becomes a passion.

"Life" is perhaps the drug, the agent of death; this stanza presents the same kind of ambiguity as in stanza 4. The issue of control versus loss of it is the paradox: the speaker does the "thrusting" in an act of will. To gain control over life and death becomes a passion. But that passion is also the desire utterly to lose control.

> Death's a sad bone; bruised, you'd say,
> and yet she waits for me, year after year,
> to so delicately undo an old wound,
> to empty my breath from its bad prison.

Death is a sad bone and it is, by implication, in her bones—bones can signify both the skeletal outside and the very core or essence. "You'd say" that death is a sad bone, "bruised" in the sense that the desire for it results from a wound that can be healed. "You" refers directly back to the listener. From the last several stanzas, the poem has involved itself so totally in rendering the suicidal experience that the reader, if the poem has achieved the proper effect, is taken far away from the sun, the lawn chair, and the sympathetic questioner of the first stanza, even if the reader began by identifying with that questioner. "You'd" say—you, who do not want to admit that death waits from the beginning, that a person can be born sad. If the "old wound" is life, death undoes that by emptying the breath from her body and releasing her. But the poem has taught its readers to expect ambiguity; the old wound may be the unsuccessful suicide attempts the speaker mentioned earlier. In that case, death is still there, waiting to open the wound again, break open the scars, pull out the stitches, and let her die.

> Balanced there, suicides sometimes meet,
> raging at the fruit, a pumped-up moon,
> leaving the bread they mistook for a kiss

This use of language is bewildering no matter what you do with it. The poem has now progressed almost entirely into that "special language," and it is here that it will leave behind any reader who has not listened closely to the suicidal idiom. This stanza speaks of the suicide's nearly complete isolation from the comforting world of human touch, the total breakdown of predictable relationship between the human and the natural, the alienation from all people and objects, with the exception of the accidental "meeting" that can occur between one suicide and another. All the moorings of ordinary life are gone when the suicides are "balanced there," in a limbo of distortion and hallucination, on the boundary between life and death. To reflect this state of spirit, the poet "balances" the poem "there," on the boundary between intelligibility and incoherence. It's exactly at this point that "reading" the poem in the formal sense stops working; the process of translation fails. This is purely the suicide's language. The speaker has turned inward to other suicides, and away from her listener,

> leaving the page of the book carelessly open,
> something unsaid, the phone off the hook,
> and the love, whatever it was, an infection.

The speaker has become part of the recollected experience, and it is now through her disappearance from the world of the listener that the poem persuades. True to its subject, the poem has become a kind of suicide attempt.

In my experience, college students are rigorously normal in their response to suicide. In a discussion before we looked at this poem, the class in which I first taught it asserted positively that wanting to die because you are suffering physically is understandable; wanting to die without what they called "a real reason," by which they meant a physical one attached to disease, is sad. Not merely sad, but bad, reprehensible, morally irresponsible, ethically debased. Depression, unlike cancer, said my students, must be reasoned with and always cured. One may never simply give over the struggle. My students almost uniformly denied the legitimacy—even the credibility—of an attitude that says from the beginning, "I would rather not live." (I think of Bartleby, who would always prefer not to, and who, by god, does not.)

I did not discuss these issues with my students as they relate to Anne Sexton's personal agony. Whether or not Sexton's own desire to die could be traced to situational factors or to chemical imbalances in the DNA is irrelevant to the assumptions and commitments of this poem. We concentrated on the poem as poem, and in the world created by this poem, it's useless to say that the speaker "shouldn't" feel like dying. My class, full of good students who were also good people, wanted to engage in humane and helpful and therapeutic argument with the absent speaker.

But through an explication of the kind I have reconstructed here, my students came to an uneasy, genuine understanding of the suicide's "special language." When we reached the final two stanzas, and came up against the limitations of explication, I still felt obligated to "finish the poem" by examining the remaining imagery and anatomizing the language. That had proved, after all, to be the right way into the poem, a poem that concerns itself with translation of language. To end here would be, I thought, to leave "the page of the book carelessly open, something unsaid." I was met with blank faces, but not the kind a teacher meets with when students are uninterested, bored, or even confused. This was the silence of compassionate insight. Finally, one student said, "It's idiomatic." Another said, "It doesn't translate." A third said, "There's nothing left to say." Class simply ended with a fourth comment: "The phone is off the hook." "Wanting to Die" ends in the silence of suicide because, for me and for the students to whom I taught it, the poem is a successful attempt. As one of my students said, "This poem self-destructs."

Perhaps successful suicide attempts, figurative or otherwise, are strange things to celebrate. I do not mean to suggest that there were any converts to suicide in my class. That was not the intention of the poem, and it certainly wasn't the purpose of my class discussion. The speaker of this poem asks only to be understood, to explain herself; she does not recruit company for her agony. Clearly, I did and do find something here to celebrate. "Wanting to Die" taught my students more about poetic process than any other single poem. It is one thing to learn that language is a powerful tool. It is another but related thing to know that language can be a mediator of this kind, that it can work either to alienate people or to bring them together in an understanding of their disparate and painfully separated selves.

"Suicide Note" is the only death poem Anne Sexton cast in this form, and the decision creates formal peculiarities of expectation and response. In many respects it is like the other suicide poems, all of which are written from slightly differing perspectives, all of which tell this suicide's story from a new narrative angle, all of which provide new images for understanding this state of mind. But the carefully constructed multi-stanza "note" is alone among the poems in that it purports to be a communication left to a "dear friend" prior to the speaker's suicide.

Situated as it is in *Live or Die,* a collection shaped by the decision implied in the title, "Suicide Note" is part of the group of "Die" poems that includes "Wanting to Die," "Sylvia's Death," and "The Addict," among others. These poems anatomize the desire to die, the ways of doing it slowly, the post-attempt explanations, but no other poem is situated in time *before* a planned attempt, whether that attempt is fictive, or really about to take place, or real but remembered.

It is an odd experience to read an artfully constructed, cool, restrained note to one the speaker assumes will have survived her, one who will want to know why. It would feel peculiar even if the poet were not now dead. But the actual ironies are denser than that: this is a 1965 poem, published in a collection which concludes with the decision to "Live," the title of its final poem. Anne Sexton, the poet and *perhaps* the speaker—I insist on the separation at the moment for specific reasons—killed herself nearly ten years after this poem was written. Reading it nearly ten years after her death and almost twenty after its composition, I find it difficult to refrain from experiencing it as what it purports to be and yet is not: a suicide note.

Having been content to collapse speaker and poet in many other poems, I am wary of the ease with which I might do so in this case. Aside from the sad fact that to equate speaker and poet in a poem with this title is to invite scorn, I find this among her most aloof and "literary" productions, entirely different in tenor from, say, "Sylvia's Death," in which Anne Sexton the potential suicide nearly overwhelms Anne Sexton the poet and craftsperson. To call this speaker "Anne Sexton" is to risk minimizing the impact of poetic technique and tight control. For this poem which presents itself as "note" before killing oneself is actually a highly formalized poetic epistle, written to a constructed self as much as to another addressee.

> Better,
> despite the worms talking to
> the mare's hoof in the field;
> better,
> despite the season of young girls
> dropping their blood;
> better somehow
> to drop myself quickly
> into an old room.

The beginning is presented as a conclusion reached after consideration. It is "despite" the worms and the young girls' blood that the speaker finds it "better" to die. The worms and the girls' blood are both ambiguous in their emotional content and their relation to life and death: while one seems primarily death-directed and the other life-directed, both are at the intersection of fertility and decay. The worms "talking to the mare's hoof" are the rich yeast of the soil on which the horse walks and from which it gains sustenance; yet the worms will ultimately speak not only of nurture but of decay. The season of menarche is the season of greatest potential for life, but blood-letting is also symbolic of destruction. "Despite" the mares and the girls, whose being at this time of year (it is June) affirm life as well as death, the speaker wants to escape into the "old room" of her death. For she has decided that it is better "not to be born" at all; and far better "not to be born twice," as women are (see "String Bean," *Live or Die*).

Now, having already presented her conclusion, the speaker introduces the "dear friend" to whom she speaks, telling him or her that "I will enter death / like someone's lost optical lens." In contrast to her own sense of smallness—"I will be a light thing"—she says that "life is half enlarged." Describing her own distorted vision, she speaks of life tilting "backward and forward." Close to the natural world of mares and blood, she feels the fierceness of fish and owls on this portentous day. Having made her decision to die, she observes these portents unaffected: "Even the wasps cannot find my eyes." Nothing can sting her now, for she is immune, and her sight has turned to vision by means of distortion and reduction. Once those eyes were "immediate," and "truly awake"; now they have been "pierced."

Recalling her old "hunger" for Jesus, whom she has loved as suffering man more than as God, she thinks of him as a fellow suicide, who "rode calmly into Jerusalem / in search of death" *before* he grew old. She has tried this herself before, but failed. This time, she does not ask for understanding,

> and yet I hope everyone else
> will turn their heads when an unrehearsed fish jumps
> on the surface of Echo Lake;
> when moonlight,
> its bass note turned up loud,

> hurts some building in Boston,
> when the truly beautiful lie together.

These rich lines begin with a disclaimer that the ensuing lines seem to renege on: "I . . . do not ask for understanding, and yet . . . " what is it that she hopes? That everyone will be sorry she has died? That the natural and man-made world—fish, moon, buildings, people—will take note of the moment of her death? Perhaps. But the lines are larger than that; they may mean almost the opposite: that everyone who has not dropped "quickly into an old room" because of the inability to stand the pain and beauty of life, will respond to that beauty and pain. This is the "understanding" she solicits: that she cannot deal with an "unrehearsed" fish breaking the surface of still water in a surge of lifeforce; that she cannot bear the "bass note" of moonlight bursting on walls; that she is unable to be, or to see, the "truly beautiful" who lie together. Like the images with which the poem begins, these are tonally poised, tilting "backward and forward" as life does for the speaker, refusing a readerly desire for definitive emotional form and statement. (Were her eyes "pierced" so that she could see "the whole story?" Or does that piercing render them unable to see at all?) Ambiguous as this series of images is, the weight of the lines that follow presses toward the more generous appraisal of motives and meaning:

> I think of this, surely,
> and would think of it far longer
> if I were not . . . if I were not
> at that old fire.

She has reminded herself of the painful beauty of life, and the memory might make her hesitate, if she were not "at that old fire," needing death. She knows, she says, that she is "only a coward," but she feels compelled to this death as moths are forced to "suck on the electric bulb" (see interviews and letters on Sexton and Plath at Boston workshops). She offers what defense she can. Now that defense takes a form similar to "The Death Baby," a poem Sexton was to write years after "Suicide Note":

But surely you know that everyone has a death,
his own death,
waiting for him.
So I will go now
without old age or disease,
wildly but accurately,
knowing my best route,
carried by that toy donkey I rode all these years,
never asking, "Where are we going?"
We were riding (if I'd only known)
to this.

If everyone has his own death waiting anyway, if we are all
only riding "to this," the speaker will choose her own moment,
without the infirmities of old age or disease, just as she earlier
suggests Christ did when he rode into Jerusalem "in search of
death." And like Christ, she will ride on a donkey. Three years
before the composition of "Suicide Note," Sexton had ridden
her donkey out of madness and out of "this sad hotel," the
mental hospital, in "Flee on Your Donkey," the third poem in
Live or Die.

Anne, Anne,
flee on your donkey
flee this sad hotel,
ride out on some hairy beast,
gallop backward pressing
your buttocks to his withers. . . .

Now she rides the same beast out of life, into a madness that has
much method: "wildly but accurately, / knowing my best
route. . . ." That she has never asked "where are we going?"
has the same content as never asking "Why build?" in "Wanting
to Die."

The final stanza is an attempt to assure the addressee that the
speaker has no illusions about the effect of her death on either the
world she leaves behind or the one she goes to. No guitars
playing, no kiss from her mother's mouth, no major disturbance
in the natural world ("The snakes will certainly not notice") or
in the man-made world ("New York City will not mind"). She

will die in June "so concrete with its green breasts and bellies"; the "note" ends where it began, with the abundance of life that the speaker cannot endure. Only the bats will take notice, beating on the trees, "knowing it all, / seeing what they sensed all day."

In "Suicide Note," we are given the formal framework that is all artifice, the pretense of suicide note which is *not* suicide note, but rather a deliberate re-creation of a state of mind that the speaker could hardly be in at the moment of composition, else she could not compose. The very form is artful ruse, the kind of lie we may need to hold in check such intensely emotional content.

NOTE

1. Kim Carpenter discussed "Wanting to Die" from a similar standpoint in "Four Positions on Suicide," *Journal of Popular Culture* 14, no. 4 (Spring 1981): 732–39. The "Indepth Section" of that issue on "American Attitudes toward Death" was coedited by me and by Malcolm Nelson; Ms. Carpenter's reading of "Wanting to Die" was the result of extended conversations among the three of us, and in that respect, the current reading is an extension of Carpenter's work with us.

EUGENE POOL

Anne Sexton, Her Kind Mix Poetry with Music

Anne Sexton and Her Kind at Jordan Hall Saturday night was not an all-girl band but a Pulitzer Prize-winning poet and a chamber rock ensemble of her friends (electric piano and organ: Bill Davies, flute and sax: Ted Casher, guitar: Steve Rizzo, bass: Mark Levinson, drum: Harvey Simons) who put Mrs. Sexton's poems to rock, blues, and jazz in such a very moving way that, if you weren't there, you should have been.

Although it may seem surprising that a poet should get together with a group of musicians, it really shouldn't, since it's been happening ever since the Beats in the fifties went into coffeehouses to read to jazz. They built up quite an audience for poetry, and then Bob Dylan stole it by reversing the procedure and mixing music with poetry, and ever since the poets have been trying to get it back.

Sexton read selections from her books *To Bedlam and Part Way Back, All My Pretty Ones,* and *Live or Die,* all as intriguing as the titles themselves. The audience in the balcony was sufficiently involved to complain at the end of the second poem that they couldn't hear her well. So Anne Sexton and Her Kind very graciously paused while those in the balcony moved downstairs. The performance was that informal and warm and there was no real interruption out of respect.

For Anne Sexton and Her Kind do deep and moving work about insanity, lost love, death, and life hopes that is emotionally cataclysmic strung out against Her Kind's eerie, insinuating music. "The Addict" and "For Johnny Pole" are two unforgettably prickling excursions into the human consciousness.

Boston Globe, May 27, 1969. Reprinted courtesy of The Boston Globe.

Able to be humorous as well, the performers blasted their way through "Woman with Girdle" (she is fat and hard pressed to get it off) and "Cripples," and brought down the house.

Ted Casher and Steve Rizzo were the most noticeable musicians, the former for his peppy leadership onstage, the latter for his young, firm rendition of "From the Garden." He sang it so far back from the mike some words were lost, but he's too talented to let that happen again. Only in his twenties, he scored almost all of the music.

You should watch for Anne Sexton and Her Kind and go to see them. The Jordan Hall audience loved them, and so will you for what they can tell you about yourself and your happy, hurting life.

CHARLES MARYAN

The Poet on Stage

*I'm not a playwright. I just wrote this on a grant. I like to read my poems. I
don't know anything about the theater. I got this grant.*
— *Anne Sexton to Charles Maryan*

In 1969 I was sent two plays by a literary agent. One play was
called *Tell Me Your Answer True*. The agent said that she did not
think that it was commercial but she wanted me to read it and
perhaps I would be able to get the play on. "The author," she
said, "is a poet and won a Pulitzer Prize." The author she re-
ferred to was Anne Sexton, and the play was to be retitled *Mercy
Street* and presented ten months later at the American Place
Theatre.

I kept no journal or notes on *Mercy Street,* so I must depend
totally on recall. Also Anne and I never corresponded during our
collaboration. We either worked together or talked on the
telephone.

The impact of reading Anne's play for the first time was not
immediate. The first version was set in a dreamlike carnival
atmosphere with a ringmaster who called people from their seats
on stage into a center ring to act out their lives. It seemed to me
Dantesque in atmosphere, but the actual scenes were very real-
istic within this amorphous structure.

At various times after I had read the play I would find myself
thinking about it quite unconsciously. I read it again and decided
I had to see the play staged. I called the agent and said that I was
interested in doing the play and that I wanted to show it to the
American Place. She said okay but they had already seen it;
however, if I wanted to try again, go ahead.

I called Wynn Handman, the artistic director of the American
Place, who said, "We've read it," and I said, "Read it again,"

From *Anne Sexton: The Artist and Her Critics,* edited by J. D. McClatchy (Bloom-
ington: Indiana University Press, 1978). Reprinted by permission of the author.

and he did. Wynn called me a couple of weeks later to say that he was interested. Now, to this point I had never met Anne Sexton. I am not sure that I had ever read her poetry, and so at Wynn's suggestion Anne was asked to come in from Boston to meet with us and talk about doing a two-week work-in-progress on the play—that is, if Anne approved of me as the director. By the time the meeting occurred I had reread the play several times and felt that the limbo atmosphere and carnival idiom had to be either reinforced or changed, but I was convinced that what was there was a very gifted first play by a writer who could and should write plays. That feeling never changed.

We met in Wynn's office around noon. Anne did not say much except that she would like to see her play done. Wynn and I exchanged ideas and then Anne and I went off to lunch. There may have been a phone call before this but this was our first real meeting. What we actually talked about I don't remember, but what was established at this first meeting was that we could talk. Anne would listen; she listened as well as anyone I've ever known and permitted me to say whatever I needed to say and responded simply and directly. She expressed then and maintained always that she knew little about the theater but liked it and invested us theater people with special knowledge that she did not have. We agreed to work on the play for two weeks and see what would happen. She left the casting to me and so in the spring we began.

We did not touch the script before we gave it to the actors. The main character of *Mercy Street* is a woman named Daisy, and the play follows her odyssey through her recollections and immediate problems. My first choice for the part was Marian Seldes, and I spoke with her even before I had met Anne. Marian and I worked together before and I thought that she was just what the role needed. She also is very sensitive to poetry and is often asked to read on television. Her reaction was, "I'll do it." I said I would send her a script as soon as I had one to give out, and she replied that she would trust me and that she loved Anne's poetry so that I could count on her.

The rest of the cast for the reading was assembled in much the same way—actors whom I knew and who for the most part knew each other. The most remarkable thing about the casting was the resemblance between Marian and Anne. They actually looked like sisters and their relationship was always, even from the first, one of real understanding and caring.

We read the play through and I remember Anne saying that until she heard the actors, especially Marian, she thought she read her own work very well but now she had doubts that she should do it. She was excited and concerned and totally open to what the actors said. We read the play frequently. We worked on scenes; however, getting a handle on the play was hard. Again the problem was connecting the scenes: where are we? Which event follows which?—it wasn't clear. Also, there seemed to be a climax to the play in the first part rather than the second. We were working against a deadline and in two weeks we had to show Wynn Handman and his staff a staged reading that they would want to produce fully for their next season. At one point during a rehearsal Anne and I were discussing a scene and the problem of where it was placed, when Marian looked at us from the stage and said, "Why don't you just reverse the acts?" Neither Anne nor I had thought of the solution, but we agreed with Marian and that began the form of the play that we finally presented.

No one committed the script to memory and I staged the play with a minimum of movement. The actors sat in chairs and moved only to play a scene with the scripts in their hands. There were about six of us in the theater for the presentation. Anne and I thought it went very well, and we began the waiting period to hear if the American Place would do it.

Anne wanted the play done. She was excited. She liked what we did and enjoyed the few rehearsals she attended. She fit in easily and we loved her. Exactly how long we had to wait I can't remember. Wynn Handman and I spoke several times. The problem was how to present the material. By doing a reading we could ignore where the play actually took place, but with a full production the individual scenes had to be dealt with physically; therefore a literal setting representing the many locales would be too expensive and too boring. The American Place was then housed in an actual church and I suggested that the whole play could happen in a church within a mass. Daisy could come to this church to decide whether to live or die—the priest could be transformed into the psychiatrist and by rebuilding St.

Clement's into a theatrical church setting we could make the physical transformations in and out of the mass.

I called Anne. She was receptive. The reality of having to come up with a satisfactory concept for a producer was not hard for her to grasp, and thematically she thought it would work since Daisy spoke about Christ and the religious imagery was constant in the play, but we would have to work the mechanics out together.

I then went to Wynn and gave him the entire play in the concept; there were a series of phone calls—Wynn to Anne, Anne to Chuck, Chuck to Wynn—and finally silence. I would call Anne and started feeling the burden of not hearing. We were like two kids waiting to hear—conspiring—angry that we had to wait so long, but hopeful. Then it came. The word that we would open the season with Anne's play, still called, at this time, *Tell Me Your Answer True.*

It was now June—we started rehearsal September 2 and we had to fit the play with a concept. My knowledge of a High Episcopal Mass—that was the one we picked and Anne thought it best—was zero. Anne's actual knowledge of religious practices was not much better, so my first trip to Weston was for a weekend so that we could go to church and start our collaboration.

She made me feel very comfortable in her house, as did the whole family; we drank a lot, talked a lot, and Sunday morning we drove into Boston to the one High Episcopal Church. Anne and I tried to follow the service—in order to see how the play would fit. I was to learn the mass and write a plan of how the scenes would fit. She would work on the timing, the clarification of the scenes, and write connecting material, but she was adamant. I had to know the mass. We worked that weekend in the kitchen and in her study, but somehow the kitchen was the place where we could spread out and drink coffee. It was the right room for us. Anne's dog, a Dalmatian, took some getting used to. The dog was not used to me and was very protective of Anne and guarded her study. We had some visitors, usually late in the afternoon—Lois Ames, Maxine Kumin and her children. We would work from 9:00 A.M. to 4:00 P.M. and then break entirely.

Our next meeting was for a longer period of time. I think

four or five days. By then, I had a better grasp of the mass. Scenes needed work—clarity was our objective—and at one point we were stuck. I was convinced that one scene was not right. Anne wrote, rewrote, and finally, after several attempts, she said to me, "You write it." I protested but Anne said, "No, you write it and I'll get some idea, maybe." I sat down in the kitchen and wrote the scene. Anne worked on something else. When I had finished she read it and said, "This is terrible but I think I know now what you mean." It worked. She rewrote the scene and it was excellent.

The late summer and early fall were devoted to going to church, studying the mass, casting, and getting a design for the show. We were complete by September 2. Two actors had changed because the originals were not available. It was hot. The American Place was not air-conditioned. Anne came to New York with Lois Ames, and took up residence at the Algonquin. She, like most people new to New York, was not used to walking, so at the first rehearsal she noticed that Marian Seldes was wearing slippers. Marian gave Anne her slippers to wear, which she kept, and she would sit, cigarette, a can of beer, wearing gold slippers, and watch us work. Again she fit in beautifully.

We had to change the great-aunt. That was a must. We could not find an older woman who would say the text; it was filled with sexual fantasy, and so we found a young woman who could play it, Me'l Dowd, and the family became complete again. There were two characters in the play who were merely voices—demons really of the characters' madness. They were difficult to integrate into the play due to the new concept of the mass, but I loved them. I had a long talk with Anne about these voices, because she actually had experienced a good deal of hallucinating that she could recall and discuss. She could and would talk to me and the cast about her madness, her experiences, her feelings at various times as casually and as cheerfully as one would remember an incident from one's past. There was no hesitation in her attitude about revealing herself. Any autobiographical reference was always explained, talked about calmly, "Yes, sometimes they took shapes and then sometimes they were just voices. They can be whatever you want them to be, Chuck."

Wynn wanted them out; I wanted them in; Anne had to decide. Anne respected Wynn a great deal. The implications of producers are obvious and he *had* produced Robert Lowell—the voices were cut and I was not able to stop it. It was the beginning of doubts that, for Anne, kept growing, if only because the incident had fed her lack of self-confidence. The play was taking real shape, and Wynn again wanted cuts. The amorphous quality of the atmosphere, which I believed helped the play, and the set-ups for the voices that made transitions possible that Anne knew instinctively were right, were cut. It was always me saying no, Wynn saying cut, and Anne having to decide, and as we approached the opening the strain began to show. I was not experienced to know how to keep this from happening. The culmination came in Wynn's office after a rehearsal before we were to play to our first audience. Wynn was after clarification about the great-aunt. I thought we had clarified too much and Anne froze. She kept repeating one phrase over and over. She had come to the realization that her living, breathing work was going to be shown. There was not a consensus of positive opinion and theater critics are scary enough for the toughest author. I finally saw that Wynn had not a clue about Anne's condition. She was, to use her phrase, doubling off, and so I said let's go home, Anne, you're getting nutty, and we left.

All this time our work was done very joyfully. Before we opened we were told that we were extended a week because there was so much interest in the play. Anne became more tentative and withdrawn but the spirit of the production was very positive, unlike most shows at the American Place. The night we opened we never changed or rewrote—we let it stand. We, the cast and I, were happy with what we had. Anne approved and said she liked it. Wynn and his staff were enthusiastic. The critics were positive, for the most part, but no "money" notices. We played our six weeks and closed. The spirit of the actors was that of being in a hit. We were page one four weeks in a row in the *New York Times* entertainment section. After the experience of going through a New York opening, Anne never seemed as excited about her work and we hardly ever spoke of it. She smiled, but the acceptance of her play was not like that of her books and she was more convinced than ever that she was not a playwright.

Anne, Marian, and I stayed in touch. Marian and I were

invited to her book party for *Transformations* at Sardi's, and Anne and I continued to talk every few months. I would try to prod her for a new play and she would suggest that I adapt one of her books of poems and laugh. She and Maxine Kumin drove to Beverly, Massachusetts, to see a summer show. Her enjoyment of the theater never left, and for me the hope of another Sexton play never came to an end. It has been seven years since *Mercy Street*. At least twenty times a year people mention the play to me and Marian in very complimentary terms. I am constantly asked about it by theater people all over the country. All these questions over an off-Broadway play that ran six weeks seven years ago? I think Anne was a playwright, and that was our only real disagreement.

WALTER KERR

A Woman upon the Altar

Anne Sexton, a fine poet with an astounding knack for incorporating the ugly and immediate vocabulary of the pressing workaday world into lyrics that nevertheless remain lyrics, is the author of *Mercy Street,* the current offering at the American Place Theater. "Offering," by the way, is the one right word for it. The play is constructed, quite literally, to resemble the Offertory in an Anglican or Roman Catholic Mass, and the gaunt, handsome, harassed girl in a canary yellow coat who moves down the aisle calling out responses to a priest is really offering herself up to see what sacrifice or what sense can be made of her life.

Miss Sexton's initial use of ritual is striking, particularly at a time when the theater is constantly boasting of "ritual" or promising "ritual" without having any event to make a rite about. Here the application is apt, the religious and dramatic implications are related, the two-part chant becomes, briefly, a harmony. The girl who wanders toward the altar to virtually place herself upon [it] is trapped somewhere "between Christ and madness," and she doesn't want Christ to busy Himself with His own dying until He has allowed her to catch up with Him.

She is married, a mother, she has been in a mental institution, she is ready to cut open the past to see where, before or after the age of thirteen, she severed herself from the wish to have gender, to be distinct, to be anything other than "all over skin like a fish." The past is promptly called to order by a priest who is also an analyst, and we meet a mother who cannot bear to be touched, a father who really thought he could live alone after the mother's death but who discovered that there was no one in the

Review of *Mercy Street, New York Times,* November 2, 1969. Copyright © 1969 by The New York Times Company. Reprinted by permission.

living room to say "Remember when . . . ?," a great-aunt who befriended the girl but went mad when her moral world collapsed, an image of the girl herself playing jacks at thirteen on a night when her father felt so lonely that he taught her to drink and crept into bed with her.

The exploration, in rotating flashbacks, produces some riveting line-images. The girl desperately hurls her head at a pillow after dark only to hear "the rats chewing under the lawn." Feeling responsible for her beloved great-aunt's despair, she "tries to wear her aunt's life" by revisiting the Venice she loved. In her desire to immolate herself she discovers herself, or imagines herself, to be pierced with the stigmata. Now she must hurry to a ladies' room to swiftly wash the blood from her gloves while other women nearby apply lipstick. Marian Seldes delivers these passages with a taut and abrasive clarity, skimming over nothing, making the naked words count.

The play, however, is impotent to complete itself, I think for two reasons. One is that the good things are line-images, intensely graphic as recall but not acted out as scenes. The nearest thing to an open scene in the play is the passage in which William Prince, as the father, innocently and disastrously fondles a daughter only too willing to be fondled, winking one finger in the air as though he were following a Bouncing Ball to the tune of "Daisy," blinking his eyes ruefully, in whimsical despair, as he realizes he has used words and told secrets he ought to have kept to himself. Mr. Prince is incredibly good in the sequence (and elsewhere throughout the evening); a relationship comes to exist in space.

Mostly, though, the memories exist out of space, intangibly, in fragments that won't come together to form a cause; they are bits of backlash beyond the edge of things. Why, really, does her great-aunt go mad? Why, really, did she love her so much? Why does the girl keep talking of a fire and thinking she has let everyone burn to death? The second of the play's failures is its refusal, or inability, to name the sin or the sickness at its center. We see the state that the girl is in now; we don't see the shape that shaped it. In the end, we become impatient. The victim has gone on too long without discovering enough.

WILLIAM DICKEY

Review of *Love Poems*

In the place that is my own place, whose earth
I am shaped in and must bear, there is an old tree growing . . .
                              —*Wendell Berry, "The Return"*

The poem defines both a person and a place, a world in which,
whether it is literal or metaphorical, the speaker of the poem has
in some serious way to live. Prospero on his island, Pope in
London, Prometheus on his rock—in each instance we feel that
the figure and his context are not really separable, that each
explains the other, and that only by the involvement of that
explanation can their meaningful identities be revealed. A corol-
lary about language follows. When the relationship of person
and place is understood with exactness and intelligence, when it
is understood as completely as possible, the poetic language is
able to be elegant. I mean to use the word as it is used in the
physical sciences, where elegance is a measure of rightness: an
explanation is elegant when, in the most economical and co-
herent fashion possible, it explains everything that then needs to
be explained. These questions presented themselves strongly to
me as I read the books I am to review, because it seemed to me
that when the relationship of person and place failed, so too did
the relationship of person and person. And when that happened I
thought the language too was often at fault, reduplicating itself,
detaching itself from an honest representation of objects and
from its necessary source in idiomatic speech.

The book which struck me most sharply as establishing no
serious relationship between person and context was Anne Sex-
ton's *Love Poems*. For while Sexton's world is full of objects,
they have no independent validity; they exist as projections of
her own indulgent emotional states:

Reprinted from "A Place in the Country," *Hudson Review* 22 (1969), by permis-
sion of the author.

> On the day of breasts and small hips
> the window pocked with bad rain,
> rain coming on like a minister,
> we coupled, so sane and insane.
> We lay like spoons while the sinister
> rain dropped like flies on our lips
> and our glad eyes and our small hips.

Anne Sexton's pattern is one of momentary connections and assertions of different kinds: "On the day of," "We lay like spoons," "minister-sinister." Their problem is that they do not reinforce one another—indeed, they often seem hardly to understand one another. If they could do so, their coherence might itself provide what would be understandable as a world. But Anne Sexton rejects that possibility:

> The hand had collapsed,
> a small wood pigeon
> that had gone into seclusion.
> I turned it over and the palm was old,
> its lines traced like fine needlepoint
> and stitched up into the fingers.
> It was fat and soft and blind in places.
> Nothing but vulnerable.

> And all this is metaphor.

I said "indulgent" because indulgence seems to me to behave this way: to admit everything but a sense of relative importance; to permit all metaphors and then to dismiss them as metaphor. The emotional consequence of such an admission is pathos: we are asked to respond to an epiphenomenon, to emotion detached from judgment; to believe in the existence of a center because things are so busy at the peripheries:

> So I fell apart. So I came all undone.
> Yes. I was like a box of dog bones.
> But now they've wrapped me in like a nun.
> Burst like firecrackers! Held like stones!

The more closely one looks at these images, the less increment they are able to provide. Anne Sexton skims from the surface of an exterior world what is moment by moment most like her, and refuses the resonances an object may have in itself. In doing so she loses the force of an accumulating structure. She also loses, I think, the ability to judge the possible extent of language:

> She took you the way a woman takes
> a bargain dress off the rack
> and I broke the way a stone breaks.
> I give back your books and fishing tack.
> Today's paper says that you are wed.
> At night, alone, I marry the bed.

The final line of this stanza, from "The Ballad of the Lonely Masturbator" is a refrain line, and is repeated seven times. Here, rather than rejecting natural possibilities of association, Anne Sexton attempts to force resonance on a line which has very little inherent complexity. The line begins by sounding flat, and comes eventually to sound absurd. But because Anne Sexton does not seriously connect her emotions with a continuous world outside them, absurdity, the failure of believable human proportion, is the last thing she can be expected to identify.

PAUL LACEY

The Sacrament of Confession

To distinguish the Robert Lowell of *Life Studies,* Anne Sexton, W. D. Snodgrass, and Sylvia Plath, among others, as "confessional" poets has been useful primarily for calling attention to a subject matter and attitudes toward it. After a generation of criticism which insisted that the "I" of a poem was not to be identified with the writer, the *real* John Keats, T. S. Eliot, or W. B. Yeats, but was to be seen strictly as a persona in the poem, we have returned—in some of our most vital poetry—to first-person utterances which are intended to be taken as auto-biographical. Thus M. L. Rosenthal speaks of Lowell's "Skunk Hour" and Sylvia Plath's "Lady Lazarus" as true examples of confessional poetry because "they put the speaker himself at the center of the poem in such a way as to make his psychological vulnerability and shame an embodiment of his civilization,"[1] and he goes on to speak of how the poems show us Lowell's sickness of will and spirit, or Sylvia Plath's self-loathing, leading on to her suicide.

Of course, the relation between the writer and his persona in a poem is still as complex as ever. Though some critics have cited the passage in "Skunk Hour" where the speaker tells of spying on lovers in their cars as evidence of Lowell's illness, the incident, in fact, comes from one of Walt Whitman's letters.[2] Similarly, readers have been so persuaded of the factual foundation for Anne Sexton's "Unknown Girl in the Maternity Ward," that they have assumed the poet herself must have had an illegitimate child—which she has not. The dramatic lyric or monologue still sets up some distance between writer and character; but a new openness, a willingness to make poetry of experience unmediated by such doctrines of objectivity as the mask, the persona, or

From *The Inner War,* copyright © Fortress Press 1972. Used by permission of the publisher.

the objective correlative, a preoccupation with extraordinary experiences—mental breakdown, infidelity, divorce—these are some of the hallmarks of "confessional poetry." And, with deep gratitude for the lessons in close reading taught us by the criticism which insists that we must read each poem as "a little world made cunningly," without reference to biography, history, or the body of work created by the same artist, we must nevertheless apply those lessons in new ways, especially when confronted with writers who consciously refuse to write within that critical canon. "There is always an appeal open from criticism to nature," said Dr. Johnson.

To interest us for very long, poetry must offer more than the *frisson* of shocked pleasure which accompanies our learning that someone else acts out our fantasies; it must be more than a casebook example of abnormal psychology; and it must make more demand on our attention than that—in the words of many novice writers—"this really happened to me!" Which is to say that, whatever the adjective "confessional" tells us about subject matter, the noun it modifies, "poetry," points us once more to the question of style and form. A poem gives shape to experience so that both the experience itself, in all its density and complexity, with whatever tastes, sights, feelings, and textures are peculiar to it, and the "meanings"—the insights, reflections, consequences, emotional and spiritual implications of the shaped experience—become available to us.

When we write poetry, we do so in order to relive or celebrate experience, to put things that have happened to us together with others that have not—things we have imagined or appropriated from our reading, our observations, or our friends. But we also write poetry to play with language, to obscure or mediate experiences through words, images, and rhymes. Starting perhaps with an emotion we wish to preserve, we become concerned with how things sound or look, how the rhythm builds or breaks, how emotions are generated and channeled by what we are saying. Looking for release or discovery, we also become interested in making the poem *work,* in saying things well. The poem, then, looks two ways, toward expression and toward communication. It organizes our responses as we write, but it also organizes responses in the audience we begin to imagine.

As readers of poetry we look for the signals from the poem

which organize our responses, which tell us we are reading aright and confirm our satisfactions in seeing what is really there. The poem creates its own frame of reference, establishing the norms—ethical, emotional, social, personal—by which we understand it. The poem tells us how to regard its statements, how to read a pattern of metaphors, when the stance is ironic, when it is successfully or unsuccessfully finished. It leads us to make judgments by comparing it with other works in its genre, or with a similar theme or tone.

What organizes our responses, whether we are writing or reading poetry, and leads us to satisfaction or dissatisfaction with the final result, is form, what Robert Frost calls "the figure a poem makes."

> There is a big change after you write a poem. It's a marvelous feeling, and there's a big change in the psyche, but I think you really go into great chaos just before you write a poem, and during it, and then to have come out of that whole, somehow is a small miracle, which lasts for a couple of days. Then on to the next.[3]

The satisfactions Anne Sexton speaks of have to do with moving from and through chaos into wholeness. They are both aesthetic and psychological, both impersonal and highly personal, and they come together in the process of finding adequate form, or, to put it another way, in exerting control over the chaos and making it yield up meaning. "For one lyric poem I rewrote about three hundred typewritten pages. . . . You have to look back at all those bad words, bad metaphors, everything stated wrong, and then see how it came into being, the slow progress of it, because you're always fighting to find out what it is you want to say."[4]

The pleasures of writing poetry are not the same as those we anticipate in reading it, however, and while most poets might speak in a similar fashion about the pains and pleasures of composition, the reader of "confessional" poetry seems faced with a particularly complex set of claims on his responses. What are his satisfactions? What entrée does he have into the poem? If the reader is being addressed in some special "confessional" sense, what is his role? Is he hearing confession like a priest, granting or withholding absolution? Is he the client-victim of such a judge-penitent as the narrator of Camus's *The Fall* or Coleridge's *Ancient Mariner?* Do we overhear an unwitting confession, as we do in "The Bishop Orders His Tomb" or "My Last Duchess"? Or are we suddenly drawn into the life of the poem by a violation of the distance established by the form, as Eliot draws us into the action of "The Waste Land": "You! hypocrite lecteur!—mon semblable,—mon frère!"

Equally important, what protection does the poem offer the reader from too much harrowing, too dangerous an evocation of psychic material within himself? The content of any confession is likely to be threatening to one who hears it. If it occurs in a context where one cannot imitate the detachment of a priest, or where the response demanded is too revealing, one may only withdraw or block all response. A reader is at once the most defenseless and the most powerful of men; he may be moved and manipulated by every intonation and gesture the poet gives, but he may also close the book and go away.

All these are questions which must be raised about most poetry, but asking them about Anne Sexton's poetry leads us directly to problems of poetic form as she has faced them.

It has been relatively easy for some critics to dismiss Anne Sexton's poetry by concentrating on its subject matter. Reviewing her first book, James Dickey begins:

> Anne Sexton's poems so obviously come out of deep, painful sections of the author's life that one's literary opinions scarcely seem to matter; one feels tempted to drop them furtively into the nearest ashcan, rather than be caught with them in the presence of so much naked suffering.[5]

Hayden Carruth speaks of a mind almost in control of her material; Denis Donoghue speaks sympathetically of the experiences Anne Sexton has gone through, but he concludes that she has tried too hard to make the material into poetry. Carruth, again, argues that the literary qualities of her poems are impossible to judge, that they are still documentaries of experience which might be starters for other poems where images and ideas "may be strengthened and consolidated in more fully objictified, imagined poems."[6] Flatness, lack of concentration, an unfinished quality to the poetry, or, alternatively, works which try too hard to be poems: these are the standard criticisms of Anne Sexton's works.

But a careful reading of her four books of poetry reveals, not the lack of form which these critics emphasize, but a continual preoccupation with both thematic and technical means for giving significant shape to her poetry. Many of the poems have elaborate rhyme and metrical patterns. Each of the books is shaped by ruling themes, carefully chosen epigraphs, or a chronological or developmental pattern. The title *To Bedlam and Part Way Back* precisely indicates the arc which the book describes, and which each poem is designed to advance: from sickness toward health; from possession by the ghosts and demons of guilt toward exorcism; from disownment toward inheritance. The book's epigraph describes the method by which the way back can be won: making a clean breast of it in the face of every question; pushing the inquiry further, even in the face of appalling horror.

All My Pretty Ones announces the themes of the book, total loss and the affliction of memory: "I cannot but remember such things were, that were most precious to me." And, just as for Wordsworth recalling emotion and experience under the control of artistic creation brings new health and strength, the aim of remembering for Anne Sexton is to learn to exorcise the evil and celebrate the good. The book's second epigraph, taken from a letter by Franz Kafka, tells us what to expect in the way of method and goal for the poetry, which will "act upon us like a misfortune," and "serve as the ax for the frozen sea within us." The epigraphs do not promise the satisfaction of resolution or the sense of a completed journey. At the most, they promise to take us to the edge of things, the boundary situation, where, for good or ill, the frozen sea within us begins to break up.

Live or Die is the appropriate next stage of development in the poetry. The choice announced by the title is real for the poet, but the poems, printed in the order of their composition from 1962 to 1966, do not simply move from death- to life-wish. "Live or die, but don't poison everything," says the epigraph, and the poems enact the process by throwing off the poison which makes them read, as Anne Sexton says, "like a fever chart for a bad case of melancholy." In the final poem, "Live," she gathers up the ruling words, images, and themes of the book to express a new equilibrium.

> So I won't hang around in my hospital shift,
> repeating The Black Mass and all of it.
> I say *Live, Live* because of the sun,
> the dream, the excitable gift.

Finally, in *Love Poems,* she quotes from a Yeats essay about the teaching of Mohini Chaterjee, "Everything that has been shall be again." The poems affirm the body in a way not to be found in her earlier poetry. Whereas in the first three books the body is apt to be described as a prison cell or a house inhospitable to its occupant, in this last book the whole body and its separate parts are celebrated and delighted in. Images of the lover as architect, builder, and kneader abound. The poetry asserts the creative power of love and is less self-conscious of its own nature. The eternal cycle described by Mohini Chaterjee brings a sense of peace to the poems gathered in this book.

This brief examination of one means by which Anne Sexton has shaped her collection of poems does not argue that carefully chosen titles, epigraphs, and influences will improve or justify a particular poem, any more than showing that a poem is a perfect Petrarchan sonnet or in terza rima proves that it is a successful work. What may be argued from such conscious shaping of her books, however, is first, that we must read and evaluate each poem in its larger context, just as we read each line or extended image of a poem in the context created by the whole poem; and second, that the confessional mode requires such shaping influences to give both the distance and familiarity a reader needs for handling the material. Speaking of *All My Pretty Ones,* May Swenson notes:

Her method is as uninhibited as entries in a diary or letter . . . , the diction seems effortless, yet when we examine for form we find it solidly there, and its expertness is a pleasurable thing in contrast to the merciless *debridement* taking place in the content.[7]

Just as any confession must provide signals telling us how to respond and protections from too much danger, confessional poetry must balance horror with comfort, threat with relief, merciless *debridement* with pleasure, in order to keep us engaged. So the wrenching loss described in "Unknown Girl in the Maternity Ward" and the claustrophobic terror of "The Moss of His Skin" are lightened by the hopeful ritual of "The Lost Ingredient" and the lyrical self-control of "For John, Who Begs Me Not to Enquire Further":

> Not that it was beautiful,
> but that I found some order there.
> There ought to be something special
> for someone
> in this kind of hope.

To convince us that we have experienced something true, and that we can live *by* and *with* what we have experienced, is the supreme accomplishment of art. Anne Sexton has said, "I think all form is a trick in order to get at the truth." The remark underlines the importance for her of shaping the lived or imagined experience into the truth. She says in her interview with Patricia Marx that in the poems which are hardest for her to write, she imposes some exceptionally difficult metre or rhyme-scheme, which *allows* her to be truthful. "It works as a kind of super-ego. It says 'You may now face it, because it will be impossible to get out'!"

The *content,* it must be insisted, does not make the poem truthful. Even the most autobiographical poet distorts or suppresses *facts* for the sake of making a fiction which will tell more of the essential truth. To reach its readers, the poem must persuade us that the truth it tells is worth the price it exacts; it must lead us to appropriate and satisfying reactions. Form operates to say to the reader what it says to Anne Sexton: this is a pattern which allows you to be truthful.

The thematic and technical forms she uses in the books establish the distance from the material which allows us first to contemplate it and then to approach it more closely. The Greek tragedians were able to handle the most psychically dangerous material we know—incest, parricide, and matricide—precisely because the stylized language, acting, masks, and costumes established sufficient distance between the protagonist and the audience that the latter could have its fear and pity tempered by the pleasure of seeing an action imitated. The playwrights of our own time who handle equally volatile materials have adapted many of the same ritualistic elements for their plays; the reduction of dialogue to ritual or its parody in Beckett, Pinter, Ionesco, and others; the nonrealistic acting styles of many absurdist plays—all have as their purpose setting distance between audience and play. The poets who handle the most dangerous materials are also most concerned with poetic form. Anne Sexton says:

> I used to describe it this way; that if you used form it was like letting a lot of wild animals out in the arena, but enclosing them in a cage, and you could let some extraordinary animals out if you had the right cage, and that cage would be form.[8]

Anne Sexton employs a great variety of thematic and technical shapers on her poetry, so many, in fact, that it might be more accurate to critize her unsuccessful poems for having too much rather than too little form. Thematically her poems are often built around such paired contrasts as guilt and love, truth and falsehood, mobility and fixity, illness and health. Other themes develop incrementally from poem to poem: the double image, the mirror, and the portrait—all used to speak of the past and present confronting each other, the conflicts of parent and child, or the testing of identity by measuring it against family history; sin, guilt, belief, grace, and love worked through a number of poems about Christ or traditional Christian faith; the connection of writing to finding health.

One preoccupation in her poetry which acts as an informing principle for both theme and technique is ritual. This preoccupation expresses itself in her use of words or images commonly associated with rituals—"sacrament," "ceremony," "rites," "ritual," "magic," "exorcise," "communion." These, and words with similar connotations, occur frequently in enough of the poems to indicate at the very least a kind of compulsive pattern by which the poet tries to make sense of what she is saying. Similar effects come from poems built on the rhythms of children's rhymes which, as M. L. Rosenthal says, "catch the note of the self reduced to almost infantile regress."[9] These patterns provide a framework in which irrational acts can be understood or order imposed on chaos.

More important in the poetry, however, is the making of rituals, or the discovery of ritual meaning in an ordinary action. Without claiming to exhaust or fully distinguish all the rituals in Anne Sexton's poetry, we may speak of three kinds which predominate: rites of *mastery,* in which power is tested or exorcised; rites of *initiation* or *cleansing,* in which the poet looks for confirmation of a new insight or stage of growth, or experiences testing, purification, or absolution; and rites of *communion,* where some gesture or order of words opens up a sense of oneness with others.

"You, Dr. Martin," the first poem in her first book, is about power, but this subject is explored by acting out rites of mastery. The poem is addressed to a therapist under whose power the hospital inmates stand. He represents order, "god of our block, prince of all the foxes." The inmates "stand in broken lines," awaiting "the shibboleth" which will open the gates and let them go to dinner, where they "chew in rows." The images emphasize the helplessness and childishness of the patients and the false connections of words and ideas which characterize madness—"the frozen gates of dinner," "we move to gravy in our smock of smiles." But they also illustrate the meaninglessness of this order; the rows and broken lines lead to nothing, the order is for its own sake. Because it demands helplessness and childishness, the poet perceives this order as judgment. The doctor has a "third eye," a magical way to see into lives; it is "an oracular eye in our nest." Dr. Martin symbolizes power. In his name, the shibboleth is pronounced, the intercom calls; his eye is the oracle which both sees and speaks. And the poet responds "of course, I love you"—an act of submission and abnegation.

Another power is present in the poem, however, and it is also evoked in ritual terms. This is the power of submission and childishness: the unraveled hands, the foxy children who fall. The poet asserts herself as "queen of this summer hotel" and even "queen of all my sins / forgotten." The power has no channel or focus yet, "we are magic talking to itself," but it is more genuine and capable of meaning than the perfect order imposed by the hospital. "Once I was beautiful. Now I am myself," and it is from that standpoint that she asserts her power in the rituals she makes out of naming and counting.

"We are magic talking to itself" introduces a connection between therapy and making poetry. In "Said the Poet to the Analyst," the poet says, "My business is words. . . . Your business is watching my words." Where the analyst wants to make words refer to facts or events so he can determine whether they correspond to the truth, the poet speaks of words as "like swarming bees," alive and vital, creating their own shape. They do not tell the truth, they control it; they are ritual or magic.

In "The Black Art" the theme is repeated. The events of life are never enough, either as experience or as meaning.

> A woman who writes feels too much,
> those trances and portents!
> . . . .
> A man who writes knows too much,
> such spells and fetiches!

The poem is not concerned primarily with distinguishing women from men or feeling from knowing; instead, it separates these ways of entering and valuing experience—each conceived of as magical—from the trivial data of experience itself. A writer is a spy or a crook, one who discovers or steals secrets, in the poem. He is also a perverter of order for the sake of nature. "With used furniture he makes a tree."

"You, Dr. Martin" is concerned with two kinds of power—the power of the therapist-parent who imposes a mechanical order on the patient, and the power of the patient-child, who discovers a deeper order or a more meaningful disorder through madness and poetry. Many of the other poems explore other kinds of power and sources of order. Sometimes our perception of the triviality of order comes through a poem's rhythm. "Ringing the Bells" develops like the final verse of "The House that Jack Built" in one long run-on sentence where no event or impression is subordinate to any other. Neither causality nor chronology matters as a means of explanation; "and" or "who" introduce each new element in the poem to operate at the same dead level.

> And this is the way they ring
> the bells in Bedlam
> and this is the bell-lady
> who comes each Tuesday morning
> to give us a music lesson

Patients, attendants, and music therapist become automatons, revealed by the childlike telling of the verse, which continues in one sentence for twenty-eight and half lines, until the whole illusion of meaningful pattern and activity is demolished in the last lines of the poem:

> · and although we are no better for it,
> they tell you to go. And you do.

Settling family estates and disposing of the remains of history provide the narrative peg for several of Anne Sexton's poems. Here putting things in order becomes a weighty ritual action which issues in either an exorcism or a benediction. In some of the poems, the poet expresses her love simply by retracing the steps of a relative or ancestor. "Tonight I will learn to love you twice," she says in "Some Foreign Letters," addressing the old maid aunt whose letters reveal her secret sins and desires. In "Walking in Paris" she reenacts the youthful past of the old aunt, measuring herself against that other life as though she were the old woman's twin:

> You are my history (that stealer of children)
> and I have entered you.

In "Funnel" she makes yet another ceremony of meeting the ancestors, in this case celebrating the richness and openness of the past, the mouth of the funnel.

> I sort his odd books and wonder his once alive
> words and scratch out my short marginal notes
> and finger my accounts.

Sorting becomes the chief ritual of mastery in these poems. "Funnel," "All My Pretty Ones," "Elizabeth Gone," "The Division of Parts" begin or end with the act of sorting and arranging the relics of the past. From this imposed, perhaps arbitrary, order, remembering, forgiving, and releasing can follow.

"All My Pretty Ones," generated and sustained by old documents and photographs, becomes a meditation on inheritance—on how to "disencumber" the dead father and the living child from past failures. Sorting means putting proper value on the past and knowing what may be discarded, and what must be kept "to love or look at later." The father's nature—"my drunkard, my navigator, / my first lost keeper"—must be affirmed, and so the poet keeps a three-year diary which documents the father's alcoholism, for

> Only in this hoarded span will love persevere.
> Whether you are pretty or not, I outlive you,
> bend down my strange face to yours and forgive you.

Discarding the past does not disencumber us. Moving back through one's history means painfully untying each of its knots all over again, forgiving one's past and the actors in it. On the surface, *sorting* is simply the method anyone uses for making the judgment whether to keep or discard, but as it becomes the process by which the poet relives the past, celebrates times, places and people, and arrives at conclusions, it takes on some of the characteristics of *sortilège,* omen-reading or casting lots, a word to which it is etymologically close.

For M. L. Rosenthal the successful confessional poem must achieve a fusion of "the private and the culturally symbolic," and be more highly charged than other poems.[10] One strategy for achieving such a fusion is to turn private idiosyncratic gestures into formal rituals or to play the private rite off against the public one.

An exceptionally rich poem which brings together ordering, exorcising, and the traditional patterns of Christian observance is "The Division of Parts," where things which are simultaneously debts, "obstacles," and "gifts I did not choose," must be sorted. Against that action proceeds the observance of Good Friday and the anticipation of Easter, in which a similar working out of debts and unchosen gifts occurs on the public level. *Dividing* is a key to the poem: making the distinctions which separate gifts from debts and performing the acts which turn debts into gifts are the acts which disencumber the past and allow the poet to claim her real inheritance. Two kinds of inheritances are at issue, the effects left by the dead mother—money, "letters, family silver, / eyeglasses and shoes"—and the complex of attitudes, emotions, doubts, and guilts with which children must also come to terms as their heritage. In this poem that second kind of inheritance is symbolized by "the clutter of worship" taught the poet by the mother, of which she says:

> I imitate
> a memory of belief
> that I do not own.

The poet must come to terms with both her mother and with Christ, and in both cases this means asserting her adulthood in defiance. Defiance causes guilt, but it also opens the way for genuine grieving. Or, to put it in the terms established through the rituals in the poem, the mother, described variously as "sweet witch," "worried guide," and "brave ghost," must first be exorcised before she can be invoked. The poet must "shed my daughterhood," an image sustained by a series of references to inherited clothes, the coats, stones, and furs which "settle on me like a debt." The same cluster of images establishes an identity between Christ and the mother.

> And Christ still waits. I have tried
> to exorcise the memory of each event
> and remain still, a mixed child,
> heavy with cloths of you.

In an earlier stanza the poet has identified the mother and Christ in images recalling the crucifixion—the thieves and the casting of lots for Jesus' garments—but also establishing the complex relationship between guilt and grief.

> . . . I have cast my lot
> and am one third thief
> of you. Time, that rearranger
> of estates, equips
> me with your garments, but not with grief.

Daughterhood, the heavy cloths, the clutter of worship must all be shed until they can be owned, both acknowledged and possessed. The poet must reject the "dangerous angels" who call on her to convert and the tempting image of Christ, on whom so many have "hitched" in trouble, and find another way which is her own. It is not the way of conversion but the way of deprivation, imaged by Jesus, the "ragged son" of Easter. Her way, tentative and incomplete even when the poem is finished, is suggested by the exorcism-invocation of the last stanzas. The poet has a dream while wearing her mother's nightgown, a dream which reenacts the struggle for mastery which is at the heart of the poem and the particular ritual patterns which shape it. What greater power can there be than the power over spirits which characterizes Jesus in the Gospel of Mark? The mother, "divided," climbs into the daughter's head, only to be cursed and expelled, *"Dame / keep out of my slumber. / My good Dame, you are dead."* Recalling this at noon on Good Friday, the beginning of Christ's agony on the cross, the poet sums up her ambivalence by speaking of both cursing and summoning her mother through her "rhyming words." And indeed, the entire next to last stanza in part 4 of the poem is made up of epithets by which the mother is invoked, celebrated, and finally laid to rest. The grief, which would not come when the poet "planned to suffer," because it was blocked by guilt, flows now into the phrases of invocation and benediction:

> my Lady of my first words,
> this is the division of ways.

The conjunction of the dream and the hours of sorrow commemorating the crucifixion recalls the journey to the underworld to meet the parents which is so often found in ancient myth and epic. The hero goes to meet the past, calls up his parents to learn about the future, and then returns to the world in which he is about to meet his most important adventures. Surely it is not strained ingenuity to see the same psychological pattern being worked out in "The Division of Parts," the ritual acting out of the passing of power from parent to child. The child asserts maturity, now, by taking an independent course. And, because the relationship with Christ has also been one of childlike dependence, or a temptation to "convert" to another's expectations, He too must be taken leave of, so that the poet can come into the real inheritance from Him. Therefore the last stanza of the poem shows us Christ fastened to His crucifix, still the ragged son and sacrifice, not the triumphant Lord who might demand obedience. The poet identifies with the tormented man, not with a theology of sin and salvation which might keep her a child. Christ remains on the cross "so that love may praise / his sacrifice / and not the grotesque metaphor." And as Christ has no power over her, neither has the mother, now only a "brave ghost" who *fixes* in the poet's mind, incapable of giving or withholding "praise / or paradise," but by that very incapacity setting the poet free to enter and affirm her real inheritance.

What we have called rituals of mastery occur elsewhere in the poems. Typically, they shape either the poet's response to the guilts of the past or to the making of poetry as a way of imposing order on life. In "A Story for Rose on the Midnight Flight to Boston," for example, the poet controls memory and fear of death on an airplane ride by making a story of them. In "Mother and Jack and the Rain," the tensions of the poem revolve around the "haunting" and "cursing" of the rain outside and the "affirming" of the room and the "endorsing" of the poet's womanhood by her memories; but the tensions are resolved by the making of poetry, by the poet's "conjuring" her daily bread. The thematic and formal significances of rituals of mastery come together:

> With this pen I take in hand my selves
> and with these dead disciples I will grapple.
> Though rain curses the window
> let the poem be made.

Whereas the rites of mastery tend to dramatize conflicts with the God-like authority figures of doctors and parents, those of initiation and cleansing tend to dramatize the poet's role as mother to her children, or to be concerned with moving from shame for the body to affirmation of it. Such a statement of the case is too schematic to be true, of course, but it separates out a tendency in the poetry which rewards close examination.

Houses, rooms, cells, caves, and other images indicating close confinement symbolize the body, especially in the volumes *All*

My Pretty Ones and *Live or Die,* as though the self were an unwelcome inhabitant in a hostile environment. "Housewife" develops this pattern of imagery most clearly, opening with the assertion "Some women marry houses. / It's another kind of skin . . . ," and closing with "A woman *is* her mother. / That's the main thing." Here two equivalences, woman equals house, and woman equals her mother, establish the sense of entrapment against which the rituals of cleansing or initiation work, for their effect is to help the poet find escapes from the trap for herself or her daughters. In "Those Times . . . " the poet describes a "bedtime ritual," "nightly humiliations" when she was "spread out daily / and examined for flaws," at the age of six. She describes her body as "the suspect / in its grotesque house," locked all day in her room, behind a gate. In defense against a mother who keeps her a prisoner to prevent divorce, the poet withdraws even further, withholding herself from the mother's breasts, from the well-made dolls, retreating into the closet, "where I rehearsed my life." Rehearsing fantasies becomes planning growth into womanhood "as one choreographs a dance"; meanwhile, she acts out another kind of fantasy, "stuffing my heart into a shoe box." The poem exploits images of testing and probing, especially through the bedtime ritual on the bathroom tiles, to express guilt and shame for being female. There is no cleansing or release here, though the poet looks forward to the time of maturity, when "blood would bloom in me / each month like an exotic flower" and children "would break from between my legs." The poem, though it speaks of rituals, and shows us a child making ceremonies to protect herself, does not lead us to a resolution in those terms. Instead, menstruation and parturition become the adult counterparts of or fulfillments of the shameful rituals.

"Those Times. . . " can serve as a gloss for other poems where the ceremonies are efficacious. "The Lost Ingredient" is one such poem. It deals with many kinds of loss—the lostness of the past, of the salt sea which was our beginning, of "rites," and of the "ingredient." The word "lost" appears six times in the twenty-four-line poem, all but once at the end of a line, and is echoed in the near-rhymes "last," "loosed," and "lust" which close four other lines. "Steal" or "stole" and its near-rhymes end seven more lines. These two key words, "lost" and "steal," shape not only its rhyme but also the poem's thematic development. The gentle ladies in Atlantic City bathe in salt water to gain "impossible loves," "new skin," or "another child," but they sit in bathtubs, "smelling the stale / harbor of a lost ocean." In the second stanza the poet swims in the Salt Lake, "to wash away some slight / need for Maine's coast," and to "honor and assault" the Salt Lake "in its proof." As the gentle ladies of the first stanza wished to recapture lost rites, the poet makes her own washing an evocation of something she calls "proof," some confirmation of the self. She goes on to associate this with Reno, where she also performs the ceremonies of gambling for the sake of a "better proof." This evidence, or lost ingredient, must be wrested from life, from time, from the salt sea; the rite becomes the way into this evidence, a gamble to "keep us calm and prove us whole at last." But in the poem the ingredient stays lost, not even identified in its absence; all we know is that salt, money, or lust have no power to uncover it. The poet has made a ritual action out of ordinary events, and we are aware of the enormous organization and control which informs the poem, but the reader remains aware only of loss and mystery.

Initiation into being a woman, which the poet calls being twice-born, controls the action of the poem "Little Girl, My String Bean, My Lovely Woman." The child, poised on her twelfth year, inhabits a body which is about to be possessed by the new powers of fullness and ripeness. The poet speaks of the daughter's body as a "home" or "place" about to be entered by the ghost hour, noon, when the sun is at its zenith. The images work together to hint at magic and mysterious powers, a divine possession of the soon-to-be-fruitful girl, but the poem also associates this new becoming with the original birth, when the child was "a world of its own, / a delicate place." The change in the body does not come from outside, however, but from within; even so, it must be greeted with an act of initiation, and on that account the girl is described as separated from her body, needing to let it into her self:

> Oh, darling, let your body in,
> let it tie you in,
> in comfort.

To be initiated is to learn some new truth by having it acted out before or with one. So it is here; the body's changes are confirmed and celebrated—"there is nothing in your body that lies. / All that is new is telling the truth." Initiation rites often have to do with possessing something; and here too the poem provides confirmation. The daughter is not an alien in the house of her body; at the end of the poem she possesses it, and the poet urges her to "stand still at your door, / sure of yourself, a white stone, a good stone." Let the noon hour in, let the sun in, let the body in, let newness and the truth in, then stand at the door, in possession of the house: so the ritual of initiation goes in the poem.

Perhaps the best example of the ritual of cleansing and initiation—and a fine poem—is "Pain for a Daughter." The title itself suggests some of the meanings working in the poem—the daughter's pain, the poet's pain on behalf of the daughter. The poem grows out of the contrast between blindness in several metaphorical senses and seeing or knowing. The daughter is described variously at the beginning of each stanza as blind with love, then with loss, pain, and fear. As she moves through these feelings, from love to fear, she loses her mastery over situations in return for knowledge. In her first stanza, blind for love of horses, she overcomes her squeamishness to treat her pony's distemper, draining the boil and "scouring" it with hydrogen peroxide. In this case her love makes her blind to the distastefulness of the job and lends her a capacity she did not have. "Blind with loss," she asserts her mastery over the neighbor's horses, but is injured and returns home, hurt and frightened. Here her father performs "the rites of the cleansing" on her injured foot, cleaning it with hydrogen peroxide, and, for the first time, her eyes are mentioned: "eyes glancing off me," "eyes locked / on the ceiling, eyes of a stranger." Though the eyes do not see, they are an index to her *knowing* in the face of her pain. She cries to God for help, where a child would have both cried to and believed in her mother. The rites of cleansing have introduced her into the adult world, symbolized not by a cry of hope but by one of despair. Her seeing parallels her mother's, who sees her daughter's life stretched out, her body torn in childbirth:

> and I saw her, at that moment,
> in her own death and I knew that she
> knew.

Anne Sexton speaks of writing as putting things in place, having an ordering effect on her own life. "I mean, things are more chaotic, and if I can write a poem, I come into order again, and the world is again a little more sensible, and real. I'm more in touch with things." It is not surprising, seeing how the poems work, that Anne Sexton thinks of form as a kind of magic for discovering the truth.

> I'm hunting for the truth. It might be a kind of poetic truth, and not just a factual one, because behind everything that happens to you, every act, there is another truth, a secret life.[11]

Nowhere do we see her commitment to the discovery of the secret life behind things more clearly than in those poems, many of them dealing directly with the figure of Jesus or the traditions of Christianity, built around rites of communion, prayer, and gift-giving. These poems are her most complex work, for they do not simply rest on traditional forms of words and actions to counterpoint or frame the struggle for peace or unity, they explore a profound ambivalence about the Christian understanding of life. Christianity, in the full force of its explanation of human existence, entices her, as the epigraph from Guardini in *All My Pretty Ones* indicates: "I want no pallid humanitarianism—If Christ be not God, I want none of him; I will hack my way through existence alone. . . ." The prayers or acts of communion in the poems, then, are neither ironic parodies nor secularized ceremonies; they are, rather, expressions of the deepest human needs in the full consciousness that "need is not quite belief."

"With Mercy for the Greedy" illustrates the point. It is addressed to a friend who has urged the poet to ask a priest for the sacrament of confession and has sent her a cross to wear. The poet prays, not to the cross, but to its shadow, detesting her sins and trying to believe in the cross. But what draws her is the crucified man—"I touch its tender hips, its dark jawed face, / its solid neck, its brown sleep"—just as in "The Division of Parts" she affirms the sacrifice and not "the grotesque metaphor." The cross around her neck taps like a child's heart, "tapping secondhand, softly waiting to be born," but it cannot come alive for the poet precisely because it represents so complete and final an answer. As Yeats resolves the debate between Soul and Heart in the Heart's favor—"What theme had Homer but original sin?"—Anne Sexton chooses the sacrament of poetry over the sacrament of confession. Or rather, she chooses the particular kind of sacrament of confession which poetry is, its kind of mercy, its wrestle with words and meanings.

We cannot know whether prayer, confession, or communion would lack efficacy for the poet; we only know that she cannot permit herself to yield to them. When they occur, they are magic incantations or childish pleas for a miracle, as in "The Operation."

> Skull flat, here in my harness,
> thick with shock, I call mother
> to help myself, call toe of frog,
> that woolly bat, that tongue of dog;
> call God help and all the rest.

Here is an implied answer to the pious believers who brag that there are no atheists in the trenches; one will believe or try anything, if only the fear is great enough, but it will be in shame at the reversion to such immaturity. In "Letter Written on a Ferry While Crossing Long Island Sound," the poet pleads for a comic miracle, that God should let four nuns break loose from the pull of gravity and float through the air, doing "the old-fashioned side stroke," and then she imagines it happening, with the four nuns crying out *"good news, good news,"* as well they might.

"For the Year of the Insane" is subtitled "a prayer," and addressed to Mary, but order and form are fragmented; "There are no words here except the half-learned, / the *Hail Mary* and the *full of grace*." The beads lie *unblessed,* and hammer in on her like waves as she counts them, for the poet knows herself an unbeliever. The words and beads associated with the worship of Mary do not convey a sense of grace but of further condemnation, as the poet moves further into silence and madness. The fragmented prayer gives way to an equally fragmented holy communion, where the bread and the wine also become images of damnation; the wine burns, and the poet says, "I have been cut in two." Mary does not respond, the bread and the wine do not change, no communion occurs: the prayer for grace, for "this crossing over" is denied, and the poet remains "in the domain of silence."

Communion occurs both between man and God and between man and man; and the efficacious ritual symbolizes and facilitates both kinds of communion. It is not accidental or arbitrary that such rituals include eating and drinking. They represent what Philip Wheelwright calls "assimilative ritual," which he says "consists in reaffirming and attempting to intensify man's continuity and partial oneness with nature, or with the mysterious creative force behind nature."[12]

The hunger for communion is the hunger for assimilation, oneness with others, and with what Anne Sexton has called a "secret life" behind things, and for self-transcendence, getting out of oneself and "in touch with things." In "For the Year of the Insane," no one but the poet appears; she is handed wine, and she invokes Mary, but the prayer for self-transcendence only confirms her isolation.

> O little mother,
> I am in my own mind.
> I am locked in the wrong house.

"Hunger" is a ruling word in *Live or Die*. In "Flee on Your Donkey" and "Suicide Note" the same line appears, "O my hunger! My hunger!" The former poem describes madness as a kind of hunger, and the poet finally turns, not to answers to save her, but to her hungers, exhorting them to turn and "For once make a deliberate decision." In "Suicide Note" we are told that "Once upon a time / my hunger was for Jesus," but again there was no fulfillment. Roman Catholic theology speaks of taking communion in a state of sin as eating and drinking damnation, precisely what "For the Year of the Insane" commemorates. So does "Wanting to Die," where a suicide attempt becomes a kind of black mass, a perverted communion service aimed at overcoming the enemy, who is both life and death.

> Twice I have so simply declared myself,
> have possessed the enemy, eaten the enemy,
> have taken on his craft, his magic.

The hunger for death in Anne Sexton's poems is equally a hunger for meaningful life, for choice, and for affirmation. Being hungry need not mean there has been no communion, only that it was not enough for the speaker's appetite; so she can say of the suicide attempt, "To thrust all that life under your tongue! — / that, all by itself, becomes a passion." "The Addict" further elaborates images of communion to speak of the lure of suicide. The pills are "a mother," "loaves," and "a diet from death," but they also keep the speaker in practice for another attempt to die. This addiction to "goodnights" is "a kind of a marriage. / . . . a kind of war"; it is a ceremony and a sport, filled with rules, and taking the pills demands

> . . . a certain order as in
> the laying on of hands
> or the black sacrament.

All these images work to suggest the complexity of the hungers to be met by this communion service, for the ritual brings together the best and worst relations human beings have with one another—war and marriage—and tries to make sense within those limits. The poet takes the pills and lies on her altar, "elevated by the eight chemical kisses." No consecration occurs on this altar, however, just as no love or affection come with chemical kisses. We know what the poet wants, what the ceremony tries to evoke, only by their absence: self-acceptance, "I like them more than I like me," maturity, "I'm a little buttercup in my yellow nightie," and a sense of love and sacramental order. The final lines are a child's jingle, mocking the longings which shape the poem.

A suicide attempt means taking one's life in one's own hands, being responsible for it; this addiction parodies suicide and gives up responsibility for one's life. In many of her poems Anne Sexton tries to impose order on events by inventing ceremonies or insisting that something is a rite, that a bed or a stretch of beach is an altar, that irrational gestures or forms of words could hold off events, as in "Lament," or gain forgiveness, as in "Christmas Eve." Rituals, like symbols, grow out of their own inner principles, however; we cannot invent meaningful rituals, we can only discover them. In Anne Sexton's poetry there are a great many rituals which do not work *as ritual,* though many of them help the poems work.

That distinction may seem forced and arbitrary, since poetry has always been close to, when not a form of, magic, and the connection between prophet, priest, and poet is as real as it is ancient; nevertheless, distinguishing the effects of ritual, especially that rooted in traditional Christianity, from those of the poetry which supports or grows out of it, in Anne Sexton's poetry, is essential. For of the three kinds of rituals discussed here, those which most closely depended on traditional Christian imagery and gestures were also those in which the meaning of the poems was most widely separated from the meaning of the rituals. What I have called rituals of mastery, where the poet struggled for ascendency over the God-like doctor, the authoritarian parent, or the chaos of past history, succeeded in and through the poems, on the two levels demanded by Rosenthal, the personal and the culturally symbolic.

Poems which employed ritual language to speak of cleansing, initiation, prayer, or communion often succeeded in being culturally symbolic precisely to the extent that they revealed an isolation and anxiety on a personal level which was not to be relieved by rituals. The poet's intense attraction to Jesus, the man who suffers for others, and Mary, the perfect and all-forgiving mother, always stands at odds with the worship which attends both those figures. Anne Sexton's poetry chronicles a struggle to come of age: to work through the conflicts with the parents in order to forgive and be forgiven; to break free from the guilts and inadequacies of the past and become open to others; to become the kind of parent who sets her children free and thus breaks the cycle of guilt and shame which has marked her family history. If we are to believe some theologians, the need of our time is also to come of age, to set aside the comforts of cult and ceremony and live affirmatively in a totally secular world. "Need is not quite belief," Anne Sexton has said, and that is a kind of gloss on our times. So is the description of Protestants she puts in an eight-year-old's mouth in "Protestant Easter":

> Those are the people that sing
> when they aren't quite
> sure.

A. R. Jones says of Anne Sexton's poetry that "her framework of reference is ultimately religious,"[13] that is, that the values she insists on are traditional religious ones. The argument of this chapter is that her poetry is largely shaped by attempts to enlarge a traditional Christian framework which has been a chief source of the psychological suffering she has endured. It would be a mistake to say that she is working her way out of that framework, since the same issues, questions, and answers have a way of recurring over and over in a lifetime, and her first play, *Mercy Street,* takes place during a celebration of Holy Communion, but the evidence of *Live or Die* and *Love Poems* supports the opinion that the poetry has worked its way to a new level of apprehension of that framework. *Live or Die* closes significantly with the poem "Live," which gathers up most of the major themes and preoccupations of her previous work and looks ahead to the affirmations of her last book, *Love Poems.* Surveying the course of her life, as it has been charted in the book, the poet acknowledges how things have been distorted by her "dwarf-heart's doodle," and how turned inward and entrapped she has been. The attempts to tell the truth became lies; the body was naked, even when she dressed it up. Now she asks a question whose answer implies a judgment on her strategies for making sense of things, especially the psychological, social, and personal rituals she has invented, "Is life something you play?"

Now, however, life opens up within her; the sun, which has been an important image in a number of the earlier poems, where it has gone from being a threat to being benign, now shines from within, purifying her. This inward change is confirmed by the love of her family, who replace her ceremonies and rituals with games and playfulness.

> If I'm on fire they dance around it
> and cook marshmallows.
> And if I'm ice
> they simply skate on me
> in little ballet costumes.

Love Poems by its very title leads us to expect a change from the earlier books of poetry, and the poems bespeak the self-acceptance toward which "Live" has moved. Even unhappy love and the sorrow of being the other woman exist in the context of hope. Truth and the secret life do not now come through obscure or tortured rituals; things are their own meanings—the pleasures of physical love, delight in the human body, trust in the lover, pain and anger at loss. Whereas many earlier poems seemed to impose meaning by insisting on the sacralization of things, the ceremonies of *Love Poems* are all playful, desacralized, celebrating the simply human. A ritual completes some kind of action and confirms its meaning by referring to the secret life underlying ordinary life. Making, constructing, building, harvesting, all of them key terms in *Love Poems,* are ordinary human occupations; they complete actions, too, but according to a plan or blueprint. When these terms become metaphors for lovemaking, they take us into a new way of creating ceremonies. "But your hands found me like an architect." "I am alive when your fingers are." "Oh, my carpenter, / the fingers are rebuilt." "He is building a city, a city of flesh."

In her work so far, Anne Sexton has penetrated deeply into chaos and has tried a number of strategies for working her way through it. In some of these strategies therapy and poetry have come together; confession has brought relief by putting things in order in the process of sharing the shame and suffering; the devices which protect the reader from too much reality also protect the writer. And if these ways of handling her material have narrowed the range of her themes, that may be a necessary price to pay for the depths she has reached. If, as seems to be the case, the poetry *has* been therapy, and the fever chart now points toward greater health, a major index of this—and perhaps something of a cause as well—is the movement from the tight confinement which rituals of mastery, initiation, and communion are attempts to break to the playful games of lovemaking which characterize Anne Sexton's last book of poems.

It is no disparagement of those earlier poems to say that *Love Poems* shows more health than the previous three books, since without them no such change can be imagined. They are the record of spiritual struggles which have issued, however tentatively and provisionally, in new degrees of self-acceptance and affirmation of love and human communion. They are also testimonies to the power of poetic forms to give point and substance to spiritual struggles. As Anne Sexton says, in speaking of what constitutes the truth in her poetry, "The effort is to try to get to some form of integrity when you write a poem, some whole life lived, to try to present it now, to give the impact."[14]

NOTES

1. M. L. Rosenthal, *The New Poets: American and British Poetry Since World War II* (New York: Oxford University Press, 1967), 79.

2. Robert Lowell, "On 'Skunk Hour,'" in *Robert Lowell: A Collection of Critical Essays,* edited by Thomas Parkinson (Englewood Cliffs, N.J.: Prentice-Hall, 1968), 133.

3. Patricia Marx, "Interview with Anne Sexton," *Hudson Review* 18, no. 4 (Winter 1965–66): 570.

4. Marx, 562.

5. James Dickey, "First Five Books," *Poetry* 97, no. 5 (February, 1961): 318–19.

6. Hayden Carruth, "In Spite of Artifice," *Hudson Review* 19, no. 4 (Winter 1966–67): 698.

7. May Swenson, "Poetry of Three Women," *Nation,* February, 1963, 165–66.

8. Marx, 568.

9. Rosenthal, 134.

10. Rosenthal, 80.

11. Marx, 563.

12. Philip Wheelwright, *The Burning Fountain* (Bloomington: Indiana University Press, 1954), 179.

13. A. R. Jones, "Necessity and Freedom: The Poetry of Robert Lowell, Sylvia Plath and Anne Sexton," *Critical Quarterly* 7 (1965): 25.

14. Marx, 564.

MYRA STARK

Walt Whitman and Anne Sexton

A Note on the Uses of Tradition

"I celebrate myself," begins Walt Whitman's *Song of Myself*.[1] Anne Sexton's title, "In Celebration of My Uterus,"[2] is the first indication of her deliberate use of the Whitman poem. Although it is only sixty-one lines long, Sexton's poem echoes the diction, the images, the very techniques of *Song of Myself*. Drawing as she does on a major American poem which took as its subject the nature of man and his relationship to the world, Sexton enriches her song of the woman self. She invokes Whitman to place what might be considered startling or unusual about her poem within a literary tradition. After all, one of Whitman's challenges in *Song* reads: "And I say it is as great to be a woman as to be a man" (85). "In Celebration of My Uterus" can be viewed as [being] written in praise of Whitman's statement.

A central impulse behind Whitman's *Song* is the affirmation of the oneness of spirit and physical being: "I am the poet of the Body; / And I am the poet of the Soul" (85). For Whitman there is no duality; all is part of life, and his insistence throughout the poem is on the sensual, sensuous, and sexual facts of existence as well as the spiritual. When Whitman asks, "What is a man, anyhow?" he answers, "hankering, gross, mystical, nude" (83). Sexton's praise of the uterus serves the same function: the choice underscores her insistence on accepting the physical woman body. Stanza one is written in denial of those who would claim that her womb is sick, old, empty, and are eager to cut it out. Lovingly, she calls it, "Sweet weight." Whitman says, "I find no sweeter fat than sticks to my own bones" (83), and again, "Clear and sweet is my Soul, and clear and sweet is all that is not my Soul" (63). For both poets, then, the affirmation of the unity

---

Notes on Contemporary Literature 8, no. 4 (1978). Reprinted by permission of the author.

of being is also an affirmation of the goodness of the human being.

The movement of both *Song* and "In Celebration" is from the self to others, from the self to the world. Both poets stress the essential unity between the self and others; the central self identifies with the human universe. The identification permits the world to flow in upon the self as the self transcends the limits of the ego and interpenetrates with others. "I am the man," Whitman insists throughout the poem, "I suffer'd, I was there" (107). "Everyone in me," says Sexton. The long and frequent catalogues in *Song,* which move backward and forward in time and roam freely throughout space, are a means of expressing the unity while at the same time celebrating the diversity of life. What is perhaps Sexton's most deliberate echo of Whitman's poem—the catalogue of women in stanza 3—serves the same purpose. "Many women," Sexton intones, and invokes one, "straddling a cello in Russia," one, "tying the cord of a calf in Arizona," one, "wiping the ass of her child," one, "in a shoe factory cursing the machine." This catalogue stresses the essential unity of women while expressing the uniqueness of their lives. "One is / anywhere," says Sexton, "and some are everywhere and all / seem to be singing," and they "are singing," she claims, "together of this." Through the catalogues both poets affirm life's abundance and find in it satisfaction; both, in fact, use the same metaphor to express this delight. "This is the meal set," says Whitman, "All this I swallow, and it tastes good" (107). Sexton's poem makes reference to the bountiful harvest and concludes with "the supper."

In both poems, food, harvest, and vegetation imagery are interlinked. In *Song,* the grass is the symbol of the unity and the continuity of life: "The smallest sprout shows there is really no death" (68). So Whitman can say, "I moisten the roots of all that has grown." Similarly, Sexton can move easily from the self and its affirmation of goodness—"I dare to live"—to the natural world of the harvest—"Hello to the soil of the fields." "Welcome," she says, to "roots." "'It is good this year that we may plant again / and think forward to a harvest.'" Both poets find all life encapsulated in each individual manifestation. Whitman says, "I believe a leaf of grass is no less than the journey-work / of the stars, / And the pismire is equally perfect, and a grain of sand . . . " (97). Sexton echoes, "Each cell has a life."

Both poems rise to moments in which a mystical affirmation of life and its goodness takes place. For Whitman, immersion in the life of the universe leads to intuitive understanding: "Swiftly arose and spread around me the peace and knowledge that pass all the argument of the earth" (66). Indeed, *Song of Myself* has been read as the poetic equivalent of mystical experience, ritually moving through the ascending stages of spiritual understanding. "In Celebration of My Uterus" is a record of a similar moment of mystical insight and acceptance: the last line of the poem is the single affirmation, "yes." After the catalogue of women, during which Sexton transcends the confines of her self to identify with women all over the world, she moves in the last stanza to a ritual invocation of sacred images: "let me carry bowls for the offering," she chants, "let me suck on the stems of flowers . . . / Let me make certain tribal figures. . . ." All these, she says, are "for the kissing, / for the correct / yes." "In Celebration," then, is a poem which begins with a consideration of a rejected part of the body ready for surgical excision and ends in ecstatic affirmation.

It is clear that there is a conscious effort in Sexton's "Celebration" to invoke *Song of Myself,* to return to and draw from the Whitman poem. Sexton uses *Song* as a literary ancestor can be used, as echo and counterpoint, to enrich and enlarge. She does so, no doubt, out of sympathy with Whitman's themes and techniques, but in the process invests her meditation upon the woman body and soul with the dignity of an accepted literary tradition. *Song of Myself* stands behind Anne Sexton's song of the woman self.[3]

NOTES

1. Walt Whitman, "Song of Myself," in *Leaves of Grass, The Portable Walt Whitman* (New York: Viking, 1955), 61. All subsequent references to this poem will be included in the text.

2. Anne Sexton, "In Celebration of My Uterus," *Love Poems* (Boston: Houghton Mifflin, 1969), 12–13. All subsequent references to this poem will be included in the text.

3. Whitman's influence on Sexton's work is far more extensive than just in this one poem. The first poem in *Love Poems,* for example, is called "The Touch"; touching is a dominant image in *Leaves of Grass.*

WILLIAM H. SHURR

Anne Sexton's *Love Poems*
The Genre and the Differences

At least half of Anne Sexton's published volumes of poetry show a tight unity of construction. Though virtually all of the poems were published separately in various periodicals, and thus each can stand by itself as a complete poem, in the collections they are brought into programmatic relation to one another. This is most obvious in *Transformations,* where the subjects are all known fairy tales and the speaker and the format of presentation is in every case the same. But study of *Love Poems, The Death Notebooks,* and *The Awful Rowing Toward God*—and, to a lesser extent, *Live or Die*—can uncover a similar continuity of experience. In the remaining volumes the reader finds suites of poems in which each can be taken separately but which yield a still "higher" synthesis when taken together.

Love Poems (1969)[1] is more than simply a collection of love poems; it is the record of a love affair which, as it is presented in the volume, lasted about four years. As shaped in the volume the experience was characterized by intense moments which the lovers had together as well as frequent separations, and it finally ended definitively. One senses in *Love Poems* a conscious attempt to isolate the experience from all others, to shape it into a unity and present the stages of its evolution as typical. A clue to Sexton's intention in shaping the collection is the forcefully suggestive passages from Yeats with which she introduced it:

> One should say before sleeping, "I have lived many lives. I have been a slave and a prince. Many a beloved one has sat upon my knees and I have sat upon the knees of many a beloved. Everything that has been shall be again."

Modern Poetry Studies 10, no. 1 (1981). Reprinted by permission of the author.

What we are to make of this is perhaps that Sexton is searching for essential contours, for a pattern of events that is repeatable and has been repeated a billion times in human history. Any collection of love poetry, or any suite of love poems, celebrates essentially the same sequence: the fascination, the awakening, the consummation, the celebration, the love-sickness in absence, the parting and the end of the affair: "Everything that has been shall be again." But so intensely lived is the experience that it seems to the lovers that it must be their unique experience alone; John Donne would persuade us that no other lovers had ever existed, that he exists as priest to unfold the wonders of this experience to the laity, gradually, according to their ability to understand. As Sexton introduces her poems, through the quotation from Yeats, she would interpret the genre to us as one in which we may appreciate again the universal moments in the experience and look as well for her own personal heightenings and insights.

By far the most highly dramatized moment of the collection, and the most intensely erotic, is the poem which celebrates "That Day." The poem has some elements of the medieval *alba:* reliving the experience and celebrating its stages in lavish detail, praising the lover's beauty (here, the details of the erection which she herself has manipulated), the union, and watching over the lover's sleep afterward. In the Troubadours, the sexual reward is the Lady's "gift," and Sexton rewrites and modernizes the tradition, "I bore gifts for your gift." Also in medieval love poetry, one finds the convention of the lovers' prayer to avoid the excesses of the unfortunate lovers of old. Medea is mentioned, and more frequently Dido, the Queen of Carthage who wanted to marry Aeneas even though she knew the Fates had decreed another wife for him, who begged at least to have a child by him as a permanent reminder of their love, and who finally committed suicide. Sexton's prayer, against this background, is chilling:

> Then I knew you in your dream and prayed of our time
> that I would be pierced and you would take root in me
> and that I might bring forth your born, might bear
> the you or the ghost of you in my little household.

The lovely eroticism of "That Day" is further heightened, interpreted, by its own framework. The typical dawn setting of the *alba* has been displaced. The experience of "That Day" is recounted the *next* day; the beloved is absent. In his place, quite literally where he had been, the mechanical typewriter is now in her hands. The end is foreseen and her aloneness frames the poem. The last lines read: "but this is the typewriter that sits before me and love is where yesterday is at."

"That Day" is the fifth poem of the collection and is preceded by three poems of preparation: the awakening of "The Hand," which will touch the beloved for the first time; the awakening of "The Kiss," which suddenly becomes adult, erotic: the awakening of "The Breast," which finds its best function in giving and receiving pleasure, in mothering the lover. What is perceived and repeated in each of these poems is the transition to a higher plane of being, the unfolding of a different function and a different kind of experience. The consummation of these preparations in "That Day" is then orchestrated with a powerful unleashing of new emotional forces. Some of Sexton's most striking lines appear in these three poems. In a vivid image, she describes the hand, before its awakening, as "sealed off / in a tin box." An image of transformation at the end of "The Kiss" arrests the attention: "Darling, the composer has stepped / into fire." In each case the suspension caused by the enjambement adds to the effect. Where the musical suggestion is here Wagnerian, it becomes playful in the next poem, "The Breast," where she describes her previously childish body as "A xylophone maybe with skin stretched over it awkwardly."

The natural flow, however, seems arrested by the difficult fourth poem in this initial group of five. It is called "The Interrogation of the Man of Many Hearts." It interrupts the continuity of the three preparatory poems with the following fulfillment poem. While the attention it requires seems to break the erotic line of development, it nevertheless clearly defines the situation of the affair and states themes which develop later as the painful dimension of the experience. It is as if Sexton were deliberately interrupting the pleasant expectations of the reader, to insist on the full reality of the matter.

"The Interrogation of the Man of Many Hearts" probes the

psychology of the male, who obviously enjoys the sexual experience with the interrogating woman, but who will inevitably rest in a more permanent married relationship with another woman. His instinct to marry another is not entirely reasonable. He acknowledges that

> She's my real witch, my fork, my mare,
> my mother of tears, my skirtful of hell,
> the stamp of my sorrows, the stamp of my bruises . . .

But still, he says, "I'm caught deep in the dye of her." The poem is a sequence of questions from the woman, with answers from the man. Once again the tradition of medieval love poetry comes to mind. Andreas Capellanus states that, among the rules for Courtly Love, marriage is actually an impediment to romantic love; the experience is heightened to its fullest only by the excitement of being extramarital, adulterous. Still another poetic technique of the Troubadours, the conversation between the lovers, the alternating *débat* between the man and the woman, is embodied in these lines.

The woman is sympathetically aware of the compulsive drives of the male. He admits that his polygamous instincts conflict with her essentially monogamous needs; what is a temporary need for him is permanent need for her:

> I have not only bedded her down.
> I have tied her down with a knot.

Sexton leads the reader through the nuances of reality, deeply felt and rendered with clear verbal intelligence. The wisdom she retrieves from this painful interrogation is the fact of the mutability of all experience, an ancient piece of wisdom traceable through Spenser and Boethius back to Ecclesiastes. Whether sanctioned by society and traditions or not, the final lesson of human experience is the same:

> *and every bed has been condemned,*
> *not by morality or law,*
> *but by time.*

Insertion of "The Interrogation of the Man of Many Hearts" at this point in the collection—between the awakening poems and the consummation poem—immediately elevates the meditations to a plane of high seriousness, from erotic romance to profound realism.

The rest of the poems in *Love Poems* are in fact rays from this initial cluster. A second sequence can be discerned in which the subject is the sexual awakening of the woman. "Song for a Red Nightgown" is the lightly humorous attempt at a precise description of a woman's night dress, the costume that signals the change from caterpillar to butterfly: "the butterfly owns her now." In another poem, "It Is a Spring Afternoon," the girl senses the change of seasons as parallel to her own profound and silent maturing. She falls in love with her new body, "her animal loveliness," in a series of healing and healthy images:

> Because of this
> the ground, that winter nightmare,
> has cured its sores and burst
> with green birds and vitamins.
> Because of this
> the trees turn in their trenches
> and hold up little rain cups
> by their slender fingers.
> Because of this
> a woman stands by her stove
> singing and cooking flowers.
> Everything here is yellow and green.

The swiftness and completeness of the transition is expressed in diction borrowed from Robert Frost's poem, "For Once, Then, Something":

> The face of the child wrinkles
> in the water and is gone forever.

The most striking of these "awakening" poems appears at the beginning of the sequence and bears the flagrant title "In Celebration of My Uterus." The poem fits into the collection only because of the context there. It derives, actually, as the opening lines make clear, from the medical problem Sexton had in 1959, when she feared that she had cancer, the disease from which her mother had recently died. The diagnosis and operation, however, disclosed only a benign tumor which was removed. The event itself was described in clinical detail in the poem called "The Operation" from *All My Pretty Ones* (1962). But, while the event itself happened several years before the affair began (as dated in *Love Poems*), still we may judge that this celebration of her womanly sexuality, where "each cell has a life," has been successfully inserted into its present place in the volume. The poem has been noticed by others, and while it may not be her strongest one there are elements in it that suggest a further respect for Anne Sexton's poetry as a whole. From this point of view, the Whitmanesque diction of the poem assumes primary importance. She invents a twelve-item catalogue, for example, of typical women; toward the end of the poem, the same phrase "Let me . . . " introduces eight separate lines of rhythmically parallel syntax; further, the Whitmanesque word "sing" and its variations occur prominently some half-dozen times, as does Whitman's divine "I am" phrase. Where Whitman celebrates the phallus, Sexton assumes the role of female counterpart, celebrating the uterus. There are reasons for seeing Sexton in the tradition of Whitman; she creates a female singer of the Self to match his male persona.

A third sequence of poems can be discerned later in the volume, celebrating the affair at its height. Leaving open the possibility that other poems and parts of poems touch the same subject, we can list the following as poems which follow without interruption in this sequence: "Now," "Us," "Mr. Mine," "Song for a Lady," and "Knee Song." The poems are characterized by innocence and spontaneity, by the security that the moment of love is eternal. In such a situation, play is the characteristic activity: "We are here on a raft, exiled from dust." The motifs rise to a high point in the final poem, where Molly Bloom's soliloquy is mined for dramatic effect: "yes oh yes yes yes . . . yes yes yes." The poems are lovely as erotic celebration. The sensual details are fresh and moving. "Song for a Lady" is a small gem of a song intricately rhymed. But even within this sequence can be heard time's winged chariot, which chills all lovers. Crystallized in a unique trope, this startling image is her version of the *carpe diem* theme:

> The shoemaker will come and he will rebuild
> this room. He will lie on your bed
> and urinate and nothing will exist.
> Now is the time. Now!

This suggests the theme of a fourth discernible sequence in *Love Poems,* a series of poems on the bitter aftermath of the affair. Once again, Sexton's placement of the poems is telling. Actually, this series comes third among the four sequences I have been suggesting, after the awakening poems and immediately before the fulfillment poems just described. It is as if Sexton would mold our responses to a harsh reality, as she had in the opening sequence of five poems: the most intense sensual pleasures are the most compelling reminders of our temporariness. It is as if Sexton were holding herself to the fire to find all the wisdom she could in a moment that was as transitory as it was beautiful. The poems that follow without interruption in this sequence are "Just Once," "Again and Again and Again," "You All Know the Story of the Other Woman," and "Moon Song, Woman Song." The sequence is ended by the powerful "Ballad of the Lonely Masturbator."

The first poem, which was actually written and published several years earlier, describes the affair as definitely over and ends with the irony that "these constants" are now "gone." The following poems are filled with bitterness: a frog "sits on my lips and defecates"; "the blackness is murderous"; she senses herself as having been used and abandoned; all lovers are "full of lies. / They are eating each other." On first reading, it is perhaps "The Ballad of the Lonely Masturbator" which strikes the reader as most original, but the poem that precedes it may have profounder rewards. "Moon Song, Woman Song" is a meditation into the ancient archetype of the moon as woman, virgin, goddess, the betrayed lover. The poem sets the speech in the mouth of the moon:

> I have been oranging and fat,
> carrot colored, gaped at,
> allowing my cracked o's to drop on the sea

The male is present in the poem as violator, "tall in your battle dress." The opposition of figures is ancient and worth considering again, but for this most recent version of the story Sexton suggests a modern context that strikingly authenticates the perennial applicability of the archetypal story. The male is lightly suggested as astronaut by the phrases "coverall man" and "blast off," and the moon passively awaits still another rough assault from him. The poem ends with a further insight; the ends of the male and the female are eternally unreconcilable: for him she is only "headquarters of an area," whereas she sees herself as "house of a dream."

Tight as the generic unity is, two poems seem to resist inclusion in *Love Poems*. The first is called "The Break," and since it follows "For My Lover, Returning to His Wife," the title suggests a smooth sequence of events. But the poem is an account of the broken hip she actually suffered from an accidental fall downstairs, on November 9, 1966. The fall and the subsequent operation were to leave her a virtual invalid for nearly a year. The muses of poetry were handing her difficult materials to transmute into a series of love poems. But poetry has rules that are different from those of biography and another careful reading is required for signs of Sexton's intention in placing the poem here. A key phrase appears: "I'm Ethan Frome's wife," and the reader recalls the end of Edith Wharton's story, where the two intense lovers are crippled and embittered finally, with the betrayed wife left to move them around at whim. The poem then suggests guilt and the fear of retribution, of poetic justice: a broken hip is the "right" punishment for an adulterous relationship. An earlier allusion, to Icarus, in line 13 confirms this suggestion of poetic justice. Congruent with this point of entry is the contrast, developed throughout the poem, between the broken hip and the broken heart. The poem begins, "It was also my violent heart that broke"; it ends with the acceptance of reality of her situation, the broken hip and "the violent heart." Her final comment draws on the phrase from the New Testament (John 2:17) to summarize her situation: "The zeal / of my house doth eat me up"—the driving energies of the violent heart have somehow resulted in the crack-up of the body. The seven other references to "heart" in this poem confirm the connection. The heart, "old hunger motor," "thought it could call all the shots." "The heart burst with love and lost its breath." With some problems, then, the poem inserts itself within the thematic patterns of *Love Poems*, suggesting that the love is a guilty one, that such overreaching cannot long escape the notice of the gods. If this is the intent of the poem, as it finds its place in *Love Poems*, then two lines in the third stanza arrest the attention:

> Yes. I was like a box of dog bones.
> But now they've wrapped me in like a nun.

In the last collection of poems she was to see through the press, *The Awful Rowing Toward God,* her love becomes a mystical love for the divine; her use of "Ms. Dog" indicates some marital relation to its reverse, "God." The lines above suggest some earlier beginning of this perception; the failure of human love isolates her for the divine.

The second poem which resists inclusion into the unity of *Love Poems* is "The Papa and Mama Dance." The poem is the recollection of a fictional brother and herself, as children, dressing in their parents' old clothes, and engaging in some intensely incestuous behavior. Sexton had no brother and the fantasy is the same as those found in other volumes of her poetry, in "For Johnny Pole on the Forgotten Beach" in *To Bedlam and Part Way Back* (1960), and in the Christopher poems in *The Death Notebooks* (1974). These poems, including the present one, are like the other moments when Sexton manufactures "autobiography" for the more intense personalization of her experiences. While "The Papa and Mama Dance," then, seems to come from another corner of the poet's mind, it is worth recalling that the convention of lovers pretending to be brother and sister, to heighten the erotic intimacy of the relationship, is at least as old as the Song of Solomon. There is, in addition, another detail which ties this poem to the present collection. It begins with the sister criticizing the brother for not burning his draft card, for going off to war instead. In the concluding sequence of the book ["Eighteen Days without You"], in the poem "December 9th," she complains to her lover:

> Two years ago, Reservist,
> you would have burned
> your draft card . . .

This poem as well, then, has multiple ties to the collection in which it appears.

An early reviewer of *Love Poems* complained that the volume seemed to him to suffer from hasty construction, and that "most of the poems seem to have been written far too quickly, as if she were rather nervous of overcooking emotional raw material."[2] It can be argued, however, that just the opposite is true, that the materials of the collection are quite cooled, quite thoroughly manipulated and artistically arranged, that the *impression* of raw emotion was precisely the one the poet was eager to convey. For example, the reader of Linda Gray Sexton's book, *Anne Sexton: A Self-Portrait in Letters,* comes to realize that two poems, "The Nude Swim" and "Loving the Killer," derive their setting and quite likely their personae from Anne's European trips with her husband.[3] Still another poem, "Just Once," fits the composite picture of *Love Poems* perfectly, but it was first published in 1958, several years before the affair began according to the internal datings of the volume. The raw experience has been cooked here quite thoroughly. Sexton had a talent for "pseudobiography," for the presentation of her poems as if they were raw emotional experiences. What embarrassed some early critics even, as unsanctionable invasion of her own privacy, turned out, at least at times, to be an intense fictional realism, the inventive talent of the poet-storyteller.

Love Poems, then, merges the possibilities of the ancient genre of erotic love poetry with the immediacy of modern experience. The contours of the genre which Sexton has emphasized are the awakening, the experience, the enjoyment and celebration of love, with the bitter aftermath of the definitive break as the controlling context for the whole. Individual poems are alive with a pulse of their own; the cool, ironic *encadrement* is the timeless theme of Mutability.

NOTES

1. Anne Sexton, *Love Poems* (Boston: Houghton Mifflin, 1969).
2. Ronald Hayman, "New Books of Poems," *Encounter* 35 (December, 1970): 77.
3. *Anne Sexton: A Self-Portrait in Letters,* edited by Linda Gray Sexton and Lois Ames (Boston: Houghton Mifflin, 1977), 299–301.

VERNON YOUNG

Review of *Transformations*

I'm relieved not to have to cope with Anne Sexton's customary war on her own gender. In *Transformations,* while her impatience with biology and destiny remains, she pursues another beast. She undermines the fairy tale with deadly address and a merciless employment of city-American idioms: occasionally vulgar, often brilliant, nearly always hilarious, to *my* cruel mind! She is no Thurber; the elegant master-spook of the graphic and English arts was a True Believer. His versions of Grimm or Andersen, however salty, set out to rival the originals; his ear was in thrall to Lewis Carroll and his wit, in this area, was less clinical than linguistic. Anne Sexton is out to *get* the brothers Grimm, armed with illuminations supplied by Freud but as much by the wised-up modern's experience of having been victimized by grandmother and recaptured by the pragmatic test. In such endeavors, tone is everything. Here's how she launches "Cinderella":

> You always read about it:
> the plumber with twelve children
> who wins the Irish Sweepstakes.
> From toilets to riches.
> That story.

> Or the nursemaid,
> some luscious sweet from Denmark
> who captures the oldest son's heart.
> From diapers to Dior.
> That story.

Reprinted by permission from "Lines Written in Rouen," *The Hudson Review,* Vol. XXIV, No. 4 (Winter 1971–72). Copyright © 1972 by The Hudson Review, Inc.

And here's how she ends the tale:

> Cinderella and the prince
> lived, they say, happily ever after,
> like two dolls in a museum case
> never bothered by diapers or dust,
> never arguing over the timing of an egg,
> never telling the same story twice,
> never getting a middle-aged spread,
> their darling smiles pasted on for eternity.
> Regular Bobbsey Twins.
> That story.

Corner-of-the-mouth stuff? Ideal for reading aloud to friends or to guests who won't thaw? But there are other passages where, sustained by her fine art of inflection and an uncanny choice of impertinent simile, she achieves a truly diabolical lyricism: in "Hansel and Gretel," in "One-Eye, Two-Eyes, Three-Eyes," in "Briar Rose (Sleeping Beauty)" (where Briar Rose audibly becomes Electra) and in "Rapunzel," from which this romping stanza:

> Rapunzel, Rapunzel, let down your hair,
> and thus they met and he declared his love.
> What is this beast, she thought,
> with muscles on his arms
> like a bag of snakes?
> What is this moss on his legs?
> What prickly plant grows on his cheeks?
> What is this voice as deep as a dog?
> Yet he dazzled her with his answers.
> Yet he dazzled her with his dancing stick.
> They lay together upon the yellowy threads,
> swimming through them
> like minnows through kelp
> and they sang out benedictions like the Pope.

The drawings of Barbara Swan incisively complement the poems. Their designs are what they should be: importunate and macabre; Gothic and placental.

BRIAN GALLAGHER

The Expanded Use of Simile in Anne Sexton's *Transformations*

Anne Sexton is, in all ten volumes of her published poems, a poet who relies relatively heavily on the use of simile and metaphor. However, in *Transformations,* her collection of sixteen Grimm fairy tales retold in poetic form, similes occur with much more than usual frequency—and metaphors with much less.[1] Often similes come in series, momentarily shifting the mode from narrative to comparative:

> She cried on her stumps
> as sweet as lotus water,
> as strong as petroleum,
> as sure-fire as castor oil.
> Her tears lay around her like a moat.[2]

At other junctures simile serves as a basic descriptive methodology:

> Once there was a witch's garden
> more beautiful than Eve's
> with carrots growing like little fish,
> with many tomatoes rich as frogs,
> onions as ingrown as hearts,
> the squash singing like a dolphin
> and one patch given over wholly to magic—
>
> ("Rapunzel," *T,* 39)

The reason for this increased reliance on simile in *Transformations* lies in the volume's particular nature. Like *Love Poems*

Notes on Modern American Literature 3, no. 3 (1979). Reprinted by permission of the editors and the author.

(1969), *The Death Notebooks* (1974), and *The Awful Rowing To-ward God* (1975), *Transformations* is a collection of Sexton poems unified by a single concept, except that in the place of a direct treatment of powerful, broad abstractions (love, death, the re-ligious impulse), *Transformations* works directly from a literary source. In fact, Sexton, although she certainly adds much in her retellings, is quite scrupulous in adhering to the basic narrative line laid out by the Brothers Grimm.[3] Rather than reworking the stories, Sexton has structured her poetic narratives to pro-vide herself with ample room to comment upon and analyze her chosen fairy tales. Each poem contains a prefatory section (rang-ing from a single stanza in "Godfather Death" to three pages, nearly half the poem, in "Red Riding Hood"), in which the persona, in a voice distinctly contemporary in tone, diction and syntax, reflects upon the meaning of the tale to follow. Some-times the import of the remarks is general: "A woman / who loves a woman / is forever young" ("Rapunzel," *T*, 35). Often the poems open with a combination of casually hip language and modernistic imagery:

> No matter what life you lead
> the virgin is a lovely number:
> cheeks as fragile as cigarette paper,
> arms and legs made of Limoges,
> lips like Vin Du Rhône,
> rolling her china-blue doll eyes
> open and shut.
> > ("Snow White and the Seven Dwarfs," *T*, 3)

Several of these "prefaces" introduce a personal referent:

> And I. I too.
> Quite collected at cocktail parties,
> meanwhile in my head
> I'm undergoing open-heart surgery.
> > ("Red Riding Hood," *T*, 74–75)

A few of the poems contain sardonic afterwords, such as this one from "Iron Hans," which recalls the realm of modern mad-ness so often depicted in Sexton's poetry:

> Without Thorazine
> or benefit of psychotherapy
> Iron Hans was transformed.
> No need for Master Medical;
> no need for electroshock—
> merely bewitched all along.

(*T*, 50)

Obviously these prefaces (and afterwords) are a major means of "transforming" the fairy tales into a modern psychological idiom, for here Sexton can, in her familiar voice, reflect upon the universal import of the terror, stupidity, fear, and wonder encapsulated in these stories. In the narrative sections of these poems, however, Sexton cannot be so direct in her remarks. Rather she resorts to several devices, most particularly simile, to provide a "running commentary" on the fairy tale she is unfolding.

Her expanded reliance on simile in the narrative sections works in three ways. Most importantly, it permits the poet to provide a host of suggestive modern parallels for the characters and action of the fairy tale. For instance, Snow White's stepmother "had a mirror to which she referred— / something like the weather forecast" (*T*, 5), and when the hunter brought her what was supposedly Snow White's heart, this evil queen "chewed it up like a cube steak" (*T*, 5). The lecherous parson in "The Little Peasant" stands exposed "as real as a soup can" (*T*, 30). In "The Twelve Dancing Princesses" the dozen maidens are pictured dancing "like taxi girls at Roseland / as if those tickets would run right out" (*T*, 91). In such instances Sexton not only "modernizes" the story without distorting its original shape, but she also introduces, *beside* the simple, single tone of the folk-based Grimm original, a complex, knowing, worldly tone. Many of these "modernizing" similes produce a comic effect via their duality—that is, they are both valid and absurd. When the queen in "Rumpelstiltskin" is described "as persistent / as a Jehovah's Witness" (*T*, 15) we identify both a comparison (a wearyingly solipsistic attitude) and a disjuncture (the impossibility of precisely this type of door-ringing, *Watch-tower*-hawking evangelist in the vaguely medieval Germanic landscape). Several poems draw a number of similes from a single "modern" realm. For instance, the narrative section of "The Twelve

Dancing Princesses" contains three similes based on the equipment used in organized sports: the shoes of each princess appear every morning "as worn as an old jockstrap" (*T*, 89); each prince who previously tried to solve the mystery of the princesses' nocturnal activities failed and "was beheaded. / Poof! Like a basketball" (*T*, 90); and at the wedding of the triumphant soldier and the eldest princess the other "princesses averted their eyes / and sagged like old sweatshirts" (*T*, 92). In other poems the "modernizing" similes serve to link the primitive, symbolic terror of the fairy tale narrative with twentieth century embodiments of such terror in a political framework:

> It was a matter of gymnastics.
> Gretel,
> seeing her moment in history,
> shut fast the oven,
> locked fast the door,
> fast as Houdini,
> and turned the oven on to bake.
> The witch turned as red
> as the Jap flag.
> Her blood began to boil up
> like Coca-Cola.
>
> ("Hansel and Gretel," *T*, 104–5)[4]

Although most of the similes in the narrative sections of the poems are meant to extend the stories in time by relating them to present circumstances, other of the similes serve to extend the scope of the stories. These are chiefly similes drawing on classical literature. The blinded prince in "Rapunzel" "wandered for years" as "blind as Oedipus" (*T*, 41). When Iron Hans dipped his hair into the golden stream his hair turned "as gold as Midas' daughter. / As stiff as the Medusa hair of a Greek statue" (*T*, 48). A princess drinks from a cup shared with a frog "as if it were Socrates' hemlock" ("The Frog Prince," *T*, 98). The intent of this type of simile is simple, but significant: to situate these tales in a larger mythopoeic context, thereby extending the meaning of the tale, quite legitimately, beyond the ken of the *Volk* who originated and preserved it.

The third expanded use for simile in *Transformations* is to make the latent content of these tales, especially their latent sexual content (since rage and terror lie close to their surface), more apparent. The princess's encounter with the prince bewitched into a frog is full of erotic similes meant to suggest the young woman's half-conscious feelings of fear and excitement over her sexual initiation: "Her fork trembled / as if a small machine / had entered her" (*T*, 98)—and when the spell is removed, the prince appears in a most phallic simile: "Like a genie coming out of a samovar" (*T*, 99). Snow White's journey through the "wildwood" (itself a common Freudian symbol for a plunge into the depths of the unconscious[5]) is rank with threatening sexual similes:

> At each turn there were twenty doorways
> and at each stood a hungry wolf,
> his tongue lolling out like a worm.
> The birds called out lewdly,
> talking like pink parrots[6]

(*T*, 6)

One of the more remarkable aspects of the poems in *Transformations* is how much they sound like "Anne Sexton" and how, at the same time, they remain faithful to the stories recorded by the Brothers Grimm. Simile is Sexton's principal device for creating this dual effect, for it allows her a series of witty, cruel, ironic comparisons, while it also permits her to keep the fairy tale narrative within the vague, "once upon a time" world where it can—and probably must needs—flourish.

NOTES

1. A rough estimate would be that the poems in *Transformations* contain two to three times as many similes as the poems in the other nine volumes, and that metaphors are employed less than half as often.

2. Anne Sexton, "The Maiden without Hands," *Transformations,* preface by Kurt Vonnegut, Jr., illustrated by Barbara Swan (Boston: Houghton Mifflin, 1971), 82. *Transformations* is cited hereafter as *T.*

3. At several points in his influential *The Uses of Enchantment: The Meaning and Importance of Fairy Tales* (New York: Vintage, 1977),

Bruno Bettelheim pauses to laud Sexton for her faithfulness to the primal Grimm narrative in the face of the superficial sophisticators from Perrault to Disney. See p. 210n and p. 290n.

4. The simile of the "boiling" Coca-Cola coming after the allusion to the Holocaust and the simile of the blood-red flag of Japanese imperialism would appear to suggest, by its very yoking of a seemingly neutral modern substance with two of the more malign political movements of the century, an attitude which finds more direct expression in Sexton's other nine volumes of poems—namely that the modern world is a particularly threatening and disorienting place in which to try to survive.

5. See Bettelheim, p. 94 and passim, on this.

6. This passage resembles, in both its imagery and its depiction of the world's insistent forcing of sexual innuendo on the child, a passage from a poem in the volume directly following *Transformations:*

> Who was he, Father?
> What right, Father?
> To pick me up like Charlie McCarthy
> and place me on his lap?
> He was bald as a hump.
> His ears stuck out like teacups
> and his tongue, my God, his tongue,
> like a red worm and when he kissed
> it crawled right in.

("Friends," part 5 of "The Death of the Fathers," in *The Book of Folly* [Boston: Houghton Mifflin, 1972], 48–49)

ALICIA OSTRIKER

That Story

The Changes of Anne Sexton

I

Anne Sexton is the easiest poet in the world to condescend to.
Critics get in line for the pleasure of filing her under N for
Narcissist and announcing that she lacks reticence. A recent ex-
ample: "She indulges in self-revelation without stint, telling all
in an *exposé* of her innermost workings that amounts to literary
seppuku." The critic wonders whether "such messy preoccupa-
tions will remain to stain the linen of the culture for long or
whether good taste bleaches out even the most stubborn stain
eventually."[1]

In letters as in life, to expose a personal fragility is to invite
attack. Cruelty and contempt follow vulnerability, just as re-
spect follows snobbishness; it is a law of human nature. Having
been on both sides of this reflex, I suspect that the sneer derives
from fear—a fear of being stung into imaginative sympathy—
and in Anne Sexton's case I suspect that the fear is threefold.

First of all, Sexton's material is heavily female and biological.
She gives us full helpings of her breasts, her uterus, her men-
struation, her abortion, her "tiny jail" of a vagina, her love life,
her mother's and daughters' breasts, everyone's operations, the
act of eating, the way her father's "serpent, that mocker, woke
up and pressed against me / like a great god" when she danced
with him after much champagne at a wedding, even the trauma
of her childhood enemas. Preoccupied with the flesh, she swings
between experiencing it as sacred and fertile and experiencing it
as filthy and defiled. This distinguishes her from Plath, for
whom the body is mainly an emblem of pain and mutilation.
But the distinction will not be an interesting one to the timid

American Poetry Review 11, no. 4 (1982). Reprinted by permission of the author.

reader. Far more than Plath, Sexton challenges our residual certainties that the life of the body should be private and not public, and that women especially should be seen and not heard, except among each other, talking about their messy anatomies. We believe, I think, that civilization will fall if it is otherwise.

Second, Sexton is assertively emotional. A love junkie who believes "touch" is "the kingdom and the kingdom come," she is driven by an unquenchable need for acceptance and caresses, and by bottomless guilt that she herself has been insufficiently loving to others. Simultaneously, the poetry presses intimately toward its audience. Feel what I feel, it says. Accept me, love me, love everything about me, my strength, my weakness. This of course is very much a feminine sort of demand, or rather it is a demand we discourage men from making explicitly (disguised versions are acceptable) and encourage women to make, with predictable results. Remember Marilyn Monroe? The egotistical sublime we tolerate; not the egotistical pathetic. The demand for love is narcissistic and childish. It is usually self-defeating, since most of us respond to another's need for love with aversion. Insofar as we manage (barely) to keep the upper lip stiff in our own lives, we judge neediness (in excess of our own) to be immoral. In the same way, wealth judges poverty and success perceives failure to be a consequence of low character. We understand that beggars and cripples exist, but do they have to put themselves where we can see them?

But what is most distressing about Sexton, I think, is her quality of unresignedness. She writes more fiercely than any poet in our time about physical and mental bliss and the holiness of the heart's affections. Her explorations of pathology are feverish attempts to "gnaw at the barrier" dividing us from each other and from the "weird abundance" of our creative capacities. She is sure not only that poetry saved her own life but that it can save others' lives. Many of her poems are gestures of rather pure human generosity. "For My Lover Returning to His Wife" and "December 12th" [from "Eighteen Days Without You"] in *Love Poems* are two examples. Typically her work enacts a pitched battle between Thanatos and Eros, self-loathing and self-love, suicide and survival. This too is irritating. "The mass of men lead lives of quiet desperation," wrote Thoreau above a century ago, trying to twit them out of it.

"We think of the key, each in his prison, / Thinking of the key, each confirms a prison," wrote Eliot a half-century back, on the way to his conversion to Christianity. But consider how much of our literature, our high literature especially, and most especially our high poetry, confirms the prison. We are instructed perhaps in its interior decoration, but not encouraged to seek escape. John Fowles's Daniel Martin muses "how all through his writing life, he had avoided the happy ending, as if it were somehow in bad taste . . . offensive, in an intellectually privileged caste, to suggest publicly that anything might turn out well." If each in his cell believes himself locked up forever, the last thing he wants to hear from a neighboring cell is the noise of scratching, poundings, screamings for the jailer.

Antipathy to a writer like Sexton makes sense if we assume that poetry must somehow be decorous. Obviously a great deal of poetry, both great and trivial, is so. But I see no real reason why poetry should be limited to tasteful confirmations of my psychic *status quo ante,* or indeed why it should be limited in any way. Reticence and good taste are excellent things, but unscrewing the doors from their jambs is a good thing too. Our original sin as humanists is a tendency to forget that nothing human is alien to any of us. This means that the crazy suicidal lady is not to be condescended to by me. It also means that she is one of the inhabitants of my own proper attic, whom I deny at my peril. A poem does not have to be, yet may legitimately be, "the ax for the frozen sea" of sympathy and self-recognition "within us," provided only that its language be living and its form just.

This brings me to the vexed question of Anne Sexton's artistry, where I must say immediately and with regret that she is not a *fine* artist. At her best she is coarse. Musically her instrument is the kazoo. If Plath, say, is porcelain and Robert Lowell bronze, Sexton is brightly painted earthenware. Reading every book of hers but *Transformations,* I burn with the desire to edit. She repeats herself without noticing. Her early poems before she hits her stride tend to be too stiff, her late ones tend to be shapeless. Her phrasing is sometimes sentimental, her endings sometimes flat.

And yet the writing dazzles. Sexton's colloquial line, vigorous, flexible and earthy, is not only a standing rebuke to every sort of false dignity but a strategy for redeeming the common life.

Her organic and domestic imagery captures species of phenomena for poetry that were never there before. Her metaphors, breathtaking as ski-jumps, direct attention both to the play of language and to the writer's intelligence—which is not the same as bookishness—and sheer capacity to describe. One does not rapidly exhaust the significance of a poem about the mad that says "what large children we are" and mentions the night nurse who "walks on two erasers," or a poem about a hospital stay concluding with the lines "and run along, Anne, and run along now, / my stomach laced up like a football / for the game." Is one's body really a toy? To others; to the self? Consider a fantasy of dying that says, "I moved like a lobster, / slower and slower," or a quick allegory of the poet's life in which Jonah, finding he cannot escape the whale, "cocked his head attentively / like a defendant at his own trial," or the simile of "tears falling down like mud," or the story of Eve giving birth to a rat "with its bellyful of dirt / and its hair seven inches long" that she did not realize was ugly. It is writerliness and nothing else that enables Sexton to re-create the child-self more keenly than Roethke, to define inner demons more clearly than Lowell, and to evoke the complicated tensile strands of intimate relationships, which include physical need and revulsion, affection and fear, pride and guilt, resentment, jealousy and admiration, better than most novelists. As to the primitive style, anyone who thinks it is easier to write "raw" than "cooked" should try it.

Often Sexton's best poems in the early books are not the harrowing accounts of private trauma which understandably most gripped her first readers, but poems where self-knowledge makes possible the verbal crystallization of some larger piece of the human condition. "Housewife," a ten-line poem with four hairpin turns and a final two lines that are as important as the first two of "The Red Wheel Barrow," is a good example. It is this that brings me to my main subject. Though Sexton is always a strong poet of the subjective self, in the middle of her career her center of gravity shifted. Beginning with *Transformations*, which was a sort of poetic self-initiation, she set the uninhibited self to work interpreting prior, external, shared cultural traditions. The texts I want to examine are *Transformations*, which is her most successful single book because of its brilliant fusion of public with personal matter; "The Jesus Papers" in *The*

Book of Folly, which is her most shocking and subversive work; and the poetry of spiritual quest in *The Death Notebooks* and *The Awful Rowing Toward God,* which is her most tragic. I believe that "confessional" or not, all these poems change the way we must look at our shared past. As their themes are increasingly ambitious, their conclusions are increasingly significant culturally. Obviously they also change the way we must look at Sexton.

II

In the winter of 1969–70, with four volumes of intimately personal poems behind her, Anne Sexton embarked on a new sort of venture. The early work dealt with the poet's family, her struggles against madness, her loves, her terrors, her desires. "That narrow diary of my mind" was laid publicly bare both as a personal necessity and in the faith that to reveal rather than conceal one's private nightmares was to perform a poetic service. The orientation of her poetry was psychoanalytic, as befitted a poet who began writing as a form of therapy following mental breakdown, who enacted in her poems the analysand's self-probing through examination of relationships with others, and who explained the vitality of their images by saying that "poetry, after all, milks the unconscious." Of all the poets subsequently labeled confessional or extremist—Snodgrass, Lowell, Berryman, Plath—she was the least reticent personally, and the most eager to have her poems "mean something to someone else." Public popularity had spectacularly confirmed Sexton's convictions. For much of 1969 the poet immersed herself with the aid of a Guggenheim grant in the autobiographical drama *Mercy Street,* a work of extreme self-saturation which played for some weeks in the fall at the American Place Theatre to mixed but respectful reviews. Up until this point, Sexton had not tried "to give you something else, / something outside of myself."[2] Self was the center, self the perimeter, of her vision.

Concerning the new series of poems which retold sixteen fairy tales from the Brothers Grimm, neither the poet nor her publishers expressed great confidence. Houghton Mifflin wondered whether she should publish them at all, and wanted to consult an outside reader. Sexton was defensive and apologetic, worrying that "many of my former fans are going to be disappointed that these poems do not hover on the brink of insanity," and acknowledging that they were "a departure from my usual style . . . they lack the intensity and confessional force of my previous work." To persuade herself and her publishers that the work was good, she solicited an opinion from Stanley Kunitz. To boost it with the public, she arranged for an admiring preface by Kurt Vonnegut, Jr.

Transformations breaks the confined circle of a poetic mode Sexton had needed but outgrown, that of the purely personal. That folktales carry a heavy cultural burden has been understood since they were first collected. Mircea Eliade tells us they represent "an infinitely serious and responsible adventure" which he identifies with the universal ordeal of initiation, "passing by way of a symbolic death and resurrection from ignorance and immaturity to the spiritual age of the adult." Bruno Bettelheim believes they provide children with models for the mastery of psychological problems, teach them the necessity of struggle, and embody through fantasy "the process of healthy human development." We see these tales, in other words, as the expression of a social mandate favoring individual growth.

Sexton does not alter Grimms' plots. Her fidelity to the stories preserves what Eliade calls the "initiatory scenario," and this may partially explain why a poet who was perennially torn between remaining a child and assuming adulthood was attracted to these tales in the first place. Formally, the plot lines give her what she never had before: something nominally outside of her personal history to write about. What she does with this material is to seize it, crack it open, and *make* it personal. The result is at once a brilliant interpretation and a valid continuation of folktale tradition—and a piece of poetic subversion, whereby the "healthy" meanings we expect to enjoy are held up to icy scrutiny.

Syntax and diction in *Transformations* are conspicuously and brazenly twentieth-century American, stripped to the colloquial bone, in a mode probably generated for American poetry by Eliot's "Journey of the Magi." The technique brings us closer to the unsentimental pre-Christian origins of these stories, much as the language of Eliot's "Magi" intends not to deflate the significance of Christ's nativity but to force the reader to confront it more nakedly. But unlike Eliot (or Pound, or their imitators), far from being interested in the past for its own sake, Sexton makes the time of the tales our own. In her "Snow White and the Seven Dwarfs":

> the virgin is a lovely number:
> cheeks fragile as cigarette paper,
> arms and legs made of Limoges,
> lips like Vin Du Rhône,
> rolling her china-blue doll eyes
> open and shut.

This is the opening tale and sets the tone. Of the miller's daughter in "Rumpelstiltskin," threatened with extinction if she does not spin straw into gold, the narrator condoles, "Poor thing. / To die and never see Brooklyn." In "Cinderella" the heroine

> slept on the sooty hearth each night
> and walked around looking like Al Jolson.

The reader's initial response to these anachronisms may be one of delighted shock—Cinderella and Al Jolson, yes, of course, think of the parallels—it is like a blue volt leaping a gap. We need to remember that just such modernization and adaptation, making the tales locally meaningful, is what peasants and poets have done with traditional lore for millennia. The stories would never survive without it. But Sexton's telescoping of past and present is also a surface manifestation of a more profound interpretive activity.

The poet's effort to understand her stories on her own terms precipitates a transformed view of traditional social values, particularly those associated with feminine life patterns: love and marriage, beauty, family, and most radically, the idea of goodness and moral responsibility, all of which she slices through like butter. The fairy-tale ending of marriage, supposed to represent romantic and financial security ever after, becomes, ironically, "that story"—incredible in the first place, and, were it credible, pathetically dull:

> Cinderella and the prince
> lived, they say, happily ever after,

like two dolls in a museum case
never bothered by diapers or dust,
never arguing over the timing of an egg,
never telling the same story twice,
never getting a middle-aged spread,
their darling smiles pasted on for eternity.
Regular Bobbsey Twins.
That story.

Half of Sexton's tales end in marriage, and most of these marriages are seen as some form of either selfishness or captivity. Regarding the value of beauty, we learn in "Snow White" that an innocent virgin's unconscious beauty makes her a stupid doll, a commodity, while an experienced woman's conscious beauty makes her not only cruel but doomed. "Beauty is a simple passion, / but, oh my friends, in the end / you will dance the fire dance in iron shoes." Moreover, since "a woman *is* her mother," at the wedding celebration during which the stepmother gets tortured to death in those iron shoes, Snow White chillingly begins "referring to her mirror / as women do." Describing the sacred emotion of mother-love, Sexton in "Rumpelstiltskin" remarks with pure contempt:

He was like most new babies,
as ugly as an artichoke
but the queen thought him a pearl.
She gave him her dumb lactation,
delicate, trembling, hidden,
warm, etc.

While none of the protagonists in Sexton's versions is described in terms of his or her virtue, which is Grimms as it should be, pre-Disney and amoral, "evil" characters and deviant behavior commonly receive her sympathy. The witch in "Hansel and Gretel" is cannibalistic and terrifying, as in the original, and her death is represented as poetic justice. But the poem's prologue has been a fantasia on the theme of a normally affectionate mother's desire to "eat up" her son, and the epilogue provocatively suggests that in a world governed by eating or being eaten, the witch in "the woe of the oven" has been a sacrifice "like something religious." Does Sexton mean that the witch is a Christ figure? Is this a reference to the subduing of the mother-goddess by a civilized daughter allied with the patriarchy? (Louise Glück's "Gretel in Darkness," by the way, raises similar questions.) In "Rapunzel," Sexton sees the witch as a lesbian in love with her imprisoned girl, and the poem stresses the emotional poignance of the older woman's loss, while perfunctorily dismissing the normality of the heterosexual lovers. "Rumpelstiltskin" and other stories follow a similar pattern, prodding us toward identification with antagonist-loser instead of protagonist-winner.

By the same token a number of characters we have conventionally accepted as good are made repellent. In "The Maiden without Hands," the king who weds the mutilated girl is motivated by "a desire to own the maiming / so that not one of us butchers / will come to him with crowbars." So long as the queen is a cripple, the king will feel secure in his own wholeness. (This, by the way, is one of the few occasions when Sexton writes, albeit allegorically, about her own marriage. Asked in an interview whether she was not afraid of hurting others by her intimate revelations of family life, she explained that she wrote mainly about the dead who could not be hurt, and avoided saying painful things about the living.) In "The Twelve Dancing Princesses," which is transformed to an Eros-versus-Logos, or Pleasure-Principle-versus-Superego parable, Logos unfortunately wins, in the person of the clever young man who finds out where the irresponsible princesses do their dancing. His mean-minded success brings an end to their enjoyable night life. The shocking final poem, "Briar Rose (Sleeping Beauty)," eliminates the heroine's mother and makes the father not merely the possessive maintainer of his daughter's prepubescent purity— "He forced every male in the court / to scour his tongue with Bab-o"—but its incestuous exploiter. Sleep in this poem brings "a voyage" into regressive infantilism. Wakened after her hundred-years' sleep, Briar Rose cries "Daddy! Daddy!" What she will see for the rest of her life when she wakens from the nightmares that plague her is

> . . . another kind of prison.
> It's not the prince at all,

>   but my father
>   drunkenly bent over my bed,
>   circling the abyss like a shark,
>   my father thick upon me
>   like some sleeping jellyfish.

Here and everywhere Sexton's interpretations discover and release elements already implicit in the stories. Over and over one thinks "of course." Were we to look at these poems as moral texts, we would have to see in them a demand for some transvaluation of social values.

But the appeal of the tales is primarily neither moral nor immoral. They are, as the central fact of magic in them partially indicates, rooted in and addressed to something less rational in our natures than the impulse toward social reform. Joseph Campbell makes the obvious point that folktale, like dream and myth, derives ultimately from the individual psyche, modified by the successions of cultures it travels through, and that its images are not simply relics of religious or superstitious periods in cultural history but projections of universal and primitive human desires and fears. It is proper, therefore, that Sexton's handling of these tales, while unconventionally personal and morally skeptical, is nevertheless designed to maintain, not reduce, their psychic impact. The poet does not rationalize or explain. She narrates, and with great swiftness and skill. She is funny, which makes sense since comedy is a major element in the traditional stories. She is intensely vivid. Her style excites, rather than soothes, the senses. Her imagery, to borrow a term from tabloids and horror movies, is sensational, full of food and feeding, sexuality, greed, and death—often fused, in a kind of synesthesia of appetites.

"Snow White," the first story in the volume, is sensationally and gratuitously oral. It tells us that the virign is "unsoiled . . . white as a bonefish," and a few lines later that her stepmother has been "eaten, of course, by age." Where in Grimm the evil queen wants Snow White's heart merely as proof of her death, Sexton's stepmother expresses a cruder longing: "Bring me her heart . . . and I will salt it and eat it." Brought a boar's heart by the compassionate hunter, "the queen chewed it up like a cube steak."

Proceeding with the story, Sexton embroiders. Snow White on entering the strange cottage eats "seven chicken livers" before sleeping, and then we meet what I and most of my students regard as the best single metaphor in the book, "the dwarfs, those little hot dogs." Revived after her first coma, her heroine is "as full of life as soda pop." When she bites the poison apple, the dwarfs "washed her with wine / and rubbed her with butter," though to no avail. "She lay as still as a gold piece." The passive coin, recalling Plath's "I am your jewel, I am your valuable, / The pure gold baby," parallels food in its appeal to greed.

Other poems similarly ply us with images of the tactile, the expensive, the devourable. The girl in "Rumpelstiltskin" is "lovely as a grape." The dwarf commits suicide by tearing himself in two, "somewhat like a split broiler." Feeding and sexuality are cheerfully identified in the bawdy poem "The Little Peasant," tragically identified in "Rapunzel," where women in love "feed off each other." In "Little Red Riding Hood" and "Hansel and Gretel," Sexton again implies the interchangeability of feeding and being fed on, in dramas of death and rebirth.

Where the Grimm stories are violent, Sexton does not skimp on pain and gore, but describes with inventive detail:

> First your toes will smoke
> and then your heels will turn black
> and you will fry upward like a frog
>
> ("Snow White")

When Cinderella's sister cuts a toe off to fit the shoe, we see

> . . . the blood pouring forth.
> That is the way with amputations.
> They don't just heal up like a wish

and both sisters at Cinderella's wedding have their eyes pecked out, leaving "two hollow spots . . . like soup spoons." Well over half the tales include death or mutilation, and both in the individual poems and cumulatively, Sexton's images of killing and eating in *Transformations* seem not merely childish but infantile.

That, I think, is the point. The evocation of these desires and terrors reminds us of powers we can scarcely control even as adults, in our lives and in the world. We are reminded of the helpless ur-self whose whole world is touch and taste, who fantasizes omnipotence, who dreads annihilation in a thousand ways. And it is this self, we understand when reading *Transformations,* that generates fairy tales.

III

Although Sexton did not again write in the manner of *Transformations,* the volume marks a turning point. She had learned how to interpret the impersonal by means of the personal, the symbol belonging to a culture by experience belonging to the self. She had exercised for the first time a gift for iconoclasm regarding social and moral conventions. She had acquired, as her later work shows, a taste for the quasi-mythic narrative. Her final finished books, *The Book of Folly* (1972), *The Death Notebooks* (1974), and *The Awful Rowing Toward God* (1975), return to a predominantly autobiographical mode. But they are bolder in language, formally more experimental, and readier to challenge convention, than any of her earlier work. In them the poet increasingly sees herself not as merely a private person, certainly not as a psychoanalytic case study, but as the heroine in a spiritual quest. At the same time, the question of what it means to be feminine—not simply to the self but to the culture and within the religion created by that culture—deepens and darkens. In an early (1965) *Hudson Review* interview, Sexton says, "It's very hard to reveal yourself . . . I'm hunting for the truth . . . behind everything that happens to you, every act, there is another truth, a secret life." What the late books reveal is that behind the "live or die" struggle in Sexton's life was another struggle, which led her first to a re-envisioning of Christian myth, then to a re-imagining of God the Father. I am tempted to say that Sexton's final wrestling was between loving and loathing God, and that she lost it because she knew too much.

The Book of Folly makes us think about gender in a way that moves a step past the deflating techniques of *Transformations.* It includes a group of *persona* pieces which enable the poet to imagine the violent personalities of one-legged man, assassin, wife beater—all of them castrated figures for whom woman is enemy, all of them evidently *animus*-figures for Sexton, as are "the ambition bird" in the finely sardonic and self-critical opening poem, and the destructive doppelgänger in "The Other." In "The Red Shoes," a spin-off from *Transformations,* ambition is secretly and shamefully handed down from mother to daughter, is uncontrollable, and destroys them. "Anna Who Was Mad" and "The Hex" are secular salvation and damnation poems struggling with the poet's guilty fear that her ongoing life is responsible for the madness and death of the beloved aunt whose namesake she is. In "Mother and Daughter" Sexton's tone is glad and proud as she relinquishes "my booty, my spoils, my Mother & Co." and celebrates the daughter's growth to womanhood, but what womanhood means is:

> carrying keepsakes to the boys,
> carrying powders to the boys,
> carrying, my Linda, blood to
> the bloodletter.

There is a figure in the carpet here.[3] In all these poems self-sacrifice is the condition of self-acceptance, and to be feminine is to be either powerless or punished. The "Angels of the Love Affair" sonnet sequence, inspired by Rilke, challenges a set of elemental angels to know and exorcise what the poet knows of shame, defilement, paralysis, despair and solitude. In the one poem where the poet remembers herself taking a pleasurable initiative (stealing grandfather's forbidden raspberries), the angel is a punitive lady "of blizzards and blackouts." The three prose narratives in *The Book of Folly* still more clearly identify passive feminine roles (daughter, wife, erotic object) with victimization and self-victimization. The one figure who seems to escape passivity, the protagonist's adventurous friend Ruth in "The Letting Down of the Hair," finally finds Christ—and kills herself. Sexton does not tell us why. But the series of seven short poems entitled "The Jesus Papers" may explain.

Prior to *The Book of Folly,* in occasional poems dealing with Christ, Sexton had evidently identified with him as sufferer and public performer. "When I was Christ, I felt like Christ," she said of "In the Deep Museum." "My arms hurt, I desperately wanted to pull them in off the Cross. When I was taken down off the Cross, and buried alive, I sought solutions; I hoped they were Christian solutions." "That ragged Christ, that sufferer, performed the greatest act of confession." In "The Exorcists," an early poem about abortion, the title implies ironically that an aborted fetus is being cast out like a demon, but the poem's text, with its "I know you not" refrain, implies that on the contrary it is a Christ whom the speaker is betraying. Many of Sexton's letters depict an intense need for faith undermined by solid skepticism: "In case it's true, I tell my Catholic friend . . . in case it's true, I tell myself, and plead with it to be true, after all. No matter what I write, I plead with it to be true!" (*Letters*, 125).[4] "God? spend half time wooing R. Catholics who will pray *for* you in case it's true. Spend other half knowing there is certainly no god. Spend fantasy time thinking that there is a life after death, because surely my parents, for instance, are not dead, they are, good god!, just buried" (*Letters*, 235). "Oh, I really believe in God—it's Christ that boggles the mind" (*Letters*, 346). "Yes, it is time to think about Christ again. I keep putting it off. If he is the God/man, I would feel a hell of a lot better. If there is a God . . . how do you explain him swallowing all those people up in Pakistan? Of course there's a God, but what kind is he?" (*Letters*, 368–69). Sexton also experienced visions, of varied duration and of great physical urgency, of Christ, Mary, God, the martyred saints, the devil, in which "I feel that I can touch them almost . . . that they are part of me . . . I believed that I was talking to Mary, that her lips were upon my lips," she said in an interview. None of this data, however, explains the radical vision of "The Jesus Papers," which is a systematic and structured—if miniature—reinterpretation of Christian myth, as *Transformations* is of Grimm. The subject is of course far more audacious; indeed, only two other poets in English have attempted it, Milton in *Paradise Regained* and Blake in *The Everlasting Gospel*. Was Jesus a man? Very well then, let the poet imagine what manner of man. Let her begin, since much Christian iconography dwells on his infancy, by imagining what manner of infant, and take it from there. Allowing for the vast difference in scale, Sexton's Jesus is as disagreeable as Milton's in *Paradise Regained*—and perhaps as unintentionally so.

The opening poem, "Jesus Suckles," consists of three sections of dwindling length. As so often in Sexton we are in the mind of someone utterly dependent on love. The language at first is erotic-playful, rich, organic, unstructured—one of Sexton's catalogs in which the condition of happiness is expressed through images of fertility. There is a tone of amplified gratification, rather like that of "In Celebration of My Uterus," and for the same reason. It is the mental effect of physical bliss:

> Mary, your great
> white apples make me glad
> . . . .
>
> I'm a jelly-baby and you're my wife.
> You're a rock and I the fringy algae.
> You're a lily and I'm the bee that gets inside.
> . . . .
>
> I'm a kid in a rowboat and you're the sea,
> the salt, you're every fish of importance.

But then:

> No. No.
> All lies.
> I am small
> and you hold me.
> You give me milk
> and we are the same
> and I am glad.
>
> No. No.
> All lies.
> I am a truck. I run everything.
> I own you.

First metaphor is killed, then the love, joy and sense of universal connection that generated the metaphor. We have a tidy drama of pleasure-principle succumbing to reality-principle, with both natural and supernatural implications. The poem reminds us that to a god, or a boy child, grateful love and helplessness are "all lies," and that reality—assuming the dualistic universe that Christianity does assume—means power, repugnance toward the flesh, and rejection of the mother. The relevant Biblical text attributes this moment of brutality to Jesus' adolescence: "Woman, what have I to do with thee?" Sexton merely pushes the time back. Blake's "To Tirzah" is a comparably cruel poem on the same text. The initial imagery implies that Mary is Mother Nature, or the pre-Christian goddesses who represent her divine fertility. Man and God are her privileged superiors and historical conquerors. The modern technological outcome of the split between Flesh and Logos which Christianity sacralizes is modestly accommodated by the synecdoche "truck."[5]

The succeeding poems trace what follows from the initial willed division of Jesus from Mary, boy child from mother, the will to control from the willingness to fondle and nurture. While the rest of the human and animal kingdom frolics and propagates, Jesus fasts. "His penis no longer arched with sorrow over Him"—the rainbow image recalling God's forgiving covenant with Noah and mankind—but "was sewn onto Him like a medal," an outrageous metaphor that not only disparages Jesus' celibacy but calls into question that Christian replacement of sexual love by *caritas*. Though he still desires Mary when asleep, he subdues his need, uses his penis as a chisel à la Rodin, and produces a Pietà so that they will be united in his death. *Civilization and Its Discontents* is the necessary gloss for this poem. For the next one *Justine* might do. When Jesus encounters the harlot Mary Magdalen being stoned ("Stones came at her like bees to candy / and sweet redheaded harlot that she was / she screamed out *I never, I never*"), he raises her up and efficiently heals her "terrible sickness" then and there by lancing with his thumbs her breasts, "those two boils of whoredom," until the milk runs out. Sexton's deadpan combination of biblical and contemporary language here is typical:

> The harlot followed Jesus around like a puppy
> for He had raised her up.
> Now she forsook her fornications
> and became His pet.

In "Jesus Cooks" and "Jesus Summons Forth" we get the miracle of the loaves and fishes as a sleight of hand act and the raising of Lazarus by assembling his bones as if he were a model airplane kit. "Tenderness" appears in a single line and appears to be part of the instructions. As with the poems on Jesus' sexuality, the poet's wry self-projection is important here. The roles of food-provider and healer were Sexton's, as was the role of public performer for whom feeling was part of the act. In the bitterly comic "Jesus Dies," the crucifixion is like an ultimate Sexton poetry reading, where Jesus' self-revelation of his sore need for God—a "man-to-man thing" that is half-competitive, half-desperate—is mingled with furious irritation at his audience's sensation-seeking.

From crucifixion Sexton does not move on to resurrection, but drops back to another woman-poem, "Jesus Unborn," which turns out to be, like "Jesus Suckles," a judgment of the Virgin's role in Christianity. It is the moment before the Annunciation, and again the imagery is lushly natural. Mary sits among olive trees, feels lethargic as an animal, wants to settle down like a camel or doze like a dog:

> Instead a strange being leans over her
> and lifts her chin firmly
> and gazes at her with executioner's eyes.

So much for how many centuries of Mariolatry? how many centuries of sacred iconography? But in case Sexton has not made herself clear, she appends to "The Jesus Papers" a final poem entitled "The Author of the Jesus Papers Speaks," which defines the place not only of Mary but of all womankind in Western religion. It is a dream-poem in three tiny episodes. First, Sexton milks a great cow, but instead of "the moon juice . . . the white mother," blood spurts "and covered me with shame." Several related readings are possible here: blood may be menstrual blood, shameful because taboo, sign of female pollutedness; or blood as sign that mothers surrender their own lives for others' lives, like beasts; or a reminder that all life leads to death. The cow might be Nature, or Mother-goddess, or Sexton's own mother who shamed and blamed her and whose "double image" she was. We have the beginnings of a rich female drama but there is no development, for at this point God speaks to Sexton and says, "People say only good things about Christmas. If they want to say something bad, / they whisper."

This is a change in tone as well as a non sequitur, it is funny, and it gives us a God who, like a boss or an earthly father, is half-uncomfortable with the way his governing role divides him from those he governs. God seems to be interrupting a mother-daughter interview, making a bid for attention—and sympathy—for his own concerns. But why should anyone say bad things about Christmas? Is God paranoid? Or guilty? Or, if this dream is taking place in the twentieth century, might we say that He doesn't know the half of it? In any case, Sexton's response is to go to the well and draw a baby out, which in her own drama means she moves from daughter-role to mother-role, and in God's terms means she produces the Christ. Judging by the poem's final seven lines, this is the submissive gesture God was looking for.

> Then God spoke to me and said:
> Here. Take this gingerbread lady
> and put her in your oven.
> When the cow gives blood
> and the Christ is born
> we must all eat sacrifices.
> We must all eat beautiful women.

Now the changed tone tells us that God has been, as it were, reassured and confirmed in His Godliness by Sexton's feminine compliance, much as a man tired and complaining after work will have his dignity renewed by a wife or daughter laying out a perfect dinner. This final speech is authoritative not only in the sense of issuing commands but in the sense of assuming verbal command over the poem's prior structure of symbols. Nature and femaleness (cow, moon, milk, blood), at first large and powerful, are reduced to domesticity and powerlessness. Dream-cow becomes cookie. "We" must at the advent of Christianity not *make* sacrifices but eat them, and God's pseudo-cosy "we" is the velvet glove of paternal imperative. The substitution of gingerbread lady for the bread that is Christ's body reminds us that the Christ-cult (and the Passover feast it builds on) takes its symbolism from earlier Middle Eastern religions in which the object of primary worship was the fertile and nourishing mother. Perhaps it implies that the misogyny of the Church and its need to subordinate ("sacrifice") women derive ultimately from a forgotten time of usurpation and a dread lest the "cow" move again to the forefront of our dream.

As a comment on "The Jesus Papers" sequence, the epilogue is a recapitulation of the theme of divine male power and mortal female submission. But it also fixes the position of its author as one who is by no means protesting the images of herself and other women within Christianity. On the contrary, she complies, she obeys, in this final dream, just as Mary and the harlot comply within the sequence. For herself, and on behalf of all beautiful women, she accepts humiliation. We may even say, since after all the dream is her invention, that she requires it.

IV

I need some such explanation to understand Sexton's religious poetry in *The Death Notebooks* and *The Awful Rowing Toward God*. For in these books, like a defeated athlete, she hurls herself again and again into a contest that her own poetry should have showed her she could not win, trying to imagine—trying to experience—a God she could both believe in and be loved by. The decisive intelligence which dismantles religious myth is no match for the child-woman's ferocious need for cosmic love, and so what we see in the last two books is a poet attempting to give imaginative birth to an adequate Godhead. But since her need is no match for her doubt, what we see is heroic failure. Or rather, perhaps, her need is no match for her sense of the significance of divine power, which is the power of the parent writ very large.

The Death Notebooks begins with a seriocomic quest poem, one of Sexton's funniest and best. It also contains the "Furies" series; the cycle of "Psalms" written in the manner of Christopher Smart, who becomes her imaginary twin and ally; and two semisurreal figures for the omnipresent Thanatos and the frustrated Eros of the poet's soul: the icy "death baby" and the despairing yet smark-aleck "Ms. Dog." *The Awful Rowing* is a series of quest poems written at breakneck speed "in a frenzy of despair and hope" shortly after her divorce in November 1973, and scarcely revised. "I cannot walk an inch / without trying to walk to God. / I cannot move a finger / without trying to reach

God" is the burden of these poems. Both books are attempts to locate the self in a context of the objectively sacred, but with Sexton implicitly insisting that the realm of the sacred must answer to her private experience of reality, that the objective and subjective must be one, as she was able to make them one in *Transformations*. She is once again working through a prior tradition (God is no post-Tillich moral abstraction but an omnipotent male person), but now as if her life depended on it. Poems like "Civil War" and "Frenzy" imply, in fact, that only by an unremitting effort to create a God coextensive with her own imagination can the poet hope to be saved. This is strenuously antinomian religion, an American specialty, and a risky business in any case, riskier when the worshipper's ego is as frail as Sexton's.

"Let there be a God as large as a sunlamp to laugh his heat at you," begins the "First Psalm" of "O Ye Tongues." She prays in the course of the psalms "that God will digest me," and at the end declares "for God was as large as a sunlamp and laughed his heat at us (i.e., Anne and Christopher) and therefore we did not cringe at the death hole." Sexton wants to imagine God as simultaneously transcendent and immanent within all flesh. He is a jigsaw with thousands of pieces, "dressed up" like a whore, an old man, a naked child, present within all domestic routines and especially present within human sexuality:

> When they fuck they are God.
> When they break away they are God.
> When they snore they are God.
> In the morning they butter the toast.
> They don't say much.
> They are still God.

Such a God is necessarily benevolent. The sustaining of even a small faith will bring him into one's hands the way a dime used to bring forth a Coke. He has no body but wishes he had one, envying humans their bodies as we envy him his soul. If Sexton can reach him he will remove and embrace the "gnawing pestilential rat" which is her figure for her sense of inner vileness. On good days he gives milk (cf. the cow in "Jesus Papers" and Isaiah 66:12) and she has the pail. Salvation depends on her ability to keep "typing out the God / my typewriter believes in.

/ Very quick. Very intense, / like a wolf at a live heart. / Not lazy" ("Frenzy").

Sexton is full of startlingly "right" modern analogues for traditional images in Christian writing. Her lifelong rowing against the wind is the emotional equivalent of the journey in *Pilgrim's Progress*. Her "sunlamp" God emits an eerie charge that the word "sun" no longer has in our language. Her infinitely multiple jigsaw or typewriter God is oddly like Milton's figure in *Areopagitica* of the scattered body of Truth, whose form all true men must be engaged in gathering up limb by limb throughout human history, until the Second Coming "shall bring together every joint and member." Almost every poem has something like this.

What defeats Sexton is in part a sense of her own evil, the "rat" or "bowel movement" her mother tried to force out of her child-self but that still fills her to the fingertips. Hers is not a conventional sin divisible from her bodily being, and priests are unable to shrive or even comprehend it. In the long sequence of faith-doubt poems beginning with "The Dead Heart" and ending with "Is It True?," a mocking self-disgust is inextricably mingled with God's unbearable departure. The tone strongly resembles that of Hopkins in the Terrible Sonnets, and Sexton's habitual oral imagery touches close on Hopkins's "I am gall, I am heartburn. God's most deep decree / Bitter would have me taste; my taste was me." There are hints that the problem is insoluble because Sexton cannot or will not deny her identification with the flesh that divides her from God:

> We are all earthworms,
> digging into our wrinkles.
> We live beneath the ground
> and if Christ should come in the form of a plow
> and dig a furrow and push us up into the day
> we earthworms would be blinded by the sudden light
> and writhe in our distress.
> As I write this sentence I too writhe.

Logically, theologically, it is inconsistent to imagine a God immanent in all bodies and a body unable to tolerate God's blinding presence. But immanence in Western religion is a heresy, and for the image of God as blinding glory there are precedents going back at least to Dante, while Christ with his plow is one of the most forceful images of Revelation. What I earlier called an "adequate" God—one powerful enough to love and accept Sexton and all of us ratlike "cursed ones falling out after"—must also be powerful enough to reject and annihilate. It is such a God, closer to Scripture than Sexton's hopeful fantasies desire, who dominates *The Awful Rowing*. Through most of the volume the tone is frenzied and agonized. God is distant, indifferent. Near the close, God is "surgical andiron." In the penultimate poem, when the poet trembles to utter her faith that God is in all matter, "heaven smashes my words."

The final poem of *The Awful Rowing* was, I think, intended to be a happy ending. When the poet finally arrives at her island, God challenges her to a game of poker. She thinks she wins because she holds a royal straight flush. God wins because he holds five aces. Here is the end of the poem and the book:

> As he plunks down His five aces
> and I sit grinning at my royal flush,
> He starts to laugh,
> the laughter rolling like a hoop out of His mouth
> and into mine,
> and such laughter that He doubles right over me
> laughing a Rejoice-Chorus at our two triumphs.
> Then I laugh, the fishy dock laughs
> the sea laughs. The Island laughs.
> The Absurd laughs.
>
> Dearest dealer,
> I with my royal straight flush,
> love you so for your wild card,
> that untamable, eternal, gut-driven *ha-ha*
> and lucky love.

To my ear there is something appalling in such an ending. Is the "lucky love" of that dreadfully lame last line supposed to be the wild card God triumphs with? What I hear sounds like a grotesque attempt to placate and conciliate a God of our Fathers who is being experienced as atrocious, brutal, a betrayer.

"Out of His mouth / and into mine . . . He doubles right

over me." Is God conceivably a rapist? This power-figure, who also inhabits the last poem of "The Jesus Papers" and the last poem of *The Death Notebooks:* is he also the father-lover of the last poem in *Transformations?* John Donne too wanted to be raped by God; yet "Batter my heart" and "The Rowing Endeth," comparable in their yearning for divine union expressed in this shared metaphor, are utterly different in emotional resonance. Reading Donne, I am able to believe the paradox of Christian surrender: "for I / except you enthrall me, never shall be free, / Nor ever chaste except you ravish me." Perhaps the reason there are so many excellent devotional writers who are men, so few who are women, is that the feminine experience of submission is for a man a rounding-out of his usual personality, hence truly a fulfillment and kind of freedom. "Absolute sovereignty is what I love to ascribe to God," Jonathan Edwards announces, and convinces us that this is "not only a conviction, but a delightful conviction." For a woman it merely reinforces her usual social role.

On October 4, 1974, after reading galleys of *The Awful Rowing,* Sexton killed herself. In the same year, Mary Daly published *Beyond God the Father,* an attack on patriarchal religion. Among feminist theologians and historians of ideas it has subsequently become a commonplace assumption that the passive-female imagery of Western religion is inadequate for women's spiritual needs, and a countercultural women's search for goddess figures has become something of a cultural brushfire in England and France as well as America. Sexton has no part in that search. She is not a protest poet. Her religion is determinedly patriarchal. Her God is not Self but Other.

There is a precedent for Sexton's painful ambivalence in this matter of God the Father. Emily Dickinson, a poet aesthetically poles removed from Sexton, seems also to have modeled her God on the image of a father. One of her roles with him is that of coy little girl, a pose that makes modern audiences twitch. But girlishness was an approved tone in Dickinson's own time, especially for unmarried women, as we know by its ubiquitous titter in many of her letters. (There is a similar aggravated girlishness in Plath's letters to her mother.) Behind anything so ostentatiously agreeable, we feel, something disagreeable must lurk. Dickinson's portrait of God, when she does not draw him flatteringly as nice daddy, is, like Sexton's, the portrait of an indifferent brute ("Of course I cried! And did God care?"), a bully, an "Inquisitor" who may or may not grant one "the liberty to die," a foe whom one must love because defiance is impossible. "Burglar! Banker—Father!" is only the most famous of her tense portrayals. And like Sexton, Dickinson seems genuinely to have adored and needed this divine antagonist. Ancestress of rebels, she is none herself. At times it is difficult to distinguish Lord from Lover in both poets. Sexton's "rowing" figure itself has an antecedent, coincidentally or not, in Dickinson's most erotic poem, addressed to an unknown love:

> Wild Nights—Wild Nights!
> Were I with thee
> Wild nights should be
> Our luxury!
>
> Futile—the winds—
> to a Heart in port—
> Done with the Compass—
> Done with the Chart!
>
> Rowing in Eden—
> Ah, the Sea!
> Might I but moor—Tonight—
> In Thee!

The range, the demands and the risks of Sexton's poetry increased throughout her lifetime. If she failed to achieve "a Heart in port," she was not alone in that.

NOTES

1. Rosemary Johnson, "The Woman of Private (but Published) Hungers," *Parnassus* 8, no. 1 (1980): 92.

2. The early volumes, all published by Houghton Mifflin, are *To Bedlam and Part Way Back* (1960), in which the apologia-poem "For John, Who Begs Me Not to Enquire Further" appears; *All My Pretty Ones* (1962), *Live or Die* (1966), for which she received the Pulitzer Prize, and *Love Poems* (1969). Sexton's *Complete Poems,* with an excel-

lent introduction by Maxine Kumin, was published by Houghton Mifflin in 1981. The interviews I quote are in *Anne Sexton: The Artist and Her Critics,* edited by J. D. McClatchy (Bloomington: Indiana University Press, 1978).

3. I mention this, I must confess, in specific irritation with W. H. Pritchard's authoritative pronouncement that "there is no figure in the poetry's carpet to worry about discovering—it's all smack on the surface," and that the late Sexton jettisoned "whatever modest technical accomplishment she possessed in favor of getting down the excitingly grotesque meanings" ("The Anne Sexton Show," *Hudson Review* 31, no. 2 [Summer 1978]: 389, 391). He does not specify *what* meanings. But we do not see what we do not look for.

4. Sexton's letters are collected in *Anne Sexton: A Self-Portrait in Letters,* edited by Linda Gray Sexton and Lois Ames (Boston: Houghton Mifflin, 1977).

5. This image appears also in "Those Times . . . " of *Live or Die,* where Sexton writes of childhood humiliations inflicted by her mother and says "I did not know that my life, in the end, / would run over my mother's like a truck." The distance between earlier and later poems makes a good index of Sexton's development. The earlier poem is private and familial; the later one locates the private scenario within a mythic context. The earlier poem is strictly autobiographical and describes the self as passive; in the later, "Jesus" becomes, among other things, a figure for active and aggressive (i.e., "male") elements in her character which she was reluctant to acknowledge while writing as a woman.

CYNTHIA A. MILLER
[CYNTHIA M. ANTONELLI]

The Poet in the Poem

A Phenomenological Analysis of Anne Sexton's "Briar Rose (Sleeping Beauty)"

Confessional poetry differs in content and style from other types of poetry. Confessional poets present in their works intensely personal life experiences of their own suffering and crises; thus, the content of confessional poetry is a projection and reflection of the author. Ralph J. Mills notes that confessional poetry concerns the "more intimate aspects of life, areas of experience that most of us would instinctively keep from public sight."[1] M. L. Rosenthal indicates that the "private life of the poet himself, especially under stress of psychological crisis, becomes a major theme."[2] The authors of confessional poetry expose highly subjective worldviews in the attempt to come to terms with themselves and their reality. The style of confessional poetry allows the author to deal with the subject matter in an unrestrained manner. Robert Phillips comments that "openness of language leads to openness of emotion. . . . The confessional poets, at the risk of all else, return that which is uniquely human to poetry. Rather than fearing emotion, they make it their stock-in-trade."[3] Confessional poetry reveals the author's innermost existential struggles. This unique classification of literature offers an opportunity to uncover and understand the author's experience within the work.

Anne Sexton, a contemporary confessional poet, uses poetry

From *The Existential Coordinates of the Human Condition,* edited by Anna-Teresa Tymieniecka (Dordrecht: D. Reidel, 1984). Reprinted by permission of the author.

to express her painful and extremely personal experiences. On some level, which is not always clear to her, Sexton is able to grasp her private life through poetry. She confesses,

> Sometimes my doctors tell me that I understand something in a poem that I haven't integrated into my life. In fact, I may be concealing it from myself, while I was revealing it to the readers. The poetry is often more advanced, in terms of my unconscious, than I am. Poetry, after all, milks the unconscious. The unconscious is there to feed it little images, little symbols, the answers, the insights I know not of.[4]

From the motifs of guilt, mental illness, fear and suffering, Sexton constructs a poetic world of reality with the persona at the center. A. R. Jones states that Sexton's poems, "create largely the world of her *persona,* the 'I' of the poems which undergoes continuing development and is clearly related, intimately and painfully, to the poet's autobiography."[5] In Sexton's works, her personae convey aspects of her own existence or being-in-the-world. No research has yet explored, phenomenologically, how the experience of confessional writers is conveyed in their works, and specifically, how the experience of Anne Sexton emerges in her poetry.[6]

Phenomenological criticism, a criticism of the creating consciousness in literature, offers a way to explicate Anne Sexton's experience as conveyed in her works through her personae. To discover the existential experience of an author, the Geneva School of phenomenology[7] employs this intrinsic approach to literature by treating the poem as "a self-contained world where human experience takes shape as literature."[8] The Geneva School contends that every piece of literature offers traces of the author's experience because the work cannot be cut off from the author's intentionality in the act of consciousness which creates it. Robert Magliola explains this point of view, stating that,

> Precisely because language is gestural, is expressive, the literary work bears within itself the unique imprint of the author's own consciousness. The Geneva critic considers the author's unique imprint immanent in the literary work and critically available there.[9]

Georges Poulet, of the Geneva School, asserts, "To understand a literary work then is to let the individual who wrote it reveal himself to us in the work. It is not the biography which explicates the work, but rather the work which sometimes enables us to understand the biography."[10]

The confessional poetry of Anne Sexton offers a rich source from which to discover more about the author's experience in her work. *Transformations*,[11] a collection of Grimms' fairy tales recast by Sexton into contemporary and shocking parables, lends itself to phenomenological criticism. Fairy tales, in their original form, confront the human existential predicament. Bruno Bettelheim posits that "the fairy tale . . . takes these existential anxieties and dilemmas very seriously and addresses itself directly to them: the need to be loved and the fear that one is thought worthless; the love of life and the fear of death."[12] And, he adds,

> As with all great art, the fairy tale's deepest meaning will be different for each person at various moments in his life. . . . When given a chance, he will return to the same tale when he is ready to enlarge on old meanings or replace them with new ones.[13]

In *Transformations,* Sexton revisits the fairy tale and recreates the story to confront problems in her own life. In the narrative mode, through the voice of the persona (speaker) telling the story, the author is able to examine her own experience by distancing her emotions. Poulet suggests that painful experiences become more manageable when they are buffered by time, and there is a "new chance which is given us to enter once more upon the existence of our lived moments, but, this time, at a distance, at an interval remote enough to allow us to rectify them."[14] Sexton acknowledges in a letter to Kurt Vonnegut, dated November 17, 1970, that the story form allows her to explore her consciousness: "I think they [poems in *Transformations*] end up being as wholly personal as my most intimate poems, in a different language, a different rhythm, but coming strangely, for all their story sound, from as deep a place."[15] The modernized fairy tales in *Transformations* offer Sexton a new perspective from which to contemplate her way of being-in-the-world.

This study examines one poem from *Transformations,* "Briar Rose (Sleeping Beauty)," and focuses on one facet of Sexton's consciousness, the experience of time. "Briar Rose" is especially appropriate for phenomenological analysis because the poem contends with the basic issues of life and death—a struggle interwoven with the author's experience of time. This analysis describes the persona's experience of time in relation to the character Briar Rose, reduces the description to the persona's experience of time, and interprets the meaning of the experience of the persona in relationship to the author's life.[16]

1. Description

The first section of "Briar Rose" is a lyric prologue. The persona objectifies her experience by narrating in the third person. As the poem opens, the persona asks the reader to reflect upon a girl's emotional experience. "Consider," the persona implores, "a girl who keeps slipping off . . . into the hypnotist's trance." A state of suspended animation, frozen time, allows the girl to drift into a "spirit world speaking with the gift of tongues." The religious allusion to prophecy implies that the girl can see into the future while in the trance. The persona observes that, during this experience, the girl feels "stuck in the time machine," as if she were wedged in time, unable to pull free.

The time frame then shifts "suddenly" and the persona reports that the girl retreats uneasily into the past, "two years old . . . as inward as a snail." Time, for the girl, is not only a diachronic experience of moving chronologically backward, but also a synchronic experience of turning inward, as if for protection. The "voyage" is overlaid with conflict and the persona states that the girl must swim "further and further back, up like a salmon." The journey into memory is exhausting as the girl confronts a strong flow of feelings and must pull herself through and over emotional tides. The metaphor involves the future as well as the past. The reference to fish fighting the current to spawn is prophetic because, like the salmon, one must inevitably face death. The girl regresses into the past and draws inward to peer at the future.

The persona relates that the girl, now firmly in her memory, dwells on a past experience with her father which carries the imaginary insinuation of death. The girl's father becomes a death-figure as he beckons seductively, "Little doll child, come here to Papa." Death proffers the appeal: "I have kisses for the back of your neck." "A penny for your thoughts, Princess," is a further tendering of consultation and support. His entreaty, "I will give you a root," is enticing, promising stability and fulfillment. The solicitation is assuring, yet malodorous and corrupt. The persona acidly describes the trip into the girl's past as "that kind of voyage, rank as honeysuckle." The advent of death compels an inviting and overpowering fragrance while simultaneously exuding the putrid smell of evil.

In the second section of the poem, the persona moves into the narrative mode: "Once a king had a christening for his daughter Briar Rose." The fairy tale exists in a state of timelessness that belongs to all stories that begin, "Once upon a time," and is thereby distanced from the present moment. The baptismal name portends the double nature of the character, which is beautiful and alluring and, at the same time, repulsive and hurtful. The ceremony intimates protection, sanctioning the future of the child. But, an unexpected and intrusive guest appears at the "grand event," the thirteenth fairy. The uninvited and forboding fairy arrives with an "evil gift" of doom, prophesying that Briar Rose will make the choice to die when she shall "prick herself on a spinning wheel" and "then fall down dead." The king is aghast; he "looked like Munch's *Scream*," a hideous shrieking face surrounded by darkness. Then, tongue-in-cheek, the persona remarks, "Fairies' prophecies, in times like those, held water," understating the certainty of death. However, the twelfth fairy mitigates the curse, changing "that death into a hundred-year sleep." The promise of life seems as powerful as the prophecy of death, and the ogre is temporarily assuaged.

The persona tells that the king then wards off the evil spirits to protect Briar Rose by ordering "every spinning wheel exterminated and exorcized." The persona remarks sarcastically that "he forced every male in the court to scour his tongue with Bab-o." The King's desire to give her a secure and pure life only results in a sterile, imprisoning environment. The persona comments, "she dwelt in his odor. Rank as honeysuckle." The reference to the king's odor suggests again, a smell that is stimulating but offensive; the king's presence is comforting yet repugnant.

The persona continues that on Briar Rose's fifteenth birthday, the prophecy is fulfilled. The princess "pricked her finger," choosing to live in a sleeplike death. In this time state, all activity halts as, "the clocks stopped. . . . The fire in the hearth grew still and the roast meat stopped crackling." Objects and people became petrified nonentities as "trees turned into metal and the dog became china," and "they all lay in a trance, each a catatonic." The suspended existence is like being "stuck in the time machine" from which there is no escape. The persona states that "only a bunch of briar roses grew forming a great wall of tacks around the castle." The princess's wall of safety attracts with blossoms yet repels with thorns. In sleep, the princess is protected from intruders who "had not scoured their tongues."

The persona's statement that "in *due* time a hundred years passed and a prince got through" [emphasis mine], suggests that the princess must pay her debt to the prophecy of death. The only event that arouses Briar Rose is the prince's brief kiss and "She woke up crying: Daddy! Daddy!" Unnerved and frightened by her new ability to feel, Briar Rose harks back to the life-giving protection of her father. The excitement of the prince instills a new freedom from her deadened existence and "Presto! She's out of prison!"

The persona reports that the princess now lives in dreaded anticipation of the future, which may bring back the numbness of sleep. The persona avers that "all went well except for the fear—the fear of sleep." The princess is anxiously aware of the dangers of inertness. The persona contends, "Briar Rose was an insomniac. . . . She could not nap or lie in sleep without the court chemist mixing her some knock-out drops." The princess realizes that sleep is an existence too close to death, and in this state she becomes powerless to really live. The princess also dreads sleep because there she foresees her death. The princess states, "I must not dream for when I do I see the table set and a faltering crone at my place, her eyes burnt by cigarettes as she eats betrayal like a slice of meat." The withering old woman resembles the evil fairy of death and sits ready, waiting to consume.

In the third section of the poem, as the fairy tale ends, the persona's lyric voice emerges from the dialogue of Briar Rose. The persona, using "I," describes a sleeplike existence equivalent to death: "I must not sleep for while asleep I'm ninety and think I'm dying." The persona feels petrified and weighted down in this condition, stating, "I wear tubes like earrings. I lie still as a bar of iron." The line, "I'm all shot up with Novocain," expresses the persona's diffident and stuporous emotional state. In time of sleep, "this trance girl" is completely submissive and "yours to do with." She feels as if she were dead already and reflects in disgust, "you could lay her in a grave . . . and shovel dirt on her face." The persona feels self-loathing, characterizing herself as an "awful package." The persona refers to herself in the third person to objectify the realization that intense sensations of the moment alone set her free from her passive state of imprisonment: "But if you kissed her on the mouth her eyes would spring open and she'd call out: Daddy! Daddy! Presto! She's out of prison." Although the persona believes temporary stimulation will free her from a life of resigned confinement, she cries for support and supervision from her father.

The persona uses the past tense in her lyric voice to delve into her memories. The character feels at some point in her past, "there was a theft," wherein part of her personhood was stolen. She states, "I was forced backward. I was forced forward." As a passive participant, she was pushed into being submissive and childlike, and thrust into being self-sufficient and adult. In the first case, she feels her growth was stunted; in the latter, her maturation was too quickly advanced. In either event, the persona believes she was treated as a nonperson or object, stating, "I was passed hand to hand like a bowl of fruit." Due to these incidents, the persona states, "Each night I am nailed into place and I forget who I am." Her past influences her passive resignation in the present, where she is suspended in time. Her allusion to the crucifixion reveals her feelings of deadened existence.

The persona reflects on the father image, stating, "Daddy? That's another kind of prison." The life-giving protection of her father, though safe, is recognized as a loss of freedom to live as an individual. This vision of her father represents a type of death. She posits that her father is "not the prince at all," but a figure "drunkenly bent over my bed, circling the abyss like a shark, my father thick upon me like some sleeping jellyfish." The father image is not the prince of sustenance, but a dangerous, deathlike predator. However, this kind of death does not strike quickly; it is a dormant, enveloping force which may smother her.

In the final lines of the poem, the persona examines the moment of writing as she asks herself rhetorically, "What voyage this, little girl? This coming out of prison?" The persona accepts that writing is a journey which provides stimulation and escape from her life's routine.

The persona works through her private experiences by referring to herself in the third person in the prologue, by transferring her experiences to Briar Rose in the fairy tale, and by speaking openly in the lyric "I" in the final section. The persona recognizes that the poem will live into the future, and "God help—" she pleads, this part of me as well, that is immortalized in the poem, "this life after death?"

2. Reduction

The major theme for the entire poem is the persona's voyage through time. First, the persona journeys into her past, regresses to childhood, and, through memory, predicts her future. Next, the persona travels into the timelessness of the fairy tale. The persona then navigates from the fairy tale to the present and dwells on her current and past life. Her trip through time brings her to the poem, "What voyage this, little girl?" The moment of writing is recorded now and propels into the future. Writing is the harbor of safety from which the persona travels through time. The entire voyage, winding into past, present and future, permits the persona to examine the tension between life and death.

The motif of the father-king is significant in that the image explicates the struggle of living and dying in the persona's experience of time. In the past, the father-king offers sustenance and life. Yet, in this sterile existence, the persona escapes from living fully. There is a strong pull towards this safer condition, but revulsion from its captivity. In the present, a sleeplike passive state simulates the secure life with the father-king. Moments of genuine feeling provoke the persona to call his name for protection. In the future, the father-king symbolizes ultimate death: a provocative, magnetic force and, concomitantly, a repulsive, dreaded power. Death's double nature is concretized in the sexual metaphor. The persona is drawn toward the sensual experience but senses the danger therein. Death, lurking in the future, is an enticing escape, but the stultifying end to all life.

The prison theme throughout the poem is a graphic metaphor of the persona's experience of time. In the present, the persona feels captive to time. Weighted down and reluctant to move through time, she restrains herself from feeling and living fully. Present time is a confinement from which she tries to escape. The persona lives for moments of excitement when, "Presto! She's out of prison." Only those moments of special stimulation, represented by a kiss, liberate the persona from her inert life. Writing is also acknowledged as a stimulating experience, a "coming out of prison," which offers escape. The past is yet "another kind of prison." Memories of her father are correlated with smothering overprotection. This time dimension represents her loss of freedom to be an autonomous self. The future is also implicated when the persona remembers her father. Her memories project the message of her death. A prisoner of time in the present and past, she views her death as the final escape; thus, there is an impelling attraction towards the future.

Grammatical structure further illuminates the persona's experience of time in the past. The persona employs "-ing" verbs, such as "learning," "swimming," "struggling," as she describes her retreat into memory. The verb forms depict the persona's active participation in attempting to understand her past. The choice of verbs reveals that her efforts require mental and physical exertion. Later, the persona describes her past using passive verbs such as "was forced" and "was passed." The verb mood shows her feelings of being acted upon and being ineffectual. The persona desires to understand her past, but her memories are repellent. The persona's conflicting sensations about this time period make resolution difficult.

Other themes from the poem shed light on the persona's experience of time in the present. The persona is mired in the present, "stuck in the time machine." A time machine usually implies access to past or future events; however, the persona is held fast in the present, unable to travel easily in time. Trapped in her existence, she chooses to escape from time through "trances" and "sleep." In these synonymous passive states, the persona confronts life. In the fairy tale, the elaboration of images shows the persona's fascination with cessated time. Activity slows down; animals are immobilized; people are depersonalized. The persona, like an object, becomes dull to all feeling. Although frozen time appears safe, the persona likens the experience to death. She begins to fear sleep, her catatonic prevalence. Suspended in time, the persona chooses to exist in passivity, a state of nonbeing, to cope with reality.

The motif of prophecy explicates the persona's experience of time in the future. Although the twelfth fairy changes the curse of death to sleep, death remains inevitable. The persona dwells on her future and predicts her own death as she refers metaphorically to the salmon and the enticement of her father. In her dreams, she envisions the withered crone, death. The persona is obsessed with sleep as death. Sleep, which is likened to death, becomes intolerable. Fear causes her to live in anxious anticipation of time, and yet, she recoils from the future.

The metaphors of time in the poem related by the persona reveal her conflicting impulses. The persona longs to journey freely in time. She desires to visit the safe memories in her past and to move with excitement through the moments of the present. However, the persona is bound in her past by feelings of throttling restraint and is [made] a captive in her present by feelings of nonbeing existence. A prisoner of time, the persona seeks escape in the future.

3. Interpretation

In the poem, "Briar Rose," as narrated by the persona, Anne Sexton's experience concerning her self-image emerges. The persona feels as if she faced reality as an impotent and incapable child. Sexton expressed her own feelings of inadequacy in a letter, dated November 5, 1963: "As the salmon fight upstream to spawn I fought to stay in Europe. . . . But I began to feel smaller and smaller, unreal."[17] The persona assumes the role of princess, which allows her to romanticize her need to be safeguarded. Sexton's battle between her roles and her own identity was reflected in a letter to her husband, dated October 6, 1963:

I want to become MORE than Princess Anne (much as I want to be her) . . . I want to become a woman who lives side by side with Kayo. Not a princess, not a queen, but a friend. . . . I must learn to be a woman, not a child. Yes, I'm your princess and want to have you say it . . . also your dearest friend, your companion, your mistress, your mother. I'm me.[18]

Sexton struggled with the process of realizing her full potential in the adult world. She was pulled between the desire to remain in the secure childlike role of princess and the need to become an adult person. The persona in "Briar Rose" possesses such a poor self-image that she feels self-abhorrence. In the same letter to her husband, Sexton disclosed her own self-aversion stating, "Kayo, sometimes I *am* ugly."[19] In the poem the persona becomes so distressed with the existential struggle that she chooses sleep. Anne Sexton also opted for a passive condition when life became too stressful. She poured out her feelings of alienation and inertia to a friend, writing, "I'm like a Jew who ends up in the wrong country. I'm not a part. I'm not a member. I'm frozen."[20] The author's wish to grow and cope with life was complicated by the exigence to learn to like herself. Sexton's conflicting self-image and the strife of everyday life resulted in the inability to deal effectively with her existential predicament.

Sexton's life, as related in the poem, is revealed in the writer's statement, "I always have this desperate feeling about time."[21] In [the same] collection of letters, there exists corroborating evidence that Anne Sexton, like the persona, experienced time in the past with conflict and anger. The persona is unable to reconcile past protection with wanting safekeeping in the present. While the events in Sexton's past are different from incidents in the poem, the prevailing mood is similar. Linda Gray Sexton and Lois Ames write that Anne Sexton's

> memories were of a childhood studded with physical and mental abuse. Yet her older sister Blanche saw Anne as a "much-loved child, over-indulged—the center of attention." Whatever the reality, an early sense of rejection was to haunt Anne throughout her life and shaped much of her poetry.[22]

Although Sexton did not believe she was overinsulated in her past, she and the persona felt as if they were treated as objects and thereby lost some of their self-identity. The author and persona experience their memories with tension, and their remembrances are bitter. The persona goes into a hypnotic trance to delve into her past. Sexton's biographers reveal that "Dr. Martin had used hypnosis with some success."[23] Sexton used psychiatric aid to heal her past experiences, and complained to her husband in a letter that "the trouble with therapy is that it makes life go backwards . . . and I am so tired of that old suffering."[24] During her entire life, Sexton struggled with her feelings toward time in her past.

Like the persona in the poem, Sexton also experienced time in the present as unbearable. She, as does the persona, searched for different avenues of escape. In a letter Sexton disclosed her obsession with a sleep-like existence: "I want to sleep all day and night (i.e., not live but not quite die)."[25] Her biographers contend that Sexton withdrew from the present, "not only by repeated suicide attempts but by various forms of hysteria, including trances, as well."[26] In correspondence to a friend Sexton admitted,

> I have blackouts. I don't mean I pass out. I mean everything goes black. . . . I was having them at least every day, sometimes seventeen a morning. . . . I've had these blackouts and this heart condition for four years. . . . I attributed it to anxiety and took seven 50 mg. Librium.[27]

The idea of death is frightening, yet Sexton toyed with the prospect through suicide. In a letter to someone close, Sexton voiced her wish to die: "I don't want to live. I'm only writing to tell you about it, not warn you. . . . Only me do I threaten. Only me do I kill. No one else. Now listen, life is lovely but I CAN'T LIVE IT."[28] Sexton felt mired in present time and was drawn toward death for relief; yet, she could not quite forsake life. Sexton and her persona chose to cope with time in the present by retreating from life.

Sexton was made to feel alive during moments of intense sensation, like the persona who is stimulated only by a kiss. Sexton found ways to wrench herself from a nonfeeling existence for brief spans of time. She wrote of her passive condition and her attempts to arouse herself: "I am like a stone that lives . . . locked outside of all that's real. . . . And because I'm just so frozen I drink to simulate [stimulate?] it; a drug up too [sic]."[29] One source of animation for the persona in "Briar Rose" is the experience of writing, which provides her a way to work out her stress. Sexton understood the value of writing in maintaining her own sanity. She wrote, "All is an emotional chaos. Poetry and poetry alone has saved my life."[30]

Sexton, as well as the persona, experienced time in the future as both provocative and horrifying. The future summoned both with promises of death, the ultimate flight from time. As Sexton and the persona lived in a deathlike state and dwelt on their final death, future time became a persistent and disturbing preoccupation. In an interview, Sexton discussed her obsession with her future and death in frequent talks with Sylvia Plath:

> Sylvia and I would talk at length about our first suicide, in detail and in depth. . . . We talked about death with burned-up intensity, both of us drawn to it like moths to an electric light bulb, sucking on it . . . as if death made each of us a little more real at the moment.[31]

Sexton was equally frightened over the prospect of death. As the persona wishes sleep would take her unaware, Sexton wanted to relinquish control over her future. The author confessed, "I wish, stupidly [,] that someone but me would kill me and take the responsibility away."[32]

Thus, the fairy tale, "Briar Rose," is essentially the story of Anne Sexton's self-fulfilling prophecy. The childhood tale is the nexus of Sexton's own modernized adult script. Flirtation with death and deathlike images pervade both. The memories of her past are suffocating and intolerable. In the present, Sexton withdraws into trancelike states in which she is numb to all feeling, a waking death. Stimulation from drugs allows her to function and to feel as if alive. Contemplation of suicide proves exhilarating and demonstrates her preoccupation with death. Unable to cope with past, present, or future, as she is pulled between life and death, Sexton becomes a prisoner of time.

Anne Sexton took her own life on October 4, 1974.

4. Conclusion

By phenomenologically analyzing "Briar Rose (Sleeping Beauty)" through the subjective perspective of the persona, a simple poem has taken on deeper meanings. The themes embodied in the language of the poem become the vehicle which enables us to project ourselves into the persona's consciousness and to understand her experience of time. The motifs have not only given us information about the persona's experience in the world of the poem but also told us the import and meaning of that experience for [the] author. Sexton's ambivalence toward time, as reported through the persona, is not a mysterious happening, but a meaningful reaction based on her existential struggle with life and death.

Confessional poetry becomes a significant genre when analyzed phenomenologically. This approach to literature returns the emphasis to the authors' unconscious experiences in the poems and turns attention away from the lives of the authors outside the poems. Therefore, the authors' experiences embedded in the works becomes primary, and biographical information which may elucidate the works becomes secondary. Because confessional writers are openly struggling with their existential dilemmas, their poetry is a rich source for understanding the deeper meaning of their lives. Uncovering the authors' ways-of-being-in-the-world in confessional poetry is a starting point for understanding our own existential plight.

NOTES

1. Ralph J. Mills, Jr., *Contemporary American Poetry* (New York: Random House, 1965), 156.

2. M. L. Rosenthal, *The New Poets: American and British Poetry Since World War II* (New York: Oxford University Press, 1967), 15.

3. Robert Phillips, *The Confessional Poets* (Carbondale: Southern Illinois University Press, 1973), 10.

4. "The Art of Poetry XV," *Paris Review* 52 (Summer 1971): 162.

5. A. R. Jones, "Necessity and Freedom: The Poetry of Robert Lowell, Sylvia Plath, and Anne Sexton," *Critical Quarterly* 7 (Spring 1965): 15.

6. Various analyses of confessional poetry are available. Ralph J. Mills in *Contemporary American Poetry* employs biographical criticism; M. L. Rosenthal in *The New Poets: American and British Poetry Since World War II* and Robert Phillips in *The Confessional Poets* feature formal analysis. Phenomenological analyses of poetry, other than confessional poetry, do exist. Janet Larsen McHughes discusses "A Phenomenological Analysis of Literary Time in the Poetry of James Dickey" (Ph.D. diss., Northwestern University, 1972). David Halliburton focuses on poems by Edgar Allan Poe in *Edgar Allan Poe: A Phenomenological View* (Princeton: Princeton University Press, 1973).

7. Sarah N. Lawall's book on the Geneva School, *Critics of Consciousness* (Cambridge: Harvard University Press, 1968) offers a summary of Genevan practice. Robert R. Magliola in *Phenomenology and Literature* (West Lafayette, Ind.: Purdue University Press, 1977) expands the list of Geneva critics and focuses on the importance of phenomenological philosophy and aesthetics to this practice.

8. Lawall, 6.

9. Magliola, 28.

10. Georges Poulet, "The Phenomenology of Reading," *New Literary History* 1 (October 1969): 58.

11. Anne Sexton, *Transformations* (Boston: Houghton Mifflin, 1971).

12. Bruno Bettelheim, *The Uses of Enchantment: The Meaning and Importance of Fairy Tales* (New York: Random House, 1977), 10.

13. Bettelheim, 12.

14. Georges Poulet, *The Interior Distance,* translated by Elliott Coleman (Baltimore: Johns Hopkins Press, 1959), 80.

15. *Anne Sexton: A Self-Portrait in Letters,* edited by Linda Gray Sexton and Lois Ames (Boston: Houghton Mifflin, 1977), 367.

16. Chapter 2 of *Phenomenology and Literature* by Robert R. Magliola presents an exhaustive account of the phenomenological methodology of the Geneva School which closely follows the early teachings of Edmund Husserl. A summary is presented on pp. 45–46.

17. *Letters,* 226.

18. *Letters,* 213–14.

19. *Letters,* 213.

20. *Letters,* 252.

21. *Letters,* 60.

22. *Letters,* 3.

23. *Letters,* 225.

24. *Letters,* 191.

25. *Letters,* 252.

26. *Letters,* 225.

27. *Letters,* 364–65.

28. *Letters,* 251.

29. *Letters,* 251–52.

30. *Letters,* 81.

31. "The Art of Poetry XV," 170.

32. *Letters,* 252.

BEN HOWARD

Shattered Glass

Two of the most conspicuous features of postwar American verse have been its drift toward simplicity of style and its preoccupation with self-disclosure. Of the dozens of influential poets who have exemplified one or both of these tendencies—Lowell, Berryman, Plath, James Wright, to name only a few—no one has done so more dramatically than the late Anne Sexton. And nowhere in Mrs. Sexton's work are these tendencies carried to greater extremes than in the three present volumes. In these final statements the poet lays her most private moments—and her nastiest fantasies—at the reader's feet, and she reduces a once-graceful style to its barest, crudest essentials. Whatever one might think of these poems, it would seem unwise to underestimate their importance. To begin with, they are the last testament of a gifted and widely recognized American poet. Beyond that, they are a form of evidence: a field of glass around a shattered windshield. In their extremity they prompt the question of where American poetry has been during the past decade, and where it might be heading.

Anne Sexton began her career fifteen years ago as a formalist poet. Her early poems were anguished in tone and autobiographical in content, but they were well-made, polished pieces, formally inventive and often ironic. In view of their subjects, they were remarkably reticent:

> The town does not exist
> except where one black-haired tree slips
> up like a drowned woman into the hot sky.
> The town is silent. The night boils with eleven stars.

Review of *The Book of Folly, The Death Notebooks,* and *The Awful Rowing Toward God, Poetry* 127 (1976). Copyright © 1976 by The Modern Poetry Association. Reprinted by permission of the author and the Editor of *Poetry.*

> O starry starry night! This is how
> I want to die.
>
> ("The Starry Night")

Over the years Mrs. Sexton abandoned the formalist manner. Her imagery grew bold, her syntax elemental. She seemed determined to share with her growing audience the most intimate details of her private life, and she seemed increasingly indifferent toward subtlety and polish. The solidity of her early work survives in her *Love Poems* (1969), but in *Transformations* (1971), her colloquial renditions of Grimms' fairytales, it is almost nowhere to be found. And what becomes of style in these final poems? "*Gods*" will suffice as an example:

> Mrs. Sexton went out looking for the gods.
> She began looking in the sky—
> expecting a large white angel with a blue crotch.
>
> No one.
>
> She looked next in all the learned books
> and the print spat back at her.
>
> No one.
>
> She made a pilgrimage to the great poet
> and he belched in her face.
>
> No one.
>
> She prayed in all the churches of the world
> and learned a great deal about culture.
>
> No one.
>
> She went to the Atlantic, the Pacific, for surely God . . .
> No one.
>
> She went to the Buddha, the Brahma, the Pyramids
> and found immense postcards.

No one.

Then she journeyed back to her own house
and the gods of the world were shut in the lavatory.

At last!
she cried out,
and locked the door.

Naming herself, the poet mocks herself. Reducing diction, imagery, and syntax to their simplest terms, she reduces her religious anxiety and religious quest to a kind of verbal cartoon. The episodic structure and pattern of comic humiliations call to mind nothing so much as the daily comic strip, or even more, the animated cartoon, whose miniature anti-hero suffers a string of defeats. Here the sought object is not a mouse or roadrunner but an elusive company of gods, and the chase is mysteriously successful. But the two structures are otherwise much the same. The pathetic figure of "Mrs. Sexton" reminds one less of St. Teresa than of Charlie Brown.

Episodic structure is prominent in these three volumes, both in the syntax of individual poems and in the structural relationships of poems grouped as sequences. *The Death Notebooks* contains three such sequences—"The Death Baby," "The Furies," and "O Ye Tongues"—and *The Book of Folly* three more: "Angels of the Love Affair," "The Death of the Fathers," and "The Jesus Papers." Poetic sequences have become common in postwar American poetry, but to my knowledge there have not been any sequences quite like these. On the whole, they create little or no sense of progression, whether dramatic or thematic, nor do they present multiple perspectives on a single subject or situation. More than anything, they evoke a sense of succession and repetition, of events following one another in predictable and usually empty patterns. The poems themselves generate a similar mood, with their frequent catalogs ("the hating eyes of martyrs, / presidents, bus collectors, / bank managers, soldiers"), their parallelisms ("Sing me a thrush, bone. / Sing me a nest of cup and pestle. / Sing me a sweetbread for an old grandfather. / Sing me a foot and a doorknob . . . "), and their elemental narratives:

Oysters we ate,
sweet blue babies,
twelve eyes looked up at me,
running with lemon and Tabasco.
I was afraid to eat this father-food
and Father laughed
and drank down his martini,
clear as tears.
It was a soft medicine
that came from the sea into my mouth,
moist and plump.
I swallowed.
It went down like a large pudding.
Then I ate one o'clock and two o'clock.
Then I laughed and then we laughed
and let me take note—
there was a death,
the death of childhood
there at the Union Oyster House
for I was fifteen
and eating oysters
and the child was defeated.
The woman won.

("Oysters")

Mrs. Sexton's reduction of syntax and structure to an episodic, child-like simplicity has its counterpart in the diction of these poems, which is often that of the nursery. Diverse voices can be heard, among them Sylvia Plath's ("Beware. Beware." "my own little Jew"), Theodore Roethke's ("Sing me a thrush, bone." "Someone lives in a cave / eating his toes, / I know that much"), the mature voice of Mrs. Sexton's *Love Poems* ("I talk to God and ask Him / to speak of my failures, my successes, / ask Him to morally make an assessment"), and the offhand colloquial voice of *Transformations* ("If someone had brought [daisies] / to Van Gogh's room daily / his ear would have stayed on"). But the dominant voice is that of the cute, defiant, and often naughty little girl. "Why shouldn't I pull down my pants," the poet asks, "and show my little cunny to Tom / and Albert? They wee-wee funny." "I am wedded to my teddy," she declares, in a poem addressed to her mother. And speaking of the biblical Jonah, whose predicament she likens to her own: "Give praise with the whale who will make a big warm home for Jonah and let him hang his very own pictures up." It remains puzzling, at least to this reader, why an artist capable of eloquence should have chosen so limiting an idiom. In the sequence entitled "The Death of the Fathers," Mrs. Sexton employs the childlike voice as part of an effort to re-create scenes from her childhood and to confront, among other things, the question of whether her alcoholic father, who appears variously as Santa Claus, the skipper of a Chris-Craft, a dancing partner, and a storyteller, is her "real" father. Elsewhere, the childlike voice serves an ironic purpose, dramatizing the disparity between childlike innocence and adult experience: "She is the house. / He is the steeple. / When they fuck they are God. / When they break away they are God." Most of the time, however, Mrs. Sexton's reduction of speech to the level of Run-Spot-Run is merely distracting. It may represent an effort to satirize childish elements in herself and in the social role she felt compelled to play. But it has neither the variety nor the acute focus of effective satire, and it very soon wears thin.

If one of Mrs. Sexton's purposes is, in fact, to satirize her predicament as an American woman, she is well-assisted by her imagery, which in these last poems becomes a bizarre blend of Gothic and domestic. Here, as in her previous work, her metaphoric range is unusually wide. By turns her imagery is sentimental, sexual, violent, freakish, surreal, maternal, religious, and scatological. She puts bees in her mouth and hatpins through the pupils of her enemies. She presents us with a one-legged man, a man with a knife in his armpit, and a "Hitler-mouth psychiatrist." Words become squash-balls in one context, and in another, dung. The sea turns into the pond of urine; the poet dreams that she can "piss in God's eye"; and the penis of Jesus is made to sing "like a dog." For all its sensationalism, Mrs. Sexton's imagery does carry conviction, and it is sometimes striking in ways that are not sensational, as when she supplicates her doctor to let her "dilate like a bad debt," or when she speaks of "someone drowning into his own mouth." Her most characteristic kind of metaphor fuses imagery of violence and death with imagery of the kitchen, suggesting a close, even inevitable relationship between them. Rarely have poems been so well-stocked with household products and brand-names—Kleenex, Lysol, Clorox, Bab-O—and with domestic objects generally. The immediate effect of such imagery is to evoke the Mad Housewife, driven to distraction by suburban confinement. More seriously, Mrs. Sexton's images evoke the horror of suburban sterility, the suppressed violence and irrational fear of a woman enmeshed in domestic routine. "Blood fingers" tie the poet's shoe; she discovers blood in her gravy; and blood flows from the kitchen pump. Mrs. Sexton has traveled leagues from Dr. Johnson, who objected to the use of the domestic "knife" in tragic drama. To a large extent, however, Mrs. Sexton's personal tragedy seems to have been bound up in domestic objects, both as literal impediments and as symbols of her role; and through those objects she seems to have been developing, at the end of her life, a vision of her predicament. That vision is far from integrated or fully realized in these poems, but its discrete elements, set in close proximity, speak with force and insight.

Mrs. Sexton's household is also the theater for her religious struggle. These poems often call to mind T. S. Eliot's description of the poet's capacity to amalgamate Spinoza and the smell of cooking, forming new wholes of disparate experiences. In these poems Mrs. Sexton amalgamates the smell of cooking—and cleaning, and laundry—with a wide spectrum of religious sentiments and attitudes, which range from sarcastic irreverence to a desperate, if self-ironic, religious striving. In some poems the domestic order appears as an impediment to spiritual fulfillment. "Hail mary coffee toast," the poet prays; and speaking of her death she asks, "God, you don't mind if I bring all my kitchens." At other times the poet's quarrel is with the perverse indifference of a God who "has turned his backside to us," who is "too busy / to be here on earth," and who is compared to "that washerwoman / who walks out / when you're clean / but not ironed." In the absence of a sympathetic personal God the poet invents substitutes, declaring that "All the cocks of the world are God" and even "I am God, la de dah." Or she strikes a pose of nonchalance:

> Interrogator:
> Why talk to God?

Anne:
It's better than playing bridge.
("Hurry Up Please It's Time")

But indifference is a thin disguise for a poet who knows that "To pray . . . is to be a man carrying a man" and who speaks often of being "swallowed" by a God who is even now "opening His teeth." Mrs. Sexton's "rowing toward God" is indeed awful, in the oldest sense of that word. Beneath the domestic clutter and confused self-mockery of these last poems there runs a current of religious terror, as though the poet were writing, willy-nilly, her personal "Dies Irae."

What she was not writing, it seems clear, were suicide notes. Nor, for the most part, are these poems cries for help. On the whole, their character is that of a preparatory ritual, in advance of a death which could come at any time. At one point, Mrs. Sexton explicitly rejects the role of the "suicide bitch," declaring (to an imagined "Herr Doktor"), "I am no longer the suicide / with her raft and paddle. . . . I'll no longer die / to spite you. . . ." Obsessed as she is with her death, the poet's imagination plays not upon forms of suicide or its effect upon her survivors but upon the necessary preparations for the final event. At the center of these preparations lies the imagining of that event. She portrays herself dying "like a nice girl / smelling of Clorox and Duz." She presents herself as a spectacle, attracting *voyeurs*:

> But when it comes to my death let it be slow,
> let it be pantomime, this last peep show,
> so that I may squat at the edge trying on
> my black necessary trousseau.
> ("For Mr. Death Who Stands with His Door Open")

And in the last of her nine "psalms," the final poem of *The Death Notebooks,* she seems to speak with confidence, as though she had recovered her faith and had faced her deepest fear:

> For God was as large as a sunlamp and laughed his heat at us
> and therefore we did not cringe at the death hole.

*

It has been little more than a year since Mrs. Sexton's death, and it is surely too soon to attempt an overview of her life and work. How much help these last books will provide remains to be seen. Mrs. Sexton's last poems provide many glimpses of her private life, and they express her sense of spiritual deprivation. But nowhere do they provide a statement of belief, or a rejection of belief, or a fully developed vision of the poet's life and the forces threatening it. Perhaps that is too much to ask of so troubled a poet. The task might best be left to those who will pick up these sharp-edged and sometimes radiant pieces.

What these last poems do provide, however, is an extreme instance of a common predicament, namely that of American poets in the aftermath of formalism. For all her uniqueness, Mrs. Sexton was one of a large number of American poets who have rejected the conventions of formalism and its doctrine of impersonality and have had to shape a style and a coherent aesthetic to replace them. In this sense Mrs. Sexton's shattered art speaks not only for a troubled American psyche but for the poets of her generation and the one presently succeeding it.

JOAN NUCIFORA

"The Awful Babble of That Calling"

The negative view of poetry in *The Book of Folly*, like everything else in Sexton, has its antecedents, for Sexton's attitude toward poetry has always had an undercurrent of destructiveness, embodying as it does an alliance of poetry with chthonic or demonic forces. In spite of Sexton's comment in her reminiscence of Plath that the poem is the opposite of suicide (and her use of it as such in, for example, "Mother and Jack and the Rain" in *Live or Die*), we may observe that even as far back as the *Bedlam* poems "Said the Poet to the Analyst" and "Portrait of an Old Woman on the College Tavern Wall," poetry was at least in part as much a way of covering up, or falsifying, for the poet as of revealing. We have seen, too, in her interviews her emphasis on the paradoxical nature of poetry as truth-telling through "lies," "magic tricks," illusions. And even in her *Bedlam* apologia, "For John, Who Begs Me Not to Enquire Further," she claims for her poetry not "beauty" but "order" and admits that when it fails to communicate with her reader, it seems to her an "awkward bowl, / with all its cracked stars shining / like a complicated lie."

The view of poetry as lie or negation, a view that is only latently or intermittently lethal in the earlier books, becomes in *The Book of Folly* explicitly and consistently so, as the encroachment of art as an alien force on the poet comes to epitomize the more general infiltration of map consciousness on every aspect of Sexton's personality. In essence, we may say that Sexton, in

---

From "'The Awful Babble of That Calling': The Personal Myth of the Madwoman in the Poetry of Anne Sexton" (Ph.D. diss., University of Wisconsin, 1978). Edited version reprinted by permission of the author.

The placement of this essay and the one following it departs from the chronological arrangement of the volume in order to present these two treatments of *The Book of Folly* together.—ED.

attempting to substitute art (which one can mold to the heart's desire) for life (which constantly confounds those desires), runs up against her perennial dilemma. That is, in withdrawing further and further away from healthy, dynamic life, or garden reality, into a schematized, polarized knowledge, or map "rationality," Sexton is once again resorting to the creation of an artificial and rigid mental construct or system similar to the false-self system that in "protecting" one from nature and life, leaves one only with artifice and death. In making art a bulwark against reality and the self, the poet transforms it from a creative to a destructive act, and the urge to immortality based on poetry of this kind becomes but an impulse to self-immolation. Thus it is that the art that had at times been a source of spiritual sustenance has now become a spiritual drain, a source of suffering. And thus it is that the poetic inspiration that in "Flee on Your Donkey" in *Live or Die* had been the poet's "muse, *that good nurse*," is now but another of the sirens beleaguering the poet and luring her to death. . . . This is a poetry of annihilating extremism, of a balance precariously maintained only by a countering of one wild shift with another.

The struggle to gain self-control in this swing from destructive pole to destructive pole particularly obsesses the poet. Yet, except for an occasional poem here and there, the struggle results only in her further manipulation. She is thrown back and forth between loss of control in frenzied movement (an outpouring of words, a dance of death, "the jig") and loss of control in paralysis (verbal stasis, petrified death, the merging with an object), between involuntarily changing and witnessing change (death is "that awful change") on the one hand and being trapped in changelessness (again, the sterility of death) on the other. She is at the mercy of powers within herself—the poetic impulse, her multiple "others," or doubles—and of powers outside herself—a malignant fate, a tormenting God.

Sexton's inner life, the well of her poetry, now takes on the character of a void, a giant emptiness that threatens to obliterate her, swallow her—like Jonah's whale, the devouring parent, or the voluminous sea of earlier work. There is no longer the mourning for lost innocence; there is only the anguished nihilism of a decaying soul. The dreams of that beautiful other world in death have been replaced by nightmares of the horror of "life." The romantic has become the decadent. Tendencies discernible in *Transformations,* then, are carried to an even greater extreme in Sexton's sixth volume. The thirty-nine poems and three short stories in this collection convey a world that is stark, fragmented, surrealistic—a murky, oppressive world, an inferno defiled by blood, excrement, and disconnected body parts. The madness that Sexton had set forth in poems of rich texture and complex imagery in her earlier books is here shadowed forth in spare macabre visions.

Since so much in this volume proves to be pointless, deadly, and absurd—that is, mad—its title, *The Book of Folly,* is indeed apt. The title also, of course, echoes Erasmus's *Praise of Folly.* And Sexton does, in fact, display here in deadly earnest several of the varieties of folly described so light-heartedly in that work: the view of life as a play, an illusion, a pretense, the desire, or "ambition," to know or to be more than is proper to mortals, and the fatal preference for art over nature. Sexton, that is, seeks a "wisdom," Oedipus's and Kurtz's answer of horror, that Erasmus's speaker, Folly, warns will lead to misery and that is itself, therefore, "folly."

Sexton's fatal substitution of art for life, of the poetic urge (the other) for her own welfare (the self), is patent from the very first poem in the volume, "The Ambition Bird" (*BF,* 3–4). Here the once health-giving impulse to write has grown out of control, like a cancer, into a suicidal compulsion that drives the poet to sacrifice all—peace, sleep, human existence itself—for the sake of art. Inspiration has degenerated into neurotic fluttering. "All night dark wings / flopping in my heart" or into extravagant and bizarre wishes for transfiguration through death. Poetry has thus become but another form of domination to which the poet must submit, another enclosure of death: "It is my immortality box, / my lay-away plan, / my coffin."

In "Sweeney" (*BF,* 9–10) also, art is preferred to life, but in another way. An ardent, slightly crazy admirer of Sexton's has adopted her poetry as his personal religion:

> Your words, Sexton, are the only
>
> red queens, the only ministers, the only beasts.
> You are the altar cup and from this

I do fill my mouth. Sexton, I am your priest.

(*BF*, 9)

Sexton recognizes the human failings that contribute to this zeal, but in the end shows herself to be in agreement with it. For on the same day that Sweeney takes her out on the town, her sister is killed in a car accident. This objective event of life, the untimely death of her sister, a bride of one week, strikes the poet as betrayal and falsehood: "her death lied." She therefore renounces life (because it can disappoint, or "lie") for a reliance on words and art for an imperishable authentic reality: "Surely the words will continue, for that's / what's left that's true."

Both "The Silence" (*BF*, 32–33) and "The Hoarder" (*BF*, 34–35) show the poet's panic when this mastery over her world through the use of words fails. As in "Mother and Jack and the Rain" in *Live or Die*, the poet in "The Silence" is once again shut up in a room, in herself, attempting to use words as weapons against the encroachment of despair, but unlike the earlier poem, this one records not the power of craft to affirm but its complete ineffectuality: both words and the poet have lost control to an all-consuming nothingness, an annihilating "silence." The scene of the disturbed creative process here, in its imagery of white, black, and red, resembles that of the violent lovers in *Love Poems*, but here there is also a cancerousness and a decadence. The whiteness of the room is not that of purity but of a deathly pallor: "whiter than chicken bones / bleaching in the moonlight, / pure garbage." It is a picture of nature perverted, with its "white plants / growing like obscene virgins." The blackness, too, is deathly: the poet's dark hair has been charred "in the white fire," and her beads are "twenty eyes heaved up / from the volcano, / quite contorted."

The entire process of trying to write in this room is grotesque and bloody: words leak out of her pen "like a miscarriage"; but the silence flings them back and remains, like "an enormous baby mouth." This cavernous silence, this gigantic inner hunger and emptiness, "is death," but it is also a species of torture, a predatory white bird (again, like the ambition bird, an image of poetic inspiration gone awry) that persecutes the poet much as the eagle persecuted Prometheus. It attacks in particular the poet's faculties of sight and speech—"the black eyes / and the vibrating red muscle / of my mouth"—further ensuring the reign of blankness and muteness.

In "The Silence," words leak out of the poet's pen like a miscarriage, yet effect no change in the obliterating silence. In "The Hoarder," the poet speaks of holding words in "though they are dung," yet the poem itself is a torrent of words, thirty-seven lines of troubled digging into the self and the past, and uninterrupted throwing up of memory and image unpunctuated until the question mark at the end. The vision of words, in this and the previous poem, as the bearers of purposeless pain or shame illustrates Sexton's growing alienation from her art and her growing fear of its serving but as agent of the demon (the "other") within her usurping her self-control.

The two main motifs in the theme of the loss of verbal, or poetic, control that we have been examining in *The Book of Folly*—the violent oscillation between anarchy and rigidity (mobility and fixity) and the possession by the "other"—are the main features as well of a *general* sense of powerlessness and victimization that leads us further into the grotesque and the absurd. Both Laing and Vernon describe the genesis of the first condition in the schizophrenic. Laing states:

> It seems to us that *without exception* the experience and behavior that gets labeled schizophrenic is *a special strategy that a person invents in order to live in an unlivable situation*. In his life situation the person has come to feel he is in an untenable position. He cannot make a move, or make no move, without being beset by contradictory and paradoxical pressures and demands, pushes and pulls, both internally from himself, and externally from those around him. He is, as it were, in a position of checkmate.[1]

Vernon describes the swing from frantic movement to paralysis as a result of the individual's splitting of the me from the not-me (subjectivity from objectivity), of the void from solidity, and being caught in "an intolerable double bind" in which there is either complete self-absorption or complete self-dispersal, "two absolute polarities with no in-between":[2]

If the schizophrenic isn't directed outward, toward merging with things, then things are literally directed inward toward him. Direction in one's gestures is polarized in schizophrenia into either totally active or totally passive states, so that the person either disperses himself into the world in a salad of frenzied actions or completely withdraws into an immobility, a catatonia, bringing with him only the ability to incorporate and consume.[3]

This double-bind is presented most overtly in the short story "Dancing the Jig" (*BF*, 65–71), in which the narrator, at a party, violently alternates between, on the one hand, "dancing the jig," that is, cavorting involuntarily in a frantic (death) dance in which she loses identity and autonomy to the other-worldly sound of the music and, on the other hand, trying by intent observation to "become," that is to merge with ("to incorporate and consume") an inert "unnoticeable" object—in this case, a chair. We learn as the story proceeds that this behavior originates in and perpetuates the narrator's childhood self-division, her response to the dinner-table ridicule of her mother (her first and most confusing "other"): "Part of me is running and the other part is sitting here frozen to the chair." When the child, who at first attempts to protect herself by fixing her attention on an object (here, a napkin ring, the counterpart of the chair at the party), can no longer contain her emotion, she goes back to the other extreme, losing control in an hysterical eruption of tears, words, and gestures—the early form of "dancing the jig."

In other stories and poems Sexton deals with these extremes not by fluctuating from one to the other but by concentrating on each singly. . . . But the selection that most devastatingly treats not only the motif of purposeless, meaningless motion but that of control by a wanton other is "The Ballet of the Buffoon" (*BF*, 72–81). Here life is a *danse macabre* of cosmic insignificance presided over by a demonic magician-puppeteer who is all appearance and no reality. He is the ultimate embodiment of the schizophrenic self and universe drained of vitality by the erection of false-self systems or roles (a layered armor of masks and costumes) that succeeds only too well in keeping the true self and real universe inaccessible. . . . Sexton's Mr. Ha-ha, "A bit like the Devil himself. A bit of a rogue and a bit of a fiend," fools his fellow townsmen into killing their wives (a death set forth in terms of sexuality, the dance, and religious ritual) and protects himself from retribution by assuming one disguise after another. At the story's end, as the others cry out for pity, Mr. Ha-ha, "the archdeceiver," as the voice of death's rule, delivers the story's final message, one that repeats the idea, first extensively developed in *Love Poems,* of earthly power as the ascendancy of the male over the female, the killer over the killed. . . .

Just as the mask of the buffoon is constantly changing, so the figure of the enemy without in Sexton's other poems shows up in many guises. In "Dancing the Jig" (65–67), it is the mother; in "Sweeney" (9–10) and "Oh" (7–8), a God who feeds on humans. In still other poems, it is the doppelgänger, or double within, kin to the poetic "ambition bird," that preys on and torments the poet. In "Angels of the Love Affair" (55–62), it is "that other, the dark one, that other me" (the old dwarf heart of *All My Pretty Ones*); in "The Other" (30–31) it is a waiting "brother," "spouse," and "lover" who cries at health, giggles at blasphemy, and inflicts insomnia on the poet until it gets its way; and in "The Hex" (24–25) it is the "Nana-hex," the poet's sense of guilt for the insanity of her great-aunt, the close friend of her youth, written of in earlier poems.

The poet in *The Book of Folly,* then, has indeed reached an impasse, Laing's "checkmate," Vernon's "double bind." Action and the cessation of action, life's flux and death's stagnation, reality and artifice, the inner world of subjective aliens and the outer world of projected aliens—have all placed the poet in an unbearable trap. Nor does recourse to the familiar hoped-for supports of previous books—Christianity or family relationships—offer solutions or solace. Christianity offers little aid, for Jesus here, treated in the nine poems comprising "The Jesus Papers" (*BF*, 91–105), is even more than in earlier poems humanized—or, rather, Sextonized—into an extension of the poet's own ego, a representation of her own—especially sexual —conflicts. Jesus is pictured as one who, like Sexton, is obsessed with his mother, is urged on by his sexual nature, and relies on tricks to impress a crowd that in the end (in "Jesus Dies") views him merely as something of a freak on exhibit. The same cutting "demythifying" impulse that determined the tone of *Transformations* determines also that of "The Jesus Papers." Like the

Grimm lore, the New Testament according to Sexton is delivered in the jaded, bone-bare voice of the bloodied "middle-aged witch." In spite of the sarcasm and seeming desecration in Sexton's treatment of Jesus and Mary in these poems, however, it would be a mistake to see Sexton as careless in her attitude. Here, as elsewhere, she is beset by pulls in opposite directions. She once remarked of Jesus, for instance: "Hell, He's no goody-goody if He's worth anything! . . . I probably can't stand to have Him so much better than me."[4] The paradox is even further indicated in the epigraph to "The Jesus Papers," which asserts:

> "And would you mock God?"
> "God is not mocked except by believers."
>
> (BF, 91)

The "God" of the poems themselves, however, is one who has forsaken his creation and his son, and the "belief," consequently, is in the degraded "nature" of both.

Like Christianity, the psychoanalytic search for the source of her conflicts, the source of her madness and her pain, in excavations of the past buried in her subconscious—her childhood, her family life—turns up only guilt, doubt, and confusion. Almost half the pieces in this collection touch in some way upon the family and almost all of these are unrelievedly brutal. The relationship of husband and wife, like that of the lovers in "Going Gone" (BF, 20–21), is strewn with carnage not only in "The Ballet of the Buffoon" (BF, 72–81) but in "The Wifebeater" (BF, 13–14). The relationship of poet and daughter is also tarnished; "Mother and Daughter" (BF, 11–12) no longer expresses the motherly concern of "The Double Image" in Bedlam, "The Fortress" in All My Pretty Ones, or "Little Girl, My String Bean, My Lovely Woman," "A Little Uncomplicated Hymn," and "Pain for a Daughter" in Live or Die, but the older woman's sense of abandonment and of uselessness with her daughter's growing independence. Furthermore, the poet's ambivalence toward her own mother is maintained: we have seen the evil consuming mother in "Dancing the Jig" (BF, 65–71); we see the good nourishing mother in "Dreaming the Breasts" (BF, 26–27). And finally in a sequence of six poems called "The Death of the Fathers" (*BF,* 39–53), Sexton delineates in highly sensory terms the growing awareness of passion, sex, and death that came to her through her relationship with her father—from her first sharing oysters ("father-food") with him, through her dancing and boating with him, to the disenchantment of seeing him a drunken Santa and, finally, to her anxiety about whether he or a horrid stranger truly fathered her. Imagery of mouth, sea, and the colors blue and red pattern the inner fluctuations in the poet as she tries to come to terms with the perplexity of her own and her father's identity.

The prospect of self-knowledge and of mastery of self and craft in *The Book of Folly,* in a world where false images dominate and truth is more than ever elusive and—paradoxically—illusive, is indeed dim. Sexton has by now, in fact, moved away from her earlier tragic perspective in which suffering took place in a deeply moral universe that conferred significance on the sufferer. Now—caught up in a grotesque play or game in which each new role or "move" increasingly distances the player from reality—the poet's vision is not tragic but absurd. The playing with the demonic that began, according to her own accounts, as "fun" for the writer in *Transformations* has now carried the player away, deprived her of her freedom, and made her afraid of the ghosts and demons of self and world that she herself has invoked. But the vision of *The Book of Folly* may also be viewed as a logical stage in a journey through a self and world that, as we have seen, have been judged beforehand to be fallen, for such a self and such a world are alienated not only from goodness but from the very meaning that determines goodness.

NOTES

1. R. D. Laing, *The Politics of Experience* (New York: Ballantine, 1967), 114–15.
2. John Vernon, *The Garden and the Map* (Chicago: University of Illinois Press, 1973), 24–25.
3. Vernon, 26.
4. Margaret Ferrari, "Anne Sexton: Between Death and God," *America,* November 9, 1974, 282.

RUTH EVELYN QUEBE

The Questing Self

In "Dancing the Jig" the attempt to rescue the self by reaching greater self-knowledge only leads in a circle, and the hoped-for regeneration remains as far away as ever. Here the image of her previous self corresponds with an Edenic or innocent state. Yet, as the story attests, this is difficult to regain—though the stratagems of awareness and recall sometimes make it seem potentially available. The past only admits the continual presence of opposites and of nonreversible change.

"Dancing the Jig," one of three short stories Sexton published in *The Book of Folly*, shares with the volume's other poems and stories an overall thematic concern with the perverse, a somewhat wryly clinical tone, and the use of a narrative framework for a meditative purpose. This particular story treats the subversive self as a spontaneous rebel against social proprieties, a self that erupts into convulsive moments under the stress of change and other people's demands. Thus the physical movement, or dancing the jig, metaphorically represents emotional alienation.

Structurally, the story actually consists of a framing narrative around a core narrative. The frame describes the speaker at a party—she finds herself "dancing the jig" and hating herself for it. Meditating on the meaning and origin of her behavior, she recounts a scene from the family dinner table when she was ten or twelve years old. This core story is peopled by an abusive mother, a drunken father, an insane aunt, and two hostile sisters, all of whom together make the speaker feel worthless and disoriented. Those feelings, depicted with a simplicity and objectivity that is a fine modulation between what the child perceives first-

---

From "The Questing Self: A Study of Anne Sexton's Poetry" (Ph.D. diss., University of Texas at Austin, 1979). Edited version reprinted by permission of the author.

hand and what the woman sees in retrospect, become the basis of her adult alienation.

To a large extent, the story takes the form of a psychoanalytic session, with present behavior being explained in terms of the past. What brings the story into the realm of art is the clarity and coherence of its images, and the order of the narrative. The child, for instance, tries to explain how the insane Nana is different:

> When I do go up to her room, where we used to tell secrets and be comfy, she won't sit down with me. I will sit on her couch and try to talk with her, but she will only moan, pacing back and forth from wall to wall, twisting her veiny old hands and mumbling to herself. She won't smile. She used to. I don't understand about people being different when they were your friend yesterday. (*BF*, 70)

The adult arranges what the child has seen, in interpenetration of time common to Sexton, but particularly well done in this story.

The story ends by returning to the grown-up speaker at the party, who dwells on her fear of change and holds up a chair as the standard of perfection: "It is a relief to dwell on it—a perfect object. So fixed. So always the same" (*BF*, 71). Change, life has taught her, means deterioration, and so she would like to become a material object, like a chair or a napkin ring, to slow down time. But one part of her wants to speed up time convulsively—"The opposite of chair is dancing the jig" (*BF*, 66)— in order to grasp its anticipated destruction, just as the mother's scolding finally goaded her into a confrontation. Better to meet the worst than keep waiting for it.

KARL MALKOFF

Anne Sexton

A student of Robert Lowell, a close friend of Sylvia Plath, Anne Sexton is at the core of what M. L. Rosenthal and others have named the Confessional school of poetry. She certainly seems to draw her materials from the worlds of private torment, seeking the deep secrets of the self, even if the implications of these secrets are potentially destructive. However, if these are tendencies that serve to define a school, another fact is equally true. Confessional poetry does not necessarily amount to biography, perhaps cannot be biography. Like Lowell, Plath, Theodore Roethke, and John Berryman, she selects and distorts her experience, creates a myth of the self. Further, she introduces many personae, the events of whose lives have nothing to do with her own, while refusing to distinguish them from the reasonably consistent voice that runs through her verse or even from her own person. The assumption of early critics that "Unknown Girl in the Maternity Ward" implies an illegitimate child in Sexton's own life has apparently been dropped, but there is still controversy as to whether or not she had a brother who was killed in the war ("For Johnny Pole on the Forgotten Beach"). The poet has not involved herself in clarifying such confusions. Her point, perhaps, is that these considerations have nothing to do with her poetry, which, whatever its ultimate origins in the poet's own psyche, moves toward a universality of form and feeling.

As if in support of this thesis, the facts of Anne Sexton's life, certainly of her younger years, are not especially clear. In 1947–48 she attended Garland Junior College, but she has listed her education (in a questionnaire for *Poetry* magazine) as "none." She worked as a fashion model in Boston in the early fifties, married, and had two children. Her significant education took place in 1958–59, when she audited Robert Lowell's course in the writing of verse at Boston University, where she met Sylvia Plath. The mental breakdowns and suicide attempts recorded in her poetry are apparently true in essence, even if specific circumstances may be distorted. It is this particular area of experience that forms the subject, directly or indirectly, of most of Anne Sexton's first book of poems, *To Bedlam and Part Way Back* (1960).

The epigraph to this volume is often cited by Sexton's critics:

It is the courage to make a clean breast of it in face of every question that makes the philosopher. He must be like Sophocles' Oedipus, who, seeking enlightenment concerning his terrible fate, pursues his indefatigable enquiry, even when he divines that appalling horror awaits him in the answer. But most of us carry in our heart the Jocasta who begs Oedipus for God's sake not to inquire further. . . . (Schopenhauer, in a letter to Goethe)

This is relatively straightforward; but there are nevertheless some ambiguities that can only be resolved in the context of Sexton's poetry, and even then imperfectly. Does the poet identify with Oedipus alone, or with Jocasta, or with both? The poem "For John, Who Begs Me Not to Enquire Further," a response to poet John Holmes's objection that "The Double Image" revealed too much intimate experience, clearly alludes to the epigraph of the book, and seems to resolve the question in favor of Oedipus. But this is misleading; Sexton did not write the poem in search of truth, which she already had, but in search of form, which the truth lacked. "Not that it was beautiful, / but that I found some order there." The poet here is neither Oedipus nor Jocasta; she is perhaps Sophocles, giving shape to destructive chaos. In the quotation from Schopenhauer, Oedipus is likened to "the philosopher," while all the evidence suggests that Sexton thinks of herself as a poet rather than a philosopher. The poet's shaping impulses take her beyond the individual, beyond creating poetry for therapy. Final obligations are not to the healthiness of the self, but to the vision of reality the self has experienced.

The poem "Said the Poet to the Analyst" differentiates the business of poetry from the business of analysis, revealing at the same time important affinities. "Words are like labels," says the poet, "or coins, or better, like swarming bees." There is a distance between word and event, the poet is "only broken by the sources of things"; the words take on a reality of their own, one that is not necessarily inferior to the one the poet had in mind.

> I must always forget how one word is able to pick
> out another, to manner another, until I have got
> something I might have said . . .
> but did not.

The analyst's business, in this case at least, is "watching" the poet's words. The poet says she is at her best praising a nickel machine in Nevada; if the analyst says "this is something it is not," the poet grows weak,

> . . . remembering how my hands felt funny
> and ridiculous and crowded with all
> the believing money.

The slot machine coins, "the believing money," are the poet's words, which, when subjected to the analyst's scrutiny—and the analyst here seems to be both psychoanalyst and professional critic—leave the poet feeling uncomfortable. ". . . But I / admit nothing," is a crucial statement, highly self-protective. The imagination must be defended from the analytic eye, but the poet, almost alienated from her own experience, is on the defensive.

Two images appear in this poem that are central to the book as a whole: first, the association with bees, later an important subject for Sylvia Plath, which seem for Sexton to carry implications of time, sexuality, imprisonment, and death; second, the male antagonist, analyst, father, God, on whom the poet depends, from whom she must be freed. Both images are introduced in the book's first poem, "You, Doctor Martin." The doctor is seen walking "from breakfast to madness"; the poet, resenting, perhaps, the doctor's intermittent presence in the "antiseptic tunnel" to which she is indefinitely confined, is ". . . queen of this summer hotel / or the laughing bee on a stalk / of death." Almost casually, Sexton remarks: ". . . There are no knives / for cutting your throat." However, her feelings toward the man upon whom salvation depends cannot be wholly negative: "Of course, I love you." The doctor, like Tiresias in the Oedipus myth, holds the key to the truth, however threatening that truth might be; he is ". . . an oracular / eye in our nest." Making moccasins (surely a pun, since she is ". . . queen of all my sins / forgotten"), the poet gropes for something solid, taking the first long step toward reintegration of a fragmented psyche. Working against the threat of chaos, against an unpredictable world of charms and incantations, is the form of the poem, the rigid stanzaic pattern ($a^3b^4c^5a^3b^4c^5a^3$), the firm, cyclical structure.

The dominant images weave in and out of the poems, pulling the book together, and varying in form and context to avoid monotony. In "Ringing the Bells," the women inmates of Bedlam are described as being "like bees caught in the wrong hive, / we are the circle of the crazy ladies." In "The Moss of His Skin," Sexton's imagination is captured by the old Arabian custom of burying young girls alive next to their dead fathers as a sacrifice to tribal goddesses. The poem, rich in sexual connotation, moves into a dark room that is "like a cave or a mouth / or an indoor belly"; it ends with the doomed child pretending

> that Allah will not see
> how I hold my daddy
> like an old stone tree.

"The Double Image," Anne Sexton's long poem to her own daughter, appears in the section of the book concerned with "part way back" from Bedlam. Almost surely influenced by W. D. Snodgrass's *Heart's Needle,* this poem (actually a sequence of seven poems) is the poet's account of what has happened to her in the recent past, as told to her younger daughter. (Of *Heart's Needle,* Sexton told an interviewer: "I had written about half of my first book when I read that poem, and it moved me to such an extent . . . that I ran up to my mother-in-law's where she [her own daughter] was living and got her back.") The materials of the poem are powerful, so powerful they threaten to overwhelm the poet's powers of imagination, her mind as a whole. The poet herself has been in and out of institutions; twice she has tried to kill herself. As she struggles to regain the strength to deal with her experience and to regain her daughter, her own mother lies dying of cancer. Sexton's voice is surprisingly calm; she has her emotions firmly under control. But there is no mistaking the caldron of feeling not very far from the surface. If she relaxes one instant, she will drown. The mirror images, both reflecting and distorting, of grandmother, mother, and daughter, form the poem's dominant conceit. With pride and love and especially guilt, the poet's final remark to her daughter is: "I made you to find me." She has also made this poem, if not to find herself—though that is in a way true—at least to contain and give shape to the energies within. As in "You, Doctor Martin," the poet depends on a rigid stanzaic form, different within each poem, to help control and dominate explosive experience, as in this stanza from the sixth poem:

> And this was the cave of the mirror,
> that double woman who stares
> at herself, as if she were petrified
> in time—two ladies sitting in umber chairs.
> You kissed your grandmother
> and she cried.

As its title (taken from Macduff's outcry on hearing of the destruction of his family) suggests, *All My Pretty Ones* (1962) is devoted largely to images of guilt and terror at the human condition. There are moments of joy—Sexton does not exclude them—but they are few. They are generally connected with her daughters, as in "The Fortress," but even here joy is defensive: "We laugh and we touch. / I promise you love. Time will not take that away."

The book begins with poems for her mother and father, who died within four months of each other. The title poem, on the death of the father, concludes:

> Only in this hoarded span will love persevere.
> Whether you are pretty or not, I outlive you,
> bend down my strange face to yours and forgive you.

It is a dismal universe the poet inhabits; its only affirmative value seems to be love. Sexton calls on love to help her bear the unbearable almost as a *deus ex machina*. Love does not really invite examination; when the poet does investigate, doubts are not dispelled. In "Old Dwarf Heart," we learn that whenever the poet lies down to love, the dwarf heart negates the act. "She knows the decay we're made of." The heart, this inmost self, links love with the strange and corrupt, with terrible knowledge and terrible pain. "Old ornament, old naked fist," exclaims the poet, almost with affection, unwilling, as well as unable, to give up her well-spring of emotion,

> even if I put on seventy coats I could not cover you . . .
> mother, father, I'm made of.

At this stage of her development, poems for Sexton explore the darker recesses of the imagination, reveal the ugliness and the decay that lurk behind even images of beauty. Sexton enters the world of Christ crucified, who wakes in his tomb to find himself being eaten by rats, the performers of the miracle ("In the Deep Museum"), and the world of Van Gogh, mad, of starry night, as "The night boils with eleven stars" ("The Starry Night"). The purpose of poetry is, in fact, defined at the end of "With Mercy for the Greedy":

> . . . This is what poems are:
> with mercy
> for the greedy,
> they are the tongue's wrangle,
> the world's pottage, the rat's star.

All My Pretty Ones must, in short, join the company of those works of art whose affirmation lies not in their philosophy, but in the very fact that they exist at all.

Live or Die (1966), winner of the Pulitzer Prize, contains some of Anne Sexton's finest poetry. The epigraph this time is from a draft of Saul Bellow's *Herzog:* "With one long breath, caught and held in his chest, he fought his sadness over his solitary life. Don't cry, you idiot! Live or die, but don't poison everything. . . ." In an author's note, Sexton apologizes for, or at least attempts to justify, the gloominess of her work by quoting Gide: "Despite every resolution of optimism, melancholy occasionally wins out: man has decidedly botched up the planet." However, in comparison with earlier work, the tone of this book is practically sunny. Forcing herself to make a choice between nihilism and affirmation (or at least acceptance) as a poet, literally between death and life as a human being, Sexton's decision is in the title of the book's last poem: "Live."

This decision is reached, however, only with misgivings, with unresolved doubts. The chronological order of the poems suggests a randomness that renders affirmation accidental; what if the book had ended elsewhere, at, for example, "Sylvia's Death"? "Thief!" Sexton accuses Sylvia Plath,

> how did you crawl into,
>
> crawl down alone
> into the death I wanted so badly and for so long

What if it had ended at "Pain for a Daughter," in which the poet hears her daughter, whose foot has been injured by a horse, cry out for God rather than for her mother. Sexton sees her daughter's life "stretch out":

> I saw her torn in childbirth,
> and I saw her, at that moment,
> in her own death and I knew that she
> knew.

What differentiates the visions of despair in this book from those of earlier ones is that Sexton has found a language for her love, made it a believable force in the universe rather than a desperate, scarcely credited hope. Look, for example, at the conclusion to "A Little Uncomplicated Hymn," written for her daughter Joy:

> I wanted to write such a poem
> with such musics, such guitars going;
> I tried at the teeth of sound
> to draw up such legions of noise;
> I tried at the breakwater
> to catch the star off each ship;
> and at the closing of hands
> I looked for their houses
> and silences.
> I found just one.
>
> you were mine
> and I lent you out.
>
> I look for uncomplicated hymns
> but love has none.

For the first time, a predominance of Anne Sexton's poems are written in free verse, rather than in exacting, if personally derived, forms. This is important, for now the discipline and control that prevent the poems from becoming undifferentiated shrieks of terror—to use a phrase applied by Stanley Kunitz to a poem by Theodore Roethke—reside in the language itself rather than in stanzaic patterns. Whether a sign of greater emotional health or increased poetic mastery, the result is the same: a stronger voice. Anne Sexton is not through with tighter forms; she uses them here and she will use them again. But she is less dependent on them.

One would have thought by the mid-sixties that the Confessional poets had opened as much new ground to the poetic imagination as they were going to. But *Love Poems* (1969) makes it clear that although sexual behavior was already a commonplace theme, a certain amount of restraint had been operative. Titles such as "The Breast," "In Celebration of My Uterus," "The Ballad of the Lonely Masturbator," suggest a new range of possibility. In these poems Anne Sexton is writing of what is normally considered the spiritual side of love as an expression of the total organism:

> . . . in celebration of the woman I am
> and of the soul of the woman I am
> and of the central creature and its delight
> I sing for you. I dare to live.
> Hello, spirit. Hello, cup.
>> (from "In Celebration of My Uterus")

Celebrating her uterus, she celebrates herself, her womanhood. One does not stand for the other; it is the other. *Love Poems* continues a journey begun in *Bedlam;* it furthers the reintegration of the self. Love is experienced as a tangible reality. There is a good deal of pain involved, but there is also joy; there is anxiety, but there is also the strength to endure.

Having led the way for Sylvia Plath many times in the past, it is now Anne Sexton's turn to be influenced by her. She has learned from the *Ariel* poems the ability to isolate the sharp, piercing image, which emerges with a clarity so brilliant it gives pleasure even when the subject is painful, as in the last lines of "For My Lover Returning to His Wife." The poet is sending her lover back to his solid, substantial wife: "As for me, I am a watercolor. / I wash off." Or the last line of "The Breast": "I burn the way money burns." Or the beginning of "The Kiss": "My mouth blooms like a cut."

The book's first poem is appropriately entitled "The Touch," for it is this sense that is emphasized throughout, to a far greater extent than in previous volumes. While contact is not always unequivocally ecstatic, it is always evidence of life, evidence that Anne Sexton has followed the exhortation of the final poem of her previous book: "Live."

In *Transformations* (1971), Anne Sexton explores a new mode of plumbing the depths of the self. The book contains the retelling of seventeen Grimm fairy tales, each preceded by an introductory section that generally makes connections between the stories in particular and the human psyche in general. "Rumpelstiltskin," for example, begins "Inside many of us / is a small old man / who wants to get out"; "The Gold Key" opens with

"The speaker in this case / is a middle-aged witch, me." Fairy tales can be thought of as collective dreams, or parables, that reveal the world as perceived by the child who still lives in all of us. And these perceptions, concerning our loves and fears, are precisely those we are most likely to have suppressed in the interest of a less disturbing sense of reality.

It would seem, then, that in these poems, which deal with archetypal rather than personal experience, Sexton is abandoning the Confessional mode. This is only superficially true, for, as she demonstrates in this book, the insights made available to us through myths lie not in the myths themselves but in our relation to the myths. Sexton relates to the tales with a kind of sardonic wit that does not eliminate terror but does win at least a temporary victory over it. The wolf in "Red Riding Hood," for example, is ". . . dressed in frills, / a kind of transvestite." The ball dropped in the well by the princess in "The Frog Prince" is a moon, a butter calf, a yellow moth, a Hindu hare. "Balls such as these are not / for sale in Au Bon Marché." Finally, it is not simply by tone and interpretation but by imagery as well that a poet masters his material, as can be seen in this passage near the conclusion of "Briar Rose (Sleeping Beauty)":

> Daddy?
> That's another kind of prison.
> It's not the prince at all,
> but my father
> drunkenly bent over my bed,
> circling the abyss like a shark,
> my father thick upon me
> like some sleeping jellyfish.

In "The Hoarder," from *The Book of Folly* (1972), Anne Sexton writes: "I am a hoarder of words / I hold them in though they are / dung." Since *The Book of Folly* is her third book in four years, it is difficult to take these lines too seriously. Many of the poems could have appeared in earlier volumes, but even in these her continuing development is evident in lines that seem shorter, often breathless rhythms, sharper imagery. In addition, there are now formal sequences of poems: "The Death of the

Fathers," "Angels of the Love Affair," and "The Jesus Papers." And there are three short stories, which may not be prose poems, but in which language overwhelms event. Anne Sexton is reaching out to broaden the possibilities of her art. Her dominant theme has not been altered, however; as at the beginning of her career, it is still Oedipus' search for the truth—at all costs.

SUZANNE JUHASZ

"The Excitable Gift"
The Poetry of Anne Sexton

This study of Anne Sexton's poetry was written before her death in October 1974. In it I describe her growing power through poetry, a triumph of life over death. Now it is apparent that the lure of death—always present, as her poems attest—grew too strong for her, despite the poetry. Yet her death does not negate either her art or the strength that she achieved through it. For the years in which she wrote, she held death at bay and with her poems sent a powerful awareness of life into the world. It was her tragedy, like that of others before her, to be both woman and poet. The struggle in this double-bind situation between such conflicting role demands is excruciating for all who will not choose between being "woman" or "poet." Anne Sexton's poetry is a testament to her courage and ability to be both for as long as she could.

"To Rage in Your Own Bowl"

Anne Sexton came to poetry through psychotherapy. She became a poet after having experienced the traditional woman's roles of wife, mother, housewife; *because* she had experienced them and needed a way, a form, a voice with which to deal with the fact of being a woman. "Until I was twenty-eight I had a kind of buried self who didn't know she could do anything but make white sauce and diaper babies," she remarked in 1968 to a *Paris Review* interviewer:

From *Naked and Fiery Forms: Modern American Poetry by Women—A New Tradition* (New York: Harper and Row, 1976). Copyright 1976 by Suzanne Juhasz. Reprinted by permission of the author.

All I wanted was a little piece of life, to be married, to have children. I thought the nightmares, the visions, the demons would go away if there was enough love to put them down. I was trying my damnedest to lead a conventional life, for that was how I was brought up, and it was what my husband wanted of me. But one can't build little white picket fences to keep nightmares out. The surface cracked when I was about twenty-eight. I had a psychotic break and tried to kill myself.[1]

After she began to write poems, her therapist encouraged her: " 'Don't kill yourself,' he said. 'Your poems might mean something to someone else someday.' That gave me a feeling of purpose, a little cause, something to *do* with my life, no matter how rotten I was."[2]

Since Betty Friedan first analyzed "the problem that has no name,"[3] psychologists, sociologists, and others writing about women have described the kind of situation in which Sexton found herself and have provided extensive insight into the sources of the kind of madness that she experienced. In discussing the poetry that she created, it is essential to observe that her "confessionalism" grew out of the therapy situation, but that the therapy was occasioned by her womanhood itself, by the very real strains and conflicts that Sexton experienced while attempting to exist in her world as a woman.

The poems from *To Bedlam and Part Way Back* (1960)[4] to the volume appropriately titled *Live or Die* (1966)[5] closely follow the psychoanalytic model. They move in concern from the present or near past, from the trappings of madness (its hospitals, inmates, doctors, pills) to the more distant past in which the madness grew. It is a past not so much of events as relationships—relations with blood kin: mother, father, daughters. Endlessly exploring herself as she has been created by these interpersonal relationships, Sexton probes for the truth. The way back to sanity is through understanding, yet we may understand better with the unconscious than with the conscious mind. As artist, Sexton wills the memories with her conscious mind (sometimes, as in "All My Pretty Ones," "Walking in Paris," "Some Foreign Letters," photographs or letters are carefully used as occasions to awaken memory), but the unconscious mind, it is hoped, will supply the images, the connections and associations that will give access to the truth. "The poetry is often more advanced, in terms of my unconscious, than I am," she tells the interviewer. "Poetry, after all, milks the unconscious. The unconscious is there to feed it little images, little symbols, the answers, the insights I know not of."[6] Thus in her poems she describes herself as patient: "And I am queen of this summer hotel / or the laughing bee on a stalk / of death" ("You, Doctor Martin");[7] her mother: "That was the winter / that my mother died, / half mad on morphine, / blown up, at last, / like a pregnant pig. / I was her dreamy evil eye" ("Flee on Your Donkey");[8] her daughter: ". . . I just pretended / you, small piglet, butterfly / girl with jelly bean cheeks" ("The Double Image").[9]

The most characteristic form for these images is the simile or epithet-metaphor: "Words are like labels, / or coins, or better, like swarming bees," she writes in "Said the Poet to the Analyst."[10] The following litany to her dead mother is based upon her understanding (consistent with psychoanalytic theory) of the power of naming itself to define and to exorcise.

Now it is Friday's noon
and I would still curse
you with my rhyming words
and bring you flapping back, old love,
old circus knitting, god–in–her–moon,
all fairest in my lang syne verse,
the gauzy bride among the children,
the fancy amid the absurd
and awkward, that horn for hounds
that skipper homeward, that museum
keeper of stiff starfish, that blaze
within the pilgrim woman,
a clown mender, a dove's
cheek among the stones,
my Lady of my first words,
this is the division of ways.

("The Division of Parts")[11]

First the naming, difficult enough; then, frequently, the definition expanded into a complex image: "I must always forget how one word is able to pick / out another, to manner another, until I have got / something I might have said" ("Said the Poet to the Analyst"). Thus Sexton "sees" her maternal guilt this way:

> . . . Ugly angels spoke to me. The blame,
> I heard them say, was mine. They tattled
> like green witches in my head, letting doom
> leak like a broken faucet;
> as if doom had flooded my belly and filled your bassinet,
> an old debt I must assume.
>
> ("The Double Image")

"The Double Image," a long poem in eight sections from *To Bedlam and Part Way Back,* offers a good example of the method by which Anne Sexton in her early poetry analyzes the nature of her madness and her identity in terms of personal relationships: here, with her mother and her daughter. The poem begins in the present tense: mother and daughter stand by a window in November, watching the leaves fall. Yet this mother and child have been parted for three years because of the mother's madness and attempted suicide; the physical fact of their reunion is the result of a series of psychological facts, and events, which the poet, explaining to her daughter, explores by going back in time and memory. When the child, Joyce, asks where the yellow leaves go, her mother answers rather cryptically, that "today believed / in itself, or else it fell." She continues:

> Today, my small child, Joyce,
> love your self's self where it lives.
> There is no special God to refer to; or if there is,
> why did I let you grow
> in another place.
>
> (part 1)

She then offers, in six poems, her memories to explain this advice.

Briefly, she describes her first suicide attempt (directly resulting from her guilt over the child's first serious illness) and the mental hospital. Then she focuses on the years when she was "part way back from Bedlam," living with her mother ("Too late, / too late, to live with your mother, the witches said") while her' child lived elsewhere, occasionally visiting. The poem moves in anguish back and forth between the partial, inadequate relationship between the poet and her mother—

> I cannot forgive your suicide, my mother said.
> And she never could. She had my portrait
> done instead.
>
> (part 2)

Only my mother grew ill.
She turned from me, as if death were catching,
as if death transferred,
as if my dying had eaten inside of her.
That August you were two, but I timed my days with doubt.
On the first of September she looked at me
and said I gave her cancer.
They carved her sweet hills out
and still I couldn't answer.

(part 3)

—and the partial, inadequate relationship between the poet and her daughter:

> Once I mailed you a picture of a rabbit
> and a postcard of Motif number one,
> as if it were normal
> to be a mother and be gone.
>
> (part 3)

I could not get you back
except for weekends. You came
each time, clutching the picture of a rabbit
that I had sent you. . . .
. . . .
The first visit you asked my name.
. . . I will forget
how we bumped away from each other like marionettes

337

on strings. It wasn't the same
as love, letting weekends contain
us.

(part 7)

The fragmented nature of these relationships is poised against
the poet's constant recognition of a profound underlying
identity between herself and her mother, herself and her
daughter: "Your smile is like your mother's, the artist said"
(part 2).

> During the sea blizzards
> she had her
> own portrait painted.
> A cave of a mirror
> placed on the south wall;
> matching smile, matching contour.
> And you resembled me; unacquainted
> with my face, you wore it. But you were mine
> after all.

(part 4)

The poet is caught between two images of herself that reflect her
to herself, but each only partially; because as reflections they rely
on her for their identity as much as she relies on them. And she
has no sense of herself, of who she is, only guilt for the kind of
daughter and mother she thinks she might be.

To talk about a condition of simultaneous separation and
identity, the poem projects a series of "double images." The
central double image is the pair of portraits, mother and daugh-
ter, in "the house that waits / still, on top of the sea," where
"two portraits hang on opposite walls" (part 5). Yet mirrors,
windows, and people themselves also reflect the idea, as the
poem's words describe the portraits:

> In south light, her smile is held in place,
> her cheeks wilting like a dry
> orchid; my mocking mirror, my overthrown
> love, my first image. She eyes me from that face,

that stony head of death
I had outgrown.
. . . .

And this was the cave of the mirror,
that double woman who stares
at herself, as if she were petrified
in time—two ladies sitting in umber chairs.
You kissed your grandmother
and she cried.

(part 6)

Analyzing those years of the portraits in part 5, the poet is, I think, also describing the movement of her poem:

. . . And I had to learn
why I would rather
die than love, how your innocence
would hurt and how I gather
guilt like a young intern
his symptoms, his certain evidence.

(part 5)

Part 7, the poem's final section, returns to the present tense of part 1: "Now you stay for good / . . . You call me *mother* and I remember my mother again, / somewhere in greater Boston, dying." It returns to mother and daughter at the window, looking out on the world, another double image. Yet the poem ends with a final memory, the mother's memory of her child as an infant, "all wrapped and moist / and strange at my heavy breast. / I needed you," in order that the poet may offer her understanding of herself to her daughter:

I, who was never quite sure
about being a girl, needed another
life, another image to remind me.
And this was my worst guilt; you could not cure
nor soothe it. I made you to find me.

(part 7)

The initial realization of her connection with her daughter had led the poet *into* madness: "as if doom had flooded my belly and filled your bassinet, / an old debt I must assume" (part 1); now an understanding of the same connection has led her out of madness. The difference, predictable in psychoanalytic terms, lies not in any severing of the connection, but in a dissolution of the guilt that arose from it. "I made you to find me," says the poet. And why not, because surely in some ways I am you and you are me, a girl child that I have made in my woman's body; and in other ways you are not me, I am not you, for I am mother, while you are child. We are a double image.

The ending and beginning of the poem focus upon the poet and her daughter, because this relationship, although dependent for its very being upon that other double image, the poet-daughter and *her* mother, can lead into life, while the other one cannot. This is not only because the poet's mother is literally dying, but because the guilt involved with that relationship is not gone. Whatever understanding has been achieved is partial and has come too late: "Too late to be forgiven now, the witches said" (part 2). The mother had accused her daughter of causing her death, and the poet could not answer, feeling the truth of the accusation, and feeling guilty for it.

The poem has demonstrated what the poet meant when in part 1 she advised loving oneself's self where it lives. True relationships between people, any kind of relationships, but especially those between people of blood ties, where a profound connection or identity exists, cannot occur unless each member of the pair is secure in her own identity. Granted that that identity may depend upon and even arise out of the relationship, it must yet be distinct: the person cannot *confuse* herself with the other person in the relationship. The double image can be both positive and negative, as it is in this poem: negative when it reflects beings who are creating their identities out of the reflections that they see, that in turn are creating identities out of the reflections that they see, that in turn, and on and on, into infinity; positive when each watcher sees another person who is like herself, who reflects herself, but who also reflects her own self!

If, as "The Double Image" and many of her early poems reveal, the cause of Sexton's madness and its accompanying desire for death has been her woman's situation, experience, identity, it is also true that the affirmation of life at which she arrives through the acts of her poems is founded in her womanhood. "Live," the final poem in her third book, *Live or Die,* helps her to locate the source of and reason for life in woman's situation, experience, identity.

> Today life opened inside me like an egg
> and there inside
> after considerable digging
> I found the answer.
> What a bargain!
> There was the sun,
> her yolk moving feverishly,
> tumbling her prize—
> and you realize that she does this daily!
> I'd known she was a purifier
> but I hadn't thought
> she was solid,
> hadn't known she was an answer.
>
> ("Live")

Life, of course, comes from inside herself—spiritually as well as physically. It is an egg, is life; and an egg is the sun, for the sun is an egg, for the sun is life; and it is not outside herself at all, for her to bask or not to bask in its (reflected) light. No, it is *inside* herself, and it is she who must deliver it, give it birth, make life happen. It is she who makes the world; it is an extension of her very body. "So I say *Live* / and turn my shadow three times round":

> So I won't hang around in my hospital shift,
> repeating The Black Mass and all of it.
> I say *Live, Live* because of the sun,
> the dream, the excitable gift.

Being a poet causes Anne Sexton to understand herself as possessor of "the excitable gift," because the act of poetry unites understanding with experience; its vision is insight. Though her poetry begins as therapy for her personal salvation, because it is a public act it reaches out to others. Yet it is always rooted in her personal self, her private life, as is the sun. It does not, like much of the "confessional" poetry of men, abstract or generalize upon its own experiences, either explicitly or implicitly; nevertheless, it communicates to others and offers its gift. In an early poem, "For John, Who Begs Me Not to Enquire Further" (*To Bedlam and Part Way Back*),[12] Sexton herself tries to explain how this gift works. Commenting upon her explorations of self, of "that narrow diary of my mind," she finds their purpose to have been, not beauty, but "a certain sense of order there." If she had tried "to give [him] something else, / something outside of myself," he would not then know "that the worst of anyone / can be, finally, / an accident of hope." Generalizing, in other words, destroys the very meaning sought.

> I tapped my own head;
> it was glass, an inverted bowl.
> It is a small thing
> to rage in your own bowl.
> At first it was private.
> Then it was more than myself;
> it was you, or your house
> or your kitchen.
> And if you turn away
> because there is no lesson here
> I will hold my awkward bowl,
> with all its cracked stars shining
> like a complicated lie,
> and fasten a new skin around it
> as if I were dressing an orange
> or a strange sun.
> Not that it was beautiful,
> but that I found some order there.
> There ought to be something special
> for someone
> in this kind of hope.
>
> ("For John, Who Begs Me Not to Enquire Further")

"A Middle-aged Witch, Me"

Love Poems (1969),[13] the volume that follows *Live or Die,* is a further extension of the decision for life into the living experience of love; it is almost a postscript to the previous volume. It is with the next book of poems, *Transformations* (1971),[14] that a major development, if not a transformation, does in fact begin to occur. Here Sexton shows where her journey from patient to poet has led her. It has led her to understanding the positive potential of herself as "middle-aged witch, me." Previous to this volume, she has equated madwoman and witch: "I have gone out, a possessed witch, / haunting the black air, braver at night" ("Her Kind," *To Bedlam and Part Way Back*). The refrain of "Her Kind" develops as follows: "A woman like that is not a woman, quite. / I have been her kind"; "A woman like that is misunderstood. / I have been her kind"; "A woman like that is not ashamed to die. / I have been her kind." The green witches of "The Double Image" who spoke inside Sexton's head of truth asked for death in payment for insight. Madness must lead to death, because the mad are "magic talking to itself, / noisy and alone" ("You, Doctor Martin"). "Talking" is a key word here, and equally so is "alone." Nobody listens; the language of the mad, like the world of women, is private. Nobody (the world) *cares* to hear, to know; for the world would not like what it learned. Yet if no one listens, the voice destroys itself with its truths. As has often been pointed out, the distance between fool or madman and poet is not great. Nor is the space between madwoman and woman poet, but it is less frequently traversed. Madwomen are doubly relegated to the private world, as mad and as women, while "poet" traditionally belongs to the male, the public world. The voice of the poet is a public voice; the poet's words affect other people: they may even cause changes, action. It is a voice of power. As Sexton's analyst had told her, poems can mean something to someone. For Sexton, as woman, the move from patient to poet has been a voyage from dependence and powerlessness to independence and power. By rooting her public voice in her private experience, by creating a public persona, witch, out of her private self, witch, she is able to discuss the race in addition to herself. The witch is a wisewoman, storyteller, seer. A witch works magic: her magic is and has always been the magic of words, so that the word "magic" in the line from "You, Doctor Martin" is also a key word. Thus it is fitting that Sexton's poetic language itself, from *Transformations* on, embodies and expresses this development.

Her power as poet arises from the power, the magic of words: the witch/poet's spells make things happen; they plant "words in you like grass seed" ("Iron Hans").[15] In her early poetry, Sexton, as madwoman and potential suicide (only "part way back"), had to control her images, her metaphors and similes of association, by the conscious forms of meter, rhyme, and the sentence itself, which consistently supplied the links between images of insight. In *Transformations* Sexton begins to abandon a great deal of this "control," because, I think, she feels in control. Now bold figures of association cast their spell with little to mediate their effect.

In *Transformations* Sexton begins to extend her original themes. In later volumes, *The Book of Folly*[16] and *The Death Notebooks*,[17] she will make her own myths. Here, she is warming up on Grimms' scales. She retells *Grimms' Fairy Tales*, with "the speaker in this case / . . . a middle-aged witch, me." These tales do for the history of the race what the earlier poems did for Sexton's personal history: they attempt to create the truth by bridging the gap between the present of adult experience, the potential madness underlying the everyday, and the past of childhood, dream, and archetype. Like the earlier poetry, these poems move from present to past (the therapy situation), not from the traditional once-upon-a-time to the moral that encompasses the present and all future time. They begin with present-day examples of situations of which the tales are archetypes, and Dame Sexton feels no compunction against using herself as a present-day example.

> If you danced from midnight
> to six A.M. who would understand?
> . . . .
>
> The night nurse
> with her eyes slit like Venetian blinds,
> she of the tubes and the plasma,
> listening to the heart monitor,
> the death cricket bleeping,
> she who calls you "we"
> and keeps vigil like a ballistic missile,
> would understand.
>
> ("The Twelve Dancing Princesses")

Many are the deceivers:
. . . .
And I. I too.
Quite collected at cocktail parties,
meanwhile in my head
I'm undergoing open-heart surgery.
The heart, poor fellow,
pounding on his little tin drum
with a faint death beat.
The heart, that eyeless beetle,
enormous that Kafka beetle,
running panicked through his maze,
never stopping one foot after the other
one hour after the other
until he gags on an apple
and it's all over.

("Red Riding Hood")

Here Sexton's characteristic figures of association are especially bold: the juxtaposition of seemingly incongruous material that, upon contact, produces sparks, shocks of definition, revelation—"her eyes slit like Venetian blinds"; "keeps vigil like a ballistic missile"; "The heart, that eyeless beetle, / enormous that Kafka beetle." The similes and epithet-metaphors embedded in the "fairy" part of the tales are particularly interesting, as they enact in microcosm the present to past movement of the poems: "tenor" belongs to the tale, the past, while "vehicle" belongs to the present, specifically modern situation—"[Rumpelstiltskin] tore himself in two. / Somewhat like a split broiler"; "The King looked like Munch's *Scream*"; "at the wedding the princesses averted their eyes / and sagged like old sweatshirts."

The tales that Dame Sexton chooses from Grimms' collection deal with her favorite themes: madness, death, and women. A cluster of the stories, "Snow White and the Seven Dwarfs," "The White Snake," "The Little Peasant," "Rapunzel," "Cinderella," "Red Riding Hood," "The Twelve Dancing Princesses," and "Briar Rose (Sleeping Beauty)," project without idealism the possible roles for women in the world. Young girls, heroines and princesses, begin in a state of mindless natural beauty, in an innocence and purity that is defined by its total physicality: "a daughter as lovely as a grape . . . / Poor grape with no one to pick. / Luscious and round and sleek" ("Rumpelstiltskin"); "The princess was as ripe as a tangerine. / Her breasts purred up and down like a cat" ("Godfather Death"):

> No matter what life you lead
> the virgin is a lovely number:
> cheeks as fragile as cigarette paper,
> arms and legs made of Limoges,
> lips like Vin Du Rhône,
> rolling her china-blue doll eyes
> open and shut.
> Open to say,
> Good Day Mama,
> and shut for the thrust
> of the unicorn.
> She is unsoiled.
> She is as white as a bonefish.
>> ("Snow White and the Seven Dwarfs")

They move to the inevitable corruption of sexuality—"They lay together upon the yellowy threads [Rapunzel's hair], / swimming through them / like minnows through kelp / and they sang out benedictions like the Pope" ("Rapunzel")—and thence to either meaninglessness or madness (or both).

> Meanwhile Snow White held court,
> rolling her china-blue doll eyes open and shut
> and sometimes referring to her mirror
> as women do.
>> ("Snow White and the Seven Dwarfs")

> Briar Rose
> was an insomniac. . .
> . . . .
> Each night I am nailed into place
> and I forget who I am.
> Daddy?
> That's another kind of prison.

> It's not the prince at all,
> but my father
> drunkenly bent over my bed,
> circling the abyss like a shark,
> my father thick upon me
> like some sleeping jellyfish.

("Briar Rose")

Like proper fairy tales, these abound with witches, for the witch has been traditionally the figure of the woman past middle age. Many of these women are embittered ex-princesses, like the wicked stepmother of "Snow White," "a beauty in her own right, / though eaten, of course, by age," or embittered spinsters, like the thirteenth fairy of "Briar Rose," "her fingers as long and thin as straws, / her eyes burnt by cigarettes, / her uterus an empty teacup." Primarily, their power is for evil, evil to aid in the corruption of innocence, corrupting the young into their own state of bitter age. Only Dame Sexton herself, because she is a poet, has broken the system and works for truth, if not goodness:

> And then I knew that the voice
> of the spirits had been let in—
> as intense as an epileptic aura—
> and that no longer would I sing
> alone.

("The White Snake")

There are no mothers and daughters in these tales, only daughters and lecherous fathers or evil stepmothers. Only once does Sexton attempt an analysis of a kind of mother-daughter relationship in the story of "Rapunzel," and here both the questions and the answers are fraught with ambiguity, as Sexton trods on dangerous ground in postulating any possible kind of salvation for women in the real world.

"Rapunzel" begins this way: "A woman / who loves a woman / is forever young." It is the tale of a witch, Mother Gothel, who had a magic garden, "more beautiful than Eve's." But this witch, unlike Eve, is a spinster. When a pregnant woman yearns for a magic root in her garden, the rampion, "a kind of harebell more potent than penicillin," the witch strikes a bargain, "typical enough in those times," with the woman's husband whom she catches in the garden: he promises his child to her. This is, of course, Rapunzel, "another name for the life-giving rampion." The witch vows that none but she will ever see or touch the beautiful girl and locks her in a high tower. Together, the pseudo-mother and daughter "play mother-me-do / all day." The witch sings:

> Give me your nether lips
> all puffy in their art
> and I will give you angel fire in return.
> We are two clouds
> glistening in the bottle glass.
> We are two birds
> washing in the same mirror.
> We were fair game
> but we have kept out of the cesspool.
> We are strong.
> We are the good ones.
> Do not discover us
> for we lie together all in green
> like pond weeds.
> Hold me, my young dear, hold me.

But the prince comes, as he always seems to do. Rapunzel is startled at this "beast . . . / with muscles on his arms / like a bag of snakes," by the "moss on his legs," and the "prickly plant" that "grows on his cheeks."

> Yet he dazzled her with his answers.
> Yet he dazzled her with his dancing stick.

When the so-called happy ending has occurred, Sexton pronounces upon it this way:

> They lived happily as you might expect
> proving that mother-me-do
> can be outgrown,
> just as the fish on Friday,

just as a tricycle.
The world, some say,
is made up of couples.
A rose must have a stem.

As for Mother Gothel, her heart shrinks to the size of a pin, never again to say "Hold me, my young dear, / hold me, / and only as she dreamt of the yellow hair / did moonlight sift into her mouth."

These tales are insistent upon the uncompromising reality of the real world, a place where neither childhood (tricycles), nor ideals (the fish on Friday), nor fantasy (dreaming of yellow hair) have any place or power. The love of Mother Gothel for her "daughter" seems to belong to all three; and although the plot of the poem, of the fairy tale, allows her no recourse, the language of the poem seems to be holding out for some other kind of validity: the bag of snakes and the dancing stick are posed against the two birds washing in the same mirror, the two clouds glistening in the bottle glass. The prince seems like a figurative as well as a literal comedown for Rapunzel, the "cesspool" out of which lesbian love with Mother Gothel had been keeping her. The other tales support this interpretation, with their portrayals of the fate of princesses. After having read all their happy endings (Cinderella and her prince, for example, living "they say" happily ever after, "like two dolls in a museum case / . . . never telling the same story twice, / never getting a middle-aged spread, / their darling smiles pasted on for eternity. / Regular Bobbsey Twins"), one might prefer the moonlight of Mother Gothel's dreams. Yet the questions remain: Were Rapunzel and Mother Gothel "the good ones?" Ought mother-me-do to be outgrown?

"For We Swallow Magic and We Deliver Anne"

The Book of Folly (1972) and *The Death Notebooks* (1974) are experimental, bold, frightening. The poet consorts with angels, Furies, Mary, Jesus, gods, and death in the writing of stories, poems, psalms. These works make it clear that she trusted her vision, wherever it might take her. The old themes are in no way gone, but their expression frequently occurs in a new dimension. It is difficult now to label this poetry "confessional," because the talking voice, immersing itself in memory and experience, is gone; the voice now chants or sings, and experience has been transformed into myth. Nevertheless, the poems still refuse to generalize, to abstract: the "awkward bowl" of Sexton's consciousness is more of a "strange sun" than ever: it is a dangerous and magical world of visionary truth-saying.

In her middle forties, Anne Sexton continued to be faithful to her own perceptions. Death became a major element in what she perceived: the death of age, the result of commitment to life. Two poems to her daughter Linda, at ages eleven and eighteen, about the coming of womanhood, document this change in tone. In "Little Girl, My String Bean, My Lovely Woman" (*Live or Die*), the poet says: "How can I say that I've known / just what you know and just where you are?"

> Oh, darling, let your body in,
> let it tie you in,
> in comfort.
> What I want to say, Linda,
> is that women are born twice.
> . . . .
> What I want to say, Linda,
> is that there is nothing in your body that lies.
> All that is new is telling the truth.
> I'm here, that somebody else,
> an old tree in the background.

In "Mother and Daughter" (*The Book of Folly*), the mother is at another stage in the process of physical connection and identification with her daughter, even as the daughter is at another stage, now a woman grown:

> Linda, you are leaving
> your old body now.
> You've picked my pocket clean
> and you've racked up all my
> poker chips and left me empty
> . . . .
> Question you about this
> and you will see my death

> drooling at these gray lips
> while you, my burglar, will eat
> fruit and pass the time of day.

"The Death Baby," a poem in six parts from *The Death Notebooks,* explores the nature of death in terms (now familiar) of woman's roles of daughter and mother. Death may be generalizable, and universal, since like birth it is an experience that all humans share; but one's own death is personal, private, peculiarly one's own. In this poem, Sexton is trying to know her death.

The poem is a process, perhaps of initiation: one knows death when one is ready, and when death is ready to be known. This process has six stages. In the first, the poet explores death in dreams; the "exploration" is not an analysis but a vision of dream death: her own death, as a baby, in the dreams of her older sister. The second death is by fantasy: the vision of a doll's death. The third is the lesson of death attempted, premature or false death: the vision, in the dream of the would-be suicide, is of an ice baby, an ice baby that rocks the dreamer and is rocked by the dreamer. The fourth is death by proxy: the vision is of the death of her mother, in which death becomes her mother's child, so that she can be neither her mother's daughter nor her mother's mother. The fifth is death averted: the vision of the attempt to kill death by friendship, a false vision. The sixth is death encountered in vision: death as a baby, to be rocked and to rock, where death is mother to its baby, baby to its mother, in an unending circle of mother and child. The poem is, of course, circular, its end in its beginning, but that is only to be expected in myths.

The poem begins:

> I was an ice baby.
> I turned to sky blue.
> My tears became two glass beads.
> My mouth stiffened into a dumb howl.
> They say it was a dream
> but I remember that hardening.

> (1. "Dreams")

Her older sister had dreamed, "nightly," of the death of the new baby: "'The baby turned to ice. / Somebody put her in the refrigerator / and she turned as hard as a Popsicle.'" But dreams are real experience, says the poem, and so the poet remembers "that hardening." Tears into glass beads, mouth stiffening into howl; and the refrigerator, too, the milk bottle hissing like a snake, caviar turning to lava, because "the rhythm of the refrigerator / had been disturbed" by the alien presence of a dying baby inside. (In yet another of her sister's dreams, the dogs think she is a bone, licking her apart, "loving" her until she is gone.) As always, it is the language of this poetry that effects its transformations. Yet it is difficult now to talk of metaphor or simile. "I was an ice baby"; "I turned to sky blue"; "The tomatoes vomited up their stomachs." Where is the comparison, either explicit or implicit? What is figurative here? Either nothing, or everything; but metaphor's transfer *from* literal *to* figurative is missing. This is, in fact, literal description of a visionary world, where any and all transformations into truth are possible. This is ritual, mantric language, with its significant repetitions and gnomic pronouncements: "I died seven times / in seven ways / letting death give me a sign, / letting death place his mark on my forehead" (3. "Seven Times").

The Dy–dee doll of part 2 has only two lives. Once the child Anne "snapped / her head off / and let it float in the toilet"; another time she melted under the sun lamp, "trying to get warm."

> She was a gloom,
> her face embracing
> her little bent arms.
> She died in all her rubber wisdom.

The deaths of the doll are another form of experiencing death in imagination and thus without its finality. The doll dies in misery and knowledge, embracing herself.

From the doll's two deaths, Sexton moves to her own "seven": the premature or false deaths of attempted suicide. In these attempts, she was getting to know her death, asking for a sign, asking to be marked by death: "And death took root in that sleep," in the dream experience of an ice baby; "and I rocked it / and was rocked by it. / Oh Madonna, hold me." The baby is herself; the baby is death.

The most compelling of the poem's six visions are parts 4 and 6: two pietàs. The fourth, "Madonna," I have called death by proxy; it describes her mother's death, and as any reader of Anne Sexton should know (as most women know), "A woman *is* her mother. / That's the main thing" ("Housewife").[18] Sexton's mother died "unrocked," "thrashing like a fish on the hook": "her rocking horse was pain / with vomit steaming from her mouth." It was a death of horror, for mother and daughter alike. The daughter would help, wants to "place my head in her lap / or even take her in my arms somehow / and fondle her twisted gray hair"; she wants to be mothered, to mother. But death has replaced Anne as her mother's "baby": "Her belly was big with another child, / cancer's baby, big as a football."

What sort of response can be made to death? In part 5, "Max," the poet and her friend Max make a pact "to beat death down with a stick. / To take over. / To build our death like carpenters." This entails talking turkey, shooting "words straight from the hip" when death comes; not being "polite." The pact, the talks, the conspiracy of the friends, is seen as a means, at first to avert and later to confront death. Yet it is a partial answer only, for in the moment of death one is alone.

The moment of death comes in the vision of part 6, "Baby." The description of the baby whom the poet rocks concentrates upon its eyes, which are made of glass, "as brittle as crystal." It is the ice baby of the refrigerator dreams, and the baby's sight reveals its knowledge: "Glass eye, ice eye, / primordial eye, / lava eye, / pin eye, / break eye, / how you stare back!" The death baby's gaze is like that of small children, because it knows exactly who she is: it has "worn my underwear," "read my newspaper." Poet and baby rock, locked in a death embrace:

> I rock. I rock.
> We plunge back and forth
> comforting each other.
> We are stone.
> We are carved, a pietà
> that swings and swings.
> . . . .
>
> I rock. I rock.
> You are my stone child

with still eyes like marbles.
There is a death baby
for each of us.
We own him.
His smell is our smell.
Beware. Beware.
There is a tenderness.
There is a love
for this dumb traveler
waiting in his pink covers.

This is Sexton's winter's tale, a myth that does not praise the new life that must always grow from old life but rather seeks to reconcile the death that also must grow from life. The central actors, and images, of both myths are the same, because both myths are complementary, existing always simultaneously: mother and child, child and mother—this is a woman's myth. One is born with one's death inside oneself, like an egg, or a baby. Through the process of living one transforms oneself into one's own death, through a process of hardening, stiffening, freezing. Each birth only hastens the process, so one grows from baby to child to daughter to mother: in the last act of birth, a mother gives birth to her own death, a death baby. The imagery of the poem underlines the nature of this process, beginning with its initial statement of truth: "I was an ice baby." "Ice," "I," "eyes," are all equated in the poem: death, identity, vision. Even as the ice baby of part I stiffens in that strange morgue, the refrigerator, so the poem's protagonist continues throughout the life of the poem, which follows the temporal course of her life, to stiffen, to grow towards death, until in the final pietà she and the death baby are carved stone, "a pietà / that swings and swings." They are a statue of themselves, their own tombstone. How can stone yet swing and swing? Because *rocking* is the primary act of the poem, an extraordinary pun on the word "rock" that can link stone and maternity. *Rocking:* turning into stone, mothering—I give birth to my own death. I am my mother's baby; I am my mother's death; I am my mother; I am my baby; I am my death. A cold vision, an icy vision, a crystal vision of truth, as Sexton looks into the glass beads of her own eye and finds herself, who is her death, reflected there. These reflections say that the mirroring process cannot go on ad infinitum, for glass turns to stone.

The poem ends this way:

> Someday,
> heavy with cancer or disaster,
> I will look up at Max
> and say: It is time.
> Hand me the death baby
> and there will be
> that final rocking.

There is no escaping death, but to know that one can say, "It is time. / Hand me the death baby" indicates that is the only possible way one might yet be powerful. To know and to ask.

Power. The word is everywhere in this essay; the sense of power comes through more and more strongly in the poetry of Anne Sexton. The power comes from making poems that "mean something to someone": from the power of magic, which has always been that of sending words to effect changes, to cause action. The power of the poet whose words are let loose upon the world. Yet the power in Sexton's words comes into them from her insight into herself; from her understanding of her identity in terms of both her own self and the others with whom she interacts, relates. Because she knew who she was, she could give out this knowledge. And the process was wonderfully reciprocal, circular; for she understood who she was with her poems; her words caused her to know who she was. She brought forth from herself the power of her vision, let loose upon the world with words: an egg, a "strange sun"—"the dream, the excitable gift."

NOTES

1. Barbara Kevles, "The Art of Poetry: Anne Sexton," *Paris Review* 13 (1970–71): 160–91.

2. Kevles, 161.

3. Betty Friedan, *The Feminine Mystique* (New York: W. W. Norton, 1963), 11.

4. *To Bedlam and Part Way Back* (Boston: Houghton Mifflin, 1960).

5. *Live or Die* (Boston: Houghton Mifflin, 1966).

6. *Kevles*, 162.

7. *To Bedlam and Part Way Back*, 3.

8. *Live or Die*, 8.

9. *To Bedlam and Part Way Back*, 58.

10. *To Bedlam and Part Way Back*, 17.

11. *To Bedlam and Part Way Back*, 66.

12. *To Bedlam and Part Way Back*, 51–52.

13. *Love Poems* (Boston: Houghton Mifflin, 1969).

14. *Transformations* (Boston: Houghton Mifflin, 1971).

15. *Transformations*, 44.

16. *The Book of Folly* (Boston: Houghton Mifflin, 1972).

17. *The Death Notebooks* (Boston: Houghton Mifflin, 1974).

18. *All My Pretty Ones* (Boston: Houghton Mifflin, 1962), 48.

STEPHANIE DEMETRAKOPOULOS

From "The Nursing Mother and Feminine Metaphysics"

The knowledge gained from breast-feeding is not a passing one, but a reference point in the consciousness of many women for their whole lives. Anne Sexton's poetry demonstrates the primal and permanent qualities of this knowledge. In her last poetic affirmation of life, the nine "Psalms" which conclude *The Death Notebooks,* Anne Sexton portrays milk as feminine and cosmic grace. An earlier reference in the book foreshadows the strength of the symbol of milk as transcendent and celebratory. Sexton imagines a dream mother: "At the cup of her breasts / I drew wine,"[1] an image which suggests the Holy Grail or the cup of communion. The earlier sections of the book also feature the symbol of a dead baby, which juxtaposes with and deepens the later exaltation in the "Eighth Psalm":

> For the baby suckles and there is a people made of milk for her to use. There are milk trees to hiss her on. There are milk beds in which to lie and dream of a warm room. There are milk fingers to fold and unfold. There are milk bottoms that are wet and caressed and put into their cotton.

> For there are many worlds of milk to walk through under the moon.[2]

In the last five lines of the final "Tenth Psalm," Sexton blesses with milk her personal icon of human misery—the rat, her shadow brother Christopher, and herself:

From *Listening to Our Bodies* (Boston: Beacon Press, 1983). Originally published in *Soundings* 65, no. 4 (1982). Reprinted by permission of the author.

For they hung up a picture of a rat and the rat smiled and held
out his hand.
For the rat was blessed on that mountain. He was given a
white bath.
For the milk in the skies sank down upon them and tucked
them in.[3]

The Death Notebooks thus ends in celebration of milk as the
connective tissue, the flow, the indisputable plenitude of a lov-
ing ground of being. In her later poetry, Sexton unfortunately
seeks connections with a masculine god; she no longer projects
her own feminine images into a vision of a patterned, containing
and loving universe. This, I believe, is part of what precipitated
her suicide.

NOTES

1. Anne Sexton, *The Death Notebooks* (Boston: Houghton Mifflin,
1974), 31.
2. *The Death Notebooks*, 94.
3. *The Death Notebooks*, 99.

STEVEN GOULD AXELROD

Anne Sexton's Rowing Toward God

I met Anne Sexton once, at her home, the summer before she died in 1974. Wearing a bright yellow dress, she was gracious and incredibly lovely. Unlike other poets I've met, she refused to say unkind things about rival poets. She told me that she hated roses, that her favorite flower was the daisy, which grows wild by the side of Massachusetts roads. In my mind's eye now, in her yellow dress, she looks to me like a daisy—morally innocent, her gaiety a badge of her despair. And yet *The Awful Rowing Toward God* reveals that out of this despair grew faith. Ultimately the struggle toward belief proves the single most important fact about her life, her poetry. Wallace Stevens has written that "it can lie in the temperament of very few of us to write poetry in order to find God," but that is precisely what Anne Sexton did in her more recent books, and perhaps throughout her poetic career. In this last volume, her "awful rowing" reaches its goal.

The poems of *The Awful Rowing Toward God* are written in the free style characteristic of Sexton's later volumes. In contrast to the highly crafted poems of her first books, these poems resemble episodes of consciousness rather than completed, uni-fied objects. Like many another American writer, she shed the coat of form in her drive toward naked truth. These "poems," then, should be seen as psychological jottings and prophetic notes. Frequently her "language fails," Sexton admits; yet in the manner of Whitman, the poems are not to be understood merely as a literary performance. They are acts of the mind in discovery of itself, its world, its God. For Sexton as for the other American prophets, from Whitman and Dickinson to Stevens and Gins-berg, poetry is a "church" and the words "whisper something

Review of *The Awful Rowing Toward God, Modern Poetry Studies* 6, no. 2 (1975). Reprinted by permission of the author.

holy." The volume may be roughly divided into halves, each with its own special emphasis.

The first half focuses on the poet's inner self and its painful frictions with outer environment. The section contains the kind of self-explorations we think of as typical of Sexton's art. The tone is almost unrelievedly anguished. An overwhelming, incredible self-loathing dominates her consciousness, turning every possible happiness sour. The poet thinks herself "a pig in a trenchcoat"—a swine partially disguised as a person. In other images, she describes herself as a witch, as worse than Hitler. She is internally possessed by a "gnawing pestilential rat," by "saws working through my heart," by a "beggar" who needs to be cut out with a scissors, by a "plague," by "acid," by a "crab." Images of pain abound, as if only pain can awaken. This is a world where the day drives nails into the heart, where light pokes, where courage is "a small coal / that you kept swallowing," where holy words themselves only "pinch me / into the grave." This intolerable physical pain figures the poet's psychic pain, and has several implications. It suggests her moral horror at the evil in the world—frequently symbolized by the Nazis—and at the kindred evil she carries within her. On a related level of meaning, the pain derives from her separation from or "ignorance" of God. And finally and paradoxically, the pain is the force which drives her to God.

The peripeteia comes in "The Sickness Unto Death," the poem at the exact numerical center of the book. The spiritual condition adumbrated in the preceding poems is here retrospectively summarized:

> I kept saying:
> I've got to have something to hold on to.
> People gave me Bibles, crucifixes,
> a yellow daisy,
> but I could not touch them,
> I who was a house full of bowel movement,
> I who was a defaced altar,
> I who wanted to crawl toward God
> could not move nor eat bread.
>
> So I ate myself.

But then comes a moment of grace: Jesus "put His mouth to mine / and gave me His air."

The second half of *The Awful Rowing* devotes itself almost exclusively to the quest for God. This theme, latent in all of Sexton's poetry and indeed in virtually all "Confessional" poetry, now at last becomes explicit and primary. The non-Christian reader may be initially discomfitted by these God poems, yet Sexton knows that and, indeed, shares the discomfiture: "As I write this sentence I too writhe." She reverses the process of Robert Lowell's "Beyond the Alps"; much against her will she arrives at the city of God. For me, the most compelling of her God poems is "Is It True?," which openly confronts the question of belief. Wanting to "pour gasoline over my evil body / and light it," she turns instead to Christ who forgives her everything. She does not know that Christ is divine, she imagines that he is, she needs to imagine that he is; and this need to imagine is itself a kind of evidence.

> Is it true?
> I can only imagine it is true
> that Jesus comes with his eggful of miracles,
> his awful death, his blackboard of graffiti.

The gift which the poet receives from Christ she shares with her reader in the poems that close the volume. It is the gift of "hope everywhere," of imaginative harmony of self, world and God, of believing oneself loved. In the last poem of the volume, "The Rowing Endeth," she has come through pain, despite herself, to existential faith. God, she, and "the absurd" commune in laughter. In her final words she gives thanks to God for "that untamable, eternal, gut-driven ha-ha / and lucky love." The resolution, as the poet herself knew, goes beyond poetry to belief. Yet even as poetry, *The Awful Rowing Toward God* is an effective piece of work, despite some characteristic unevenness. In its best passages, emotions are communicated with powerful intensity, and part of the world we have made and live in is revealed for us, as if for the first time.

Sexton excels at what I would tentatively term the "bourgeois image." Plymouth fenders, salad anchovies, batter, Coke bottles, tension headaches, Cannon towels, frozen haddock, pantsuits and names of hotel chains comprise the sensuous surface of this verse. These images are sometimes used satirically, but more often straightforwardly. In an age in which obscenities are part of the orthodox poetic diction, Sexton has daringly enlarged the resources of our literary tradition by including the truly quotidian, thus ratifying the importance of our everyday existences. In these poems, the extraordinary occurs in the language of the ordinary. Sexton's God leaves baskets covered with Cannon towels. Any list of the best poems in *The Awful Rowing* would probably include "Rowing," "The Witch's Life," "The Sickness Unto Death," "The Wall," "Is It True?," "Frenzy," and "The Rowing Endeth." It is consoling to know—and to think that she herself knew—that in these poems written at the end of her life Anne Sexton was writing as well as she ever had written.

MAXINE KUMIN

Sexton's *The Awful Rowing Toward God*

The poems in *The Awful Rowing Toward God* were written during a crisis time in Anne Sexton's life, a period of great personal anguish and at the same time of intense, even manic creativity. There is no psychic distance between the poet and the poem; on the contrary, the poem is an almost tangible physical extension of the psyche, a kind of third hand or eye. Robert Motherwell said, in an essay on art, "there is a certain point on the curve of anguish where one encounters the comic." So it is in these poems. They are all signed with her vivid imagery. Again and again we are tossed on the curve, saved, refreshed, by the satire, the self-mock, the comic inner lining of the macabre. Reticence forms no part of Sexton's style, nor economy, nor brusque reason. The poem is a defense against isolation, against memories so terrible that they erode the senses to the edge of hallucination.

We were for eighteen years warm personal friends. During the late winter of 1973, while these poems were being constructed out of blood and sorrow and fury, I was living in Kentucky as writer-in-residence at Centre College. We had agreed before I left Boston to divide the long-distance telephone bill; further, we had agreed to talk on the reduced-rate side of the ledger, after 5:00 P.M. or before 8:00 A.M. My rooms in Danville abutted a Baptist church with a dependable clock that pinged on the quarters and tolled the hours. And every afternoon at five, a concert of Baptist hymns. But just as the carillons embarked on their opening measure, the ringing of my phone would float up through those other bells, and we would talk across the early dark of a Boston winter into the twilight of a bluegrass one. For the most part, we dispensed with amenities of time and place quickly and got down to the professional business of the

From "A Memorial for Anne Sexton," edited by A. Poulin, Jr., *American Poetry Review* 4, no. 3 (1975). Reprinted by permission of the author.

363

poems—mostly hers, for she was writing with the urgency of a fugitive one length ahead of the posse. As indeed she was.

One other fact. As is evident from her poetry, Anne Sexton was strongly attracted to, indeed sought vigorously a kind of absolutism in religion that was missing from the Protestantism of her inheritance. She wanted God as a sure thing, an Old Testament avenger admonishing his Chosen People, an authoritarian yet forgiving God decked out in sacrament and ceremony. Judaism and Catholicism each exerted a strong gravitational pull. Divine election, confession and absolution, the last rites, these were her longings. And then an elderly, sympathetic priest, one of many priests she encountered—accosted might be a better word—along the way, said a saving thing to her, said the magic and simple fact that kept her alive at least a year beyond her time, and made the awful rowing a possibility. "God is in your typewriter," he told her. Thus she went to her typewriter and thus, according to your lights, she found, or invented Him.

CAROLE FERRIER

Anne Sexton
Demystifier or Mystic?

Sexton's poetry conveys a sense of powerfully felt experience in strikingly concrete images. Thus, she fuses a sense of emotional and psychological depths with their context of the mundane facts of women's lives. Sexton used as epigraph to her second volume, *All My Pretty Ones,* a passage from a letter of Franz Kafka to Oscar Pollak, in which he asserts that a literary work should plumb the depths of the individual psychology of the writer and find an echo in the consciousness of the reader, making her or him feel as if "lost in a forest remote from all human habitation—a book should serve as the ax for the frozen sea within us." In an interview she expressed the effort involved in producing this kind of work: "you're always fighting to find out what it is that you want to say. You have to go deeper and deeper each time."[1] This is the same search as that which Adrienne Rich deals with in her poem "Diving into the Wreck" or Sylvia Plath does in "The Colossus": a symbolic descent below the surface in quest of understanding. A more original image of the same kind of search is found in a poem from a more recent volume, *The Awful Rowing Toward God,* in which the poet imagines herself in an elevator in a New York many-storied hotel:

> These are the warnings
> that you must forget
> if you're climbing out of yourself.
> If you're going to smash into the sky.

Review of *45 Mercy Street, Hecate: A Women's Interdisciplinary Journal* (Brisbane) 4, no. 2 (1978). Reprinted by permission of the author and the publisher.

> . . . .
> Floor six thousand:
> the stars,
> skeletons on fire,
> their arms singing.
> And a key,
> a very large key,
> that opens something—
> some useful door—
> somewhere—
> up there.
>
> ("Riding the Elevator into the Sky")

But this key to the understanding of experience to which Sexton refers, like that Ginsberg imagines his mother Naomi giving in *Kaddish,* never opens the gate outside which she waits like Kafka's seeker at the door of the truth. Her evocation of the force of experience is powerful and clear, but her poems never go beyond a certain point toward analysis of the situation she so tellingly documents in an attempt to understand ways of transforming it.

Is it even reasonable to ask that a poet do this, and can poetry be expected to do it? Is it perhaps enough that the experiences are forcibly presented, and the psychological motivation clarified? The material with which Sexton is centrally concerned: "madness," schizophrenia, "love," mental hospitals, suicide, is also that upon which the anti-psychiatry school of the later sixties, notably Laing, Szasz and Cooper, built their theory. In her earlier poetry, we find Sexton dealing with these experiences in order to begin a demystification of them. Sexton's insights are conveyed in an encoded language, contrasting with the assertive mode of anti-psychiatric theory, as in, for example, Laing: "There is no such condition as schizophrenia, but the label is a social fact and the social fact a political event."[2] The social fact of the hospitalization of members of a society in order to bring their vision into line with the commonly held view is dramatised in some of Sexton's early poems. "You, Doctor Martin" draws out the patriarchal role played by the male doctor in the mental hospital. Read with Plath's poem "Daddy," the literary insight which parallels, and frequently precedes the psychological theory, in this case that of Szasz's *The Manufacture of Madness,* becomes clear.

Laing had tried to bridge the gap between theory and imaginative writing in "The Bird of Paradise," the concluding section of *The Politics of Experience.* The whole vexed question of the interaction between literary quality and clarity of political message is raised by this juxtaposition of literary and theoretical texts as vehicles for ideas and understanding. Conservative critics, conscious of the political force of some of Sexton's writing, attack it in terms of an alleged lack of artistic control: "no more than jottings from a psychoanalyst's notebook." (Simultaneously, the anti-psychiatry group are attacked as subjective and unscientific.) Sexton, in fact, is a highly conscious and careful artist who makes deliberate use of subtlety of both form and idea. The pervasively "crazy" mood of much of her earlier writing is conveyed by a use of dislocated rhythms and jumbled syntax; for an example of this we can go back again to "You, Doctor Martin":

> . . . Of course, I love you;
> you lean above the plastic sky,
> god of our block, prince of all the foxes.
> The breaking crowns are new
> that Jack wore. Your third eye
> moves among us and lights the separate boxes
> where we sleep or cry.

In this poem, the echoes of nursery rhyme and A. A. Milne are used with a sophisticated understanding of the potential of naïveté. A similar ingenuousness informs Sexton's repeated use of a Freudian frame of reference, with an at least partly ironic intention. Sexton has many poems about her relationship with her parents,[3] and particularly with her father, from the title poem of *All My Pretty Ones* to "The Truth the Dead Know" in which she expresses her lack of understanding of her relationship with them by the same means as Plath did in "The Colossus"— imaging them as cold stone figures:

> And what of the dead? They lie without shoes
> in their stone boats. They are more like stone

than the sea would be if it stopped. They refuse
to be blessed, throat, eye and knucklebone.

In her later *The Book of Folly,* Sexton includes a whole sequence
dealing with her relationship with her father entitled "The
Death of the Fathers." Insights originally expressed in works of
literature can subsequently be used to develop theory, as Freud's
use of Greek drama and the work of the anthropologist James
Fraser on the idea of the golden bough illustrate. The anti-psy-
chiatry group make little direct reference to literature, but the
parallels between Cooper's concept of the "death of the family"
and the sense of the destructive power of family relationships
embodied in work such as Sexton's poems about her father are
striking.

In the account of the position of women in relation to house-
work and childcare also, a similar process of interaction of ideas
between literature and theory can be seen. The poetry of Rich,
Plath, and Sexton preceded the first works of the second wave of
the women's movement in the U.S.—though not the lone voice
of Simone de Beauvoir, who as early as the late forties was
presenting her analysis of the condition of the second sex, in-
cluding the role played by women at home in perpetuating
bourgeois social relations:

> But she has no other job than to maintain and provide for life
> in pure and unvarying generality; she perpetuates the species
> without change, she ensures the even rhythm of the days and
> the continuity of the home, seeing to it that the doors are
> locked.[4]

This perpetual and enclosed round of housework is also de-
scribed by Sexton in the poem "Housewife":

> Some women marry houses.
> It's another kind of skin; it has a heart,
> a mouth, a liver and bowel movements.
> The walls are permanent and pink.
> See how she sits on her knees all day,
> faithfully washing herself down.

Both Plath and Sexton were originally products of the *Ladies' Home Journal* ethos of the fifties; Sexton gives an account of her situation at the age of twenty-eight as follows:

I didn't know I had any creative depths. I was a victim of the American Dream, the bourgeois, middle-class dream. All I wanted was a little piece of life, to be married, to have children. I thought the nightmares, the visions, the demons would go away if there was enough love to put them down. . . .But one can't build little white picket fences to keep nightmares out. The surface cracked when I was about twenty-eight. I had a psychotic break and tried to kill myself.[5]

Plath's poem "Lesbos" had expressed a similar encoded account of this sense of isolation and non-communication endemic to the life of the woman in the home:

> You peer from the door,
> Sad hag. "Every woman's a whore.
> I can't communicate."
>
> I see your cute décor
> Close on you like the fist of a baby
> Or an anemone, that sea
> Sweetheart, that kleptomaniac.
>
> (*Winter Trees*)

On a different level, Sexton's poem "Cinderella" from *Transformations* comments ironically on the notion of marriage as leading to living happily ever after:

> like two dolls in a museum case
> never bothered by diapers or dust,
> never arguing over the timing of an egg,
> never telling the same story twice,
> never getting a middle-aged spread,
> their darling smiles pasted on for eternity.
> Regular Bobbsey Twins.
> That story.

An important feature of the work of some women writers of the sixties and seventies is a much greater explicitness about sexuality and the physical facts of women's lives than had previously been common. While Sexton does have some poems that show this, as for example "Old Dwarf Heart" in *All My Pretty Ones,* she is, generally speaking, more preoccupied with emotional and psychological states than with actual physical situations. This ties in with her almost total lack of recognition in her work of the economic base of the oppression of women which she so incisively documents. In the posthumously published *45 Mercy Street,* a sequence of poems called "The Divorce Papers" chart the breakdown of her marriage, largely through a series of images and feelings:

> And within the house
> ashes are being stuffed into my marriage,
> fury is lapping the walls,
> dishes crack on the shelves,
> a strangler needs my throat,
> the daughter has ceased to eat anything,
> the wife speaks of this
> but only the ice cubes listen.
>
> ("Landscape Winter")

Another long poem from this sequence is "The Break Away," focussing on a bunch of daisies; moving on to a tortured image of sexual antagonism and frustration:

> The daisies absorb it all—
> the twenty-five-year-old sanctioned love
> (If one could call such handfuls of fists
> and immobile arms *that!*)

The flowers have been sent to her by the man she is leaving her husband for, but she has few illusions about escape:

> I see two deaths,
> and the two men plod toward the mortuary of my heart,
> and though I willed one away in court today
> and I whisper dreams and birthdays into the other,

> they both die like waves breaking over me
> and I am drowning a little

A similar image of suffocation is central to "The Love Plant" which Sexton portrays as growing inside her, something that is also infectious:

> Perhaps I am becoming part of the green world
> and maybe a rose will just pop out of my mouth?
> Oh passerby, let me bite it off and spit it at you
> so you can say, "How nice!" and nod your thanks
> and walk three blocks to your lady love
> and she will stick it behind her ear
> not knowing it will crawl into her ear, her brain
> and drive her mad.

The surreal imagery of this poem evokes a sense of the feeling spreading cancerlike through the body of the woman, destroying her from within; she sees herself as "a pink doll with her frantic green stuffing." Beyond a certain point, we cannot find in Sexton any way out of the contradictions of the ideology of love to which women are conditioned to adhere. Some of the poems in *The Awful Rowing Toward God* escape into a kind of mysticism posing as philosophy. "The Sickness Unto Death," for example, describes some kind of spiritual experience:

> So I ate myself,
> bite by bite,
> and the tears washed me,
> wave after cowardly wave,
> swallowing canker after canker
> and Jesus stood over me looking down
> and He laughed to find me gone,
> and he put His mouth to mine
> and gave me His air.
>
> My kindred, my brother, I said
> and gave the yellow daisy
> to the crazy woman in the next bed.

Sexton's treatment of the theme of suicide, also, expresses the contradictions of a position of romantic individualism. Plath saw coming close to death as disposing of "a trash / to annihilate each decade" in her poem about suicide, "Lady Lazarus," but her ritual proved too dangerous. Sexton also is prone to glamourising to a degree the act of taking one's life, as her early poem about Plath's death, "Wanting to Die" shows:

> To thrust all that life under your tongue!—
> . . . .
>
> leaving the page of the book carelessly open,
> something unsaid, the phone off the hook
> and the love, whatever it was, an infection.

The supremely despairing individualism that sees suicide as a "cure" also expresses itself in a preoccupation with death found in Sexton's later work, particularly *The Death Notebooks* (1974):

> There is a love
> for this dumb traveler
> waiting in his pink covers.
> Someday,
> heavy with cancer or disaster
> I will look up at Max
> and say: It is time
> Hand me the death baby
> and there will be
> that final rocking.[6]

> ("The Death Baby")

In Frame's* recent novels also we find this fusion of ideas of love and death, along with a retreat further and further away from the world of everyday social interaction. Frame's *Daughter Buffalo* and *Intensive Care* are pervaded by the idea of the physical collapse of the body, surgery, and death. *45 Mercy Street* has several poems in which these kinds of images figure prominently; in "Food" the poet comments "Your nipples are stitched

---

*Janet Frame (b. 1924), New Zealand poet and novelist.—ED.

up like sutures / and although I suck / I suck air." In "Praying to Big Jack" we find images of

> . . . The brains as
> helpless as oysters in a pint container,
> the nerves like phone wires.
> God, take care, take infinite care
> with the tumor lest it spread like grease.

For the critic Alvarez, a preoccupation with death in literature justifies itself in these terms:

> The ultimate justification of the highbrow arts in an era when they themselves seem less and less convinced of their claims to attention and even existence . . . [is that] they survive morally by becoming, one way or another, an imitation of death in which their audience can share; to achieve this, the artist in his role of scapegoat, finds himself testing out his own death and vulnerability for and on himself.[7]

Morality is not a strategy for social change, though the archetypal figure of the scapegoat has enjoyed considerable historical appeal. Sexton clearly to a degree shares Alvarez's view of the artist; her recent volumes include a range of poems in which the figure of Jesus, with whom she imaginatively identifies, appears. "Making a Living" is a more sophisticated version of the earlier death and rebirth motif:

> His whole past was there with him
> and he ate that.
>
> At this point the whale
> vomited him back into the sea.
> . . . .
> Then he told the news media
> the strange details of his death
> and they hammered him up in the marketplace
> and sold him and sold him and sold him.
> My death the same.

When Anne Sexton committed suicide in October 1974, Denise Levertov wrote a response that expressed the political problem of this preoccupation:

> But alienation is of ethical value, is life-affirmative and conducive to creativity only when it is accompanied by a political consciousness that imagines and affirms (and works toward) an alternative to the society from which it turns away in disgust. Lacking this, the alienated person . . . becomes especially a prey to the exploitation that characterises capitalism and is its underlying principle [and] concurrently . . . internalizes the exploitive, unwittingly becoming *self*-exploitive.[8]

While, to a degree, "the personal is political," Anne Sexton's highly subjective poetry, with its focus on personal and individual experience, does also avoid seeking any collective solution. There can, as she was to discover, be no individual solution to the problems of personal relationships. A passage from a poem in *45 Mercy Street* seems to give support to Levertov's argument about the tendency of writing such as Sexton's

> But today I roam a dead house,
> a frozen kitchen, a bedroom
> like a gas chamber.
> The bed itself is an operating table
> where my dreams slice me into pieces.
>
> ("The Lost Lie")

NOTES

1. Patricia Marx, "Interview with Anne Sexton," *Hudson Review* 18, no. 4 (Winter 1965–66): 562.

2. R. D. Laing, *The Politics of Experience and the Bird of Paradise* (Penguin), 100.

3. The destructive force of parent-child relationships is a central aspect of the work of many women writers. Some focus equally on both parents, as Stead does in *The Man Who Loved Children*. Others focus almost entirely upon one; Plath's poems focus almost entirely on the figure of her father, though her mother's influence upon her is described in *The Bell Jar;* Violette Leduc talks almost exclusively of the

effect of mothers, partly because she never knew her own father. Janet Frame in *A State of Siege* and Doris Lessing in the Children of Violence sequence again dwell upon the personality of the mother figure.

4. Simone de Beauvoir, *The Second Sex,* 405.

5. Barbara Kevles, "The Art of Poetry, XV: Anne Sexton," *Paris Review* no. 52 (1971): 160.

6. The Max referred to here is Maxine Kumin. For an account of her close and supportive relationship with Sexton, see Elaine Showalter and Carol Smith, "A Nurturing Relationship: A Conversation with Anne Sexton and Maxine Kumin," *Women's Studies* 4 (1976): 115–35.

7. A. Alvarez, *The Savage God* (Weidenfeld and Nicolson, 1971), 216.

8. Denise Levertov, "Anne Sexton: Light Up the Cave," *Ramparts* 13, no. 5 (December, 1974–January, 1975): 62.

KATE GREEN

Inventory of Loss

After her death Anne Sexton's poetry continues to push against
the boundaries of loss, to embody the daily nature of a despair
that is as quiet as a lit fuse. Imminent explosion, the air tense
before a storm—this is the energy of her last poems: a sensibility
leaning over the edge of control, knowing that loss is final and
inevitable. Sexton's poems have always come from the frontiers
of the personal. In fact, her work scouted vast unknown regions
of emotion for poetry and brought back word:

> Underneath the soil lies the violence,
> the shift, the crack of continents,
> the anger,
> and above only a cut,
> a half-inch space to stick a pencil in.

For this exploration, she was awarded the Pulitzer Prize in
1966. *45 Mercy Street* is her ninth book. It is brought out
posthumously, edited by her daughter and literary executor,
Linda Gray Sexton. In her introduction Linda Sexton writes that
the book was "complete" at the time of Sexton's suicide in 1974
but that the manuscript was still in the process of revision.
"Each line appears exactly as she wrote it," Linda Sexton says,
". . . although ultimately she did not find time enough for that
final perfection." This accounts for the unevenness of the book;
it lacks editing. Had she chosen to stay alive, Anne Sexton and
her editors may have cleared out certain poems and lines which
seem inaccessible, not fully surfaced out of the poet's internal
mythology. Sexton knew well how to invite the reader into a
private poem, but several of these poems seem closed, like a

Review of *45 Mercy Street, Moons and Lion Tailes* 2, no. 2 (1976). Copyright
©1976 by Kate Green. Reprinted by permission of the author.

code, though full of energy. The language emanates from an inner place that stammers and does not articulate. Many poems, though, are terribly clear. They are powerful and focused like mirrors one cannot turn from. Cutting the clouded poems would have strengthened the book; yet I am sure it was difficult to cut any of the manuscript knowing there would be no more poems.

45 Mercy Street is divided into four sections. The first contains the weakest poems, but also includes the title poem in which Sexton begins to speak about her writing, the effect of the public life on the private, the intensely personal poems which left her naked and exposed. These are the poems about the poet as poet. Some of them do not take flight; they're like phone conversations. But some, like "Leaves That Talk," gather into journeys of their own:

> . . . the branches are bare.
> The leaves lie in green mounds,
> like fake green snow huts.
> And from the window as I peer out,
> I see they have left their cages forever—
> those wiry, spidery branches—
> for me to people
> someday soon when I turn green
> and faithless to the summer.

"Bestiary U.S.A." is the second section, a series of animal poems which are fine vehicles for projections of internal states of mind. From "Bat": "Surely when first born my face was this tiny / and before I was born surely I could fly." These poems are clever and subtle. Sexton focuses on beings other than herself, and they return her reflection.

The third part, "The Divorce Papers," is the heart of the book, cut open. Here Sexton continues the surgery of her life which *is* the poems. She opens herself relentlessly, abundantly, perhaps excessively. Sometimes I cringe at what I recognize in that slicing. The poems are past being mere private cries. They begin to sing a mythology of separation, of the divorce not only of a man and a woman but also of life and spirit. These poems dive inward until, at times, the deepest internal state has become what we all know, "Drilling into the marrow of my entire bone." The poems unfold around Sexton's divorce. They have a terrifying momentum and ought to be read in sequence. We cannot fail to recognize our own losses in these poems. Her imagery, at its best, is brilliant, full of speed and wings:

> doing the undoing dance
> . . . .
>
> letting my history rip itself off me
> and stepping into something unknown
> and transparent,
> but all ten fingers stretched outward,
> flesh extended as metal
> waiting for a magnet.

The language sounds sharp. It clicks like a knife against ice, yet the images are hot. Energy is strung across this circle of opposites—erotic and frightening:

> Hands
> growing like ivy over me,
> hands growing out of me like hair,
> yet turning into fire grass,
> planting an iris in my mouth,
> spinning and blue,
> the nipples turning into wings,
> the lips turning into days that would not give birth,
> days that would not hold us in their house,
> days that would not wrap us in their secret lap,
> . . . .
>
> hands that excite oblivion,
> like a wind,
> a strange wind
> from somewhere tropic
> making a storm between my blind legs

The poems turn pain inside out. Sometimes it is hard to breathe in them, as if we were swimming down and down through dark water with no possibility of coming up:

> . . . I dream the love is swallowing itself.
> Next I dream the love is made of glass,
> glass coming through the telephone
> that is breaking slowly,
> day by day, into my ear.

Poems carved out of personal pain and suffering are often criticized for being too solipsistic, even selfish. We want dark poems to transform us. Sometimes they do. You can feel air rushing into the lines, everything slows:

> name it gentle,
> as gentle as radishes inhabiting
> their short life in the earth,
> . . . .
> name it gentle as maple wings singing
> themselves on the pond outside,
> as sensuous as the mother-yellow in the pond,
> that night it was ours,
> when our bodies floated and bumped
> in moon water and the cicadas
> called out like tongues.

45 *Mercy Street* continues a vision that is sculpted by all of Sexton's work—the violence of the world turned in upon the body, upon the self: "The flesh itself had become mad." If there is excess, it is not in the personal nature of the poems but in the images themselves, which seem, at times, to spill out of control. When Sexton is criticized for being too painful, for not lifting both herself and her audience out of despair, I cannot help thinking that the violence of the outer world has been internalized in her poems. It is under the skin, under the ground, daily as bodily functions, daily as the blue light of a television. By living so close to that fire in her, indeed by entering it, she gave us a look straight into our planet's eye: "The house of my body has spoken."

Those who have been moved by Sexton's vision, though it be one of irrevocable loss, will find a journey *through* loss in these poems. Like most journeys, however, there is no final arrival.

The tension remains, humming in the air after the poems, as the poems themselves remain after her death.

In the poem "Horse," Anne Sexton says:

> And yet and yet,
> field horse lapping the grass
> like stars . . .
> . . . .
>
> Your soft nose would nuzzle me
> and my fear would go out singing
> into its own body.

It is still singing.

KATHLEEN L. NICHOLS

The Hungry Beast Rowing Toward God
Anne Sexton's Later Religious Poetry

Although Anne Sexton began writing religious poems early in
her career, her last volumes of poetry—*The Death Notebooks,
The Awful Rowing Toward God,* and *45 Mercy Street*—reflect her
growing awareness of the imminence of death, an awareness
that seemed to cut her off from the conventional world of subur-
bia and the marriage in which she would formerly "lose [her]
frightened self."[1] Instead, with increasing absorption, she
turned to a private, self-contained mythology of God and Self
which would compensate for the sense of a lost self which had
plagued her all of her life. The compensatory function of re-
ligious myth is especially apparent in Sexton's posthumously
published volume *The Awful Rowing Toward God.* Although this
volume is controlled by the religious frame of the journey to-
ward God, the archetypal patterns evoked by her poetic descents
into the unconscious reveal her increasing need to find in death
the ideal mother and father—the male and female archetypes of
the united Self—from which she had felt severely dissociated by
her birth and, even more so, by their deaths. In *The Awful
Rowing,* these underlying psychological patterns transform her
sea journey toward God into a regressive journey back to the all-
embracing womb of the mythic mother and, contained within,
the lost aspect of self—the archetypal father-soul.

The consciously imposed religious pattern is readily per-
ceived in the opening and closing "frame" poems which set up
the sea-journey analogy. The opening poem entitled "Rowing"
records the poet's retrospective awareness that for most of her
life "God was there like an island I had not rowed to." The

Notes on Modern American Literature 3, no. 3 (1979). Reprinted by permission of
the publisher.

change of focus in middle age is shown by the rowing refrain: "I am rowing, I am rowing / though the oarlocks stick and are rusty / . . . I am rowing, I am rowing, / though the wind pushes me back."[2] This poem "ends with me still rowing," but as the title of the last poem indicates, "the rowing endeth" when she moors "at the dock of the island called God" where she finds laughter and "lucky love" (85–86). Given Sexton's progress from Bedlam in her first volume of poetry to the island of God in this one, the reader might almost be tempted to see a "divine comedy" pattern informing the entire Sexton canon.

Yet the sense of progress that this frame should provide is missing within the poetic sequence. In poem after poem, the animal and scatological images evoked from the unconscious vividly express the poet's sense of being overwhelmed by some inner, negative force against which she has no defenses. As in earlier volumes, Sexton thinks of herself as "Ms. Dog" (50), as well as a "pig in a trenchcoat" (1). Even more grotesquely, inside her is a "gnawing pestilential rat" (2) and elsewhere "clutching fast to my heart, a huge crab" which not even modern surgery can remove (28). These images of disgust become even more intense when Sexton returns to a metaphor found in her earlier poetry: man is "an outhouse" (27); "I . . . was a house full of bowel movement" (41). The "shit" with which she feels constipated "right into the fingers" is the "evil that permeates"—it is "poison / and the poison was all of me" (55). She feels "a pain in my bowels" because "the devil has crawled / in and out of me" (48), and this evil is so insidious and ubiquitous that "even in a telephone booth / evil can seep out of the receiver" (45); it "comes oozing / out of flowers at night," and she warns the reader that "it comes into your mouth while you sleep / . . . Beware. Beware" (34). Overwhelmed by this evil that "climbed into me," she wishes to "pour gasoline over my evil body / and light it" (50).

Although Sexton had struggled in her earlier poetry to find herself through a painful analysis of her family relationships, one of the unusual features of this volume is the limited number of direct references to those most problematic forces in her life—namely, to her mother and father. Yet these dominating figures, as abstract principles or idealized archetypes, still hover in the background, defining the nature of her life and transforming the meaning of her religious journey. The poet's sense of dissociation and self-loathing, for instance, is attributed to the loss of a controlling, godlike essence—a divine father who could love and "feed" the seemingly insatiable primal hungers. Sexton maintains that "to be without God is to be a snake / who wants to swallow an elephant" (38–39), and elsewhere she thinks that she can get rid of the hungry rat "gnawing" inside of her only if she can find God, who will "embrace" the starving creature (2). Male and female are viewed as conflicting forces which have created the dissociative problem of a sexually restricted identity. In one of the few autobiographical references, Sexton defines "Mother" as the repressive force which surgically fragmented the daughter's bond with the father principle. "Ms. Dog," for instance, speculates that "maybe my mother cut the God out of me" (50), leaving only the "evil" flesh—the incestuous instinct—that "separates you from God" (47). But, when "God went out of me / . . . My body became a side of mutton" (40). This instinctual appetite to find the safely distanced father is especially reflected in the sexual act which symbolically, like a rite of sympathetic magic, united the male-female aspects of Self; the sexual instincts are man and woman's "double hunger" bringing them together and driving them "to reach through / the curtain of God" (19). This ravenous hunger for the sexually complementary Self can assume hyperbolic, indeed, nearly mythic, proportions: "Man is eating the earth up / like a candy bar / and not one of them can be left alone with the ocean / for it is known he will gulp it all down. / The stars (possibly) are safe" (13–14). When the priest asks "whose God are you looking for?" the poet's reply is again in a hunger metaphor: "A starving man doesn't ask what the meal is" (50). Her "God" is obviously the male principle—the lost and idealized father who could provide recognition and meaningful transformation of the primal instincts.

In order to express her sense of psychic dissociation or loss of "soul," Sexton frequently externalizes this lost "god," but the lost self has, in actuality, been buried under the repressed and distorted instincts which often break out with dangerous intensity. However, through poetry she can "cut out the beggar" and "pry out the broken / pieces of God in me," an agonizing process which will enable her to "build a whole nation of God / in me—but united" (3–4). Her poems can become Whitmanesque "song[s] of myself" (4) or "anthems" when the controlling poetic process succeeds, as it sometimes does, in integrating the hidden and conscious selves: "my books anoint me" (11) when the inner objects inside "the room of my life" begin to "dream and wear new costumes, / compelled to, it seems by all the words in my hands" (9–10). These "miraculous" words (71) are also "fallen angels" which she "shoves" around "till something comes" (22). The importance of this poetic process of integration is suggested by the image of her typewriter as "my church / with an altar of keys" (51), yet even when she rejoices in the power of poetic control—"I carol with what the typewriter gives, / with what God gives" (80)—the same image simultaneously expresses her sense of an only partially assimilated self, for the God or male principle she writes about is the one that her *typewriter* "believes in" (76).

When this poetic integration does work, her discovery of the hidden "God" or repressed Self transforms, by "caging" or controlling in poetic forms, the hungry beasts which threaten her,[3] but a sense of only minimally fulfilled hungers or of precariousness is still implied. In several poems, her search for God leads her to "gravy" and "water," a meal, however, of bare survival (63, 65), and elsewhere God "fills" her even though "there are times of doubt / as hollow as the Grand Canyon" (70). On the other hand, the hungers of dissociation are satisfied by a falling, mannalike "snow," which she calls God's "blessed" milk—"Today God gives milk / and I have the pail" (77)—while a positively joyful note is sounded in "Welcome Morning," a poem of thankfulness for the "God / right here in my pea-green house" (58)—that is, as she phrased it earlier, in the "room of my life." But even in the exquisitely controlled poem "Small Wire," which asserts a calm, confident faith, the reader senses the precarious balance and security of a "faith" which is "a great weight / hung on a small wire." The ease with which she claims "He will enter your hands" lies in an uneasy tension with her surprising, past-tense analogy—"as easily as ten cents used to / bring forth a Coke" (78).

According to Sexton, each poetic descent into the unconscious brought a sense of wholeness—a "rebirth" which, however, lasted only a couple days[4]—which is precisely the problem, for in her poetry the integrating process must also be attempted over and over again, establishing an exhausting cycle that finally can be stopped only by death. Although Sexton externalizes her "voyage / onto the surgical andiron / of God" (82), the archetypal sea-womb images change the meanings of the surface Christian patterns. Sexton, for instance, refers to the "sea without which there is no mother, / the earth without which there is no father" (56); in her version of the Genesis story, man and woman's origins are the sea (7), and the sea is called the "mother" of God himself (68). This sea-womb association is also apparent in the many mother-child poems in which the image of the archetypal sea-mother transforms the poet's imaginative journey toward death into a fetal journey back to primal sources and an undifferentiated preconsciousness which encompasses both male and female principles. In "Mothers," for instance, a suckling child views the nursing breast as the "sea wrapped in skin" and the mother's legs "that bounce me up and down" as the "horses I will ride / into eternity" (72). Even Jesus, the male principle of divorced consciousness and suffering with which she identifies so frequently in all of her poetry, begs to be allowed to reenter the primordial world of the virgin mother's "belly" where he can "float . . . like a fish" and perhaps be reborn again "into something true," something he has not become in his previous rebirths—a real Messiah (61). This image of Jesus arouses in the poet feelings of pity and abhorrence because it fuses the ideas of continual rebirth and of eternal suffering. Therefore, when Jesus "comes with his eggful of miracles" (promises of renewal), what the poet envisions is "his guts drooping like a sea worm"—his unrelieved suffering because he "lives on, lives on" in the "awful death" (57)—which is actually his life and the consciousness of dissociation. Her distrust of the efficacy of a Christian renewal and her horror at the idea of an endless series of rebirths which never quite take are echoed in the grotesque image of the "Lord" contained within a womblike "oven" in which "He is boiled, / but He never dies, never dies" (33). Therefore, when she sees the amphibious "fish that walked" out of the sea (separated from his maternal origins), this Christ-fish which unites so awkwardly both sea and land functions only revives in the poet a "misplaced" or prenatal memory of her mother and the "salt of God's belly / where I floated in a cup of darkness." She "longs" for the "country" of the fish's origins (20–21)—for a cessation of postpartum consciousness.

Despite the religious frame of *The Awful Rowing Toward God,* Sexton's poetic descents into the unconscious release archetypal images and patterns that alter the meaning of her journey. What she imaginatively attains at the end of the volume is a wish-fulfilling reunion with her lost soul or "divine" father on a fish-shaped island floating in and surrounded by the archetypal amniotic fluid of her preconscious, maternal origins. Her final goal is the delivery unto death and the lost, archetypally distanced parents who define the missing aspects of Self.

NOTES

1. *Anne Sexton: A Self-Portrait in Letters,* edited by Linda Gray Sexton and Lois Ames (Boston: Houghton Mifflin, 1977), 24. Two typical studies of Sexton's religious poetry are A. R. Jones, "Necessity and Freedom: The Poetry of Robert Lowell, Sylvia Plath and Anne Sexton," *Critical Quarterly* 7 (1965): 11–30; and Paul A. Lacey, *The Inner War* (Philadelphia: Fortress Press, 1972), 25–30.

2. Anne Sexton, *The Awful Rowing Toward God* (Boston: Houghton Mifflin, 1975), 1–2. All further references to this edition will be included in the text.

3. Patricia Marx, "Interview with Anne Sexton," *Hudson Review* 18, no. 4 (Winter 1965–66): 586.

4. Marx, 570.

ROSEMARY JOHNSON

The Woman of Private
(but Published) Hungers

Daniel Bell in an essay in *Partisan Review* no. 2, 1978, comments upon what he perceives as the costs of the great surge of creativity in Western Culture in the last two centuries. The price has been great in his opinion, "One cost has been the loss of coherence in culture, particularly in the spread of an anti-nomian attitude to moral norms and even to the idea of cultural judgment itself. The greater price was exacted when the distinction between art and life became blurred so that what was permitted in the *imagination* (the novels of murder, lust, perversity) has often passed over into fantasy, is acted out by individuals who want to make their lives a work of art, and when, with the 'democratization' of criticism, the touchstone of judgment is no longer consensual agreement on standards but each self's judgment as to how art enhances that 'self.'"

"Self-revelation, self-vindication, this is the sole animating purpose of the writer of Confessions. For every volume of Confessions is in truth an *Apologia*."[1] Yes, but De Quincey also writes beautifully and this largely determines his place in literature. Even as he plumbs the depths of his experiences he essays style, and style presupposes a certain reticence, at least a nod in the direction of good taste. Some may say Anne Sexton is a confessional poet; certainly she indulges in self-revelation without stint, telling all in an exposé of her innermost workings that amounts to literary *seppuku*. More are likely to ask if such messy preoccupations will remain to stain the linen of the culture for long or whether good taste bleaches out even the most stubborn

Review of *A Self-Portrait in Letters* and *Words for Dr. Y.*, *Parnassus: Poetry in Review* 8, no. 1 (1980). Reprinted by permission of the Poetry in Review Foundation.

stain eventually. I feel Sexton's mark is at least as indelible as that of Mary Shelley. The Massachusetts poet resembles the Englishwoman in some gothic ways, and their work will exist as long as the climate that fostered their particular sensibilities continues. Both women weather critical acclaim and disdain alike quite well, dilapidate rather than refurbish the language and wander far off the literary track. They dabble in certain of the subterranean currents of feeling (not of thought) of the times. Power courses through Mary Shelley's novel because of her contact with the irrational—her acquaintanceship with the abnormal. Through her, to reflect Goya in his *Capricbos,* the sleep of reason engenders its monster, a creature still in lien amongst us, laying claim to the shadowy byways of our thought, embodying a pathology or at least a bastardized neuroticism, a spawn of the subconscious. Nowadays, more often than not, the progeny of the irrational are deemed legitimate issue. Calibans no longer. Merely special. Anne Sexton puts her finger on it,

> the somehow deficient,
> the somehow maimed,
> are thought to have
> a special pipeline to the mystical,
> the faint smell of the occult,
> a large ear on the God-horn.
> ("One-Eye, Two-Eyes, Three-Eyes," *Transformations)*

Anne Sexton is her own sacred monster, but it wasn't an inevitability that her work is such a curious oil-and-water mix of the absolutely commonplace and the singular, of the quite literal curdled by the incredible. However, the eddies of her madness rather than the shallows of her day-to-day suburban round give her work its prevailing tone. She personifies, in fact, the abnormal in the normal, which is how we tend to view contemporary things with a Freudian eye for peculiarity. Wallace Stevens remarks (with disapproval) of the post-Modernist period, "It is natural for us to identify the imagination with those who extend its abnormality." The poet in question comprehends this in her very marrow. No charlatan of the irrational, of *extremis,* she is certifiably able, has the good housekeeping seal of approval as it were, to act out her psychodramas. And only sometimes do her productions backslide into melodrama or slither into creature-feature when she casts herself thus: "I have no arms or legs / I am all one skin like a fish."

In feeling that her inadequacies display themselves as deformities, Anne Sexton is simply, honestly, and literally admitting a delusion we all share. One knows oneself to have somehow sustained damage, albeit hidden damage, e.g., "The dreadful has already happened" in a sense wider than Freud intended. Externally aberrant human beings—freaks, dwarfs, giants, mongoloids, and the like—compel attention because of the by-stander's complicity, his unwilling or unwitting recognition of his own carefully concealed inner shortcomings and cripplings in their all-too-visible deformities. Sexton lives this fascination. What ails Everyman afflicts her. She can never hope for the self-containment of others and she cannot trust her outer comeliness to camouflage the ugliness she feels within. She asks in effect, "Would the cripple inside of me / be the cripple that would show?" not just of one specific accident, but so often as to be the question haunting her all life long.

The poet's misfortunes are triple. Her talent for self-expression must single her out from the common run of women, yet the Fates cast her as a housewife, the keeper of the commonplace, and the Furies drove her mad. So this suburban Psyche, for Psyche was surely the first housewife, set as she was to labor purely for love at chores never done, is fated never to find fulfillment in any role nor to rest nor to attain the wholeness of those who consider themselves sane.

Although Anne Sexton toys, for effect one feels, with notions of lack of gender, androgyny, hermaphroditicism, and the like, the obvious needs to be said (were she a man, it would not have to be): the poet's perceptions and her sensibility are female, stem from her womanhood. As a woman she picks apart the seamier parts of woman's biological destiny and possibilities. She does not spare us abortion or menstruation. Nearing a hysterectomy, she writes a poem in celebration of her uterus, and she certainly grasps some of the nettles of what was to become the second wave of feminism. The description she dashes off in a letter to Erica Jong of herself as "the woman of the poems, the woman of the kitchen, the woman of the private (but published) hungers" fits. Indeed a lot of conflicting directions pull her apart. One hazards more than anything else that the life of Anne Sexton née Harvey was timed to coincide with the waxed pitfalls of what is termed the Feminine Mystique. The homely undiagnosed angst of mid-century suburbia, its loneliness and airwickness, its gentility and conformity, its good causes and consumerism, the never-ending useless tasks and its trivia are all there in her letters. Mrs. Sexton speaks with originality and courage especially in the earlier poems of this female anomie, resembling Rilke's "unlived, distained, last life, of which one can die":

> Some women marry houses.
> Its another kind of skin; it has a heart,
> a mouth, a liver and bowel movements.
> The walls are permanent and pink.
> See how she sits on her knees all day,
> faithfully washing herself down.
>
> ("Housewife," *All My Pretty Ones*)

Drugs, drink, therapy, Thorazine, travel, many were the cures undertaken by this "Mad" housewife and details of them embellish the walls of a shut-in existence like fever charts. She senses that what ails or oppresses her is to a certain extent the result of having a life full of creature comforts but bereft of real choice. She writes of one escapade—maybe an escape of a sort?—"I have deserted my husband and my children / the Negro issue and the late news and the hot baths."

Some improvement takes place. In a sense good luck dogs her footsteps. Fame smiles upon her but this leads to another reification. "The woman of the private (but published) hungers" takes over Mrs. Sexton. This woman pushes to its limits the modern idea of the artist making of his or her life a work of art, being his own raw material. Anne Sexton exposes an enormous amount of herself, leaves so little under wraps that the outmoded concept of Decorum rises from under its dustsheets to protest, so much is the reader privy to things the reader does not wish, or need, to know. However, from her point of view Anne Sexton had precious little privacy to protect. Neither in the lap of domesticity nor in the grip of her breakdowns or their aftermath could she have anything but trespassed upon existence. Her time and her mind were not always her own and furthermore it seems emotionally she could not stand alone. Her letters reveal just how much reliance she placed not only on her nearest and dearest and on her friends—even willfully absented friends—but also on her current psychiatrist—surely the "Other man" in her life. Complicity, "Years of hints / strung out" occurred. Sometimes she must worry herself over whose words are whose—unnecessarily. Anne Sexton makes her own work. Yet her analyst, her "enthusiast," makes a most sympathetic—if bought—audience and to him she says as much, "Your business is watching my words." Anne Sexton is generous and always credits where credit is due. Undoubtedly her indebtedness to the doctors is great. They stumped Rumpelstiltskin-like into her mental cul-de-sac or into her run-of-the-mill world and forced this latter-day miller's daughter into creation, into naming Names. "I have words for you, Dr. Y., / words for sale." It's an odd midwifery to an even stranger labor and the results are good. In the poem "You, Doctor Martin," for example, the good doctor walks "from breakfast to madness" into the cotton-wool world of his patients:

> . . . We stand in broken
> lines and wait while they unlock
> the door and count us at the frozen gates
> of dinner. The shibboleth is spoken
> and we move to gravy in our smock
> of smiles. We chew in rows, our plates
> scratch and whine like chalk
>
> in school. . . .
> (*To Bedlam and Part Way Back*)

Anne Sexton's concern for the inmates immured in Mental Institutions lasts all her life as her correspondence shows, but unlike Robert Lowell she never made the mad a subject for her poetry. In fact, as far as the poetry is concerned, other people really only existed for her as an audience. Her first audience was medical. Her next her dead, her parents and her great-aunt, her Nana, then the public. The poet performs miracles of loaves and fishes for the hungry living. As her popularity grows, a multitude seems to clamour for a piece of the act and Anne Sexton obliges with bread and circuses. Always she commands top billing:

> I am the only actor.
> It is difficult for one woman
> to act out a whole play
> The play is my life,
> my solo act.
>
> ("The Play," *The Awful Rowing Toward God*)

She lauds herself and takes vainglory bows, ignoring the "many boos" as the critics become increasingly harsh,

> Despite that I go on to the last lines:
> To be without God is to be a snake
> who wants to swallow an elephant.
> The curtain falls.
> The audience rushes out.
> It was a bad performance.
> That's because I'm the only actor
> and there are few humans whose lives
> will make an interesting play.
> Don't you agree?
>
> ("The Play")

The poet's absorption in her one-woman show is enormous. This may be partially excused. One cannot parcel oneself out wholesale to all and sundry and still have something left for one's nearest and dearest if one is falling to pieces. Hence in her search for wholeness Sexton is so wrapped in herself she has time only for her correspondents and in her poetry for her daughters who in their "brand-new bodies" appear as her earlier self reproduced unmarred. The poems to Joy and to Linda, her "little . . . string bean," are lovely and unforced. One of them, "The Fortress," goes crisply thus:

> My child, since July
> the leaves have been fed
> secretly from a pool of beet-red dye.

> And sometimes they are battle green
> with trunks as wet as hunters' boots,
> smacked hard by the wind, clean
> as oilskins.
>
> *(All My Pretty Ones)*

Even the delight of her girls is worm-eaten. She admits to Joy:

> I, who was never quite sure
> about being a girl, needed another
> life, another image to remind me.
> And this was my worst guilt; you could not cure
> nor soothe it. I made you to find me.
> ("The Double Image," *To Bedlam and Part Way Back*)

The tormented woman is so often not all there that perforce she must take a mental tally of her limbs and organs in order to ascertain if the props of her act—she is after all her own raw material—are present and accounted for before the show can go on:

> Left to my own lips, touch them,
> my own dumb eyes, touch them,
> the progression of my parts, touch them,
> my own nostrils, shoulders, breasts,
> navel, stomach, mound, kneebone, ankle,
> touch them.
> ("The Fury of Abandonment," *The Death Notebooks*)

Indeed the marvel grows that a person so mauled by madness and its attendant terrors emerges so often from her cage of dreads to detail, as a past mistress of the phlebotomy, the spasms of her many small deaths, whether on the analyst's couch or on the podium or in bed. But sometimes our sympathy wavers and we lose patience: for several reasons, one being a growing impatience with the poet's habit of crying wolf—too many relapses and suicide attempts in short—and another being the diminishing returns from certain kinds of voracious self-absorption. People who feed upon themselves in order to nourish their art eventually dish up pretty thin fare:

> I have come back
> but disorder is not what it was.
> I have lost the trick of it!
> The innocence of it!
>
> ("Flee on Your Donkey," *Live or Die*)

No "Hunger Artist" ever put it better. Moreover there's a trick to it somewhere. Like the proverbial lady-in-the-box being cut in half, she takes it all lying down really. Certainly the words speak out. Undeniably. They drool, spit, suck, gag, and the like, and she achieves moments of transcendence when she overcomes her condition and proclaims,

> So I won't hang around in my hospital shift,
> repeating The Black Mass and all of it.
> I say *Live, Live* because of the sun,
> the dream, the excitable gift.
>
> ("Live," *Live or Die*)

But such epiphany is rare. That sort of vision is not often granted to her if only because Anne Sexton is not really a romantic, not if one sees Romanticism at least in part as the gifted individual's intensifying of an otherwise drab existence. For this most modern poet wishes benumbment—to feel less, not more. She yearns to sink aproned against dirt, daisy-fresh, into a tranquilized tranquility, to be drugged into something quite different from the peace of mind envisioned by Wordsworth (a state, though, not incomprehensible to Keats). Anyway, she writes,

> My sleeping pill is white.
> It is a splendid pearl;
> it floats me out of myself,
> my stung skin as alien
> as a loose bolt of cloth.
> I will ignore the bed.
> I am linen on a shelf.
>
> ("Lullaby," *To Bedlam and Part Way Back*)

Passivity is hutched in her as mesmerized as a laboratory rabbit. Underneath the clamour of the italics and the hue-and-cry verbs, the thud-and-blunder syntax and the tarantula-on-a-slice-of-angel-food tone, this "Lady with a brain that broke" invites erasure. Paint her white. The quiescent verse rings the most true:

> In this fashion I have become a tree.
> I have become a vase you can pick up or drop at will,
> inanimate at last. What unusual luck! My body
> passively resisting. Part of the leftovers. Part of the kill.
> > ("Angel of Flight and Sleigh Bells," *The Book of Folly*)

Passivity is the other face of hysteria, a short-circuiting caused by emotional overloadings. Sexton's creative gift after the first four books produced increasingly strange fruit of stock either stunted or weedy, never fully matured. In a sense there was a clinical inevitability to it all. An hysteric, and it seems Sexton was one, may adopt the confessional mode—essentially the voicing of guilt—but he or she cannot truly experience guilt, for if one perceives events to be outside one's control, and an hysteric surely does this, then one cannot possibly be to blame or in any real sense responsible. The fault must lie elsewhere. Nor can such a being beset by all the others who align themselves outside his compass, and his comprehension, recognize the reality of those others except in a fragmentary way. Psychological reductionism aside, Anne Sexton does reach for the comforts of Christianity, but as she conceives herself sullied by others long before she herself fell into sin, she can grasp only the half of it. Forgiveness is possible but not contrition since the fault lies elsewhere, yet forgiveness requires a certain maturity; it is subsequent to the arrival of guilt. When Sexton gropes for guilt, it is blame she discovers. To her friend Ruth a confused explanation is given:

> My friend, my friend, I was born
> doing reference work in sin, and born
> confessing it. This is what poems are:
> with mercy
> for the greedy,
> they are the tongue's wrangle,
> the world's pottage, the rat's star.
> > ("With Mercy for the Greedy," *All My Pretty Ones*)

The mystical palindrome "rats live on no evil star" appeals to Sexton because her understanding is of such things. She believes in the hexes and jinxes of women and peasants, in the medieval signs that mark the lives of those who feel in their bones that they have been crossed by fate and who know in their hearts (and heads) control of their destinies is out of their hands. She writes to W. D. Snodgrass in November 1958, "Then at thirteen I kissed a boy (not very well—but happily) and I was so pleased with my womanhood that I told Nana I was kissed and then she went mad. . . . I tell you this not to confess, but to illuminate. At thirteen I was blameful and struck—at thirty I am not blameful (because I am always saved by men who understand me better than I understand myself)." Thirteen was ever an unlucky number even if Anne's Nana had her breakdown much later and for different reasons. Anne accuses her anagram self the Nana-Hex:

> You did it. You are the evil.
> It was the day meant meant for me.
> Thirteen for your whole life,
> just the masks keep changing.
>
> ("The Hex," *The Book of Folly*)

The ill-starred members of the house of Agammemnon learned that those whom the Fates have fingered may well be ultimately guilty of continuing to live. Sylvia Plath inherited this knowledge as may have John Berryman. Anne Sexton intuits something of it:

> Like Oedipus I am losing my sight.
> Like Judas I have done my wrong.
> Their punishment is over;
> the shame and disgrace of it
> are all used up.
> But as for me,
> look into my face
> and you will know that crimes dropped upon me
> as from a high building
> and although I cannot speak of them
> or explain the degrading details

> I have remembered much
> about Judas—
> about Judas, the old and the famous—
> that you overlooked.
>
> ("The Legend of the One-Eyed Man," *Live or Die*)

Her fractured Humpty-Dumpty ego was put together again and again by analysis, and as we may all be said to be in too many ways the sum total of what others see in us, or of what we think they see, Sexton, exposed to the delvings and deductions of psychiatric scrutiny, began to add up to being a priestess of their faith, psychotherapy—one stark raving sane and speaking in tongues of the oral and the anal. The last two works, *The Book of Folly* and *The Awful Rowing Toward God,* seem no more or less than this. She writes of vocation in *Live or Die,* testifying to the sun,

> Now I am utterly given.
> I am your daughter, your sweet-meat,
> your priest, your mouth and your bird
> and I will tell them stories of you
> until I am laid away forever,
> a thin gray banner.
>
> ("The Sun," *Live or Die*)

Rimbaud wrote that in order to attain the unknown, "It is necessary to be a seer, to make oneself a seer. The poet makes himself a seer by a long immense and reasoned unruliness of the senses. . . ." According to this Anne Sexton was a natural for the sacerdotal role.

Death figures a great deal in the poetry as a possible escape. However the one death we all live through, the death of childhood, Anne Sexton never gets over. Sylvia Plath and Stevie Smith keep her company in this. One may hear in Plath's poetry a very bad child screaming blue parricidal murder. Stevie Smith remains a wise child all her life. Anne Sexton believes she has been robbed of a seemingly happy childhood, and it galls her. Yet so often in her view of herself as a child she goes beyond the bounds of belief and fact, placing herself in a Gretel or Cinderella role, and grousing about ill treatment endured:

> I will speak of the little childhood cruelties,
> being a third child,
> the last given
> and the last taken—
> of the nightly humiliations when Mother undressed me,
> of the life of the daytime, locked in my room—
> being the unwanted, the mistake
> that Mother used to keep Father
> from his divorce.
>
> ("Those Times . . . ," *Live or Die*)

Really it's a be-ginghamed girlhood Sexton laments and celebrates, the once upon a time when virginal Anna lived long before those boots, shoes, and slippers filled with blood (Sexton's sexual imagery is quite often shod in footware). She depicts her daughter's accident in such bloodied terms it suggests the rupturing of maidenhood,

> The thoroughbred has stood on her foot.
> He rested there like a building.
> He grew into her foot until they were one.
> The marks of the horseshoe printed
> into her flesh, the tips of her toes
> ripped off like pieces of leather,
> three toenails swirled like shells
> and left to float in blood in her riding boot.
>
> ("Pain for a Daughter," *Live or Die*)

Young Anne or rather "Daisy" "sixteen-in-the-pants" "smelling of Clorox and Duz" wears clean underwear in case of just such an accident,

> For underpants I'll pick white cotton,
> the briefs of my childhood,
> for it was my mother's dictum
> that nice girls wore only white cotton.
>
> ("Clothes," *The Death Notebooks*)

When the poet strips her work down to its underwear, it's a necessary shedding of more than the proprieties; she takes off the

integuments of wifehood, shucks the present tense, turns herself
back into a girl again, listening,

> I hear
> as in a dream
> the conversation of the old wives
> speaking of *womanhood*.
> I remember that I heard nothing myself.
> I was alone.
> I waited like a target.
>
> ("Little Girl, My String Bean, My
> Lovely Woman," *Live or Die*)

Anonymous was a woman, so feminists say, and no doubt she
told fairy stories—old wives' tales which concocted remedies,
recipes for the pangs undergone during the rite of passage into
the adult world. Sexton's obsessions and regressions slip her,
hand in glove, into this tradition. She pulls off her book of
stories beautifully. *Transformations* contains her best work. In it
her sugar-and-spicing of glad-wrapped horrors is appropriate.
Her excitability chills into an iced *Schadenfreude* laced with
cynicism. She can handle things for once, no more hot pota-
toes. The literal quality of her images does her no disservice;
rather she pockets metaphors, her usual small things that
come to hand, comfortably and displays her wares with con-
fidence,

> The apple was as smooth as oilskin
> and when she took a bite
> it was as smooth and crisp as the moon.
>
> ("The White Snake")

Well might a princess smile "like warm milk." Dame Sexton
cups her realm in the palm of her hand. She copes. Everything is
as self-contained as a doll's house. Thoughts stop rampaging and
come to her call to sit quietly awaiting her bidding "In an old
time / there was a king as wise as a dictionary," The "awful
babble" is over the hills and far away, and surgically sure she
performs miracles and her familiars—for the characters are
mostly all figments of Anne—graft into herselves triumphant,

> Without Thorazine
> or benefit of psychotherapy
> Iron Hans was transformed.
> No need for Master Medical;
> no need for electroshock—
> merely bewitched all along.
> Just as the frog was a prince.
> Just as the madman his simple boyhood.
>
> ("Iron Hans")

In "Red Riding Hood" the great-aunt now grandmama gobbled up by beastly madness is restored to life. The Anna-Nana anagram rejoice at their lucky escape and they never have to cry wolf ever again,

> Those two remembering
> nothing naked and brutal
> from that little death,
> that little birth,
> from their going down
> and their lifting up.

Sexton actually corners some of her nightmares in these stories and sometimes her surrogates even succeed—not always the usual fate for the heroines of the female writer. Anyway, within the province of fairy tales, of wishful thinking, it's fine never to grow up, normal to feign innocence, and defensible to wish to be "Thirteen for your whole life." If on the other hand you are a bit the worse for wear, your shop-soiling may vanish in the twinkling of an eye:

> When I was a wild man,
> Iron Hans said,
> I tarnished all the world.
> I was the infector.
> I was the poison breather.
> I was the professional,
> but you have saved me
> from the awful babble
> of that calling.
>
> ("Iron Hans")

According to Wallace Stevens, "The final belief is to believe in a fiction which you know to be a fiction there being nothing else. The exquisite truth is to know that it is a fiction and that you believe in it willingly." Sexton catches hold of her fears one by one; holds them up wriggling and skewers them by surrogate as it were. The adulterous couple get off scot free in "The Little Peasant." The tweaks and twinges of infidelity elsewhere described in her "Love Poems" here plump out into amoral commonsensical *fabliaux*.

> The miller's wife
> smiled to herself.
> Though never again to dingo-sweet
> her secret was as safe
> as a fly in an outhouse.

At the end of "The Twelve Dancing Princesses" the escape hatch of the insomniac, the amnesiac, the drug taker, the night person clamps shut for ever, thus affecting a dreadfully mundane cure-for-your-own-good,

> Now the runaways would run no more and never
> again would their hair be tangled into diamonds,
> never again their shoes worn down to a laugh,
> never the bed falling down into purgatory
> to let them climb in after
> with their Lucifer kicking.
>
> ("The Twelve Dancing Princesses")

Marriage gets its comeuppance quite a few times. In "The White Snake" the happy couple are

>   . . . placed in a box
> and painted identically blue
> and thus passed their days living happily ever after—
> a kind of coffin,
> a kind of blue funk.
> Is it not?

"Briar Rose (Sleeping Beauty)," which ends the collection, fails as a necessary fiction. It is too close to the heart of the matter, too autobiographical. The Princess awakens from her enchanted sleep and nothing has been solved. Storytelling time is over, the lies and distortions of truth are back,

> There was a theft.
> That much I am told.
> I was abandoned.
> That much I know.
> I was forced backward.
> I was forced forward.
> I was passed hand to hand like a bowl of fruit.
> Each night I am nailed into place
> and I forget who I am.
> Daddy?
> That's another kind of prison.
> It's not a prince at all,
> but my father
> drunkenly bent over my bed,
> circling the abyss like a shark,
> my father thick upon me
> like a sleeping jellyfish.

She has come full circle. Her former self writes to Thoreau, Kind Sir,

> I have turned around twice with my eyes sealed
> and the woods were white and my night mind
> saw such strange happenings, untold and unreal.
> And opening my eyes, I am afraid of course
> to look—this inward look that society scorns—
> Still, I search in these woods and find nothing worse
> than myself, caught between the grapes and the thorns.
> ("Kind Sir: These Woods," *To Bedlam and Part Way Back*)

NOTE

1. G. Douglas, ed., Introduction to *The Confessions of an English Opium Eater,* by Thomas DeQuincey (London: Everyman's Library, 1907).

KATHERINE F. MCSPADDEN

The Self in the Poetry of Anne Sexton
The Religious Quest

I am pretty God Damn religious if you want to look at it.

—Letters

Whatever else she seeks—a loving relationship with a supportive mother-figure, a reconciliation with the father, an end to the mental turmoil which plagues her, even death—Sexton's quest for self-realization has an underlying religious motivation. Her spiritual quest has been belittled by some critics, who see it as another manifestation of her dependency, of her need for a protective father or mother. However, her religious poetry reflects the same dogged Oedipus-like spirit of inquiry and the same concern with the nature of the self that characterize her other works.

Sexton condemns superficiality both in the Protestant worship in which she was reared and in the "pallid humanitarianism" of those religions which refuse to grapple with the problematic duality of Christ's identity and settle instead for a system based on ethical values. She insists that "need is not quite belief" and sets out to do exactly what Guardini recommends in the lines with which she introduces a section of *All My Pretty Ones*[1]—to "hack [her] way through existence alone," searching for new spiritual truths in which she can believe (*CP,* 60). She never abandons Christianity completely, but in questing for spiritual values outside orthodoxy she finds meaning in aspects of reality that institutional Christianity has deemphasized, namely, physical nature and the human dimensions of Jesus' identity. Neither does she accept the orthodox view that the trials of earth are a preparation for a fuller life beyond the grave. In her version of the Lazarus story, Lazarus is grateful to be

From "The Self in the Poetry of Anne Sexton" (Ph.D. diss., Loyola University of Chicago, 1985). Edited version reprinted by permission of the author.

403

restored to life because "in heaven it had been no different. / In heaven there had been no change" ("Jesus Summons Forth," *CP*, 341–42). Thus she finds potential for transcendence in the here and now, and even in the negative aspects of human identity, a transcendence which can be reached only by a full acceptance of and immersion in physical—and human—nature. Likewise, the thousands of ordinary, even trivial details of daily life—cuts and scratches, frying pans, dolls, sunbathing, rowboats, the birth of puppies—are inseparable from the spiritual life, contrary to the more traditional ascetic view that the business of life tends to crowd out spiritual awareness.

Throughout her poetry and letters, Sexton expresses a strong desire to embrace wholeheartedly the Christian religion in which she was raised and a persistent inability to do so. The Christian message fails to satisfy her, either as a way of coping with and finding value in her limited, misguided identities or as a means to a transcendent, transformed self that connects her with all of reality, including God, other human beings, nature, and the universe. One poem in which she explores the ways in which Christian worship has failed her, "Protestant Easter" (*CP*, 128–31), reflects her ever-present need to probe ceaselessly for the truth about identity, in this case the identity of Jesus. The worshippers in Sexton's poem make no serious attempt to fathom the troublesome uncertainties of the central Christian question of Christ's dual identity as God and human being. Neither are they awed by the mystery of the possibility of an intersection of human and divine selfhood, nor motivated by the implication that they too might bear the seeds of divinity within themselves. These worshippers, imbued with the Jocasta-like spirit which Sexton abjures, are content with a shallow, unexamined form of religion and are instead preoccupied not with the possibilities for transcendence of human failures but with materialistic competitiveness— whose Easter bonnet is the prettiest.

What Sexton seeks most from religion is a means of overcoming the guilt-ridden, bone-fragile, death-fearing, unloved childself that plagues her. While Jesus comes close to representing a God who, having taken on a human identity, shares human suffering, and accepts human limitations, she cannot quite bring herself to accept him as an image of the "mercy" she longs for. While the Christian message is forgiveness, for which she feels an intense need—as indicated by the kind of confessional poetry she writes—she cannot bring herself to trust religious confession to satisfy this need. Her poem, "With Mercy for the Greedy" (*CP*, 62–63), forthrightly recognizes the difference between believing and merely needing to believe. A Catholic friend, Ruth, has sent Sexton a crucifix and urged her to make an appointment for confession. The poet is touched by this gesture, especially because the cross has been worn by her friend and thus represents vividly an extension of her friend's selfhood:

> your own cross,
> your dog-bitten cross,
> no larger than a thumb,
> small and wooden, no thorns, this rose—

Sexton prays to "its shadow," which is "deep, deep." The shadow and the repetition of the word "deep" suggest her wish that the mysteries of Christ's identity could lead her to the kind of enlargement that she seeks. But though she admires Jesus and is able to identify with his physical suffering, this sense of identity does not lead to belief:

> True. There is
> a beautiful Jesus.
> He is frozen to his bones like a chunk of beef.
> How desperately he wanted to pull his arms in!
> How desperately I touch his vertical and horizontal axes!
> But I can't. Need is not quite belief.

Thus, though she is able to empathize deeply with Jesus' suffering and to see her own desperate need to believe as akin to his desperate state of agony and desolation, such identification does not lead to affirmation. She regards her poems as fulfilling her need for confession:

> My friend, my friend, I was born
> doing reference work in sin, and born
> confessing it. This is what poems are:
> with mercy
> for the greedy,

> they are the tongue's wrangle,
> the world's pottage, the rat's star.

Thus, again, she draws a connection between her spiritual quest and her poetry. The above lines constitute the most explicit definition of poetry that Sexton ever gives, and they clearly suggest that she finds more "mercy" forthcoming from her public poetic confessions than she believes institutional religion, with its emphasis on reform, is capable of.

Sexton imagines a God who is a companion on earth rather than in a remote heaven in "Rowing" (*CP,* 417–18), the first and title poem in her volume of religious poetry, *The Awful Rowing Toward God.* In this guise God extends to her the kind of mercy and acceptance of self that she longs for. She calls the poem "my tale," thus suggesting that it reveals matters essential to the self. She reiterates the aspects of her negative, restricted self which have prevented her from developing her full identity and an expansive self:

> I was stamped out like a Plymouth fender
> into this world.
> First came the crib
> with its glacial bars.
> Then dolls
> and the devotion to their plastic mouths.
> Then there was school,
> the little straight rows of chairs,
> blotting my name over and over,
> but undersea all the time,
> a stranger whose elbows wouldn't work.
> Then there was life
> with its cruel houses
> and people who seldom touched—
> though touch is all—
> but I grew,
> like a pig in a trenchcoat I grew,
> and then there were many strange apparitions,
> the nagging rain, the sun turning into poison
> and all of that, saws working through my heart

This summary of her life repeats succinctly the many other autobiographical poems in which she describes her child self as lacking an identity, frozen, unloved, her only love objects plastic dolls which were as dead as she. School only intensified her feelings of a lack of self-identity and reinforced her passivity and sense of being an awkward misfit—"a pig in a trenchcoat." A lack of community has seemed to characterize her adult life as well, so that she has continued to feel out of place and lacking in wholeness. This lack of selfhood has culminated in madness and self-destruction. Thus far she has been in a state of spiritual deprivation as well: "and God was there like an island I had not rowed to, / still ignorant of Him."

Now, however, she has arrived at middle age, though still "about nineteen in the head," and the embarkation on the quest has awakened her from her passive state:

> I am rowing, I am rowing
> though the oarlocks stick and are rusty
> and the sea blinks and rolls
> like a worried eyeball,
> but I am rowing, I am rowing,
> though the wind pushes me back

Though she is rusty, her quest is invigorating and expansive, overcoming the years of lack of identity and purpose and pitting her against larger realities and forces, represented by the worried and threatening sea and the contrary wind. The poem ends with a description of her goal. Relief from her frozen, pestilential self comes not through a violent merger with the cosmos, as in "The Starry Night," but from a quiet acceptance by a merciful God of her flawed self. No transformation is required:

> . . . I know that that island will not be perfect,
> it will have the flaws of life,
> the absurdities of the dinner table,
> but there will be a door
> and I will open it
> and I will get rid of the rat inside of me,
> the gnawing pestilential rat.

God will take it with his two hands
and embrace it.

She thus elevates the search for self-understanding and self-ac-
ceptance, which is also the journey of psychological analysis, to
the level of the spiritual quest. Her God is to be sought through
the earth and the body, not outside them.

Sexton longs to share in this divine identity too. In addition to
her desire to fully experience her human identity, she hungers to
transcend the limitations and constrictions of her human self and
to become an extension of some powerful, superhuman being.
Always death, usually a violent death, is a means of achieving
this identification. Such visionary poems, in which she imagines
herself in some sort of transformed state, involve throwing off
her human identity to take on some larger self, or joining her
weak and unsatisfactory human self with some more potent
being.

One of Sexton's early visionary poems is "The Starry Night"
(*CP*, 53–54), her poetic contemplation of Van Gogh's famous
painting of the same title. In this poem, the prime mover of the
universe is "the old unseen serpent," a mythological cosmic
figure. The poem is an important one because it reflects two
elements basic to Sexton's world view, namely, her faith in
nature and also in art as avenues of redemption superior to re-
ligion. The use of Van Gogh's painting as the organizing meta-
phor of the poem indicates that she finds in him an artistic fore-
bear for these views. Indeed, this sense that she is an extension of
Van Gogh becomes explicit in the epigraph to the poem, a
quotation from a letter of Van Gogh to his brother:

That does not keep me from having a terrible need of—shall I
say the word—religion. Then I go out at night to paint the
stars.

The power of the painting is effectively transmuted into
words in Sexton's poem. She longs for death as a way to become
part of this power, which represents for her a violent expansion
of self:

> The town does not exist
> except where one black-haired tree slips
> up like a drowned woman into the hot sky.
> The town is silent. The night boils with eleven stars.
> Oh starry starry night! This is how
> I want to die.

The town, which can be seen to represent life as the poet experiences it in the here and now, is passive and insignificant compared to the boiling universe. The only thing in the earthly landscape that is not passive and silent is the tree, which has a female identity and seems to embody the desire for merger with "the hot sky." References in other poems to a desire for—or fear of—drowning suggest an identification here between the tree and the poet herself; drowning in Sexton's work seems desirable or threatening, depending on the mood of a particular poem, as a means of a loss of individual identity and an opening to an expanded, cosmic self. In "The Starry Night" nature is ominous, but the speaker wishes to experience and become part of the violence of the universe:

> It moves. They are all alive.
> Even the moon bulges in its orange irons
> to push children, like a god, from its eye.
> The old unseen serpent swallows up the stars.
> Oh starry starry night! This is how
> I want to die:
>
> into that rushing beast of the night,
> sucked up by that great dragon, to split
> from my life with no flag,
> no belly,
> no cry.

In Sexton's starry night, everything in the universe is alive and threatening. The god powering this turbulent cosmos is the serpent, with whom she desires to be united. This god is a part of nature, and paradoxically, she finds something godlike in a creature that is generally considered dark, ugly, and evil. Here it is the serpent's devouring quality that attracts the poet; she desires to experience the great "rushing" movement of the cosmos. Paradoxically in this portrayal of a turbulent universe, the spiritual quest takes the form of a desire for a complete loss of identity. Not a trace is to remain: no flag to mark the place of her disappearance, no tears of bereavement by those left behind, no "cry" from her, betraying a reluctance to go.

In her religious poetry, Sexton views the self as "a whole nation of God," made up of many selves, some limiting and self-destructive, some nurturing and reaching out to larger realities. For her, the spiritual quest involves escaping the confines of those aspects of her various roles and selves which are narrow and constricting and opening herself to deeper and more expansive selves.

NOTE

1. Anne Sexton, *The Complete Poems* (Boston: Houghton Mifflin, 1981). Cited in text as *CP*.

DIANA HUME GEORGE

How We Danced
Anne Sexton on Fathers and Daughters

"Love Grew Rings Around Me":
With Father in *Bedlam*

In *To Bedlam and Part Way Back,* Anne Sexton began composing the mythopoeic music of the father-daughter dance, which echoes now as a swan song for her poetic and personal lives. "We bent together like two lonely swans," she later wrote in "How We Danced," a central poem in "The Death of the Fathers" sequence in *The Book of Folly.* The father-daughter motif is equalled in resonance and poignance in Sexton's canon only by the mother-daughter relationship, and for similar reasons: Sexton saw the nuclear family as the microcosmic analogue of the social and psychic structure of her culture. What began as a poetic journeying into the "narrow diary of my mind" became first "more than myself" in relation to people she knew and loved. "It was you, or your house / or your kitchen." But even very early, in "For John, Who Begs Me Not to Enquire Further," "you" widens to include a fully peopled world: "your fear is anyone's fear. . . ."

Sexton's ablest critics have located the shift from personal to "transpersonal" or "cultural" in Sexton's work in her fourth volume, *Transformations.*[1] While I agree that in *Transformations* such a shift is mythically embodied and newly garbed, there is within the "narrow diary" of even the early poems a structural outline for the psychic biography of a gender, and particularly for what Phyllis Chesler calls "woman's 'dependent' and 'incestuous' personality" in relation to her father[2]—a pattern long known to and exploited by psychoanalysis, to the degree that therapeutic method colludes with patriarchy. If Anne Sexton

Women's Studies 12, no. 2 (1986). Reprinted by permission of the author and the publisher.

learned about her own incestuous dependencies from Freud and his proxies during the early stages of her life as a career mental patient, hers was still the first contemporary voice outside of the psychoanalytic world to describe the normative relationship between father and daughter from the daughter's perspective.[3] Sexton's early poetry both represents and dissects the subtle and pervasive psycho-social pattern that Phyllis Chesler would later discuss, and damn, in *Women and Madness,* and which now, in the wake of feminist inquiry, seems almost obvious: "romantic" love in the western world is "psychologically predicated on sexual union between Daughter and Father figures."

The "normal" woman in western society, whether or not she is a poet, and whether or not she is fully aware of the psychic dynamics, falls in love with her father, who delights her, despises her, seduces her, betrays her, and dies. The father who dies in 1959 in the poet's personal life undergoes a series of resurrections as man and imago—husband, doctor, lover, priest—and is finally reborn as the diety of *The Awful Rowing Toward God.* Burial and resurrection of the fathers becomes a central theme in Sexton's poetry, as it is in the personal lives of her contemporaries and the collective life of her culture. In all of his incarnations in Sexton's poetry, the father finally fails himself and his daughter, for he is a god not sufficiently omnipotent, a man not sufficiently human, a male principle not sufficiently able to accommodate feminine powers and desires. But this ultimate failure is never judged harshly in Sexton's poetry, never evoked without the empathy that always accompanies insight; for the shortcomings of the father-god in a patriarchy are nearly definitive of the failures of the human enterprise, one in which all men and all women engage. This is not to say that Sexton's poetry lacks anger, or what Blake called "prophetic wrath": that is quite another matter. (In her personal life, Sexton seems to have saved her wrath for herself, a wrath "prophetic" only in the most mundane sense; that, too, is another matter.) In the world of Sexton's poetry, the men born into their myths are often as helpless and hapless as the women born into theirs; Sexton was inclined to portray the sad worthiness of all human effort, however doomed. Although she saw, reluctantly, the relentless "gender of things," her poetic eye was androgynously kind. (Too kind? Again, another matter.)

To Bedlam and Part Way Back lays the foundation for Sexton's version, or inversion, of Freud's *Totem and Taboo,* in which the father in the family evolves into the defiled and then worshipped God. Five poems in *Bedlam* establish the father figure as god, doctor, and cultural myth, as well as biological parent and great-grandparent. The collection opens with "You, Doctor Martin," which immediately establishes the therapist as modern mediator between the religious and the familial. He is the confessor who is the "god of our block," the father of all the "large . . . foxy children" who inhabit Bedlam.

"You, Doctor Martin, walk / from breakfast to madness." The speaker, a patient in a mental institution, narrates both from within and outside of her own madness. Mad enough to be among the "moving dead," mad enough to be "queen of this summer hotel," mad enough to "make moccasins all morning," she is sane enough to look at the anatomy of her relationship to her confessor with insightful equanimity: "Of course, I love you." That calm awareness of psychic process (specifically, of the clinical phenomenon of transference) does not stop her from being "mad," nor does the madness inhibit her clear-sighted analytic knowledge. The speaker knows that the patient always "loves" the doctor, the sinner always loves the confessor, the daughter always loves the father. Speaking out of her own awareness of individual pain and comfort, the narrator is nevertheless detached enough to see exactly how that individual situation is an enactment of a paradigmatic drama, in which she plays her inevitable role of the crazy daughter in a scenario with the grown-up father-doctor whose very business is the eminently sane management of madness. He is the "god of our block, prince of all the foxes."

> . . . Your third eye
> moves among us and lights the separate boxes
> where we sleep or cry.
>
> What large children we are
> here. All over I grow most tall
> in the best ward. Your business is people,
> you call at the madhouse, an oracular
> eye in our nest. . . .

> . . . You twist in the pull
> of the foxy children who fall

> like floods of life in frost.

Although the speaker talks of the doctor's third eye, she gazes from her own third eye, painfully and sanely aware of the psychic dynamics she and her fellow inmates play out. She ironically and consciously regards the doctor as both god and father, herself as queen and daughter. His "third eye" is "oracular," prophetic and all-knowing, for it has, godlike, known all the separate sins of his patients. With his third eye he is able to "light" their separateness, illumine their pain, comfort merely by his presence. But he is also only human, a man attending to his "business": treating sick people. He is not, after all, one of them, for he only "calls at the madhouse" after his breakfast. With her own third eye, the speaker sees that they have all become his children, whom he can leave only by extricating himself from their desperate and clever grasps. The third eye is the doctor's blessing, his ability to see and to cope, but it is also his curse; perhaps the speaker-poet's own third eye is her blessing and curse as well, for when the father-god has gone, the patients become "magic talking to itself, / noisy and alone." When the magic of therapy departs, leaving only the magic of madness, the speaker turns her third eye toward what we might call "vision," toward the magic of the poem. The poem she writes is a hymn of praise to her doctor, the daughter-patient's version of Donne's "Hymn to God My God, in My Sickness." As Donne is Adam, Sexton's speaker is Eve, both paying tribute to their gods, both supplicants who ask: "Receive me, Lord."

"You, Doctor Martin," serves as frontispiece not only for the theme of madness, but for the further explorations of the father-daughter relationship in this first volume, one that ends with an extended discussion of the other and feminine source of the self—what Sexton will later call, in "Old Dwarf Heart," the "mother, father, I'm made of." During the transference process of psychoanalysis, the therapist *becomes* in his person a condensation of all the images of the mind; although, ideally, he will "become" mother as well as father, his gender and the patriarchal nature of the process identify him most clearly with the gods and fathers, rather than the goddesses and mothers, of one's memory. The tightly condensed father-god figure of "You, Doctor Martin" fragments into his component parts in subsequent poems of *Bedlam,* becoming father, great-grandfather, Apollo, and, in a transcultural and quasi-mythic incarnation, a dead Arabian father buried with his daughter.

"Mother, Father, I'm Made Of": *All My Pretty Ones* and *Live or Die*

Sexton's second collection, *All My Pretty Ones,* takes place in an ever-present past, in the "deep museum" of entombed memory carved with words into a monument of the living dead. Here, perhaps more deliberately than in any other single volume of Sexton's poetry, the ambiguity of inheritance is the single strongest issue. The "frozen sea within us," Sexton knew, is always iced by consciousness, which keeps us from the depths of both pain and pleasure that arise from breaking the surface and plunging into the past that actually creates the present. The poems are not restricted to the speaker's personal losses, but range instead into poignant portraits of unknown people, unknown lives ("Doors, Doors, Doors"), lives that never were ("The Abortion"); and they reach from the sacred to the profane with the ease that will more and more characterize Sexton's religious quest. The "mother, father, I'm made of" is the mother and father we are all made of, in which the concept of deity resides. So profoundly did Anne Sexton believe that family relationships are the foundation of all tragedy, all joy, that even God's plight is best understood through his son.

The second section of *All My Pretty Ones* is preceded by a Guardini epigraph: "I want no pallid humanitarianism—If Christ be not God, I want none of him; I will hack my way through existence alone." In this section, Sexton explores this other and related betrayal: that God is, after all, only the mortal father whose child inherits his weakness, which ends in her own death. The grandfather enters as mediator of this process in the final poem of the volume, "Letter Written During a January Northeaster," in which the speaker is alone, awaiting a lover's letters that never come. The poem begins on a Monday, with snow falling upon "the small faces of the dead," in particular the mother and father. Divided into six days, the poem is an elaborate pretense: "I have invented a lie. / There is no other day but Monday." By this narrative device, the poet emphasizes the repetition enacted in time, the stasis underlying movement. The letters do not come.

> The mailman is an impostor.
> He is actually my grandfather.
> He floats far off in the storm
> with his nicotine mustache and a bagful of nickels.

Tenderly evoking the grandfather to whom Sexton dedicates the last section of poems in this volume, the speaker reveals the identity not only of the mailman, but of the letter, the word, as mediator between the present beloved (who is absent) and the past beloveds (who are dead). "Now he is gone / as you are gone." The grandfather, too, is dead; the lover is absent and in his absence as good as dead; and the mailman who should have brought the lovers together through the efficacy of words has proved an imposter. But he, grandfather-mailman, "belongs to me like lost baggage." As the mailman recedes into the storm, so does the figure of that grandfather; unlike the mailman, and like the lover, he belongs to her in the same way that lost baggage still belongs to its owner. "Letter" establishes the virtual identifications of its imagined components: of one day with the next, of the present lost lover with the dead grandfather.

The identification of a woman's husband with her father remains implicit in the first two volumes, where it is hinted at, leapt beyond, or discussed at one remove through mythology, anthropology, or the buffer of an extra generation. In *Live or Die,* Sexton's third volume, that identification is made explicit for the first time. The speaker's father was "a born salesman" who sold wool, and a born talker "in love with maps," who "died on the road." Her husband also sells wool, also travels on the road:

> And when you drive off, my darling,
> Yes, sir! Yes, sir! It's one for my dame,
> your sample cases branded with my father's name,

your itinerary open,
its tolls ticking and greedy,
its highways built up like new loves, raw and speedy.

This is a world where women stand and wait—"I sit at my desk / each night with no place to go"—while men explore and conquer, "greedy" for the open road and all it represents: freedom, independence, possession, the familiarly "raw and speedy" litany. The salesman father and husband of Sexton's real life symbolize a cultural axiom she would later explain in *Transformations,* where the fairy tale world is one of masculine and feminine principles meeting and conflicting. The man brings home "one for his dame," who sits and waits while he conquers a world in which the highway inflicted on the countryside is the equivalent of the penis entering the body of nature—always a woman's body. The "new loves" allude to the infidelity inherent not only literally in the salesman's life, but figuratively in the desertion of the wife or daughter for that new love, the road that is always open, offering adventure.

In "Cripples and Other Stories," the father emerges as doctor once again, taking up where he left off in *Bedlam.* Responding to his laughter at a "silly rhyme" she wrote for him (*"Each time I give lectures / or gather in the grants / you send me off to boarding school / in training pants"*), she insists in sing-song rhyme that he and she both look at the facts:

> God damn it, father-doctor.
> I'm really thirty-six.
> I see dead rats in the toilet.
> I'm one of the lunatics.

The poem moves through childhood rituals that revolve around the speaker's mother and father. The child puts her hand through the wringer-washer. "My father took the crowbar / and broke that wringer's heart." Yet even if he was her champion here, he is usually indifferent, "fat on scotch" which "leaked from every orifice," or a "perfect man, / clean and rich and fat," intent only on making money and smoking cigars. The doctor is the father's surrogate, but unlike the father who "didn't know me," he responds on her behalf with tenderness instead of rage: "How strange that you're so tender!" At the end, she drops the "doctor" of the original address.

> Father, I'm thirty-six,
> yet I lie here in your crib.
> I'm getting born again, Adam.
> as you prod me with your rib.

The same process, that of rebirth through psychoanalytic therapy, of starting over and getting this time around a father who holds and kisses and is loving to her in her "fever," might be merely sentimental or silly if it were not for Sexton's choice of rhyme and meter. In carefully wrought tetrameter and trimeter lines, Sexton both exemplifies and parodies the process of therapy, through which the analysand becomes again a child responding to her parents. The process, and the poem, are thus tinged with a gentle, wry irony. Can it really work, this process? Phyllis Chesler asks the same question in *Women and Madness,* as part of her discussion of the infantilization of women in the therapeutic process:

> Can a technique based on transference, or on the resolution of an Oedipal conflict—i.e., on a romanticization of a rape-incest-procreative model of sexuality—wean women away from this very sexual model?[4]

The poet does not answer such polemical questions—that is not her role as she perceives it—but the tonal complexities of this "nursery rhyme" suggest her knowledge of the difficulties as well as the dynamics involved. Although I think we are meant to see the doctor's tenderness (he kisses and holds her in the poem) as properly humane rather than prurient in intent, there is something comically prurient in the very nature of the process as Sexton describes it: a grown woman first put in training pants by her doctor, then kept in a crib, and finally, in the regressive evolution of both the method and the poem, being reborn—all in the cadences of "This Little Piggy." And while I think Sexton's poem vindicates rather than damns the doctor's motivations, there is also no escaping the sexual overtones of the final line, in which the doctor, a new Adam, "prods" her with his "rib," corresponding neatly with Chesler's rape-incest-procreative description of psychoanalysis's *modus operandi*. This is particularly so since we are left with the image of a passive infant female being sexually assaulted (with whatever ostensibly benign motivation or effect) by an adult male doctor's prodding rib—or, in the illuminating vernacular, his hard cock.

It seems to me that Sexton neither endorses nor damns the method here, but merely subjects it to an interested and insightful scrutiny. The tone of the poem suggests that she is benefitting from this process of rebirth in which she reenacts a traumatic childhood "in your crib," and receives the love from the doctor that she was denied by his prototype, the father. The doctor may be able to bring to life the primal and potentially strong woman of the speaker's unconscious depths, and she accords him and his method this accession; but she is also suspicious, ironic, detached, a bit alarmed both at herself and at the method which seems to deny that she is "really thirty-six." Yet, thirty-six or not, if she sees "dead rats in the toilet," she needs help. And if her father is one of those dead rats, beyond either saving or damning her himself, then perhaps, she seems to say, she needs this second chance. She needs the mediation of the doctor as Father and Adam and God, in her effort to get the rats out of the toilet.

"What Voyage This, Little Girl?": *The Transformations of Daddy*

While the father of *Love Poems* is almost entirely subsumed by the lover's transmutation into the carpenter-god, he returns again in *Transformations* in differently transmuted form. The hearts of the passive princesses and daughters of *Transformations* are bonded as surely to the "mother, father, I'm made of," as are Sexton's early speakers. In "Snow White," "Cinderella," "Red Riding Hood," "The Maiden Without Hands," "The Twelve Dancing Princesses," and "Briar Rose (Sleeping Beauty)," fathers and mothers save or thwart or damn or damage or love or devour their mythic offspring in both literal and surrogate capacities. Most of the tales begin at home, with the heroes and heroines in domestic peril or at domestic peace; similarly, most of the tales end with either restoration or transformation of that domesticity. The lovers who marry the girls and women of most of the tales I mention are barely disguised fathers, protector figures who take their new wives home and live with them to dwell in infinitely protracted and infinitely patriarchal bliss. Because it most directly and sardonically addresses the subject, I will deal here with "Briar Rose."

In the Prologue, Sexton introduces us to a "little doll child":

> come here to Papa.
> Sit on my knee.
> I have kisses for the back of your neck.
> A penny for your thoughts, Princess.
> I will hunt them like an emerald.
> Come be my snooky
> and I will give you a root.

The tale Sexton has transformed here tells us only that the king dearly loved his child, and that because of this love and the fairy's curse, he overprotected her—a circumstance that, with or without a fairy's curse, is common enough to be normative in our culture. In her version of "Briar Rose," Sexton plays out the effects of such smothering and overprotective love on the part of fathers for the "purity" and "safety" of their daughters—effects also sufficiently common to be normative. Briar Rose manages to get in trouble despite her father's obsessive restrictions on her activities; in due course, she pricks her finger on the spinning wheel and falls asleep. The prince who finally gets through the briars to wake her up gets a greeting not included in Grimm:

> He kissed Briar Rose
> and she woke up crying:
> Daddy! Daddy!

Since "Daddy" is the only man she has ever been permitted to know, the single source of love and safety, the prince is her daddy for life. The only hitch is that she has become an insomniac because of her fear of sleep—her long sleep was initiated, it is probably important to remember, by her father's omission of the proprieties; he did not propitiate the proper female deities by recognizing the thirteenth fairy. When Briar Rose sleeps, she returns to a kind of death-in-life. "You could lay her in a grave, . . . / and she'd never call back: Hello there!'' Only the kiss can wake her when she gets this way, so the prince is forced to wake her always in a repetition of that initial awakening:

> But if you kissed her on the mouth
> her eyes would spring open
> and she'd call out: Daddy! Daddy!
> Presto!
> She's out of prison.

Permanently infantilized by her earlier relationship to an idolatrously loving father and a long and symbolic sleep in which no other men could come near her, she is never quite a woman, always a daughter, even to her husband.

In a rhetorical move uncharacteristic of the other "transformations" here, which have only prologues, Sexton appends an epilogue to the tale of Briar Rose. The identity of the speaker is ambiguous; because of an abrupt tone shift and a sudden change from third to first person, we cannot be sure if the "I" of the epilogue is Briar Rose or "Dame Sexton." The speaker tells us that "there was a theft," and "I was abandoned" and "forced backward." The closing of the poem also constitutes the end of the book:

> Each night I am nailed into place
> and I forget who I am.
> Daddy?
> That's another kind of prison.
> It's not the prince at all,
> but my father
> drunkenly bent over my bed,
> circling the abyss like a shark,
> my father thick upon me
> like some sleeping jellyfish.
> What voyage this, little girl?
> This coming out of prison?
> God help—
> this life after death?

The tone change is remarkably abrupt and complete. Throughout the tale Sexton has maintained that tongue-in-cheek tone so characteristic of *Transformations,* in which deadly serious matter is relieved by casual and sardonic wit. The seductive father of the prologue—"Come be my snooky / and I will give you a root"— is both doting daddy and dirty old man, and for him we are invited to feel an affectionately dismissive contempt. But the father of the prologue is a daylight daddy, a bringer of lollipops as well as that vaguely threatening "root." At only one moment does he appear truly sinister: "A penny for your thoughts, Princess. / I will hunt them like an emerald." But the father of the epilogue comes to the daughter at night, "circling the abyss like a shark." This is the flip side face of the daddy who bounces on the knee, just as this new perspective is the flip side of the daughter's irresistible seduction when she awakes: "Daddy!" If the body of the tale gives us the way in which the incestuous romance of father and daughter is carried *by the daughter* to her husband's bed, the epilogue is a sinister echo of the genesis of that behavior in the prologue. While Sexton, perhaps uncharacteristic of many contemporary women, is not afraid to acknowledge the daughter's part in the sexual drama of father and daughter, neither is she reticent to insist that the father share the blame—that, in fact, he be held responsible for its most exploitive and darkest form in the actual seduction or rape of daughters by their fathers.

We know from other sources that Anne Sexton was an insomniac and that her intensely ambivalent relationship to her father, Ralph Harvey, may have included such a "midnight visit," as she calls it elsewhere. In view of these circumstances and the internal evidence of the poem, I think it safe to say that the speaker of the final words in *Transformations* is a conflation of the mythical Briar Rose and the poet Anne Sexton. If the speaker of "Mother and Jack and the Rain" is also Sexton, we have both sides of a story Anne Sexton knew to be not only her own, but that of countless American women: fantasized seduction in which the daughter not only participates, but that she initiates in the close private recesses of her own bed and her own body, accompanied by actual seduction that becomes the source of lifelong trauma for the daughter. Of course the female child dreams of making love with her father, of bearing him a baby, of replacing her mother; and of course, when the father makes that dream come true, the daughter is betrayed. As Chesler says, in patriarchal society the father-daughter incest taboo is *"psychologically* obeyed by men and disobeyed by women." Although Chesler does not expand on this, I take her to mean something such as this: a female child, because of the stages of her psycho-social development, is nearly compelled to desire the father, while the male is not compelled to desire the daughter by that same process; rather, he will desire, and possibly find, the mother. But the *actual* disobedience of the taboo is usually initiated by the father, who is not only older, more powerful, and in a position of authority, but who is also—and this is probably crucial—a male member of a patriarchy. (The incidence of mother-son seduction is comparatively minor.) "What voyage this, little girl?" After the shark circles her in the dark, after the jellyfish is thick upon her, she will always awake crying, in more ways than one, "Daddy!"

"The Lost Signalman" and "The Train That Comes No More": *The Death of the Fathers*

Nothing for it but to put the father to death, and that is what Sexton does, mournfully and lovingly, in the sequence titled "The Death of the Fathers" in *The Book of Folly*. The death of the fathers marks the passage from innocence to experience. In "Oysters," a simple seafood meal between father and daughter becomes her rite of passage into womanhood.

Through eating oysters for the first time—which despite or because of their source in the sea the speaker calls "father-food"—the speaker incorporates and conquers the sea in herself.

> Oysters we ate,
> sweet blue babies,
> . . . .
>
> It was a soft medicine
> that came from the sea into my mouth,
> moist and plump.
> I swallowed.

While the daughter makes her first attempts to get them down, her father laughs at her fear and drinks his martini, "clear as tears." This laughter, fatherly and benign, is tinged with friendly ridicule of her fear; but the clear tears of his martini reflect, perhaps, his own disguised sorrow at the ritual into which he knows he initiates his daughter. The challenge to her to eat something soft, moist, plump, and alien, which she must swallow in order to pass a test, hovers on the border between sensuality and sexuality; this might as easily be a description of fellatio as of eating oysters.

> Then I laughed and then we laughed
> and let me take note—
> there was a death,
> the death of childhood
> there at the Union Oyster House
> for I was fifteen
> and eating oysters
> and the child was defeated.
> The woman won.

The woman becomes she who devours and incorporates the sea-creature, the alien thing that is herself. It is particularly significant that the father, alone and without the mother, escorts the speaker through this ritual while he drinks his martini, surely another father-food, surely another sexual signal. The laughter between them is canny; alone together, sans mother or siblings, father and daughter have their sweet and slightly wicked tête-a-tête. The unspoken understanding between them, one the poem itself articulates, is that the father has introduced his daughter not only to adulthood, but to the sexual ripeness of womanhood.

But this celebration of sexuality with the father, this triumph he shares with her, is also a defeat for him: "Oysters" marks one of his "deaths." By initiating her into womanhood, the father relinquishes his exclusive hold on her affections; and relinquishing the daughter-child status by which she has belonged only to him, she comes into her own. The event they celebrate together is his demise as the only lover in her life. Through this mediation from the sea, he hands her to her womanhood, and thereby to other men who will take his place.

In "How We Danced," the dramatic situation is a family wedding. The speaker is nineteen, dancing with her father as man and woman rather than as father and daughter. They dance "like two birds on fire," and "we were dear, / very dear."

> Mother was a belle and danced with twenty men.
> You danced with me never saying a word.

> Instead the serpent spoke as you held me close.
> The serpent, that mocker, woke up and pressed against me
> like a great god and we bent together
> like two lonely swans.

The mother in this Oedipal scenario is conveniently out of the way, dancing with other men as her husband and daughter perform a wedding dance that is both reflection and parody of the actual wedding. The serpent, the father's penis, speaks what he does not, disregards propriety and taboo, "mocking" both a cultural and a personal contract. His penis is like a god, because in the mythic world invoked here, incest is the paradigm, not the deviation. Together, irrevocably joined in their unspoken and by now implicitly mutual sin, father and daughter do not acknowledge what comes between them. Once again, something dies—this time, it is the swan-song of a fiction of sexless familial love, a demise that by the end of the poem compels the daughter's complicity. His "death" is his diminishment as "father," accompanied by his phoenixlike rebirth as the lover that he has always been, even if secretly, to his daughter. But the serpent is indeed a mocker, for the involuntary physical sign of his sexual desire constitutes a betrayal of his daughter *as daughter,* a betrayal of himself *as father*.

In "Santa," the speaker remembers father dressing up as Santa Claus, another all-giving father, in the yearly Christmas scenario. Playing Santa is another in the series of lies that separates children from adults, the kindly lies that make mythology of family and sanity of familial madness. "But that is over." The daughter has replaced the mother, and now Father-Santa is dead.

> And you, you fade out of sight
> like a lost signalman
> wagging his lantern
> for the train that comes no more.

The father joins dead hands with the grandfather-mailman of "Letter Written" in *All My Pretty Ones*. The mailman with his "bagful of nickels" and the train signalman are both representatives of a life that is past, that passes even as it lives.

"The Death of the Fathers" marks a series of broken taboos through which the poet rejects, reclaims, is rejected by, reclaimed by, the fathers of her life. The deaths are plural because there are many small deaths before the large and literal one represented in the poet's life by Ralph Harvey's death in 1959; and the fathers are many because, as Sexton knew, her speaker claimed and rejected that paternal presence in many guises: father, grandfather, doctor, priest, God. I think Sexton also intended a double plurality of deaths and fathers to signify the culturally representative nature of her own biography; just as Ralph Harvey was not her only father, and just as he and his surrogates were to undergo many symbolic deaths in her life, there are many Annes among her readership, each with her own several fathers and multiple deaths.

"Divorcing Daddy: Dybbuk! Dybbuk!": *45 Mercy Street*

Sexton says her final published words on the father in "Divorce, Thy Name Is Woman." The speaker tries to break that archaic and infantile tie at last, by acknowledging the nature of the marriage bond with and the divorce from her husband.

> I am divorcing daddy—Dybbuk! Dybbuk!
> I have been doing it daily all my life
> since his sperm left him.

The speaker is all women who enact the paradigmatic relationship Sexton first explored in mythic terms in *To Bedlam and Part Way Back*. The dybbuk becomes a concretion of the mythic and the personal. The dybbuk, in medieval Jewish legend, may be either the spirit of a dead person who lives and speaks through a living human; or it may be a demon that possesses the living; here it is both. The spirit of the father is the spirit of the dear dead, whom the speaker always remembers as Macduff remembers his slain wife and children; but he is also the demon who possesses the living in order to dispossess her of herself. She addresses that paradox of the human condition: that we turn to the dead, to memory, as individuals and as a culture, for our sense of identity and meaning; that we have no choice in this matter; that we piece together a sense of self out of the inheritance of family, enlarged into an inheritance of culture.

But at the same time that the legacy of the dead provides us with a raison d'être, and represents our own urge to propel ourselves into the future through the immortality of generations, it also represents the death-wish, the urge to annihilate oneself, to follow the dead to their stone graves. In a woman, the paradox is apparent in the relationship to the father who is succeeded by a reincarnation of himself in the husband. A woman may spend her life, in effect, divorcing and marrying her father. In this poem, Sexton constructs a kind of allegory for woman in western culture. The marriage of daughter to father is represented as literal.

> Later,
> when blood and eggs and breasts
> dropped onto me,
> Daddy and his whiskey breath
> made a long midnight visit
> in a dream that is not a dream
> and then called his lawyer quickly.
> Daddy divorcing me.

The "dream that is not a dream" is a psychic fact, a fact of mental life, something that "actually happens" in the netherland of unconscious primary process. The father seduces the daughter, then rejects her, disowning his own passion and hers. "I have been divorcing him ever since" in the interior world of psychic realities, where the Mother is her witness in the courtroom. The daughter keeps on divorcing him, "adding up the crimes / of how he came to me, / how he left me." Sexton's speaker takes on the voice of any woman working out her childhood love for her father, any woman still

> waiting, waiting for Daddy to come home
> and stuff me so full of our infected child
> that I turn invisible, but married,
> at last.

What Sexton speaks of here is as narrow as the room of each womb we come from, and as broad as our dedication to Classical culture. We are all implicated, fathers and daughters alike, all dwelling in a shadow world in which the realities we perceive are shadows of original forms—and of original desires. We stay in the cave willingly, perceiving reflected forms, because we cannot look upon those forms directly without becoming "invisible." Yet we seek that original form, the original desire, never quite content with its substitute.

While Sexton breaks this ultimate taboo, thereby acknowledging her self-effacement, her speaker also wants to affirm the divorce. The "solution" of the poem is a continual process of divorce, an unending courtroom scene, but one which always returns from courtroom to bedroom, where the woman is "opening and shutting the windows. Making the bed and pulling it apart." Before and after the divorce of man and wife is this continuous marriage to and divorce from the father, a permanent oscillation between two conflicting desires: to divorce and be done with; and to "marry, at last."

"The Island of God": *The Death Notebooks,* *The Awful Rowing*

Although the father is entirely absent from *The Awful Rowing Toward God* as a literal and familial presence, this entire collection has been accurately described by critics as a monument to Anne Sexton's need for a God who is the embodiment of paternal authority, absolutism, absolution; a God who will punish the "gnawing pestilential rat" inside of her, and then "take it with his two hands / and embrace it" ("Rowing"); a God who will finally guarantee her that immortality will be replication, eternal and writ large, of a perfected and idealized family circle in which she will at last win the love and acceptance and protection and approval denied her by her parents. This heavenly family will be presided over by a benevolent but exacting Papa who will drink mana instead of whiskey, punish her justly instead of capriciously, love her unconditionally instead of sporadically. Maxine Kumin calls this God of Sexton's deepest desires "a sure thing, an Old Testament avenger admonishing his Chosen People, an authoritarian yet forgiving Father decked out in sacrament and ceremony."[5] To Alicia Ostriker, the poet's attempt to "give imaginative birth to an adequate Godhead" becomes a "heroic failure," because the "decisive intelligence which dismantles religious myth is no match for the child-woman's ferocious need for cosmic love."[6] Estella Lauter finds that the "essential drama of her work in these years [1970–1974] lies in her repeated discoveries of the Father-God's inadequacy coupled with her inability to give Him up."[7]

Before I cluck too sympathetically or patronizingly at the pathetic end of Anne Sexton's quest for the Father, I must remind myself of two equally important facts, one about Anne Sexton, one about the culture of which she is both member and visionary spokesperson. First, and most humbling, is that Sexton's search for the traditional Father-God in dozens of poems that may be failures in the feminist sense—as Ostriker says, she "accepts humiliation on behalf of all beautiful women"—is an eloquent representation of an entire culture's search for that same God. The loving and admonishing Father for whom she searches is the Father for whom we have all searched, men and women alike. We have all sought his blessing, tried to conjure up his presence in times of crisis if not of ease. Even those of us who have rejected him outright in favor of no gods at all—or of gods that offend our sensibilities less, or match our politics better, or seem to us truer, more imaginative—catch ourselves wishing, or fearing, that he might exist. Sexton's failing Father-God is, in short, our own; I cannot see how it could be otherwise in a patriarchy as old and enduring as ours. The idea of such a God is not original or rehabilitating or appealing, except to those instincts that are conservative, repetitive, and fearful. But to deny his vestigial hold on us is to pridefully declare that we are not, at whatever seemingly safe remove, influenced by the conservative, the repetitive, the fearful. Who has not asked, slightly desperate at the heart, "Is it true? Is it true?" Who has not been "in this country of black mud," longing for that God through whom one could be "born again / into something true?"

Second, and more important, the poet who needs to be beaten by God in that final poker game is the same one who dreams she can "piss in God's eye" ("Hurry Up Please It's Time," *The Death Notebooks*). She is, as Ostriker and Lauter explain, the poet who dismantles religious myth and reimagines Christianity in the most daring and original ways. She undertakes to rewrite Genesis, the Psalms, and, most radically, the Gospels. She is among the most original and radical of religious poets in our literary and spiritual heritage.

With this reservation in mind, I participate in regretting the imaginatively small and fraudulent God Sexton asked herself and her readers to settle for at the end of *The Awful Rowing Toward God*. In *The Death Notebooks,* the God she searched out was still pluralistic, still appealingly heathen and varied. "Mrs. Sexton went out looking for the gods" in the first poem of *The Death Notebooks,* in lower case plural. Even *The Awful Rowing* finds God in the "chapel of eggs" with "the absurdities of the dinner table," sometimes "dressed up like a whore" or an old man or a child. He "lives in shit" and beans and butter and milk, in the poet's typewriter, in "the private holiness of my hands." It is, I think, primarily the final poem in the collection that so disturbs readers and critics.

In "The Rowing Endeth," God has diminished back into the father of "Oysters," who laughs as he drinks his martini and presides over a ritual of defeat as well as triumph for the speaker-poet. While "Oysters" may seem an oddly minor poem in thematic concerns compared to "The Rowing Endeth"—after all, one is about eating oysters for the first time and one is about rowing to the island of God for salvation—they are similar in situation, tone, even in language. Listen to the central scene in both: in "Oysters" the father is laughing at and with the daughter as she gags down her first oysters and he drinks his martini: "Then I laughed and then we laughed." We leave them laughing, celebrating "the death of childhood" and the speaker's rebirth into womanhood. In "The Rowing Endeth," God wins the poker game, probably by cheating:

> He starts to laugh,
> the laughter rolling like a hoop out of His mouth
> and into mine,
> and such laughter that He doubles right over me
> laughing a Rejoice-Chorus at our two triumphs.

In both cases, the triumph for the daughter-poet—rebirth into womanhood, rebirth into salvation—is presided over by a Father-figure who has the edge over the speaker. He is bigger, older, wiser, male. He enjoys his power over her, and she enjoys it with him. In "The Rowing Endeth," as in "Oysters," the speaker is initiated into mysteries, made privy to secrets, included, endorsed, approved of, loved. Yet in both scenarios, there is no question of who enjoys the power. Reading both poems, I feel the edge of sexual humiliation through seduction, the kind felt by a girl who is told a dirty joke by an older man; she laughs, uncomfortably and too loud, half understanding the joke, half knowing that it is directed at her. Here, as in "The Death Baby" (*The Death Notebooks*), such "love" is both erotic and deathly, both the symbol of woman's self-assurance and of her self-annihilation. Her passionate responses enact both her wish to live and her wish to die. "You have seen my father whip me. / You have seen me stroke my father's whip."

Just such an unsavory seduction takes place in an untitled 1965 poem from the posthumously published sequence of poem-letters to her psychiatrist in *Words for Dr. Y.* An unnamed male the speaker called "Comfort" reads to the speaker during her childhood, from the Bible, "to prove I was sinful."

> *For in the night he was betrayed.*
> And then he let me give him a Judas-kiss,
> that red lock that held us in place,
> and then I gave him a drink from my cup
> and he whispered, "Rape, rape."
> And then I gave him my wrist
> and he sucked on the blood,
> hating himself for it,
> murmuring, "God will see. God will see."

In this extraordinarily ambiguous seduction, the girl-child appears to initiate the ritual of blood that is both sexual and religious. But the dynamics of power are unmistakably on the side of the older male, who ironically whispers "rape" when, if there is such a thing going on, we know very well who is the victim. While the male ostensibly worries that "God will see" what they are doing, it is clear that he is playing the part of God himself, "allowing" himself to be betrayed by this Judas-child. It might be illuminating to know the identity of this male in the poet's biography, and to find it, we need only turn to *All My Pretty Ones,* to the grandfather of the "bagful of nickels" in "Letter Written During a January Northeaster," to whom the final sequence of poems in that volume is dedicated: "For Comfort, who was actually my Grandfather."

This seduction scene between granddaughter and grandfather is repeated in reverse form in the posthumously published "Leaves That Talk" in *45 Mercy Street.*

> I dream it's the fourth of July
> and I'm having a love affair
> with grandfather (his real birthday)
> ······························
>
> and in my dream
> grandfather touches my neck and breast
> and says, "Do not be afraid!
> It's only the leaves falling!"

Here the grandfather is the initiator of sexual contact, and the process he interferes with is the suicide's conversation with her voices, the "green girls"—leaves that call her to "come to us" and die. His role here as "comforter" is compromised by his seduction of his granddaughter; if his comfort were merely paternal, we could be glad of his saving presence, which calls her away from the voices that urge her to die. But the fact that he "touches her breast" lends this scene the sinister aura of the dirty old man, whose motivations in urging her away from the feminine-suicidal to the masculine-sacrificial are highly suspect.

Sexton's grandfather is a minor character in the family drama that unfolds in Sexton's poetry during the eighteen years and ten volumes of her writing career, overshadowed as he is by the poet's mother, father, daughters, and great-aunt, Nana. Yet it is he, finally, who most clearly connects the God of *The Awful Rowing* and the father-figures of the poet's personal life. Perhaps his title as "grand" father makes this connection appropriate, for what is a God in a patriarchy but a Grand Father? That he is also the person the child called "Comfort" is acutely apropos, for comfort is what she seeks from God. In "Grandfather, Your Wound" (*The Death Notebooks*), the speaker sits in a house on an "island" belonging to him.

> . . . you are a ceiling made of wood
> and the island you were the man of,
> is shaped like a squirrel and named thereof.
> On this island, Grandfather, made of your stuff

Sexton the writer stands "in your writing room" in this poem, surrounded by his belongings and mourning the absence of "Mr. Funnyman, Mr. Nativeman . . . Mr. Lectureman, Mr.

Editor." Arthur Gray Staples was indeed a lecturer and writer, editor-in-chief of the *Lewiston Evening Journal* (one of Maine's largest newspapers) and author of several books of essays. Squirrel Island was the summer home of seven five-story houses described in "Funnel" (*All My Pretty Ones*). Staples's writing room, setting for "Grandfather, Your Wound," was a spacious room with an ocean view.[8]

When Sexton moors her rowboat at the dock of the "island called God" at the end of *The Awful Rowing,* she is, I believe, mooring herself again at her beloved Squirrel Island. And "the flesh of The Island"—the flesh of God—is none other than her grandfather, that "ceiling made of wood" in "Your Wound." "I wouldn't mind if God were wooden," she writes in a peculiar and otherwise inexplicable line in "Is It True?"

> Oh wood, my father, my shelter,
> bless you

And in *The Death Notebooks,* to receive "God's Backside," the "dark negative" turned against her, is cold, "like Grandfather's icehouse" ("God's Backside"). If we need any further indication that Grandfather is God, we find it in the closing of "Your Wound," when dead "Comfort" comes back, resurrected with the same appositive/expletive construction that closes "All My Pretty Ones":

> my God, Grandfather,
> you are here,
> you are laughing,
> you hold me and rock me
> and we watch the lighthouse come on,
> blinking its dry wings over us all,
> over my wound
> and yours.

The sun has gone down, but when he comes back to her, "it comes bright again." The unspecified "wound" of which he died is the flaw that she inherits, that she, too, will die of; but his presence, a resurrection from the dead, is the assurance that he lives to be her "comfort" once again—to tell her that she is sinful, to sin with her, to love her. He, perhaps alone among all her other familial gods, endorses her as a writer. (Mary Harvey, who once wanted to be a writer, inaugurated Anne's efforts with rejections and an accusation of plagiarism, while her father and husband, whose business was wool, were not able or likely to make her feel that such activity really qualified as "work.") The God "my typewriter believes in" ("The Frenzy," *Awful Rowing*) is her grandfather as writer as well as father. Elsewhere in *Awful Rowing,* the typewriter is her "church," her "altar of keys." In her introduction to the *Complete Poems,* Maxine Kumin writes:

> An elderly, sympathetic priest she called on—"accosted" might be a better word—patiently explained that he could not make her a Catholic by fiat, nor could he administer the sacrament (the last rites) she longed for. But in his native wisdom he said a saving thing to her, said the magic and simple words that kept her alive at least a year beyond her time and made *The Awful Rowing Toward God* a possibility. "God is in your typewriter," he told her.[9]

"Your Wound" ends with the chillingly familiar scene of laughter between the daughter-poet and the father-God, but here the laughter seems genuinely mutual, truly benevolent. We may regret that in his metamorphosis from human grandfather to cosmic Grand Father, the male figure represented in this discussion by Arthur Gray Staples became such a sinister and fraudulent deity. It is difficult to "applaud" this "dearest dealer," as Sexton asks herself and us to do in "The Rowing Endeth." Doubling "right over me" in laughter, he is at least as much the circling shark and the "father thick upon me" like some "jellyfish" of "Briar Rose," as he is the benevolent "bagful of nickels" of "Letter Written," holding and rocking her as the lighthouse flashes on to illuminate the darkness. Yet what we *can* applaud is that, as Kumin says, the search for the God in her typewriter kept her going, inspired by an old priest who may have been reminiscent of her grandfather—and who certainly offered her "comfort" through affirming her worth as a poet.

I find it poignant to discover that the "island of God" may have been the island of childhood where she summered, and where, as her editors remind us in the *Letters,* "Anne's happy memories centered."[10] I also confess that I find it beautiful; I contemplate that simplicity, that perfect circle of sought-after comfort, one that brings the middle-aged poet back to the few ideal moments of a troubled and unhappy past. Perhaps anyone's idea of heaven is some such journey into the past. Did Anne Sexton know that the island of God was Squirrel Island? This most psychoanalytic, most autobiographical, most naked of all contemporary poets did not say that she knew this, either in the letters or explicitly in the poems. It seems a strange omission, from one who was so willing to be explicit. And although she was capable of the subtlest kinds of elusiveness, as all good poets are—"tell all the truth but tell it slant," as Dickinson put it—it was not this kind of subtlety she cultivated. Yet whether or not she knew, she left us a wake through the water as she rowed to the island of her God.

NOTES

All Sexton citations are from Anne Sexton, *The Complete Poems* (Boston: Houghton Mifflin, 1981).

1. Critics who have identified this shift from personal to transpersonal, cultural, or mythic in Sexton's work include Alicia Ostriker and Estella Lauter; for full citations, see below.

2. Phyllis Chesler, *Women and Madness* (New York: Avon Books, 1972), 18.

3. Karen Horney was the first to re-envision the father-daughter relationship from within psychoanalysis. See *Feminine Psychology* (New York: W. W. Norton, 1967), Horney's collected essays on patriarchal psychoanalytic theory.

4. Chesler, 111.

5. Maxine Kumin, "How It Was: Maxine Kumin on Anne Sexton," in Anne Sexton, *The Complete Poems* (Boston: Houghton Mifflin, 1981), xxiii.

6. Alicia Ostriker, "That Story: The Changes of Anne Sexton," in *Writing Like a Woman* (Ann Arbor: University of Michigan Press, 1983) 78; "That Story" also appears in *American Poetry Review* 11, no. 4 (1982): 11–16.

7. Estella Lauter, "Anne Sexton's 'Radical Discontent with the

Awful Order of Things,'" *Spring: An Annual of Archetypal Psychology and Jungian Thought* (1979): 82.

8. Editorial note, in *Anne Sexton: A Self-Portrait in Letters,* edited by Linda Gray Sexton and Lois Ames (Boston: Houghton Mifflin, 1977), 4.

9. Kumin, "How It Was," xxiii.

10. *Letters,* 4.

HELEN VENDLER

Malevolent Flippancy

The unevenness in Anne Sexton's writing makes her work hard to judge, but the publication of the *Complete Poems* demands some attempt at judgment. Many of these poems are by now famous or infamous, but a clear sense of Sexton's talent—its extent and its limitations—has yet to appear. The Sexton legend not only haunts the poems, but is unhappily perpetuated in the ladies-magazine tone of the introduction to this volume by Sexton's generous friend, Maxine Kumin. The introduction begins with a description of Sexton, "tall, blue-eyed, stunningly slim, her carefully coiffed dark hair decorated with flowers." Later we hear that "the frightened little girl became a flamboyant and provocative woman; the timid child who skulked in closets burst forth as an exhibitionist declaiming with her own rock group; the intensely private individual bared her liver to the eagle in public readings." This melodramatic and sentimental style, infected by Sexton's own hyperboles, can perhaps do no harm; but neither can it do any good. Kumin's devoted kindness to Sexton is well-known, and perhaps a friend's elegiac tribute is not the place to look for a dispassionate appraisal. Still, the poems do appear within this frame; and the lavish terms of Kumin's essay tend to coerce the reader into a somewhat single-minded view of the poet whom Kumin embarrassingly names "this gifted, ghosted woman."

The introduction is determinedly and sometimes vulgarly feminist: the earlier world view of the poet as "the masculine chief of state in charge of dispensing universal spiritual truths" (Diane Middlebrook, *The World into Words*) has eroded. Surely no one could write (Middlebrook) or quote (Kumin) such a reductive vulgarization of Shelley's "poets are the unacknowl-

Review of *The Complete Poems, New Republic,* November 11, 1981. Copyright Helen Vendler. Reprinted by permission of the author.

edged legislators of the world" without an obstinate incomprehension of what Shelley meant in his defense of poetry. Kumin adds that women poets owe a debt to Anne Sexton because she "shattered taboos": she wrote openly about menstruation, abortion, masturbation, incest, adultery, and drug addiction at a time when the proprieties embraced none of these as proper topics for poetry. Such a sentence itself enacts a new (and illogical) definition of what women poets want to, or need to, or should be allowed to, write about. After all, adultery, incest, and drug addiction are not new topics in literature—they are a staple set of Romantic properties. As for biology per se, it does not interest poetry, though the feelings solicited by menstruation or masturbation or abortion do. But lyric poetry has never demanded that the occasion for a poem be named in the poem: masturbatory fantasy, for instance, has taken many literary forms. Taboo-breaking is not in itself a poetic task. No poem is improved by having a shattered taboo in it, or an abortion in it either. It is an absurd stereotyping of women that would charge them to be priestesses of the biological or shatterers of taboos. "Anne delineated the problematic position of women—the neurotic reality of the time," says Kumin, "though she was not able to cope in her own life with the personal trouble it created." I am not sure to what the "it" here refers, but I assume Kumin means that it was the problematic position of women that created the personal trouble in Sexton's life.

Such a claim is both true and false, and in any case irrefutable. Was it "the problematic position of men—the neurotic reality of the time" that created the personal trouble in Berryman's life? The biographies of Berryman and Sexton have a good deal in common: both poets were intelligent, gifted, married, parents, multiply addicted to pills and alcohol, and often (if not always) in the care of hospitals and therapists until their respective suicides. Both cases seem resistant to simple analyses (it was the pills and drink; it was the original alienating poetic gift; it was childhood guilt; it was unloving parents; it was "the problematic position" in society of women/men). No lived reality is so easily characterized. Nor will it do to hail any poet, finally, as a "woman" poet (or a "gay" poet). Every poet is in the end only one sort of poet—a poet of the native language. The poet does well by perception in vesting it in language, or does not. The poem finds a language for its experience, or it does not. Sometimes Sexton found that language.

Kumin gives valuable testimony to Sexton's industry (even though couched in cliché—"Our sessions were jagged, intense, often angry, but also loving"). Sexton, as the earlier poems show, was eager to master all the prosodic and stanzaic variations she could find useful; Sexton's lack of success does not usually (until the latter part of her life) result from lack of labor. Sexton worked hard for her teachers—among whom I include her therapists as well as her mentors (John Holmes, Robert Lowell) and her fellow poets (Plath, Starbuck, Kumin). She worked hard too for her students, who were grateful to her for her intense advice about their writing.

What, then, did Sexton have; and what did she lack? The second question should perhaps be raised before the first.

She did not have an education. Emily Dickinson had no more formal schooling than Sexton but she did have her father's library, and a precocious appetite for poetry. Kumin takes a peculiarly American point of view when she remarks, "Untrammeled by a traditional education in Donne, Milton, Yeats, Eliot, and Pound, Anne was able to strike out alone, like Conrad's secret sharer, for a new destiny." Of course the poets of the past never thought of a traditional education as a set of fetters. Their notion, on the whole, was that in reading your great predecessors you were learning the language of poetry. So Milton read for seven years at Horton after leaving Cambridge; so Hopkins did classics at Balliol; so Keats translated Virgil in high school and read his way, underlining, through Spenser and Shakespeare and *Paradise Lost* and Chapman's *Homer*. It is anyhow an odd view of a "traditional education" that would sum it up as "Donne, Milton, Yeats, Eliot, and Pound." In any case, Sexton is said to have read "omnivorously and quite innocently whatever came to hand and enticed her." According to Kumin's list, rather little that enticed her was poetry. Kumin lists "popular psychiatric texts" (Reik, Rieff, Deutsch, Erikson, Bettelheim), and says that after Sexton took a course in Dostoevsky, Kafka, and Mann, she went on to read novels by Saul Bellow, Philip Roth, and Kurt Vonnegut—a sequence that tells something about Sexton's taste, since someone else might have gone on to

Tolstoy, Flaubert, and James. Kumin concludes the remarks on Sexton's reading by saying, "But above all else, she was attracted to the fairy tales of Andersen and Grimm . . . . They were for her, perhaps, what Bible stories and Greek myths had been for other writers." Kumin does not raise the question whether Grimm and Andersen can possibly rival as imaginative sources the Bible and Greek mythology—but the question is important in thinking about Sexton.

It was not the ethical parables of the Bible, or the fertile suggestiveness of Greek myth, but the grim tit-for-tat of fairy tales—where the unsuccessful suitors are murdered, or the witch is burned in her own oven, or the wicked wolf is himself sliced open—that appealed to Sexton's childlike and vengeful mind. The fairy tales and folktales put forth a child's black-and-white ethics, with none of the complexity of the Gospels, and none of the worldliness of the Greeks. It is characteristic of Sexton that she did use the myth of Prometheus—which reads like one of her folktales, with its rebel hero, its avenging father-god, and its grotesque evisceration by a vulture.

Sexton looked, usually in vain, for ways to stabilize her poems outside her increasingly precarious self. She based one sequence on horoscope readings, another on the remarks of her therapist "Doctor Y.," another on the life of Jesus, another on the Psalms, another on beasts. The only group that succeeds more often than it fails is the group based on folktales, *Transformations*. The tales—Snow White, Rapunzel, Cinderella, Red Riding Hood, the Frog Prince, Briar Rose, Hansel and Gretel, and others—gave Sexton a structure of the sort she was usually unable to invent for herself, a beginning, a middle, and an end. Her poems tend, on the whole, to begin well, to repeat themselves, to sag in the middle, and to tail off. She had an instinct for reiteration; she wanted to say something five times instead of once. Her favorite figure of speech is anaphora, where many lines begin with the same phrase, a figure which causes, more often than not, diffuseness and spreading of effect rather than concentration of intensity:

> . . . I will conquer myself.
> I will dig up the pride.
> I will take scissors
> and cut out the beggar.

> I will take a crowbar
> and pry out the broken
> pieces. . . .

This is a form of poetic backstitching or, to change metaphors, a way of letting the poem get stuck in one groove. The folktales, by the necessary forward motion of plot, gave Sexton a momentum and shape that, on her own, she seemed to have no instinct for.

The tales, as I have said, matched her infantile fantasy; they gave her a clean trajectory; they turned her away from the morass of narcissism. But most of all, they enabled her as a satirist. Kumin speaks disapprovingly in the introduction of a draft of a poem which she disliked. It had, Kumin says, "what seemed to me a malevolently flippant tone." And Kumin urged that it be rewritten; and it was. But Sexton's aesthetically most realized tone is precisely a malevolently flippant one, however distasteful it might seem to others. Sexton herself preferred the maudlin or lachrymose or (on other occasions) the winsome or the babyish. But in the Grimm transformations all her sharp-eyed satire was unleashed. "Snow White," for instance, indicts the bourgeois cult of hypocritical virginity:

> No matter what life you lead
> the virgin is a lovely number:
> cheeks as fragile as cigarette paper,
> arms and legs made of Limoges,
> lips like Vin Du Rhône,
> rolling her china-blue doll eyes
> open and shut.
> Open to say,
> Good Day Mama,
> and shut for the thrust
> of the unicorn.

"Rumpelstiltskin" looks sardonically at the myth of maternal doting:

> . . . a son was born.
> He was like most new babies,
> as ugly as an artichoke

but the queen thought him a pearl.
She gave him her dumb lactation,
delicate, trembling, hidden,
warm, etc.

"One-Eye, Two-Eyes, Three-Eyes" casts a cold eye on the social role of the deformed:

The Thalidomide babies
with flippers at their shoulders,
wearing their mechanical arms
like derricks.
The club-footed boy
wearing his shoe like a flat iron.
The idiot child,
a stuffed doll who can only masturbate.
The hunchback carrying his hump
like a bag of onions . . .
Oh how we treasure
their scenic value.

When a child stays needy until he is fifty—
oh mother-eye, oh mother-eye, crush me in—
the parent is as strong as a telephone pole.

This painfully graphic sketch is written by a person who is not "nice." What is occurring in such writing is not so much the shattering of taboos as the expression of an extremity of nonparticipatory vision. If Keats took part in the existence of the sparrow at his window with what we might call an objective sympathy, he could not have refrained from extending that same sympathy to the repressed virgin or the nursing mother or the hunchback. But a satirist feels under no obligation to extend sympathy. Sexton feels a slashing glee in her perfect vignettes. We see, for instance,

the night nurse
with her eyes slit like Venetian blinds,
she of the tubes and the plasma,
listening to the heart monitor,

> the death cricket bleeping,
> she who calls you 'we'
> and keeps vigil like a ballistic missile.

Sexton threw off phrases with reckless bounty. The death cricket and the ballistic missile in this passage are shafts that fly straight and true; and the night nurse enters literature. In these fiendish cartoons, Sexton is most unlike Lowell. Too often, in her poems about family members and asylum experiences and exacerbated states, she sounds entirely too much like an echo of Lowell, and a bad one:

> That was the winter
> that my mother died,
> half mad on morphine,
> blown up, at last,
> like a pregnant pig.
> I was her dreamy evil eye.
> In fact,
> I carried a knife in my pocketbook—
> my husband's good L. L. Bean hunting knife.

There is far too much of this sort of thing in the *Complete Poems,* especially in the dreadfully imitative sequence "The Death of the Fathers."

Sexton's poems read better as a diary than as poems. They then seem a rather slap-dash journal stuck with brilliant phrases. Even the most formally arranged poems have, underneath their formal structure, no real or actual structure: they run on, they chatter, they moan, they repeat themselves, they deliquesce. Or, conversely (as in the famous "Her Kind"), they stop without any particular reason—they could have been shorter, they could have been longer. If, as A. R. Ammons once said, a poem begins in contingency and ends in necessity, the trouble with Sexton's poems is that they lack that necessity—the conviction that they were meant to be just as they are, with just these words and no others, extending to just this length and no other, with each part pulling its weight. Dickinson and Bishop often make us feel that necessity; Edna St. Vincent Millay—like Sexton a facile and prolific writer—does not.

Necessity appeals to some readers more than others, needless to say, and most of Sexton's readers have read her as a gripping journalist of the strained and difficult in life. One knows her very well by the end of this book. In that sense, she succeeded as a diarist, if not as a poet. Through this diary we come to know this third daughter whose two elder sisters laughed at her; she is the daughter of a rich alcoholic father who behaved toward her with sexual possessiveness, and of an unloving mother obsessed with enemas and cleanliness. The daughter defended herself by taking on a wooden lack of feeling, from which she was partially released by therapy after a postpartum depression. But she then thought of herself as composed solely of excrement. If she saw herself as an animal, it was as a rat.

These feelings were never to disappear. Giving up her children while she was in the asylum exacerbated her guilt. She confused poetry writing with therapy, expression with restructuring. The restructuring never seemed to take hold, though the writing, like the analysis, became obsessive. She saw that she was a perpetual, avid child, "a baby all wrapped up in its red howl," demanding that her family and friends mother her. "I need food / and you walk away reading the paper," became her reproach. She recognized, and was cruelly frank about, her compulsions; but she was unable to change her insatiable nature, her "greed for love." She defined herself as "a woman of excess, of zeal and greed," and nobody could have said worse things of her than she said of herself:

> Do I not look in the mirror,
> these days,
> and see a drunken rat avert her eyes?

Eventually, she was able to work less well at revision. The fantasies spun out of control; the dreams and hallucinations began to float around in disorder, and the masochistic poems about Jesus assumed disagreeable proportions:

> Jesus slept as still as a toy
> and in His dream
> He desired Mary.
> His penis sang like a dog . . .

> With His penis like a chisel
> He carved the Pietà.

In the poems, Sexton seems only frailly connected to anything outside herself. Her children, husband, and friends have a shadowy existence here, along with various unspecified lovers, who seem temporarily valuable as means to make Sexton feel loved. There are occasional mentions of war. But the relentless centrality of the "I"—almost always indoors alone, contemplating its own anguish (even if sometimes in farcical terms)—is finally exasperating. It drives us to comparison with other "I" poets of extreme psychic states—Dickinson and Berryman come to mind. Berryman, besides his humor, possessed a perfect, even icy, recognition that Henry, his libidinal self, was just that—one restricted portion of his entire self. Berryman's intellectual self took on the derelict Henry as a case study. Berryman's moral self looked on in disapproval, and offered, in blackface, quiet judgments and calm sympathy for Henry's distracted sins. Sexton's own intellectual mercilessness saves many poems. But she had no moral sympathy for herself; and she, more often than Berryman, lost herself in tragic attitudinizing and melodrama. Dickinson had the great gift of observation—not of the freaks of the world, making common cause with them, like Sexton (the witches, the old, the sick, the winos, the crippled)—but rather of the cosmos, a universe strict, impersonal, beautiful, dangerous, and indifferent. Dickinson felt acutely the scale of the whole creation, the nature of its imperial design. When she saw human beings, she saw them in that frame:

> Grand go the Years—in the Crescent—above them—
> Worlds scoop their Arcs—
> And Firmaments—row—
> Diadems—drop—and Doges—surrender—
> Soundless as dots—on a Disc of Snow.

Dickinson's "I," though as insistently present as Sexton's, is always placed in a context—religious, philosophical, cosmic, or social—larger than itself. When Dickinson goes mad, she does not take her madness as normative; she says, "And then a plank in Reason broke." There is a normative sanity present to measure the vertigo of psychic instability. Sexton's fantasies are often self-indulgent; only rarely can she include a plumb line by which to estimate her own slant out of equilibrium. In Sexton's poems we miss the complexity contributed by the double vision of fever taking its own pulse, being at once physician and patient. This was a double vision especially rigorously practiced by Sylvia Plath at the end of her life. But Plath, unlike Sexton, had a violent need for structure and containment; chaotic inner states, however exciting, did not in her view suffice to make a poem.

As Sexton passes into the anthologies, the more obviously "feminist" poems will no doubt be chosen, and there is no reason not to represent them:

> Am I approximately an I. Magnin transplant?
> I have hair, black angel,
> black-angel-stuffing to comb,
> nylon legs, luminous arms
> and some advertised clothes.

But the evil eye (as Sexton put it) should be in the anthologies too. This "evil," unsympathetic, flat, malicious, gleeful, noticing eye is neither male nor female, but it is Sexton's most distinguishing characteristic:

> The big fat war was going on.
> So profitable for daddy.
> She drove a pea green Ford.
> He drove a pearl gray Caddy.
>
> In the end they used it up.
> All that pale green dough.
> The rest I spent on doctors
> Who took it like gigolos.

This is of course superlatively unfair to the doctors and to Sexton herself. But that was Sexton's chief flair—a knack for the flat, two-dimensional cartoon. Some of that shrewd caricature should make its way into the anthologies too.

DIANE WOOD MIDDLEBROOK

Poet of Weird Abundance

When Anne Sexton's posthumous *Complete Poems* came out four years ago, poet Katha Pollitt summarized the negative judgment many critics arrived at in their reviews: "the sheer quantity of inferior work does tend to dull one's response to the gems. One puts down this enormous book with the nagging feeling that all along a slim volume of verse was trapped inside it."[1] Contemporary poets tend to be assessed by the carat: prized for glitter, expense, durability and for scale that permits resetting in an anthology. As Pollitt says, "the gems are there" in Sexton, too.

Yet the appearance of a complete poems also presents an opportunity to pose questions about a writer whose entire body of work is the necessary critical context. How are the gems related to surrounding poems? Is the ungemlike work inferior as art, or does it represent different artistic goals? Sexton's method of writing, which she referred to as "milking the unconscious,"[2] often produced a loosely structured poetry dense with simile, freaked with improbable associations. In a poem addressed to James Wright, Sexton herself acknowledged she knew the effect offended certain tastes: "There is too much food and no one left over / to eat up all the weird abundance" ("The Black Art"). Weird: uncanny, magical, unconventional. While some of Sexton's most admired poems work, like little machines, on well-oiled armatures of rhythm or rhyme (such as "All My Pretty Ones," "The Starry Night," "Wanting to Die"), others equally powerful depend on manic or despairing or ecstatic cascades of association ("The Furies," "O Ye Tongues") that flow like an

Review of *The Complete Poems, Parnassus* 12, no. 2–13, no. 1 (1985). Reprinted by permission of the author. Quotations from unpublished materials in the Anne Sexton Archive by permission of Linda Gray Sexton, Executor of the Estate of Anne Sexton, and the Harry Ransom Humanities Research Center, the University of Texas at Austin.

open spigot. The gems, or closed forms, tend to be early; the looser style, later. In this collection, the reader can watch Sexton evolve her second style as a way of exploring a changing relation to her subject matter.

Sexton's *Complete Poems* is a compilation of the eight books she saw into print, plus an edited collection of work left in manuscript at the time of her death; Sexton's good friend Maxine Kumin supplies a valuable introduction. The early poetry (*To Bedlam and Part Way Back,* 1960; *All My Pretty Ones,* 1962) holds up very well. But as this volume shows, Anne Sexton made bolder exploration of her lifelong subject—her experiences of madness—in later work, beginning with the volume *Live or Die* (1966). Mining the realm of the unconscious as she had been taught by both psychotherapy and contemporary writing, after 1962 Sexton became increasingly preoccupied with the psychological and social consequences of inhabiting a female body.

Because Sexton's writing seems so personal she is often labeled a "confessional" poet and grouped (to her disadvantage) with poets such as Lowell, Berryman, Roethke, and Plath. But Sexton resisted the label "confessional"; she preferred to be regarded as a "storyteller."[3] To emphasize that she considered the speaking "I" in her poetry as a literary rather than a real identity, Sexton invariably opened her public performances by reading the early poem "Her Kind." These are the first and last stanzas:

> I have gone out, a possessed witch,
> haunting the black air, braver at night;
> dreaming evil, I have done my hitch
> over the plain houses, light by light:
> lonely thing, twelve-fingered, out of mind.
> A woman like that is not a woman, quite.
> I have been her kind.
> . . . .
>
> I have ridden in your cart, driver,
> waved my nude arms at villages going by,
> learning the last bright routes, survivor
> where your flames still bite my thigh
> and my ribs crack where your wheels wind.
> A woman like that is not ashamed to die.
> I have been her kind.

No matter what poetry she had on an evening's agenda, Sexton offered this persona as a point of entry to her art. "I" in the poem is a disturbing, marginal female whose power is associated with disfigurement, sexuality, and magic. But at the end of each stanza, "I" is displaced from sufferer onto storyteller. With the lines "A woman like that . . . I have been her kind" Sexton conveys the terms on which she wishes to be understood: not victim, but witness and witch.

The witch-persona of Sexton's poetry is the voice Sexton invented to tell the story of her changing relationship to a severe, incurable, but apparently undiagnosable malady. She was born in 1928 in Wellesley, Massachusetts, and lived all her life in the suburbs of Boston. Married at age nineteen to a man in the wool business, Sexton had two daughters. Severe depression following the birth of her second child deepened into a permanent mental illness for which she was treated by psychiatrists for the rest of her life. She died by suicide of carbon monoxide poisoning in 1974. Her professional interest in poetry began during the first phase of her illness, in 1956. Intensified by the death of her parents in 1959, the illness was the fixed point of reference by which she measured the reality of love, the practice of poetry, and the possibility of spiritual redemption.

Sexton's *Complete Poems* yields most when read as if it contained a narrative: an account of a woman cursed with a desire to die. Why is she different from other women? Where did the curse come from? A story line with a beginning, middle, and end takes shape in *Complete Poems* as Sexton systematically exhausts a set of culturally acceptable explanations for the condition of her kind. These are, first, a psychiatric explanation; later, a sociological explanation; and finally a spiritual explanation.

The story begins with the discovery of the poet in the sick person. The narrator of Sexton's first book is a woman "part way back" from Bedlam—that is, not yet restored to the family home as wife and mother—contemplating what took her to the mental hospital: the preference for suicide over motherhood as she had learned that role from her own mother ("The Double Image"). Bedlam has been a school which taught a valuable lesson: the power of signs.

> I tapped my own head;
> it was glass, an inverted bowl.

....

 . . . if you turn away
 because there is no lesson here
 I will hold my awkward bowl,
 with all its cracked stars shining
 like a complicated lie
("For John, Who Begs Me Not to Enquire Further")

From now on, she will be a poet of the tapped head: the mad housewife.

Condensed into the metaphor of the broken kitchen bowl are most of the meanings Sexton associates with her own liberation into poetry. Before she tapped meanings from her head, the bowl—her womanly identity—revealed but enclosed her (like Plath's bell jar); only through costly breakage did the identity begin to shine with complex significance. Breakage ruined the bowl for kitchen use but endowed it with a more precious moral utility. Further, the act of offering her own breakage as a gift shifted her relation both to her suffering and to the beholder. In the metaphor of the bowl whose cracks became stars, Sexton avows belief that her experience has been redeemed by its transformation into the social medium of language. "Star" in her personal mythology will from now on designate that place—the poetic symbol—where the language of private suffering grows radiant and magically ambiguous.

Sexton began writing poetry as a form of therapy, at her doctor's suggestion. In her first two books, she uses a good many references to this therapy and occasionally speaks of herself almost objectively as a case history. These are her most admired books. They are also her most "confessional" books in that they establish that her maladjustment as a woman is to be her subject as a poet.

By 1962 Sexton's poetry had won a respectful audience. But as a psychiatric patient she had experienced many setbacks and relapses. She had changed as an artist; as a sick woman, she did not change: repetition of destructive patterns was one of the symptoms of her illness. To survive as a poet meant to attain another, a less reportorial relation to the subject of her pathology. Beginning with poems written for her third volume, *Live or Die,* Sexton gradually abandoned the polarity sick/well

which gives underlying structure to the poems of *Bedlam* and *Pretty Ones*. In the poetry of *Live or Die* Sexton begins to explore the suspicion that what she suffers from is femaleness itself, and is probably incurable. "—I'm no more a woman / than Christ was a man," she says in a dream ("Consorting with Angels," *Live or Die*). Behind this claim are questions that eventually dominate her last, religious poems: what kinds of social significance has *her* suffering? Is it too specifically female to contain spiritual meaning? Can a woman speak for Man? More and more for Sexton the problematic will not lie between being insane and being healthy, but within being female. To be female is to be defective.

The most important poem in this transition to a new perspective on her illness is "Flee on Your Donkey" (*Live or Die*). Sexton worked it over for four years. "Flee on Your Donkey" takes its title from a poem by Rimbaud quoted as an epigraph: *Ma faim, Anne, Anne, / Fuis sur ton âne* (My hunger, Anne, Anne, / Flee on your donkey). Sexton's notes on the poem indicate that she came across this wordplay on her name one day while feeling on the verge of a psychotic episode; she wrote it onto a piece of paper she carried to her psychiatrist's office in search of therapy. A bizarre quarrel with the doctor ensued: "He had a moment of fury and hit me on the nose." At the end of the session, Sexton again entered the mental hospital—though as she remarked, "It might have made more sense to put him in the hospital, but I wasn't strong enough to know that."[4] The episode with her doctor surfaces in "Flee on Your Donkey" only indirectly, in the form of recognition that she has exhausted both her repetitious sickness and its therapies as sources of creative self-knowledge; she needs a new angle of vision.

> I have come back
> but disorder is not what it was.
> . . . .
> Turn, my hungers!
> . . . .
> Anne, Anne,
> flee on your donkey,
> flee this sad hotel,
> ride out on some hairy beast,

gallop backward pressing
your buttocks to his withers,
sit to his clumsy gait somehow.
Ride out
any old way you please!
In this place everyone talks to his own mouth.
That's what it means to be crazy.

Live or Die contains numerous poems in which Sexton writes about the effort to flee the story she has learned to tell of herself in therapy: the story of a woman disabled by illness from performing womanly roles, especially the role of mother. "Anne," the pathological identity formed in childhood, the subject of analysis in therapy, becomes for the moment *âne:* the hairy beast astride which her consciousness might escape confinement. In this metaphor the vehicle is male: is literature. Unlike that other rider of a donkey who "rode calmly into Jerusalem / in search of death" ("Suicide Note"), this rider faces backward, surveying terrain already crossed. Yet, driven by hunger, she proposes to find a new relation to the all-too-familiar landscape of her own psyche.

With *Live or Die* Sexton's style changes, too. Her first two books are full of short lyrics faceted by techniques she learned in workshops with George Starbuck and Maxine Kumin (rhyme schemes, elaborate stanza forms), and by auditing Robert Lowell's poetry course at Boston University ("He worked with a cold chisel, with no more mercy than a dentist").[5] After *All My Pretty Ones,* rhyme and meter no longer provide obvious structure in much of Sexton's poetry. Stanzas have spasmodic lengths, and move from point to point on narrative transitions (as in "Flee on Your Donkey": "Because . . ." "Today . . ." "Now . . ." "In here . . ." "But you . . ." "I have come back . . ." "This is madness . . ." "Turn, my hungers!") Poetic values lie in the intrinsic interest of the stories Sexton tells— "The Addict," "Wanting to Die," "Cripples and Other Stories," "The Ambition Bird," etc.—and in the surrealist economy of telling she devised. The lines surprise, disturb, confront, and puzzle the reader with bizarre tropes and similes, as in the gastric metaphors of "Flee on Your Donkey": "I have come back, / recommitted, / fastened to the wall like a bathroom

plunger / . . . It is my stomach that makes me suffer. / Turn, my hungers!" Her goal was "to enforest the page with images,"[6] a technique she said she learned from Neruda, whose work she met through James Wright in 1961. No use looking for gems; the treasure here is Sexton's "weird abundance."

Except for the "clumsy gait" of the free verse Sexton used after *Pretty Ones,* readers have not much remarked on the departures Sexton announced in "Flee on Your Donkey." But from now on, Sexton assumes an unconventional relation to her own madness. No longer merely its victim, she is now its interrogator.

This interesting shift can be glimpsed in two poems written early in the development of *Live or Die:* "Mother and Jack and the Rain," and "Consorting with Angels." Both have to do with the woman poet's necessary resistance to repressive social conventions. Writing from "a room of my own," Sexton identifies Mother and Jack—one dead, the other a former lover, now a priest—with intrusive custodianship of her mind and body. Like the rain, metaphor for obsessional repetition, "Mother and Jack fill up heaven; they endorse / my womanhood." The middle sections of the poem reflect back on her sexual history as an adolescent: sexually courted by father; covertly inspected by Jack. The womanhood these men, and mother, endorse is fundamental to her pathologies. To be a poet she must resist their repressive power in her psyche while maintaining access to her feeling for them.

> Haunted, always haunted by rain, the room affirms
> the words that I will make alone.
> I come like the blind feeling for shelves,
> feeling for wood as hard as an apple,
> fingering the pen lightly, my blade.
> With this pen I take in hand my selves
> and with these dead disciples I will grapple.
> Though rain curses the window
> let the poem be made.
> . . . .
>
> I come to this land to ride my horse,
> to try my own guitar, to copy out
> their two separate names like sunflowers, to conjure

up my daily bread, to endure,
somehow to endure.

Concern for the survival of the imagination is equally the
theme of "Consorting with Angels." "Tired of the gender of
things," Sexton receives an "answer" to her ennui in a dream
where she is recreated as an angel, "not a woman anymore."

> I was tired of being a woman,
> tired of the spoons and the pots,
> tired of my mouth and my breasts,
> tired of the cosmetics and the silks.
> There were still men who sat at my table,
> circled around the bowl I offered up.
> The bowl was filled with purple grapes
> and the flies hovered in for the scent
> and even my father came with his white bone.
> But I was tired of the gender of things.
>
> Last night I had a dream
> and I said to it . . .
> "You are the answer,
> You will outlive my husband and my father."
> In that dream there was a city made of chains
> where Joan was put to death in man's clothes
> and the nature of the angels went unexplained,
> no two made in the same species,
> one with a nose, one with an ear in its hand,
> one chewing a star and recording its orbit,
> each one like a poem obeying itself,
> performing God's functions,
> a people apart.
>
> "You are the answer,"
> I said, and entered,
> . . . .
> I was not a woman anymore,
> not one thing or the other.
> . . . .
> I'm no more a woman
> than Christ was a man.

Addressing "the gender of things," the poem acquires what a later generation of readers would recognize as a feminist consciousness (though Sexton herself showed little interest in feminism). Father, Mother, Jack, and others lose significance as mere people, or fit subjects of elegy and autobiography, as Sexton begins to regard them in terms of their dominance over her: to regard them, in the metaphor she chooses in a late poem, as power cards in the hand dealt at her birth, the "royal straight flush" that loses against God's aces in "The Rowing Endeth." In the books that follow *Live or Die,* Sexton's particular concerns will be with social and religious conventions surrounding female difference.

In my reading of Sexton's *Complete Poems, Love Poems* (1969) and *Transformations* (1971) form a dyad. *Love Poems* exposes the dilemma of the female poet trying to write within the conventions of the literary genre of love poetry; *Transformations* explains this dilemma by situating sexual love in its social context: the marriage contract that stabilizes the social order. Both have an unsettling, masochistic tone. The speaker of *Love Poems* experiences her body as a hoard of attributes, desirable only in dismemberment. "Love" is the anxious energy she feels as her body parts come to life under the prospective or actual gaze of a man:

> For months my hand had been sealed off
> in a tin box.
> . . . .
>
> It lay there like an unconscious woman
> fed by tubes she knew not of.
> . . . .
>
> Oh, my carpenter,
> the fingers are rebuilt.
> They dance with yours.
> They dance in the attic and in Vienna.
> My hand is alive all over America.
>
> ("The Touch")

The woman in sexual relation to a man becomes his construct. Heart, hand, clitoris, breast, mouth, womb become, under a man's attention, "households" ("That Day"), "cities of flesh" ("Mr. Mine"), "the boards, / the roof, the removable roof"

("You All Know the Story of the Other Woman"). Between her legs, "the woman / is calling her secrets, little houses, / little tongues that tell you" ("Barefoot").

Transformations also presents women as some of their parts; but since Sexton adopts here the plots of fairy tales from Grimm, by which children are instructed in the repression and displacement of libido, the consciousness is perhaps more acceptable than it feels in the radically masochistic *Love Poems*. The tale-teller of *Transformations* is "a middle-aged witch, me"—the woman who has done her hitch over the plain houses but is not a woman quite. She designates as the chosen auditor of these stories a boy of sixteen ("He is sixteen and he wants some answers. / He is each of us") who has found a gold key and is about to learn the use of it.

> Its secrets whimper
> like a dog in heat.
> He turns the key.
> Presto!
> It opens this book of odd tales

These narratives are adapted directly from Grimm; what Sexton underscores in retelling is the phallic key. The wisecracking witch supplies prologues which emphasize roles and strategies within the system of exchange where sexuality is the coin circulated among the generations to replenish the family and define differences between masculine and feminine identities. As in "Cinderella:"

> Cinderella and the prince
> lived, they say, happily ever after,
> like two dolls in a museum case
> never bothered by diapers or dust,
> never arguing over the timing of an egg,
> never telling the same story twice,
> never getting a middle-aged spread,
> their darling smiles pasted on for eternity.
> Regular Bobbsey Twins.
> That story.

Sexton said *Transformations* was "as much about me" as any of her first-person lyrics, and it is. Yet in neither *Love Poems* or *Transformations* is the pathological conceived as merely personal. If Sexton's *Complete Poems* can be read as a woman's story of her wish to die, these explore the death wish as a response to the emptiness of sexuality experienced as a commodity—its re-petitiousness, its fetishes.

In the last three books Sexton saw through publication, another appetite emerges: the hunger for redemption. Sexton reformulates, this time in religious terms, her oldest questions about the origins and meaning of her wish to die. The dyad of mother and daughter, and the oedipal triangle, scrutinized psychiatrically in earlier work, return to these volumes as potential sources of grace. In one of Sexton's most imaginative inventions, regression becomes a metaphor for spiritual quest.

The Book of Folly reintroduces the theme of the mother's power of cursing or curing a sick daughter. Sexton had, in effect, two mothering figures in early childhood, and both have roles to play in Sexton's late poems. Great-aunt Anna Dingley, the loving "Nana" of Sexton's early childhood, went insane and was institutionalized shortly after Anne told her about kissing a boyfriend at age thirteen. Sexton thus associated her own sexual development with her spinster aunt's decline, and recreated the episode in numerous poems (see, especially, "Some Foreign Letters," "Rapunzel," "The Hex") as well as in her play *Mercy Street,* in which the maiden aunt witnesses an incestuous episode with the father. In *Folly,* Sexton's yearing to recover the "good mother" lost first to insanity and then to death takes the form of desire for regression to the period before the heterosexual kiss divided them.

> Take me the gangling twelve-year-old
> into your sunken lap.
> Whisper like a buttercup.
> Eat me. Eat me up like cream pudding.
> Take me in.
> Take me.
> Take.
>
> ("Anna Who Was Mad")

Sexton's real mother, Mary Gray Staples Harvey, occupies another kind of ambivalent symbolism. In the late poems, Sexton locates the possibility of her redemption from insanity—the evil of being female—in the memory of her first connection to Mother Mary through the mouth:

> Mother,
> strange goddess face
> above my milk home,
> that delicate asylum,
> I ate you up.
> All my need took
> you down like a meal.
>
> ("Dreaming the Breasts")

Mouthing mother, her original hunger was appeased; yet appeasement was only possible in the infant stage when the female body of the mother was innocent—that is, was a source of comfort, not an object of identification. Redemption from the condition of femaleness resides, by this logic, only in the infant stage before separation has done its work and before the infant knows her name and pronoun.

In this world both symbolic and real, it is no more innocuous to be male, of course. The three ambitious sequences that end *Folly*—"The Death of the Fathers," "Angels of the Love Affair," "The Jesus Papers"—can be read as progressive confrontations with father figures, motivated by Sexton's defect-haunted sense of herself as a woman. If to mother a daughter is to press her into female roles, so to father a daughter is to expose her to male desire. "The Death of the Fathers" revisits old subject matter—young Anne Harvey's tender fascination with her father Ralph Churchill Harvey—treated in the elegiac lyrics of the earlier volumes, most poignantly in "All My Pretty Ones," "Young," "And One for My Dame." But by the time of writing *Folly*, Sexton has reduced the dead father to a mere symbolic shadow of himself. In *Folly*'s "The Death of the Fathers," he stands for the unattainable object of desire, the lover who might give her both safety and sex. But above all, he is the man she can't have: first because he's her father; again because he's a drunkard; then because he's dead; and now, when Sexton is forty-two, because his authenticity has been challenged by a usurper, a man claiming to have been her mother's lover. By 1971, of course, Sexton's memory of Ralph Churchill Harvey has been much mediated by years of psychotherapy. But in any case by age forty-two a woman's relationship to her father, even a relationship disfigured by memories or fantasies of incest, takes its place in a social realm larger than family life.

In *The Book of Folly* this realm is theological. Sexton's most inventive explanation of femaleness in the scheme of things occurs in "The Jesus Papers," the sequence of nine poems that ends *Folly*. Food metaphors dominate this sequence; most particularly, the metaphor of breast milk as a principle of generosity, a form of salvation issuing specifically from the female body. Flowing from the madonna's breast ("Jesus Suckles") it offers the infant his first knowledge of human connection—and its cognate, knowledge of separation. The experience of separation or the creation of the selfish ego becomes in these poems *the* principal human experience needing spiritual cure. Thus, the infant Jesus, separating from the breast, fantasizes himself as a truck, an image that recalls Sexton's guilty happiness at discovering her poetic gift as won at her mother's expense. ("I did not know that my life, in the end, / would run over my mother's like a truck"—"Those Times . . .").

The narrative of Jesus' acts turns on associations between various physical hungers and spiritual connection conceived as regression. He heals the harlot by lancing her breasts—"those two boils of whoredom"; this "cure" returns her to a childlike state of attachment to Jesus as to "a father / who brushed the dirt from her eye" ("Jesus Raises Up the Harlot"). Finally, the complex meaning of Jesus' death on the cross is not that he possessed a superior wisdom or supernatural power to heal others. His meaning was his hunger, learned and appeased in infancy; lingering and unappeasable in adult life.

> From up here in the crow's nest
> I see a small crowd gather.
> Why do you gather, my townsmen?
> There is no news here.
> . . . .
>
> I want heaven to descend and sit on My dinner plate
> and so do you.
> I want God to put His steaming arms around Me

and so do you.
Because we need.
Because we are sore creatures.

("Jesus Dies")

Sexton says in "The Jesus Papers" that all spiritual striving is an effort to fill the plate emptied in infancy. Christ designated his suffering as a sacrifice with the words, "Take, eat; this is my body." In "The Jesus Papers" Sexton attempts to explore meanings in this offering which are obscured by conventional reverence. More urgently, Sexton also wants to participate in whatever redemption Christ's model offers *her*. Is the female body equally a host of spiritual meaning? In "The Jesus Papers," madonna and harlot are both condemned by Jesus: the hungers their bodies nourish are merely hungers of the flesh. But the author of "The Jesus Papers," being both mother and poet, offers the world the sustenance of words also. In the last poem of the sequence, these flow from her life not in the forms she wishes—"moon-juice, . . . the white mother"—but in the form of blood. Still, God recognizes and accepts her sacrifice, which Sexton images as a middle-class American version of the Eucharist:

> In my dream
> I milked a cow,
> the terrible udder
> like a great rubber lily
> sweated in my fingers
> and as I yanked,
> waiting for the moon juice,
> waiting for the white mother,
> blood spurted from it
> and covered me with shame.
> Then God spoke to me and said:
> People say only good things about Christmas.
> If they want to say something bad,
> they whisper.
> So I went to the well and drew a baby
> out of the hollow water.
> Then God spoke to me and said:

> Here. Take this gingerbread lady
> and put her in your oven.
> When the cow gives blood
> and the Christ is born
> we must all eat sacrifices.
> We must all eat beautiful women.
>> ("The Author of the Jesus Papers Speaks")

This poem contains clues to Sexton's belief in an analogy between her suffering and that of Christ. In Sexton's version of Christian theology, Christ's death, like her own deathwish, is meaningful to others as a source of symbolisms. For God does not dispense meaning. He dispenses in infancy the hunger for meaning, and he endows the earth with meaning-makers. In Sexton as in Christ the sufferer and the symbol-maker meet: she is the hungry woman we eat as we read her words.

These, in any case, are the symbolisms carried over into Sexton's last two books: *The Death Notebooks* and *The Awful Rowing Toward God*. The baby drawn "out of the hollow water," above, returns in *The Death Notebooks* as "the death baby." Found, shockingly, in the refrigerator "between the mayonnaise and the bacon," later put among dogs as their food, the death baby is Sexton's symbol for her identity as a poet at this time. Most obviously, it represents her suicide wish, born horribly within the conventions and controls of a quiet family life in the suburbs. As horribly, the death baby represents the marketing of poetry expressing her suicide wish: it puts food on the table. Beyond these, it stands for her spiritual hunger, the desire for connection expressed in offering the breast and in taking the breast. Particularly in the sequence titled "The Death Baby," but throughout this volume, the speaker is alternately infant and mother fused in an act of rocking, symbolizing both the rhythms of maternal care and the rhythms of the poetic lines which are Sexton's sacrificial offering.

> I died seven times
> in seven ways
> letting death give me a sign,
> letting death place his mark on my forehead,
> *crossed over, crossed over.*

And death took root in that sleep.
In that sleep I held an ice baby
and I rocked it
and was rocked by it.
Oh Madonna, hold me.
I am a small handful.

("3. Seven Times")

Death,
you lie in my arms like a cherub,
as heavy as bread dough.
Your milky wings are as still as plastic.
Hair as soft as music.
Hair the color of a harp.
And eyes made of glass,
as brittle as crystal.
Each time I rock you
I think you will break.
I rock. I rock.

("6. Baby")

Sexton's firmest poems in the volume *The Death Notebooks* are built on the symbolisms radiating from this infant identity condensing hunger/sacrifice/poetry. In both "The Death Baby" sequence and, further on, in "The Furies" sequence, the successes arise from the startling originality and intelligence with which Sexton draws on regression as a source of imagery. "The Furies" appears occasionally to owe something to Theodore Roethke's sequence "The Lost Son," and the final sequence, "O Ye Tongues," is modeled after Christopher Smart's "Jubilate Agno." In both cases the models are structural, and have served to free Sexton's characteristic strength: access to the matrix of symbolism, the infant psyche from which she retrieved her subject matter throughout life.

I find "O Ye Tongues" one of Sexton's most moving and accomplished poems, formally and thematically. Her language is that most nurturing rhetoric: praise. The loose, associational structure typical of Sexton's later work is completely appropriate in these psalms, which begin grammatically in the impersonal imperative and only gradually evolve a first person voice, and only after that refer to a persona named Anne. It is not until "Fourth Psalm" that Sexton arrives at the auto-biographical subject characteristic of her last poems: the child-hood sources of her pathology—here viewed almost serenely, maternally, as the sources also of her prodigal creativity. "Fourth Psalm" is an eerily, beautifully sustained account of the emergence of the symbol-making consciousness in infancy.

> For I am an orphan with two death masks on the mantel and came from the grave of my mama's belly into the commerce of Boston.
>
> For there were only two windows on the city and the buildings ate me.
>
> For I was swaddled in grease wool from my father's company and could not move or ask the time.
>
> For Anne and Christopher were born in my head as I howled at the grave of the roses, the ninety-four rose crèches of my bedroom.
> ·
> For I became a *we* and this imaginary *we* became a kind company when the big balloons did not bend over us.
>
> For I could not read or speak and on the long nights I could not turn the moon off or count the lights of cars across the ceiling.
> ·
> For I was prodding myself out of my sleep, out of the green room.
> The sleep of the desperate who travel backwards into darkness.
>
> For birth was a disease and Christopher and I invented the cure.
>
> For we swallow magic and we deliver Anne.
>
> ("Fourth Psalm")

"Fourth Psalm" is a parable of liberation from confinement. Confinement: first in swaddling, then in childhood rooms whose wallpaper, windows, closets, and bathroom fixtures recur in Sexton's bedlam poetry. Then, confinement in bedlam itself ("Anne is locked in" is a refrain in "Sixth Psalm"; Sexton was institutionalized over twenty times between 1957 and 1974). Then, prospectively, confinement in the grave. "Birth was a disease" because it deposited her in a prison whose only exit is "the death hole"—"For she prays that she will not cringe at the death hole. / For I pray that God will digest me," ends "Second Psalm." The consciousness-bearing body, first to last, is a prison "unless God digest me." In this poem God is *invention;* from him comes forth the inexhaustible abundance of the material world—including the dark, the slimy, the hidden, the nasty celebrated in "Fifth Psalm"—which Christopher and Anne transubstantiate in their own inventions.

The serenity of "O Ye Tongues" vanishes in the poetry recording Sexton's last struggle for spiritual clarity, *The Awful Rowing Toward God.* Symbolized once more as an elusive parent, God becomes the object of a strenuous and hopeless quest.

The pair of poems that begin and end this book ("Rowing" and "The Rowing Endeth") give it a solid structure. Sexton writes in "Rowing" that she had passed her life ignorant of God as a destination: "I grew, I grew, / and God was there like an island I had not rowed to." While writing the poems of *The Awful Rowing,* Sexton was preparing to separate from her husband; projected changes in her way of life seem to lie behind Sexton's metaphor of the island as a spiritual destination with the characteristics of a new household. It "will not be perfect, / it will have the flaws of life, / the absurdities of the dinner table, / but there will be a door / and I will open it." Unlike the childhood home, unlike the "cruel houses" of married life (including the mental hospitals she has lived in), this island, she believes, houses the paternal presence who might embrace and rescue her at last.

But when she arrives, in "The Rowing Endeth," "at the dock of the island called God," she does not find the expected door. No shelter; no embrace. Instead, she and God "squat on the rocks by the sea / and play—can it be true— / a game of poker." The hand she's dealt Sexton calls a royal straight flush. Instead it seems to be a run of 9-10-J-Q-K, a suit—or family—of five headed by a King and Queen; presumably, the ace is missing from this straight run, because the winning hand is God's five aces. ("A wild card had been announced / but I had not heard it / being in such a state of awe / when He took out the cards and dealt.") God, like the salesman-father named Ace in Sexton's play *Mercy Street,* is fond of a joke, and the poem ends as loser Anne joins the winner in his "untamable, eternal, gut-driven *ha-ha.*"

God's aggressive masculine presence in the poem aligns him with other father figures in Sexton's poetry, including the doctors: those she is doomed to love from a position of compliance, but from whom she will never receive healing care. God's "wild card" signifies the privilege of Him over Her everywhere—the inscrutable possession of dominance. But the poker game with God also seems to stand for a final confrontation of her delusions as delusions. There is no "door" to pass through which will retrospectively transform her history, and no magic embrace, equivalent to God's wild card, which can "get rid of the rat inside of me."

Between the first and last poems of this volume, however, Sexton writes on a variety of themes that may be regarded as "rowing" exercises, or strategies of approach to the redemptive island. In these poems her body acquires a new set of meanings, as a site for the study of the existence of evil.

> Ms. Dog,
> why is you evil?
> It climbed into me.
> It didn't mean to.
> . . . .
> I have,
> for some time,
> called myself,
> Ms. Dog.
> Why?
> Because I am almost animal
> and yet the animal I lost most—
> that animal is near to God,
> but lost from Him.

("Is It True?")

465

The mirroring transformation that could make rats into star could make Ms. Dog into God. "Evil" is the point of view darkening the mirror:

> That's why language fails.
> Because to one, shit is a feeder of plants,
> to another the evil that permeates them
>
> ("Is It True?")

The Awful Rowing Toward God contains a number of parables and speculative lyrics which search out the star lost in rats, the god in the dog, the soul in the beating heart.

> the artery of my soul has been severed
> and soul is spurting out upon them
>
> ("The Big Heart")

> God does not need
> too much wire to keep Him there,
> just a thin vein,
> with blood pushing back and forth in it
>
> ("Small Wire")

These are poems of belief based on no theology and no consistent religious symbolism—"I carol with what the typewriter gives, / with what God gives, / as even He gives the hair on our heads" ("The Saints Come Marching In"). Their strengths do not reside in any sort of "arrival"; they manifest spirituality as an inevitable aspect of the poet's words. God is already in the typewriter, in the letters and syllables of the language, and sometimes Sexton hits the right keys.

Sexton in the first poem of *To Bedlam and Part Way Back* wrote, "We are magic talking to itself, / noisy and alone"—a line characterizing herself as mental patient in relation to doctor, but one equally descriptive of the poet of *The Awful Rowing* in relation to the God from whom she seeks a cure.

> Of course, I love you;
> you lean above the plastic sky,
> god of our block, prince of all the foxes.

> The breaking crowns are new
> that Jack wore. Your third eye
> moves among us and lights the separate boxes
> where we sleep or cry.

("You, Dr. Martin")

Always in Sexton's poetry, stationed above her in a heavenly state of knowing, possessor of the wild card or the third eye, has been this inaccessible, controlling being. Whether parent, doctor, god, he is the forceful reminder of intolerable separation. And so *Complete Poems* loops back on itself with its last poem—the last Sexton oversaw into print. "The Rowing Endeth" is a closing poem without reconciliation, integration, transformation, or any other kind of healing in its hand.

But neither is it a suicide note, or in any other way valedictory. Sexton's *Complete Poems* ends not with a "last word" but with 141 pages of unpublished work in various stages of finish. An epigraph for the book might well have been, "This story ends with me still rowing" ("Rowing"). The mysterious curse of her mental illness, and the death wish at its core, could be lifted neither by medical nor by other means; but in becoming its storyteller Sexton achieved an emancipating relation to it. "This is madness / but a kind of hunger . . . Turn, my hungers!" In the leap from madness to metaphor Sexton fled solitary confinement again and again.

Arriving at the end of Sexton's *Complete Poems* brings me to the question of merit. Sexton was in many ways an interesting writer; but was she an inferior poet?—Inferior, say, to her mentor W. D. Snodgrass, her teacher Robert Lowell, her friends James Wright and Sylvia Plath, her Boston peers Adrienne Rich and Denise Levertov?

As I have been suggesting, I find Sexton a startlingly original and valuable artist. But Sexton differs from members of this group in two important ways that make it difficult to rank her among these other writers. First, she was not an intellectual. Sexton had only a high school education; she got her training as a poet in workshops. Though she had a quick mind and read widely, her thinking was intuitive rather than systematic. She did not identify herself with a literary tradition, she did not measure herself in terms of precursors, she did not acquire a critical language by which to classify and discriminate. Hers is not a poetry of ideas—aesthetic, political, philosophical, or historical.

Second, she stopped writing the kind of short lyric that remains coin of the realm in American poetry: the lyric of perfect economy composed according to an exacting formal standard, whether in meter or free verse. Critics still praise Sexton's early work for its control of the materials of disorder by means of formal effects she dismissed as "tricks." Manuscripts of early poems reveal that Sexton often began by setting herself a design problem: a stanza template with rhyme positions designated "a, b, c," etc.; then she would write a poem into the mould. She continued this practice, with good results, through 1962: her workshop years.

As I have been arguing, Sexton's later style developed out of the demands of her subject matter: accounting for madness. The exploratory, associational method she devised gave priority to the implacable structure of unconscious processes. This method is most successful in such poems as "O Ye Tongues," "The Jesus Papers," "The Furies," "The Death of the Fathers," "The Death Baby," *Transformations*—works where the traces of a narrative adumbrate a boundary of reference within which to rationalize the flow of association. For much of Sexton's *Complete Poems,* the horizon or story line is, of course, autobiographical, focused on Sexton's attraction to death. Sexton's *Complete Poems* might be described as a psycho-narrative in verse, to which each poem is a contribution.

Moreover, the type of poem Sexton evolved was probably an inevitable creation in mid-century American poetry. It articulates the dilemma of a female recipient of certain ideas about women's place in the social order; it invests this dilemma in a single persona, a performing voice. The contemporary writings of Sylvia Plath and Adrienne Rich offer perhaps the closest analogues to Sexton's work, since their own dilemmas were equally privileged and middle class. As young *women,* all three had embraced prevailing ideologies about women's roles. All three of them seem to have been excessively susceptible to highly conventional expectations, tormented by questions about whether they were "good" daughters, students, mothers, wives. As young *artists* they had to gain recognition in a prestige system condescending to women, and the conflicts they experienced between the roles of woman and artist fueled their development. In fact, the gender specificity of much of their poetry helps us see how specifically "masculine" were the concerns of peers such as Lowell, Snodgrass, Berryman, Wright, Roethke, Ginsberg—who struggled to attain spiritual authority in the postwar consumer society littered with unusable masculine stereotypes.

But for Plath and Rich, the male-identified literary tradition eventually suggested models for transcendence uncongenial to Sexton. Both Plath and Rich essentially revised, for women's use, the poetics of romanticism which centers the poem in a visionary ego. Plath adopted the voice of a maenad; Rich evolved a powerfully personal voice of informed social criticism.

Sexton's voice remained unembarrassedly domestic. She tested notions about self and God against feelings schooled in repression, and her poems do not transcend, they explore this repression. Sexton's art celebrates word-magic, buffoonery, regression, "milking the unconscious," as inexhaustible sources of resistance to the deadly authority of the stereotypes constraining adult women's lives. Sexton's artistry was to achieve a mode of expression for this particular female consciousness, expression at once intimate and theatrical. Her audiences, mostly women, responded to that voice as the manifestation of a condition they had previously felt to be wholly personal and interior. Suddenly, poetry had expanded to acknowledge a whole new citizenry: the middle-class American woman beginning to seek liberation from confinement in domestic roles. As American poetry slowly incorporates a feminist consciousness, Sexton's work seems uncannily ahead of its time. It seems bound to endure at least as long as the social and psychological dilemmas that inspired her.

NOTES

1. *The Nation,* November 21, 1981, 534.

2. To Barbara Kevles, for an interview in *Paris Review* (1968), Sexton remarked, "The poetry is often more advanced, in terms of my unconscious, than I am. Poetry, after all, milks the unconscious. The

unconscious is there to feed it little images, little symbols, the answers, the insights I know not of." This interview is reprinted as "The Art of Poetry: Anne Sexton," in *Anne Sexton: The Artist and Her Critics,* edited by J. D. McClatchy (Bloomington: Indiana University Press, 1978), 5.

3. "The Art of Poetry," *passim.*

4. Notes on "Flee on Your Donkey," from manuscript of a lecture Sexton prepared for a course on her own poetry she taught at Colgate University, spring 1972. Manuscript in the Anne Sexton Archive, Humanities Research Center, The University of Texas, Austin; quoted with the permission of Linda Sexton.

5. "The Art of Poetry," 10.

6. Sexton's phrase, reported by her student Eric Edwards published in an interview, Cambridge, Massachusetts, April, 1983.

Bibliography

[Note: *An asterisk indicates that the work, or a portion of it, is included in this volume.*]

Primary Materials

POETRY

To Bedlam and Part Way Back. Boston: Houghton Mifflin, 1960.
All My Pretty Ones. Boston: Houghton Mifflin, 1962.
Selected Poems. London: Oxford University Press, 1964.
Live or Die. Boston: Houghton Mifflin, 1966.
For the Year of the Insane. Boston: Impressions Workshop, 1967. [Broadside illustrated by Barbara Swan.]
Poems By Thomas Kinsella, Douglas Livingstone and Anne Sexton. London: Oxford University Press, 1968. [A selection of previously published poems.]
Love Poems. Boston: Houghton Mifflin, 1969.
Transformations. Boston: Houghton Mifflin, 1971.
The Book of Folly. Boston: Houghton Mifflin, 1972.
The Death Notebooks. Boston: Houghton Mifflin, 1974.
The Awful Rowing Toward God. Boston: Houghton Mifflin, 1975.
45 Mercy Street. Edited by Linda Gray Sexton. Boston: Houghton Mifflin, 1975.
Words for Dr. Y.: Uncollected Poems with Three Stories. Edited by Linda Gray Sexton. Boston: Houghton Mifflin, 1978.
The Complete Poems. Boston: Houghton Mifflin, 1981.
Selected Poems. Edited by Diane Wood Middlebrook and Diana Hume George. Boston: Houghton Mifflin, forthcoming.

PROSE

"Feeling the Grass." *Christian Science Monitor,* June 4, 1959, 8.
Eggs of Things. New York: Putnam, 1963. [With Maxine Kumin.]
More Eggs of Things. New York: Putnam, 1964. [With Maxine Kumin.]
Foreword to *The Real Tin Flower: Poems About the World at Nine.* By Aliki Barnstone. New York: Collier-Crowell, 1968. Reprinted in "Stories for Free Children," *Ms.,* March, 1975, 69.
Joey and the Birthday Present. New York: McGraw-Hill, 1971. [With Maxine Kumin.]
[Writing Exercises (with Robert Clawson)]. In *The Whole Word Catalogue 1,*

Edited by Rosellen Brown et al., 9, 11, 45. New York: Teachers and Writers, 1972. [Examples of writing exercises given by Sexton and Clawson in the class they taught at Wayland High School in the fall of 1967, 9, 45; example of student's story, 11; excerpt from Sexton's class journal (later published in entirety as "Journal of a Living Experiment"), 45.]

[Autobiographical Statement]. In *World Authors, 1950–1970,* edited by John Wakeman, 1284–85. New York: H. W. Wilson, 1975.

The Wizard's Tears. New York: McGraw-Hill, 1975. [With Maxine Kumin.]

Anne Sexton: A Self-Portrait in Letters. Edited by Linda Gray Sexton and Lois Ames. Boston: Houghton Mifflin, 1977.

"Journal of a Living Experiment." In *Journal of a Living Experiment: A Documentary History of the First Ten Years of Teachers and Writers Collaborative,* edited by Phillip Lopate, 44–75. New York: Teachers and Writers, 1979. [Sexton's account of the English class she taught with Robert Clawson at Wayland High School in the fall of 1967.]

No Evil Star: Selected Essays, Interviews, and Prose. Edited by Steven E. Colburn. Ann Arbor: University of Michigan Press, 1985.

RECORDINGS

The Poetry of Anne Sexton. Writer's Forum Videotape Library, Department of English, SUNY College at Brockport. Videocassette. [Interview with A. Poulin, Jr., and William Heyen, September 11, 1973, SUNY-Brockport.]

Anne Sexton Reads Her Poetry. Caedmon, TC 1441, 1974. [Studio recording, June 1, 1974.]

A Conversation with Anne Sexton: The Late Pulitzer Prize-Winning Poet Talks with James Day. Center for Cassette Studies, 38840, 1974. Cassette.

The Poetry of Anne Sexton. Jeffrey Norton, 23212, 1977. Cassette. [Recording of reading at YM-YWHA Poetry Center, New York, November, 1964.]

Anne Sexton. Tapes for Readers, LIT 074, 1978. Cassette. [Contains: interview with Stephen J. Banker, February, 1974; excerpts from a live concert recording of Anne Sexton and Her Kind, Lincoln, Mass., October, 1968; discussion of performance by Banker, Emerson Meyers, and Frank Getlein; Banker reading Maxine Kumin's poem "How It Is."]

Anne Sexton. American Poetry Archive, 1983. Videocassette. [March, 1966 recording of Sexton at home, reading and discussing her work.]

Secondary Materials

Alkalay-Gut, Karen. "Last Portraits: Anne Sexton." In *Mechitza.* Women Writers Chapbook 5. Merrick, N.Y.: Cross-Cultural Communications, 1986. [Poem.]

"Anne Sexton Dies, Pulitzer Poet, 45." *New York Times,* October 6, 1974, 65.

"Anne Sexton Ruled Suicide." *New York Times,* October 9, 1974, 46.

[Announcement]. *Teachers and Writers Newsletter* 1, no. 1. [Announcement of the English class that Sexton taught with Robert Clawson at Wayland High

School in the fall of 1967. Includes excerpts from Sexton's letter to Herbert Kohl and excerpts from a letter by Clawson.]

Armstrong, Roberta R. "Sexton's *Transformations:* Beyond Confessionalism." *Iowa English Bulletin Yearbook* 24, no. 3 (1974): 57–66.

Ashworth, Debora. "Madonna or Witch: Women's Muse in Contemporary American Poetry." In *Women's Culture,* edited by Gayle Kimball, 178–86. Metuchen: Scarecrow, 1981.

Atwood, Margaret. Review of *Anne Sexton: A Self-Portrait in Letters.* In *Second Words.* Toronto: Anansi, 1982.

Axelrod, Rise B. "The Transforming Art of Anne Sexton." *Concerning Poetry* 7, no. 1 (1974): 6–13. Reprinted in *Feminist Criticism,* edited by Cheryl L. Brown and Karen Olson (Metuchen: Scarecrow, 1978), 131–41.

Axelrod, Steven Gould. "Anne Sexton's Rowing Toward God." *Modern Poetry Studies* 6, no. 2 (1975): 187–89. [Review of *The Awful Rowing Toward God.*]*

Balliro, Charles. "Interview with Anne Sexton." *Fiction* 1, no. 6 (1974): 12–13, 15.

Barnes, Clive. "Theater: Seeking Either a Priest or a Psychiatrist." *New York Times,* October 28, 1969, 43. [Review of *Mercy Street.*]

Bartlett, Kay. "No One Was Surprised When Anne Sexton Chose to Die." *Boston Sunday Globe,* November 17, 1974, A3.

———. "The Poet Who Courted Death." *Syracuse Herald-American,* November 17, 1974, 79, 82. [Based on interviews with friends and relatives of Sexton.]

Baures, Mary. "Anne Sexton's Last Year." *Bosarts,* November, 1974, 4–7.

Berg, Beatrice. "'Oh, I Was Very Sick.'" *New York Times,* November 9, 1969, D1, D7. [Interview with Sexton.]

Bixler, Frances, ed. *"The Fierceness of Female": Original Essays on the Poetry of Anne Sexton.* Conway: University of Central Arkansas Press, forthcoming.

Blankenburg, Gary Dean. "A Rhetorical Approach to Confessional Poetry: Plath, Sexton, Lowell, Berryman, and Snodgrass." Ph.D. diss., Carnegie-Mellon University, 1983.*

Boyers, Robert. *"Live or Die:* The Achievement of Anne Sexton." *Salmagundi* 2 (1967): 61–71. Reprinted in McClatchy (1978), 204–15.*

Calio, Louise. "A Rebirth of the Goddess in Contemporary Women Poets of the Spirit." *Studia Mystica* 7, no. 1 (1984): 50–59. [Comments on *45 Mercy Street.*]

Cam, Heather. "'Daddy': Sylvia Plath's Debt to Anne Sexton." *American Literature* 59, no. 3 (1987): 429–32.

Capo, Kay Ellen Merriman. "Redeeming Words: A Study of Confessional Rhetoric in the Poetry of Anne Sexton." Ph.D. diss., Northwestern University, 1978.*

Carpenter, Kim. "Four Positions on Suicide." *Journal of Popular Culture* 14, no. 4 (1981): 732–39. [Comments on "Wanting to Die."]

Carroll, James. "'Someone Is Dead, Even the Trees Know It.'" *National Catholic Reporter,* November, 1974, 1.

Clifford, Deborah A. "Anne Sexton: Determination without Self-Love in *The Awful Rowing Toward God.*" *Nassau Review* 3, no. 5 (1979): 39–43.

Cowart, David. "Anne Sexton." In *Dictionary of Literary Biography.* Vol. 5. Detroit: Gale, 1980.

Cunningham, Lawrence S. "Anne Sexton: Poetry as a Form of Exorcism." *American Benedictine Review* 28, no. 1 (1977): 102–11.

Dash, Irene. "The Literature of Birth and Abortion." *Regionalism and the Female Imagination* 3, no. 1 (1977): 8–13.

Demetrakopoulos, Stephanie. "The Nursing Mother and Feminine Metaphysics." *Soundings* 65, no. 4 (1982): 430–43. Reprinted in *Listening to Our Bodies* (Boston: Beacon, 1983), 33–44. [Comments on *The Death Notebooks*.]*

Diamonstein, Barbaralee. "Anne Sexton." In *Open Secrets: Ninety-Four Women in Touch with Our Time*. New York: Viking, 1972. [Sexton's written responses to a general questionnaire.]

Dickey, James. "Five First Books." *Poetry* 97 (1961): 316–20. Reprinted in *The Suspect in Poetry* (Madison, Minn.: Sixties Press, 1964), 33–34, and in McClatchy (1978), 117–18. [Review of *To Bedlam and Part Way Back*.]*

———. "Dialogues with Themselves." *New York Times Book Review*, April 28, 1963, 50. Reprinted in *The Suspect in Poetry* (Madison, Minn.: Sixties Press, 1964), 34–35, and in *Babel To Byzantium* (New York: Farrar, 1968), 133–34. [Review of *All My Pretty Ones*.]*

Dickey, William. "A Place in the Country." *Hudson Review* 22 (1969): 347–68. [Review of *Love Poems*.]*

Fein, Richard J. "The Demon of Anne Sexton." *English Record* 18, no. 1 (1967): 16–21.

Feldman, Rivkah. "Anne Sexton." Women's Studies Cassette Curriculum. Everett/Edwards, 5514, 1976. Cassette.

Ferrari, Margaret. "Anne Sexton: Between Death and God." *America*, November 9, 1974, 281–83.

Ferrier, Carole. "Anne Sexton: Demystifier or Mystic?" *Hecate* 4, no. 2 (1978): 65–71. [Review of *45 Mercy Street*.]*

Fields, Beverly. "The Poetry of Anne Sexton." *Tri Quarterly*, o.s. 6, no. 1 (1963): 38–47. Reprinted in *Poets in Progress*, 2d ed., edited by Edward Hungerford (Evanston: Northwestern University Press, 1967), 251–85.*

"Friends of Anne Sexton to Pay Tribute in Poetry." *New York Times*, October 29, 1974, 40.

Gallagher, Brian. "The Expanded Use of Simile in Anne Sexton's *Transformations*." *Notes on Modern American Literature* 3, no. 3 (1979): no. 20.*

George, Diana Hume. "Beyond the Pleasure Principle: Anne Sexton's 'The Death Baby.'" *University of Hartford Studies in Literature* 15, no. 2 (1983): 75–92.

———. "Anne Sexton's Suicide Poems." *Journal of Popular Culture* 18, no. 2 (1984): 17–31.*

———. "Is It True? Feeding, Feces, and Creativity in Anne Sexton's Poetry." *Soundings* 68, no. 3 (1985): 357–71.

———. "Kumin on Kumin and Sexton." *Poesis* 6, no. 2 (1985): 1–18.

———. "Anne Sexton." In *Contemporary American Poets,* edited by Ronald Baughman, 307–34. Contemporary Authors Bibliographical Series. Detroit: Gale, 1986.

———. "Death Is a Woman, Death is a Man: Anne Sexton's Green Girls and the

Leaves That Talk." *University of Hartford Studies in Literature* 18, no. 1 (1986): 31–44.

———. "How We Danced: Anne Sexton on Fathers and Daughters." *Women's Studies* 12, no. 2 (1986): 179–202.*

———. "Oedipus Iscariot: The Prophetic I (Eye) and Anne Sexton's Drama." *Poesis* 7, no. 2 (1986): 46–56.

———. *Oedipus Anne: The Poetry of Anne Sexton.* Urbana: University of Illinois Press, 1987.

———. "The Poetic Heroism of Anne Sexton." *Literature and Psychology* 33, nos. 3–4 (1987): 77–88.

———, ed. *Sexton: Selected Criticism.* Urbana: University of Illinois Press, forthcoming.

Gilbert, Sandra. "My Name Is Darkness." *Contemporary Literature* 18, no. 4 (1977): 443–57.

Gilroy, Harry. "Marianne Moore Wins Gold Medal." *New York Times,* April 14, 1967, 36. [Notice also mentions Sexton's winning of the Shelley Award of the Poetry Society of America.]

Gray, Paul. "American Poetry: School's Out." *Time,* April 26, 1976, 95–98. [Review of *45 Mercy Street.*]

Green, Carol. "A Writer Is Essentially a Spy." *Boston Review of the Arts* 2, no. 5 (1972): 30–37. [A joint interview with Sexton and Maxine Kumin.]

Green, Kate. "Inventory of Loss." *Moons and Lion Tailes* 2, no. 2 (1976): 87–90. [Review of *45 Mercy Street.*]*

Gullans, Charles. "Poetry and Subject Matter: From Hart Crane to Turner Cassity." *Southern Review* 7 (1970): 497–98. Reprinted in McClatchy (1978), 131–32. [Review of *Live or Die.*]*

Hamilton, Ian. "Songs among the Ruins." In *A Poetry Chronicle.* London: Faber and Faber, 1973.

Hartley, Margaret, ed. Special Issue on Anne Sexton. *Southwest Review* 64, no. 3 (1979). [See "The Editor's Notebook," ii–iii.]

Hemley, Cecil. "A Return to Reality." *Hudson Review* 15, no. 4 (1962–63): 612–19. [Review of *All My Pretty Ones;* also covers Stafford, Ostroff, Merrill, and Sewell.]*

Hoffman, Cindy, Carol Duane, Katharen Soule, and Linda Wagner. "Three Contemporary Women Poets: Marianne Moore, Anne Sexton, and Sylvia Plath." In *American Women Writers: Bibliographical Essays,* edited by Maurice Duke, Jackson R. Bryer, and M. Thomas Inge, 379–402. Westport, Ct.: Greenwood, 1983.

Hoffman, Nancy Jo. "Reading Women's Poetry: The Meaning and Our Lives." *College English* 34 (1972): 48–62.

Hoffman, Nancy Yanes. "A Special Language." *Southwest Review* 64, no. 3 (1979): 209–14.

Hoffman, Steven K. "Impersonal Personalism: The Making of a Confessional Poetic." *ELH* 45, no. 4 (1978): 687–709.

Honton, Margaret. "The Double Image and the Division of Parts: A Study of Mother/Daughter Relationships in the Poetry of Anne Sexton." *Journal of Women's Studies in Literature* 1, no. 1 (1979): 33–50.

Howard, Ben. "Shattered Glass." *Poetry* 127 (1976): 286–92. Reprinted in Mc-Clatchy (1978), 177–85. [Review of *The Book of Folly, The Death Notebooks,* and *The Awful Rowing Toward God.*]*

Howard, Richard. ["Anne Sexton"]. In *Preferences.* New York: Viking, 1974.

Hubbart, Marilyn Stall. "Fairy Tale Stereotypes as Unique Individuals: A Study of Iris Murdoch and Anne Sexton." *Publications of the Arkansas Philological Association* 4, 3 (1978): 33–40.

Jaidka, Manju. "Interior Events: The Poetry of Anne Sexton." *Indian Journal of American Studies* 15, no. 1 (1985): 45–55.

Johnson, Greg. "The Achievement of Anne Sexton." *Hollins Critic* 21, no. 2 (1984): 1–13.*

Johnson, Rosemary. "The Woman of Private (but Published) Hungers." *Parnassus* 8, no. 1 (1980): 92–107. [Review of *A Self-Portrait in Letters* and *Words for Dr. Y.*]*

Jones, A. R. "Necessity and Freedom: The Poetry of Robert Lowell, Sylvia Plath and Anne Sexton." *Critical Quarterly* 7 (1965): 11–30.

Jong, Erica. "Remembering Anne Sexton." *New York Times Book Review,* October 27, 1974, 63.

———. "Dear Anne Sexton." In *Loveroot,* New York: Holt, Rinehart and Winston, 1975. [Poem]

———. "Eating Death, for Anne Sexton." In *Loveroot,* New York: Holt, Rinehart and Winston, 1975. [Poem.]

Juhasz, Suzanne. "'The Excitable Gift': The Poetry of Anne Sexton." In *Naked and Fiery Forms.* New York: Harper, 1976.*

———. "The Critic as Feminist: Reflections on Women's Poetry, Feminism, and the Art of Criticism." *Women's Studies* 5, no. 2 (1977): 113–27.

———. "Transformations in Feminist Poetry." *Frontiers* 4, no. 1 (1979): 23–30.

———. "Seeking the Exit or the Home: Poetry and Salvation in the Career of Anne Sexton." In *Shakespeare's Sisters,* edited by Sandra M. Gilbert and Susan Gubar, 261–68. Bloomington: Indiana University Press, 1979.

Kammer, Jeanne H. "The Witch's Life: Confession and Control in the Early Poetry of Anne Sexton." *Language and Style* 13, no. 4 (1980): 29–35.*

Kauffmann, Stanley. "Stanley Kauffmann on Theatre." *New Republic,* November 22, 1969, 22, 33. [Review of *Mercy Street.*]

Kerr, Walter. "A Woman upon the Altar." *New York Times,* November 2, 1969, sec. 2, p. 3. [Review of *Mercy Street.*]*

Kevles, Barbara. "The Dying of a Poet." *Village Voice,* April 5, 1976, 47–48, 50.

Kihss, Peter. "Albee Wins Pulitzer Prize; Malamud Novel Is Chosen." *New York Times,* May 2, 1967, 40. [Notice also mentions Sexton's winning of the Pulitzer Prize for *Live or Die.*]

Knox, Sanka. "Honors Bestowed by Arts Academy." *New York Times,* May 23, 1963, L34. [Notice of Sexton's receipt of the first traveling fellowship of the American Academy of Arts and Letters.]

Kumin, Maxine. "How It Is." *New Yorker,* March 3, 1975, 38. [Memorial poem.]

———. "Interview with Martha George Meek." *Massachusetts Review* 16, no. 2 (1975): 317–27. Reprinted in *To Make a Prairie* (Ann Arbor: University of Michigan Press, 1979), 19–34.

———. "Four Kinds of I." In *To Make a Prairie*. Ann Arbor: University of Michigan Press, 1979.

———. "A Friendship Remembered." In McClatchy (1978), 103–10. Reprinted in Maxine Kumin, *To Make a Prairie* (Ann Arbor: University of Michigan Press, 1979), 83–92.*

———. "Reminiscence Delivered at Memorial Service for Anne Sexton in Marsh Chapel, Boston University." In *To Make a Prairie* (Ann Arbor: University of Michigan Press, 1979), 78–80.*

———. "Sexton's *The Awful Rowing Toward God*." In "A Memorial for Anne Sexton," edited by A. Poulin, Jr. *American Poetry Review* 4, no. 3 (1975). Reprinted in *To Make a Prairie* (Ann Arbor: University of Michigan Press, 1979), 81–82.*

———. "How It Was." Biographical introduction to Anne Sexton, *The Complete Poems* (1981).

Lacey, Paul A. "The Sacrament of Confession." In *The Inner War*. Philadelphia: Fortress, 1972.*

Lant, Jeffrey L. "Another Entry in *The Death Notebooks*." *Southwest Review* 64, no. 3 (1979): 215–19.

Lauter, Estella. "Anne Sexton's Radical Discontent." *Spring,* 1979, 77–92. Reprinted in *Women as Mythmakers* (Bloomington: Indiana University Press, 1984), 23–46.

Legler, Philip. "O Yellow Eye." *Poetry* 110 (1967): 125–27. [Review of *Live or Die*.]

———. Review of *Live or Die*. *New Mexico Quarterly* 37, no. 1 (1967): 89–92.*

Lento, Takako U. "The Deathwish and the Self in Contemporary American Poetry." *Kyushu American Literature* 19 (1978): 17–27.

Levertov, Denise. "Anne Sexton: Light Up the Cave." *Ramparts* 13, no. 5 (1974–75): 61–63. Reprinted in McClatchy (1978), 74–80, and in Denise Levertov, *Light Up the Cave* (New York: New Directions, 1981), 80–86.*

Lewis, Theophilus. "Mercy Street." *America* 121 (1969): 622.

Lowell, Robert. "Anne Sexton." In McClatchy (1978), 71–73.*

Lucie-Smith, Edward. "Between Suicide and Revolution: The Poet as Role-Player." *Saturday Review,* April 19, 1975, 14–18.

McClatchy, J. D., ed. *Anne Sexton: The Artist and Her Critics*. Bloomington: Indiana University Press, 1978. [Though mainly a collection of secondary critical materials, this volume does reprint three Sexton interviews, as well as the worksheets for "Elizabeth Gone." Cited as McClatchy (1978).]

McGill, William J. "Anne Sexton and God: Preeminently a Confessional Poet." *Commonweal,* May 13, 1977, 304–6.

McSpadden, Katherine Frances. "The Self in the Poetry of Anne Sexton." Ph.D. diss., Loyola University of Chicago, 1985.*

Malkoff, Karl. "Anne Sexton." In *Crowell's Handbook of Contemporary American Poetry*. New York: Thomas Y. Crowell, 1973.*

———. "A Short History of Contemporary American Poetry." In *Crowell's Handbook of Contemporary American Poetry*. New York: Thomas Y. Crowell, 1973.

Marras, Emma. "After a Conversation with Linda and Joy Sexton." *Paintbrush* 6, no. 11 (1979): 34–38.

Maryan, Charles. "The Poet on Stage." In McClatchy (1978), 89–95. [By the director of *Mercy Street*.]*

Middlebrook, Diane Wood. "Three Mirrors Reflecting Women: Poetry of Sylvia Plath, Anne Sexton, and Adrienne Rich." In *Worlds into Words*. New York: W. W. Norton, 1978. [Comments on *Transformations*.]

———. "Housewife into Poet: The Apprenticeship of Anne Sexton." *New England Quarterly* 56, no. 4 (1983): 483–503. Reprinted as "'I Tapped My Own Head': The Apprenticeship of Anne Sexton" in *Coming to Light,* edited by Diane Wood Middlebrook and Marilyn Yalom (Ann Arbor: University of Michigan Press, 1985), 195–213.

———. "Becoming Anne Sexton." *Denver Quarterly* 18, no. 4 (1984): 24–34.*

———. "Poet of Weird Abundance." *Parnassus* 12, no. 2–13, no. 1 (1985): 293–315. [Review of *The Complete Poems*.]*

———. *Anne Sexton: A Biography*. Boston: Houghton Mifflin, forthcoming.

Miller, Cynthia A. "The Poet in the Poem: A Phenomenological Analysis of Anne Sexton's 'Briar Rose (Sleeping Beauty).'" In *The Existential Coordinates of the Human Condition,* edited by Anna-Teresa Tymieniecka, 61–73. Analecta Husserliana 18. Dordrecht, Holland: D. Reidel, 1984.*

Mills, Ralph J., Jr. "Four Voices in Recent American Poetry." *Christian Scholar* 46, no. 4 (1963): 324–45. [Review of *All My Pretty Ones*.]

———. "Anne Sexton." In *Contemporary American Poetry*. Studies in Language and Literature 2. New York: Random House, 1965.*

Mitgutsch, Waltraud. "Women in Transition: The Poetry of Anne Sexton and Louise Glück." *Arbeiten aus Anglistik und Amerikanistik* 9, no. 2 (1984): 131–45.

Mizjewski, Linda. "Sappho to Sexton: Woman Uncontained." *College English* 35 (1973): 340–45.

Molesworth, Charles. "'With Your Own Face On': Confessional Poetry." *Twentieth-Century Literature* 22, no. 2 (1976): 163–78. Reprinted in *The Fierce Embrace* (Columbia: University of Missouri Press, 1979), 61–76.

Mood, John J. "'A Bird Full of Bones': Anne Sexton—A Visit and a Reading." *Chicago Review* 23, no. 4–24, no. 1 (1972): 107–23.

Myers, Neil. "The Hungry Sheep Look Up." *Minnesota Review* 1, no. 1 (1960): 97–104. [Review of *To Bedlam and Part Way Back*.]

Newlin, Margaret. "The Suicide Bandwagon." *Critical Quarterly* 14 (1972): 367–78.

Nichols, Kathleen L. "The Hungry Beast Rowing Toward God: Anne Sexton's Later Religious Poetry." *Notes on Modern American Literature* 3, 3 (1979): no. 21.*

Northouse, Cameron, and Thomas P. Walsh. *Sylvia Plath and Anne Sexton: A Reference Guide*. Boston: G. K. Hall, 1974.

Nucifora, Joan Ellen. "'The Awful Babble of That Calling': The Personal Myth of the Madwoman in the Poetry of Anne Sexton." Ph.D. diss., University of Wisconsin, 1978.*

O'Brien, John. "R.I.P. . . . Anne Sexton (1928–1974)." *Oyez Review* 9 (1975): 45–49.

Ostriker, Alicia. "The Nerves of a Midwife: Contemporary American Women's Poetry." *Parnassus* 6, no. 1 (1977): 69–87.

————. "Body Language: The Release of Anatomy." In *The State of the Language,* edited by Leonard Michaels and Christopher Ricks, 247–63. Berkeley: University of California Press, 1980. Reprinted in *Stealing the Language* (Boston: Beacon, 1986), 91–121.

————. "That Story: The Changes of Anne Sexton." *American Poetry Review* 11, no. 4 (1982): 11–16. Reprinted in *Writing Like a Woman* (Ann Arbor: University of Michigan Press, 1983), 59–85.*

————. "The Thieves of Language: Women Poets and Revisionist Mythmaking." *Signs* 8, no. 1 (1982): 68–90. Reprinted in *Coming to Light,* edited by Diane Wood Middlebrook and Marilyn Yalom (Ann Arbor: University of Michigan Press, 1985), 10–36.

————. "I Make My Psyche from My Need." In *Writing Like a Woman.* Ann Arbor: University of Michigan Press, 1983.

————. "What Are Patterns For?: Anger and Polarization in Women's Poetry." *Feminist Studies* 10, no. 3 (1984): 485–503. [Comments on "The Jesus Papers."]

Perrine, Laurence. "Theme and Tone in Anne Sexton's 'To a Friend Whose Work Has Come to Triumph.'" *Notes on Contemporary Literature* 7, no. 3 (1977): 2–3.

Phillips, Robert. "Anne Sexton: The Blooming Mouth and the Bleeding Rose." In *The Confessional Poets.* Carbondale: Southern Illinois University Press, 1973.

Pool, Eugene. "Anne Sexton, Her Kind Mix Poetry with Music." *Boston Globe,* May 27, 1969, 55. [Review of Anne Sexton and Her Kind, Jordan Hall, Boston.]*

Pool, Gail. "Anne Sexton: Poetry and Witchcraft." *New Boston Review* 3 (1978): 3–4. [Review of *A Self-Portrait in Letters.*]

Poulin, A., Jr. "Notes on the Poets." In *Contemporary American Poetry.* 2d ed. Boston: Houghton Mifflin, 1975.

————, ed. "A Memorial for Anne Sexton." *American Poetry Review* 4, no. 3 (1975): 15–20. [Includes: J. M. Brinnin, "Offices (Boston University)" (poem); Pat James, "The Angel of High Wires" (poem); Anne Maxwell, "The Unspoken—To Anne Sexton" (poem); untitled memoir by Maxine Kumin; A. Poulin, Jr., "After Photographs by Arthur Furst" (four poems); Susan Fromberg Schaeffer, "In Memory of Anne Sexton" (memoir); S. F. Schaeffer "Anne Sexton" (poem): untitled memoir by Kathleen Spivack; Lucien Stryk, "Anne Sexton" (memoir); C. K. Williams, "Homage to the Poet Anne Sexton" (prose poem).]

Pritchard, William H. "The Anne Sexton Show." *Hudson Review* 31, no. 2 (1978): 387–92. [Review of *A Self-Portrait in Letters.*]

Quebe, Ruth Evelyn. "The Questing Self: A Study of Anne Sexton's Poetry." Ph.D. diss., University of Texas at Austin, 1979.*

Reisz, H. Frederick. "Images of Christ in Contemporary Poetry." *Word and World* 3 (1983): 69–78.

[Report]. *Teachers and Writers Newsletter* 1, no. 2 (1967): 7–8. [Comments on the English class that Sexton taught with Robert Clawson at Wayland High School in the fall of 1967. Includes excerpts from Sexton's class journal (later published in entirety as "Journal of a Living Experiment"), and examples of students' writing and course evaluations. Announces plans for continuation of the class in spring semester.]

Rich, Adrienne. "Anne Sexton: 1928–1974." In *On Lies, Secrets, and Silences.* New York: W. W. Norton, 1979.

Rosenblatt, Jon. "The Limits of the 'Confessional Mode' in Recent American Poetry." *Genre* 9, no. 2 (1976): 153–59.

Rosenthal, M. L. "Poetry as Confession." *Nation,* September 19, 1959, 154–55.

———. "Other Confessional Poets." In *The New Poets.* New York: Oxford University Press, 1967.*

Rosenthal, M. L., and Sally M. Gall. "Sylvia Plath's 'Final' Poems and Anne Sexton's 'The Divorce Papers.'" In *The Modern Poetic Sequence.* New York: Oxford University Press, 1983.

Schechter, Ruth Lisa. "Where Is Mercy Street?" In *Speedway.* Midland Park, N.J.: Chantry, 1983. [Poem.]

Sheppard, R. Z. "Living with the Excitable Gift." *Time,* November 28, 1977, 124–25. [Review of *A Self-Portrait in Letters.*]

Shor, Ira. "Anne Sexton's 'For My Lover . . .': Feminism in the Classroom." *College English* 34 (1973): 1082–93.

Shurr, William H. "Anne Sexton's *Love Poems:* The Genre and the Differences." *Modern Poetry Studies* 10, no. 1 (1981): 58–68.*

———. "Sexton's 'The Legend of the One-Eyed Man.'" *Explicator* 39, no. 3 (1981): 2–3.

———. "Mysticism and Suicide: Anne Sexton's Last Poetry." *Soundings* 68, no. 3 (1985): 335–56. [An extended analysis of *The Awful Rowing Toward God.*]

Spivack, Kathleen. "Poets and Friends." *Boston Globe Magazine,* August 9, 1981, 10–13, 35–42.*

Stallworthy, Jon. "W. B. Yeats and the Dynastic Theme." *Critical Quarterly* 7 (1965): 247–65.

Stark, Myra. "Walt Whitman and Anne Sexton: A Note on the Uses of Tradition." *Notes on Contemporary Literature* 8, no. 4 (1978): 7–8. [Compares "In Celebration of My Uterus" to "Song of Myself."]*

Swan, Barbara, "A Reminiscence." In McClatchy (1978), 81–88. [By Sexton's illustrator.]*

Stessel, Harry. "Confessional Poetry: A Guide to Marriage in America." *Moderna Språk* 72, no. 4 (1978): 337–55.

Tanenhaus, Beverly. "Politics of Suicide and Survival: The Poetry of Anne Sexton and Adrienne Rich." In *Women, Literature, Criticism,* edited by Harry R. Garvin, 106–18. Lewisburg: Bucknell University Press, 1978. [Volume was also issued as *Bucknell Review* 24, no. 1 (1978).]

Thurley, Geoffrey. "The Poetry of Breakdown: Robert Lowell and Anne Sexton." In *The American Moment.* New York: St. Martin's, 1978.

Thomas, William V. "Literary Excursions into Death." *Chronicle of Higher Education,* May 12, 1975, 10. [Review of *The Awful Rowing Toward God.*]

"A Tribute to Anne Sexton." Special Awards/Anthology Issue. *Croton Review* 11 (1988).

"Twenty-Third Annual Conference of New Jersey Association for Mental Health to Be Held June 4–5 in Newark with Scheduled Speakers Poet Anne Sexton and Dr. Rollo May." *New York Times,* May 27, 1974, 37.

Vendler, Helen. "Malevolent Flippancy." *New Republic,* November 11, 1981, 33–36. [Review of *The Complete Poems.*]*

Wagner, Linda W. "*45 Mercy Street* and Other Vacant Houses." In *American Literature: The New England Heritage,* edited by James Nagel and Richard Astro, 145–65. New York: Garland, 1981.

Wagner-Martin, Linda, ed. *Anne Sexton: Critical Essays.* Boston: G. K. Hall, forthcoming.

Ward, Patricia. "Anne Sexton's Rowing Toward God." *Christianity Today,* August 27, 1976, 18–19. [Review of *The Awful Rowing Toward God.*]

Webster, Harvey Curtis. "Six Poets." *Poetry* 133, no. 4 (1979): 227–34. [Review of *Words for Dr. Y.*]

Wegs, Joyce M. "Poets in Bedlam: Sexton's Use of Bishop's 'Visits to St. Elizabeth's' in 'Ringing the Bells.'" *Concerning Poetry* 15, no. 1 (1982): 37–47.

Williams, Polly C. "Sexton in the Classroom." In McClatchy (1978), 96–101.

Wilson, Sylvia. "To Anne Sexton and Sylvia Plath, Most Deeply Admired." *Concerning Poetry* 7 (1977): 42–43. [Poem.]

Young, Vernon. "Lines Written in Rouen." *Hudson Review* 24, no. 4 (1971–72): 669–86. Reprinted in McClatchy (1978), 149–51. [Review of *Transformations.*]*

Zollman, Sol. "Criticism, Self-Criticism, No Transformation: The Poetry of Robert Lowell and Anne Sexton." *Literature and Ideology* 9 (1971): 29–36.

POETS ON POETRY   Donald Hall, General Editor

Poets on Poetry collects critical books by contemporary poets, gathering together the articles, interviews, and book reviews by which they have articulated the poetics of a new generation.

Goatfoot Milktongue Twinbird
Donald Hall

Walking Down the Stairs
Galway Kinnell

Writing the Australian Crawl
William Stafford

Trying to Explain
Donald Davie

To Make a Prairie
Maxine Kumin

Toward a New Poetry
Diane Wakoski

Talking All Morning
Robert Bly

Pot Shots at Poetry
Robert Francis

Open Between Us
David Ignatow

The Old Poetries and the New
Richard Kostelanetz

A Company of Poets
Louis Simpson

Don't Ask
Philip Levine

Living Off the Country
John Haines

Parti-Colored Blocks for a Quilt
Marge Piercy

The Weather for Poetry
Donald Hall

Collected Prose
James Wright

Old Snow Just Melting
Marvin Bell

Writing Like a Woman
Alicia Ostriker

A Ballet for the Ear
John Logan

Effluences from the Sacred Caves
Hayden Carruth

Collected Prose
Robert Hayden

Platonic Scripts
Donald Justice

A Local Habitation
John Frederick Nims

No Evil Star
Anne Sexton

The Uncertain Certainty
Charles Simic

The Character of the Poet
Louis Simpson

You Must Revise Your Life
William Stafford

A Concert of Tenses
Tess Gallagher

Reviews and Essays, 1936–55
Weldon Kees

Poetry and Ambition
Donald Hall